One Man's Journey

My Daily Journal

Following

Annotation 19

Of the

Spiritual Exercises

Of

Ignatius Loyola

Robert Hart

July 2012

This is Maggie, our five-year-old "Texas black dog." She was by my side almost every day for the nine months of the Exercises. She and I walked along this very beach many mornings to pray and reflect.

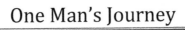

For my wife, Sallie Ann

Ignatius Loyola wrote the Spiritual Exercises over the period from 1522 to 1524 as a set of meditations, prayers and mental exercises designed to be carried out over a period of roughly 30 days in a secluded setting or retreat. In "annotation 19" of his original instructions, Ignatius provides a model for completing the Exercises over a longer period, without the need for seclusion, which he referred to as the "Exercises in Daily Life."

In late August 2011, Sister Joan Grace, of Our Lady Star of the Sea Parish in Ponte Vedra Beach, agreed to be my Spiritual Director for the Exercises. She explained that we would use as a guide the handbook written by Father Joseph Tetlow, the Director of Montserrat Jesuit Retreat House in Lake Dallas, TX ("Tetlow" or the "Tetlow handbook").

I began the exercises on September 4, 2011. Almost every day thereafter, for more than nine months, I prayed, meditated and reflected on a passage from scripture or a "thought-piece" from the Tetlow handbook. As instructed, I recorded my thoughts, feelings, and reactions to each day's exercise in a journal. This is that journal.

The Meditation Garden.

Prologue

Today I will begin the Spiritual Exercises of Ignatius Loyola. Each day for the next nine months, more or less, I will pray and meditate for about an hour. I have been instructed to find a time when, and a place where I can accomplish my exercises. Early mornings work best for me. Most days, I intend to begin my prayers in a corner of my library, which is downstairs in my house in Ponte Vedra Beach, Florida. If the weather allows it, I will take my prayers out to the garden, where I have installed a bench expressly for this purpose. From time to time, I hope to continue the process on the beach, which is only a short walk from the garden.

Ignatius Loyola was seriously injured in the Battle of Pamplona in 1521.[1] He went through a conversion during his recovery. Ignatius looked deeply into his life. He opened the "eyes of his soul" to examine his relationship with God. His effort has inspired hundreds of thousands more to follow his guide in making the Spiritual Exercises.[2]

---

[1] According to Wikipedia, "The Battle of Pampeluna (also spelled Pamplona) occurred on May 20, 1521, between French-backed Navarrese and Spanish troops, during the Spanish conquest of Iberian Navarre and in the context of the Italian War of 1521–1526. Most Navarrese towns rose at once against the Spanish, who had invaded Navarre in 1512. The Spanish resisted the siege sheltered inside the city castle, but they eventually surrendered and the Navarrese took control of the town and the castle of Pamplona. It was at this battle that Inigo Lopez de Loyola, better known as St. Ignatius of Loyola, suffered severe injuries, a French cannonball shattering his leg. It is said that after the battle the French so admired his bravery that they carried him all the way back to his home in Loyola."

[2] According to Wikipedia, "*De Vita Christi* by Ludolph of Saxony inspired Loyola to abandon his previous military life and devote himself to labor for God, following the example of spiritual leaders such as Francis of Assisi. He experienced a vision of the Virgin Mary and the infant Jesus while at the shrine of Our Lady of Montserrat in March 1522. Thereafter he went to Manresa, where he began praying for seven hours a day, often in a nearby cave, while formulating the fundamentals of the *Spiritual Exercises*. In September 1523, Loyola reached the Holy Land to settle there, but was sent back to Europe by the Franciscans. Between 1524 and 1537, Ignatius studied theology and Latin in Spain and then in Paris. In 1534, he arrived in the latter city during a period of anti-Protestant turmoil which forced John Calvin to flee France. Ignatius and a few followers bound themselves by vows of poverty, chastity, and obedience. In 1539, they formed the Society of Jesus, approved in 1540 by Pope Paul III, as well as his *Spiritual Exercises* approved in 1548. Loyola also composed the *Constitutions* of the Society. He died in July 1556, was beatified by Pope Paul V in 1609, canonized by Pope Gregory XV in 1622, and declared patron of all spiritual retreats by Pope Pius XI in 1922. Ignatius' feast day is celebrated on July 31."

When Ignatius wrote his autobiography in 1555, he referred to himself throughout in the third person. In this passage from Chapter Two of that autobiography, he introduces the idea of a journal:

> [H]e took a byway that led him to a town called Manresa. Here he determined to remain a few days in the hospital and **write out some notes in his little book**, which for his own consolation he carefully carried about with him.

In my effort to "write out some notes in my little book," I intend to follow the instructions with respect to each day's Ignatian assignment. In addition, however, I hope to weave into the tapestry of this experience the various strands of spiritual wisdom I have gathered over the past several years. I will attempt the same level of openness and honesty demonstrated by Ignatius.[3]

For me, the exercises are yet another step, albeit a major one, in a journey that began many years ago. In fact, I cannot pinpoint its exact beginning. Thomas Merton writes about our spiritual growth in his book, New Seeds of Contemplation:

> Every moment and every event of every man's life on earth plants something in his soul. For just as the wind carries thousands of winged seeds, so each moment brings with it germs of spiritual vitality that come to rest imperceptibly in the minds and wills of men.[4]

It has occurred to me that the solitude I experienced as a young boy on the family farm in Idaho was fertile soil for the seeds of spirituality. For several months each year, I moved sprinkler pipe early in the morning, and again later in the afternoon. So both while working and while waiting, I was alone, talking to myself. I like to think my discussions with myself were about important matters, including where I came from, why I was here, and what it all meant.

Certainly, some of the messages of the Mormon Church, my former faith, about God and Christ and moral values got through to me, in spite of my relative indifference to the religion. There is correspondence from my first year at Harvard and from the two years I spent as a missionary for the Mormons in Germany, all revealing a great deal of spiritual searching.

The trail grows cold in the years following my excommunication by the Mormons, but there are bits and pieces of evidence that suggest I continued to think about God, though not through any organized religion. I have always read voraciously, especial-

---

[3] I will also attempt to heed the advice of James Russell Lowell, who famously said, "Blessed are they who have nothing to say and who cannot be persuaded to say it." Some of what I have written in the past was vastly improved by editing. However, that reminds me of the great T.S. Eliot line, "Some editors are failed writers, but so are most writers."

[4] Thomas Merton, New Seeds of Contemplation, p. 40.

ly history and biography. I have been active in politics, focusing particularly on the needs of the poor and poorly represented.

I have come to believe that something beyond my own power - outside of "self" - acted on my life choices in a way that nudged me toward various forms of service. Of course, the early decisions to work with the poor were made at the end of the Sixties, when a great many of the young people in the United States were reaching similar conclusions. However, long after most of my generation lost interest in helping the people at the margins of society, I continued to try, often making decisions that put my own interest second.

I was certainly not selfless. My ego came first. In addition to whatever psychic rewards my career provided, there were always plenty of opportunities to make sure that I did rather well financially.

Five years ago, I was humbled by heart disease. My business career came to an early and, I thought, ignoble end. My initial reaction was as far from a spiritual journey as can be imagined. At the depths of depression, I looked for and found hell on earth. Only with the help and support of some incredible people, including particularly my wife Sallie Ann, and the influence of a power higher and greater than me, did I survive that physical, mental, and spiritual trauma.

I embarked in earnest on a journey toward God that would eventually lead through Rome. My journey began with an ambitious reading program, which included books from and about several different Wisdom Traditions. Buddy Tudor, my closest friend for more than forty years, walked with me on almost every step of the journey.[5] Father John Robbins, the Pastor of St. Anne's parish in Houston, counseled, coached, corrected, and comforted me along the way.[6] (Sadly, both Buddy and Father John died before I reached baptism) I went through two years of RCIA.[7] I was given the extraordinary opportunity to serve on a board with Jesuit theologians at the Woodstock Center at Georgetown University. Finally, I was baptized, confirmed, married

---

[5] Robert Beal ("Buddy") Tudor, Jr. was a general contractor in Alexandria, Louisiana. His company, Tudor Construction Company, built several housing projects for my various real estate development companies, beginning with Carver Apartments in Picayune, Mississippi, and ending with The Gables, in Bethesda, Maryland, He also built the coal preparation facility at the Inverness mine in Delbarton, West Virginia. I was at his house, on a business trip to Louisiana, when my second daughter was born.

[6] Father John Robbins was Pastor of St. Anne's Catholic Church in Houston, TX. He died on December 19, 2009. He was 66 years old. He mentored me during the first three years after my heart surgery, as I considered, and finally accepted, baptism into the Catholic Church.

[7] Rite of Christian Initiation of Adults ("RCIA") is the program of instruction for adults seeking to become Catholic. Children's Catechetical Development ("CCD") is a similar program of instruction for children.

as a Catholic, and received first communion.   All of these blessings and many more propelled me forward toward a closeness to and deeper understanding of God.

It is in that spirit, then, that I begin this journal.   I am a traveler.   This is not the beginning of my journey.   I hope it is far from the end.

Ignatius Loyola

Days of Decision

(Two Weeks)

God provides for me. We are seeking a deeper trust in the Father's care for me. How have I experienced God's providential care in the events and relationships of my life?[8]

2011

Sunday, September 4   (Luke 11:1-11)

Lord, teach us to pray

I prayed before reading these verses from the eleventh chapter of Luke:

> *One day Jesus was praying in a certain place. When he finished, one of his disciples said to him, "Lord, teach us to pray, just as John taught his disciples." He said to them, "When you pray, say:*
>
> *"'Father, hallowed be your name, your kingdom come. Give us each day our daily bread. Forgive us our sins, for we also forgive everyone who sins against us. And lead us not into temptation.'"*
>
> *Then Jesus said to them, "Suppose you have a friend, and you go to him at midnight and say, 'Friend, lend me three loaves of bread; a friend of mine on a journey has come to me, and I have no food to offer him.' And suppose the one inside answers, 'Don't bother me. The door is already locked, and my children and I are in bed. I can't get up and give you anything.' I tell you, even though he will not get up and give you the bread because of friendship,*

---

[8] The weekly assignments from the Tetlow handbook always include a "grace," which is the object of the prayer and meditation for that week. Readings, either scripture or a "thought-piece" from Tetlow, were assigned for each of the seven days between meetings with Sister Joan. I show the reading in parentheses after each date. I have included all graces and themes for the appropriate period in a blue, italicized font.

yet because of your shameless audacity he will surely get up and give you as much as you need. "So I say to you: Ask and it will be given to you; seek and you will find; knock and the door will be opened to you. For everyone who asks receives; the one who seeks finds; and to the one who knocks, the door will be opened.

I never cease to wonder at the power of grace, and its constant presence. It is always on offer. We need only accept that offer - to ask, to knock, to seek. It is not forced on us, nor is it available to purchase or acquire in trade. It is always free and unconditional. Even after wandering for forty years and sinking into deep despair, grace was right there in front of me, responding to the slightest indication that I was willing to ask for and accept it.

Tuesday, September 6   *(Luke 12:22-23)*

Why are you anxious?

The reading today is a short, but wonderful passage from Luke:

> *Then Jesus said to his disciples: "Therefore I tell you, do not worry about your life, what you will eat; or about your body, what you will wear. For life is more than food, and the body more than clothes.*

Do not worry about the superficial stuff. I sat in the garden to pray again after reading the passage from Luke, and the following several verses. All around me were both superficial things - results of the selfish and self-centered pursuit of my architectural dreams - and wonderfully natural things of beauty. How could a rose ever be more beautiful? How can man ever improve on that perfection? I listened to Bach as I sat on the bench, and, again, was moved to ask how any sound could be more perfect. Maggie, my "heart" dog,[9] searched for lizards among the rose bushes. Could there ever be anything as perfectly innocent as the simple love between a dog and her master?[10]

So, the superficiality of the manmade elements in the garden is more than offset by the profound beauty of God's presence all around me. Is this what Luke was aiming at? I am not sure, but it feels right.

---

[9] Maggie is a black dog, allegedly a cross between a cocker spaniel and a poodle, who was given to me by Sallie Ann when I returned home from heart bypass surgery. She was four years old on October 15, 2011.

[10] Note, however, that I have precious little mastery over Maggie!

Wednesday, September 7   *(Isaiah 43:1-7)*

You are precious in my eyes.

"Fear not for I am with you." I prayed this morning while walking on the beach, having read and re-read these verses. Sometimes I am overcome with doubt and unease. Where in the world are we going in this country? Will anything any of us do make any difference? How can God allow the entire middle class to sink into poverty believing the enormous lies of the politicians? How have we allowed schools and infrastructure to fall apart?

Are these the kinds of fears Isaiah spoke about?

Everyone on every side of every issue invokes God. The far right Christian Conservatives, the missionaries working with the hungry and homeless, the terrorists in the Arab countries, the orthodox Jews spreading hatred and fear with anti-Sharia legislation - to whom was Isaiah speaking?

I think the intention has to be that he was addressing the "righteous," regardless of race, religion, or nationality. Righteousness must be understandable on some basis as justice or fairness. God gave us minds to reason with, and a spark of the Divine sufficient to know right from wrong. So how can anyone hate or act to harm others, doing so in God's name?

Thursday, September 8   *(Ephesians 3:14-21)*

Paul's prayer to grow strong

"That Christ may dwell in your hearts through faith." Paul tells the Ephesians (who must be Gentiles, I assume[11]) that the Spirit will give them inner strength and great power. Maggie and I talked to the statue of St. Francis this morning.[12] Paul's words echoed in my mind. The peace I find in the garden or on the beach is powerful. It is an indwelling of the Spirit.

I struggled last night with my despair regarding the plight of a close friend. He lost his house in foreclosure recently, and is left with a personal liability for several hundred

---

[11] Generally, I consider most of the Christians Paul writes to and about to be Gentiles rather than Jews. There were Jewish communities throughout the part of the world visited by Paul, but he considered his primary mission to be preaching to the Gentiles. James, the first Bishop of Jerusalem, and other apostles considered it their primary mission to preach to the Jews.

[12] There is a large statue of St. Francis in our garden at Serendipity, which is the name we gave our house in Ponte Vedra Beach, Florida. Throughout this journal, reference will be made to the library and garden, both of which are at Serendipity, and to the beach, which is across the lagoon and the golf course from Serendipity.

thousand dollars. And he has a job! How many more just like him have been forced out of their homes, but must face the consequences without a job or health care or hope? Anyone who helps him must be very careful about his saving face. Anyway, bits and scraps of charity are no remedy for the larger problems facing us today. I am depressed.

Sunday, September 11   *(Psalm 23)*

The Lord is my shepherd.

> *The LORD is my shepherd, I lack nothing.*
> *He makes me lie down in green pastures,*
> *he leads me beside quiet waters, he refreshes my soul.*
> *He guides me along the right paths for his name's sake.*
>
> *Even though I walk through the darkest valley,*
> *I will fear no evil, for you are with me;*
> *your rod and your staff, they comfort me.*
>
> *You prepare a table before me in the presence of my enemies.*
> *You anoint my head with oil; my cup overflows.*
>
> *Surely your goodness and love will follow me all the days of my life,*
> *and I will dwell in the house of the LORD forever.*

What a wonderful message to read on this sad day, the anniversary of one of the most painful days in modern US history.[13] I cannot focus on the scripture as much as I would like, as the noise of despair drowns out all other sound. We have indeed been walking through the valley of the shadow of death, not just as so many died in New York on that day ten years ago, but in all the misguided actions ever since. Twice as many Americans have died in our wars of retribution, along with hundreds of thousands of Iraqis and Afghans. We have squandered so much treasure that we cannot properly address problems here at home.

Tuesday, September 13   *(Psalm 62)*

Hope in God alone.

"My faith rests in God alone." I prayed at length last night and this morning. The message is clear that God alone is our hope and salvation, definitely not we alone, or our leaders. Turning my life, including my fears and concerns, over to God is very hard for me to do.

---

[13] In the unlikely event that anyone reading this does not know, it was on September 11, 2001, that Al Queda terrorists attacked the World Trade Center in New York and the Pentagon in Washington.

Saturday, September 17

Sister Joan and I met for the second time this afternoon. I reported to her that I had not read three of the readings she left for me before her trip. I decided to read them all today. Maggie and I sat together in the library, watching the cloudy sky and waiting for the rain.

Let not your hearts be troubled.   *(John 14:1-7)*

As instructed, I read the passage from John last night. In the first four verses, Jesus makes it clear to His disciples that knowing right from wrong is pretty straightforward:

> *Do not let your hearts be troubled. You believe in God; believe also in me. My Father's house has many rooms; if that were not so, would I have told you that I am going there to prepare a place for you? And if I go and prepare a place for you, I will come back and take you to be with me that you also may be where I am. You know the way to the place where I am going.*

I often feel like a great deal of the mystery associated with knowing the right thing to do is self-imposed. I know what is right and good and Godly. In my experience, the overwhelming majority of life's decisions are extremely simple. Society works on rather well-posted rules, most of which do not require much, if any, moral or ethical consideration. It is right to follow those rules and wrong not to do so. In those rare instances where the rules of society clash with deeply held notions of right and wrong, I like to think I listen to an informed inner compass.

A simple sense of right and wrong has been instilled in me over a lifetime of learning how best to get along with others. I have added to this "innate morality" by reading avidly, and listening to many wise people talk about various systems of morality.

I am just insubordinate enough to chafe against most authority, including even instructions meant to be divinely inspired. However, I have seldom been told to do something by an authority that actually violated my own sense of right and wrong. In most cases where I do disagree with those in authority over me, no action is called for on my part.

In my weakness, I sometimes choose not to do what is right, hiding that choice behind the false notion that the way is not clear; that there are several choices and more information is needed to choose correctly. There are certainly some difficult decisions in all our lives, decisions where two or more alternatives have much going for them and the clear winner is not obvious. In my experience, however, these situations are extremely rare. Over most of my life, the right choice was quite apparent. The question was not what to do or which choice was preferable. Rather, the question was whether I had the courage to make the right choice.

Thomas said to him, "Lord, we don't know where you are going, so how can we know the way?"

Jesus answered, "I am the way and the truth and the life. No one comes to the Father except through me. If you really know me, you will know my Father as well. From now on, you do know him and have seen him."

John goes on to quote Christ saying "...No one comes to the Father except through me." This sentence has been used by many Christians throughout the ages to exclude all non-Christians from Heaven. It flies in the face of the concept of inclusiveness or of any ecumenical effort. I know that the Gospel cannot be approached like a delicatessen, where we are allowed to pick and choose only those bits that we like. However, I also believe that the ecumenical message of Vatican II is a valid part of our faith. I am praying for the strength to remain open and inclusive.

Do not be afraid for I am with you.   (Isaiah 41:8-14)

I have chosen you and have not rejected you. So do not fear, for I am with you; do not be dismayed, for I am your God.

I love the message so often repeated throughout both the Old and New Testaments that we are not to be afraid; that God is with us; that He has chosen us for whatever task we face. No matter how often I hear it, I take comfort from that message.

Still, I struggle with the idea that by choosing us for something, God makes the choice for us to do that thing. It is the age old question of predestination or foreordination versus free will. One of the reasons I so like the new prayer ("I choose to breathe the Breath of Christ")[14] is that it is filled with the idea that everything is choice. We have to choose to accept God's grace. Obviously, an omniscient God knows how we will choose, but He has left us with the responsibility to actually make the decision, and with accountability for the decision we make.

When I hear people say that a certain action is "God's plan," I want to say that the only part of the action that is God's plan is for the person to make the decision to take the action. In other words, God does not make our choices for us, nor is it His plan that we choose one way or the other. To suggest that God makes our decisions, or plans for us to decide in a certain way, is to suggest that God intended bad things and evil choices. In general, bad things happen because people make bad choices. All choices have consequences, and some of those consequences negatively affect

---

[14] Tetlow wrote a version of the Anima Christi that is recommended for use during the period of decision and preparation. The original Medieval Anima Christi, along with two recent versions, including Tetlow's, are included later in this journal.

entirely innocent bystanders.[15]

God's protection   *(Psalm 91)*

> *He is my refuge and my fortress, my God, in whom I trust.*

What a wonderful, hopeful message! The theme of so much of the reading this week has been God's love and the protection He provides for us. He urges us not to be afraid; to trust Him; to accept His grace.

As I complete these three readings, I come to the end of the decision period. Tomorrow, I will begin the Preparation Days.

I am more than a little excited about this journey into the vast interior of spirituality. I take great comfort from four centuries of predecessors who have paved the way, and confirmed by their own journeys that the trip is worth taking. I am happy to have Sister Joan as a guide. I am comforted by the ever present advice from the Woodstock community. I love it that Sallie Ann travels with me, at once holding my hand and chiding me to be humble.

Sister Joan agreed to meet with me weekly for the next eight to nine months. She launched the next phase of the exercises with an assignment sheet, which included a list of seven scriptural passages or thought-pieces, one for each day of the week following our meeting. She told me she would give me a similar assignment sheet for each week of the Preparation Days, the First Week, the Second Week, the Third Week, and the Fourth Week (these are "Exercise weeks," not calendar weeks).

---

[15] For me, this view of free choice and consequences works for all those situations where human choices are involved. I do recognize bad consequences that result from "acts of God," i.e., totally unrelated to any human decision or action. Examples of this include many diseases and most natural disasters. My evolving view of these situations is that God set a process of evolution in motion with the Big Bang. That process follows the rules of natural selection, free choice, and ever greater complexity. It is a process that of necessity involves winners and losers, both of which belong to the wholeness of creation.

Preparation Days

(Eight Weeks)

1. A week of Prayer

Remember first that you are in God's holy presence. Then take the passage for the day and quietly read through it. Think about it for a while and, if you find yourself moved to do so, address God our Lord with reverence. Try to remember always to end your prayer with the Our Father, since that is how Jesus taught us to pray.

Sunday, September 18 (John 4:1-14)

John's story of Christ meeting the Samaritan woman at Jacob's well is one of my favorites:

> *Now Jesus learned that the Pharisees had heard that he was gaining and baptizing more disciples than John — although in fact it was not Jesus who baptized, but his disciples. So he left Judea and went back once more to Galilee.*

> *Now he had to go through Samaria. So he came to a town in Samaria called Sychar, near the plot of ground Jacob had given to his son Joseph. Jacob's well was there, and Jesus, tired as he was from the journey, sat down by the well. It was about noon.*

> *When a Samaritan woman came to draw water, Jesus said to her, "Will you give me a drink?" (His disciples had gone into the town to buy food.)*

> *The Samaritan woman said to him, "You are a Jew and I am a Samaritan woman. How can you ask me for a drink?" (For Jews do not associate with Samaritans.)*

> *Jesus answered her, "If you knew the gift of God and who it is that asks you for a drink, you would have asked him and he would have given you living water."*

> *"Sir," the woman said, "you have nothing to draw with and the well is deep. Where can you get this living water? [12] Are you greater than our father Jacob,*

who gave us the well and drank from it himself, as did also his sons and his livestock?"

Jesus answered, "Everyone who drinks this water will be thirsty again, but whoever drinks the water I give them will never thirst. Indeed, the water I give them will become in them a spring of water welling up to eternal life."

Yesterday, Sister Joan emphasized the Ignatian approach to contemplative prayer, which she explained is a core element of the exercises. A deeper understanding of scripture can be obtained by the reader imagining himself as one of the participants in the scene described in the reading. In the case of today's scripture, the choices are limited to Christ and the woman. I imagined myself to be an onlooker, but close at hand. Happily, the fountain outside the library once sat upon a well somewhere in France (or is copied from one that did), so I knelt on the grass to the side of that fountain and read John's story again.

It is a wonderful scene, filled with so many lessons. I love every part of the Gospel that emphasizes the "big tent" of Christian faith. The woman was first of all a Samaritan, a people of mixed race who had once fought against the Jews. Talking to her or, even worse, asking for water from a jar she had touched would have been unthinkable for a proper Jew. As Father John so often said, however, the message of our faith is **inclusive**. It does not discriminate by race or ethnicity or creed. Beyond being Samaritan, the woman was immoral. Jews were permitted up to three marriages; she had been married five times, and was living then with another man outside of marriage. Yet the tent was big enough to include her; even to use her as a messenger to her whole village. As I imagined listening to the conversation in my garden next to the fountain, I could hear both the challenge, and a bit of tease in the words of the woman. Christ upped the ante, so to speak, by challenging her to risk so much more than simply speaking to a Jew – the possibility of eternal life.

I love the concept of living water. It is repeated in the prayer that I read last night to Sallie Ann and again this morning. "I choose the living water flowing from His side." Water, which is such a simple, basic substance, can, at the same time, represent eternity, the Holy Spirit, the Word, and even the journey of faith.[16] The prayer begins with "I choose to breathe the Breath of Christ that makes all life holy." Again, a substance as simple and all available as air becomes the medium for both a message and for the Holy Spirit. God's grace is as available as the air and the water that is all around us. It is just as essential for life.

---

[16] One of my favorite uses of water is its comparison to the Trinity. Just as ice, water, and steam are all the same substance, simply in a different form, one can view God, Jesus Christ, and the Holy Spirit as different forms of the one God. My own understanding of the Trinity is evolving as I incorporate a better understanding of God's role in the Big Bang, the Cosmic Christ, and the energy force field of the Holy Spirit.

The Joseph Tetlow prayer that I am reading every day this week is a wonderful version of the Anima Christi. The Anima Christi, in turn, is a medieval prayer to Jesus, possibly written by Pope John XXII.[17] It is often attributed to Ignatius Loyola, since he used it so much. In fact, it is sometimes referred to as the "Aspirations of Ignatius Loyola." However, there are several copies of the prayer dating from at least a century before Ignatius was born. The original was, of course, written in Latin. Here is the translation found in our Missal:

> *Soul of Christ, sanctify me.*
> *Body of Christ, save me.*
> *Blood of Christ, inebriate me.*
> *Water from the side of Christ, wash me.*
> *Passion of Christ, strengthen me.*
> *O good Jesus, hear me.*
> *Within Thy wounds hide me.*
> *Separated from Thee let me never be.*
> *From the malicious enemy defend me*
> *In the hour of my death call me*
> *And bid me come unto Thee*
> *That with thy Saints I may praise Thee*
> *Forever and ever, Amen*

John Henry Newman wrote another, very poetic version of the prayer more than a century ago:

> *Soul of Christ, be my sanctification;*
> *Body of Christ, be my salvation;*
> *Blood of Christ, fill all my veins;*
> *Water of Christ's side, wash out my stains;*
> *Passion of Christ, my comfort be;*
> *O good Jesus, listen to me;*
> *In Thy wounds I fain would hide;*
> *Ne'er to be parted from Thy side;*
> *Guard me, should the foe assail me;*
> *Call me when my life shall fail me;*
> *Bid me come to Thee above,*
> *With Thy saints to sing Thy love,*
> *World without end. Amen.*

Of all the versions and translations, however, I like that of Joseph Tetlow the most:

---

[17] John XXII (1244-1334) was the second Pope of the Avignon Papacy. In addition to receiving credit for the Anima Christi, John XXII famously (or infamously) condemned the Franciscans for espousing poverty.

*I choose to breathe the breath of Christ
that makes all life holy.*

*I choose to live the flesh of Christ
that outlasts sin's corrosion and decay.*

*I choose the blood of Christ
along my veins and in my heart
that dizzies me with joy.*

*I choose the living waters flowing from His side
to wash and clean my own self and the world itself.*

*I choose the awful agony of Christ
to charge my senseless sorrows with meaning
and to make my pain pregnant with power.*

I choose you, good Jesus, you know.

*I choose you, good Lord;
count me among the victories
that you have won in bitter woundedness.*

Never number me among those alien to you.

Make me safe from all that seeks to destroy me.

Summon me to come to you.

*Stand me solid among angels and saints
chanting yes to all you have done,
exulting in all you mean to do forever and ever.*

*Then for this time, Father of all,
keep me, from the core of my self,
choosing Christ in the world. Amen.*

This is a beautiful piece of poetry. Listen to the phrases, "dizzies me with joy," or "senseless sorrows," or "pain pregnant with power." Very good indeed!

Monday, September 19   *(John 10:1-21)*

In this account, Jesus had recently caused the blind man to see, but that miracle was contested by the Pharisees. After listening to the once-blind man give witness to Christ and His miracle, the Pharisees "cast him out." Jesus found him and, in earshot of the Pharisees, said "and those who see become blind." When the Pharisees asked if Jesus meant that they were blind, He answered that were they blind, they would have no guilt. However, since they were sighted, they had guilt. The scene was now set for Jesus to deliver to the Pharisees His Good Shepherd sermon. Presumably, the once-blind man was still present. As I imagine myself in the scene, my choices are to be one of the Pharisees, the once-blind man, or Jesus Himself. I see myself as the once blind man, looking on and listening to Jesus address the Pharisees.

Ultimately, Jesus states that He is the gate through which one enters the sheepfold. However, He begins His sermon saying that people entering the sheepfold other than through the gate, clearly referring to the Pharisees (and to false prophets preceding Jesus), are thieves and robbers. I continue to bristle at the suggestion that the only way into the sheepfold (read Kingdom of God) is through Jesus Christ, just as I did in reaction to John 14:1-7.

However, Jesus goes on to exclaim that He has "...other sheep that are not of this pen." While it seems clear that John understands this to mean Gentiles as well as Jews, I choose to see this as an ecumenical opening to all human beings. We are all one flock, and there is but one shepherd. While belief in and worship of Christ is the gate through which we must all pass, the powerful part of the gospel message is that obedience to the great commandment of loving our neighbors as ourselves trumps the narrow dogma of the Pharisees and Sadducees. They, the learned, righteous Jewish leadership, are the thieves who have come to "kill and destroy," while Christ and His message promise the fullness of life.

Standing in the background, I can imagine no starker contrast than the smug, dogmatic law-enforcers on one side, and the simple, humble Jesus alone on the other side. The growing dislike of Jesus is evident, as is the fear that His message threatens the very existence of this learned political class.

These are strong messages that evoke strong feelings. I wonder which side I am really on. Like the man whose role I imagined, I was blind and only gained my sight when my very life was threatened by three heart attacks. My eyes were opened by a truly extraordinary conversion process that made the simple beauty of Christ's message visible to me. It is a message that appeals directly to my inner self, entering through the heart, not the head. Yet I am drawn constantly to books and scholars and other things of the mind, lessening the impact of the feelings that Christ (and Sallie Ann) constantly emphasize.

It occurs to me now that prayer is the resolving power. It is only prayer and conscious meditation that allow me to read and study these Gospel passages with both feeling and understanding. Is that what the Ignatian method is all about? Is that the Ignatian message?

Tuesday, September 20 *(Luke 5:17-26)*

In this passage, Christ is in a room filled with Pharisees and "teachers of the law." Friends of a paralytic lower their afflicted friend through the roof, hoping that Jesus will see him and heal him. The act of dropping the poor man through the roof right into the middle of the gathering was so brazen and showed so much faith and hope that Jesus was moved to act. He announced to the man that his sins were forgiven, to which the Pharisees reacted by questioning Jesus's right to forgive sins. Only God has that power, they said. Jesus answered them with the question, "Would it have been better if I said rise up and walk?" So, after further grumbling from the crowd, Jesus did in fact tell the paralytic to rise, pick up his bed, and go home.

I try to imagine being part of the scene as one of the crowd, present either because of my profession or simply because I have heard about the new prophet performing miracles and ministering to the unclean. How truly strange it must have been for this revolutionary to go against the grain of common or ordinary practice; to challenge all taboos; to choose to work with and talk to the poor, sick, unclean, and untouchable people in the margins. As I watch the scene with the paralytic man unfold, I am particularly struck by the fact that Jesus knew what was in the hearts of the Pharisees. He only performed the healing act in the way they expected it to prove that He did, in fact, have the power to forgive.

It occurs to me that forgiveness is perhaps the first crucial step in the healing process. While I have never considered the possibility that physical ailments could be helped by forgiveness, I am now persuaded that mental anguish and depression require forgiveness. Not only is it critical to let go of resentment by forgiving others, it is even more important that we forgive ourselves for our own wrongdoing. Perhaps the adage "hate the sin, but love the sinner" is most important when applied to our own actions.

Consider the difference between the two concepts of guilt and shame. Guilt, which results from an action of some kind, is the remorse that one feels as a result of **a fault of doing**. This is the sin that we should hate. Shame, on the other hand, is the sense of worthlessness that results from **a fault of being**; a failure or falling short. This is the sinner that we should love.

I am also reminded again and again that our faith requires us to get outside ourselves. It is not a faith governed by rules, regulations, and restrictions. The Pharisees and law givers said that Jesus did not have the authority to forgive. They said that tax collectors were to be avoided. They said that lepers were unclean. Yet Christ acted in defiance of all of that, not simply to challenge the old system, but to demonstrate that the new gospel of "loving thy neighbor" was the key to salvation.

> I sought to hear the voice of God and climbed the topmost steeple, but God declared: "Go down again. I dwell among the people."[18]

We cannot be Christians without a core commitment to help the poor, sick, and outcast.

---

[18] John Henry Newman

Wednesday, September 21   *(Mark 12:1-12)*

Jesus and His disciples have walked from Galilee down through Jericho to Jerusalem. Along the way, Jesus has given sight to Bartimeaus, cursed a fig tree, and cleansed the Temple. Confronted by the chief priests and scribes, Jesus responds to various challenges of His authority. Then Jesus told them the parable of the tenants.

In order to "join" Christ and His disciples in this situation, I imagined walking with them along the dusty road with the Jordan River off to our left. I am one of the disciples, jockeying for position around Jesus. Mark's account describes the camp site in Bethany, a small community east of the city, to which our group returned after the first glorious day at the temple. It was in traveling to and from Bethany that we passed the fig tree, first with leaves and then withered. The scene is so real that I feel embarrassed that I tried to be as close as possible to Christ during the journey, but was quite happy to fade into the background when the confrontation with the chief priests and scribes began.

In this parable, the tenants are the people of Israel; the landlord is God; the initial servants are prophets; and the son is Jesus Christ. God left the people of Israel the land of Israel in trust – the people of Israel were meant to be stewards of this enormous gift from God. Prophet after prophet came to the people of Israel to demand repentance (collect the rent), and were rejected and sometimes killed. Finally, God sent His son Jesus Christ, who was also rejected and killed by the mob with the active support of the chief priests and scribes.

This is a powerful parable, but very sad. Are we today managing our roles as stewards any better? Everything we have – our talents, our energy, this planet, and the various bits of success we have achieved, whether material or in the form of respect from others – we have as a result of God's grace. We are only granted tenant rights to these gifts. It is our charge to manage them with respect and in trust, increasing them in value to honor God.

Thursday, September 22   *(Mark 9:14-29)*

Once again, I joined Jesus and His disciples this morning on their journey back to Galilee from Sidon and Tyre. This process of putting myself in the scene is beginning to take over my daily period of prayer and meditation. I do it even during times of the day other than my exercise hour.

I experience dust from the barren near-desert land north and west of Galilee, even though I am walking on the beach! I awakened this morning from a dream in which Jesus, His disciples and I are sitting around a fire in a small room.

As I read Mark in the pages just prior to the assigned scripture, I imagined myself part of the crowd of 4,000, partaking of the seven loaves. I see Jesus heal the blind man and question His disciples regarding the understanding of the people as to who

He is. When He asks Peter, James and John to join Him on His climb up Mount Hermon, I am at first hurt to be left out, and then find myself walking alongside them. I see Elijah and Moses and the transfigured Christ. It is all so amazing.

When we come down the mountain, the rest of the disciples are talking to a loud crowd, which includes some of the scribes and a father with his stricken son. The disciples have failed in their efforts to cast a demon from the son, so Jesus steps in and accomplishes the miracle. When asked by the disciples why they were not able to remove the demon, Christ answers that they need to pray more.

I take the admonition personally. I know I need to pray more, and I need to pray with greater faith. This morning, like each morning this week, I read the "Choose to Breath" prayer, followed by the Our Father. I am aware of the need to add to these prayers my own words, thanking God for all His phenomenal blessings and seeking His grace to increase my understanding. Perhaps St. Francis had a better idea:

Preach the Gospel at all times and when necessary use words.

In the silence prior to writing these words in this journal, I listened for a response. I feel God's presence, but cannot say I hear His voice. The feeling fills the room. It is like a tactile sense of grace. These mornings are truly wonderful!

Friday, September 23   *(Matthew 14:13-21)*

Maggie and I walked on the beach early this morning. I read through Matthew 14 last night, including the account of Jesus walking on the water. As I looked out at the ocean this morning, I could "see" Christ walking at the edge of a storm coming into shore. Turning south, I "saw" the other disciples walking down the beach. I prayed the Our Father a few times, and then walked in meditative silence for a while. I listened to the waves. I felt the strong sense of grace in that wave-broken peace. God was with me on that walk.

The reading this morning is preceded by Matthew's account of the death of John the Baptist. What a decadent, tragic story. Only due to being "pleased" by the dancing of his niece did Herod order the beheading of John. Jesus was so saddened to hear this from the followers of John that He "withdrew from [them] in a boat to a desolate place by Himself." It is extremely painful to imagine the sorrow (and disgust) of Jesus. I imagine myself to be one of the disciples. We reported to Jesus on His return that a large crowd had gathered and there was not enough food to feed them. I am moved to think of these five loaves and two fishes as offerings to eat in remembrance of John the Baptist. I am humbled by that memorial act.

The story of John the Baptist's death comes this week when we have watched the state of Georgia execute a man after all kinds of appeals, including one from Pope

Benedict.[19] How easy it seems for a state to take a life. Herod beheaded John because of a promise to his sister and the titillation of a young girl's dance. It seems so casual. Our Supreme Court, along with all the authorities in Georgia, seemed almost casual in their consideration of the clemency appeals. I am saddened by this.

I am back at the bench in the garden, just returned from helping the presenting CRHP[20] team prepare for the retreat this weekend. What a difference that meager effort makes! I am happy, filled with peace, and capable of looking all around me at the wonder of God. Colors are brighter. All of the plants are showing fresh growth from all of the rain. The sun is peeking out from behind clouds, even though it continues to rain lightly. The difference in surroundings is not in the plants or the sun or shimmering surface of the lagoon. The difference is inside me. I am seeing a different world because I stepped outside of myself, if only briefly, to help others. It changed me. It is the primary message of our faith.

Saturday, September 24 *(Luke 15:1-32)*

Jesus continues to preach to tax collectors and sinners, while the Pharisees and judges watched from the wings. Luke reports that these Jewish leaders scorned Jesus, challenging His decision to mingle with and preach to sinners. The three parables in this reading all relate to the issue of concern for the single loser in preference to the multitude of winners.

First, the one lost sheep gets all the attention of the shepherd, who allows the 99 sheep to run free.

Second, a passionate search for a lost coin ends in great joy when the coin is found.

Finally, the parable of the prodigal son emphasizes the joy of the father when his errant and wasteful son returns. It is the precise opposite of utilitarian morality.

Today is the first day of the women's CRHP retreat. I played a long three sets of tennis this morning, and then walked with Maggie on the beach for more than an hour. I began the day hung over with the joy of yesterday. My prayers feel hopeful.

---

[19] On September 22, 2011, Troy Davis, a black man, was executed by the State of Georgia for allegedly killing a white police officer twenty years earlier. Pope Benedict, among many other world leaders, urged that the authorities stay the execution.

[20] Christ Renews His Parish ("CRHP") is a faith and community building program that has been part of the Our Lady Star of the Sea parish program since 2005. Men and women separately participate in a weekend retreat, followed by several months of weekly meetings. Each retreat group is referred to as a "Team." The receiving team at one retreat becomes the presenting team at the following retreat.

As blessed as I am now, I have been the prodigal son, the lost sheep. Excommunicated before I was 21 and divorced before I was 26, I had marked up two of life's major failures before leaving the starting gate of the journey. Over and over again, I have taken two steps backward for each step forward. Yet each time I have stumbled thus far in my life, God's grace has been extended in the form of a helping hand, another chance, a forgiving gesture, or a welcome heart. Sallie Ann has consistently been the greatest expression of God's grace. She accepted my absence over much of the 25 years that I traveled on business. She took me back after I figuratively left her in my year of depression following my first cardiac event and the loss of my CEO position. She was there in the recovery room after my by-pass surgery. She held my hand as I journeyed through the spiritual path to Rome. She inspired Father John to embrace my decision to become a Catholic.

Luke's description of these three parables resonates very personally for me. Is that resonance the sound of God's whispered response to my prayers?

2. Praying over how I am loved by God

As you come to the end of your prayer time, try to make sure that your prayer turns into a dialog with God. You might talk with your Creator, or with Jesus of Nazareth, or with any of those who are present in your prayer.

Sunday, September 25   *(Luke 11:1-13)*

Sister Joan and I met this afternoon, opening our meeting with a prayer. Maggie sat peacefully on the floor. I read aloud the journal entries I had written since we last met. She gave me the new assignments, still part of the preparation period. At first I felt impatient, wanting to get on with the meat of the exercises. After a while, I was able to put some reason into my consideration. First of all, we are talking about a few days in the context of a nine-month program. Second, part of the message of Ignatius is to slow down, meditate, reflect, and get away from conventionally measuring time and progress.

This first reading for the second "preparation days" assignment, Luke 11:1-13, was the first reading assigned to me by Sister Joan the day we met for the first time. It was, if you will, a "pre-preparation" reading. What has changed in this past month is my appreciation of the Ignatian concept of contemplation; of imagining myself in the scene. I have developed the habit of reading the scriptures preceding the assigned reading, and sometimes a bit following the assignment, all in an effort to better understand the scene – the place, the characters, and their probable state of mind.

These ten chapters of Luke (from 9-19) recount Christ's final journey to Jerusalem. Huge crowds now form wherever Jesus and His apostles go. It is relatively easy to imagine myself one of the crowd. Jesus regularly performs miracles, preaches in parables, and asks ever more from His disciples. Among other things, Luke reports in Chapter 10 the sending out and the return of "the seventy-two." He praises a woman named Mary for choosing "the better part," and advises her sister Martha not to worry too much about less important details. Chapter 11 begins with Jesus praying alone. One of His disciples asks that Jesus "teach us to pray."

Maggie and I walked down to the meditation bench to reflect on the reading and to pray. Of course, we prayed the Our Father. How many times in my life have I prayed the Our Father? It is so simple, yet so profound. It is so often the way I have ended meetings with people I love, just as it is far and away the prayer I pray the most when I am alone.

Luke goes on to recount the somewhat confusing story of the man knocking on a neighbor's door in the middle of the night, seeking to borrow some bread. Jesus makes the point that persistence is required to rouse the neighbor from his sleep.

Thereafter follows the wonderful line "ask and it will be given to you, seek and you will find, knock and it will be opened to you." When I read this passage a month ago, I reflected on the ever present quality of God's grace. Grace is always present; always on offer. This morning, I read the commentary of the Church Fathers in Thomas Aquinas's Catena Aurea.[21] Augustine said:

But He would not so encourage us to ask were He not willing to give.

This seemed consistent with my own understanding. John Chrysostom[22] wrote:

---

[21] The Baronius Press describes its four volume edition of the Catena Aurea as follows. "St. Thomas Aquinas wrote the Catena Aurea at the request of Pope Urban IV, in order that an orthodox Patristic commentary on the Gospels was readily available to all readers. John Henry Newman, who is widely expected to be canonized next year, was responsible for its translation into English in 1841. Cardinal Newman hoped that the Catena Aurea would become a source of catechesis within the family and the Church. Cardinal Newman s edition of the Catena Aurea is one of the jewels of the 19th century Catholic Restoration, making the scholarship of the Fathers available to a wider audience. As with many 19th century texts it employs a sober, dignified style of English, which is eminently suitable to the unsurpassable mysteries of the Catholic Faith. e Catena Aurea, compiled by one of the Catholic Church's greatest minds, is of immeasurable use to priests writing homilies, lay people engaged in private or family study or of the Gospels and religious instructors will find it an invaluable help in preparing lessons. It is the perfect companion to study the Scriptures in detail and receive the wisdom of St. Thomas on particular passages. Consider the Catena Aurea as a discussion of the Gospels among the supreme theologians of the Church."

[22] According to Wikipedia, "John Chrysostom (c. 347–407), Archbishop of Constantinople, was an important Early Church Father. He is known for his eloquence in preaching and public speaking, his denunciation of abuse of authority by both ecclesiastical and political leaders, the Divine Liturgy of St. John Chrysostom, and his ascetic sensibilities. After his death in 407 (or, according to some sources, during his life) he was given the Greek epithet chrysostomos, meaning "golden mouthed" in English, and Anglicized to Chrysostom. The Orthodox and Eastern Catholic Churches honor him as a saint and count him among the Three Holy Hierarchs, together with Basil the Great and Gregory Nazianzus. He is recognized by the Eastern Orthodox Church and the Catholic Church as a saint and as a Doctor of the Church. Churches of the Western tradition, including the Roman Catholic Church, some Anglican provinces, and parts of the Lutheran Church, commemorate him on 13 September. Some Lu-

For it is the beginning of virtue to ask to know the way of truth. But the second step is to seek how we must go by that way. The third step is when a man has reached the virtue to knock at the door, that he may enter upon the wide field of knowledge.

Connecting virtue to the search for truth is brilliant. I love it that asking the way is only the beginning of a process that requires seeking or following the way, and, upon arrival, entering into the truth.

Another Greek Commentator takes the discussion further:

All these things a man acquires by prayer. To ask indeed is to pray, but to seek is by good works to do things becoming our prayers. And to knock is to continue in prayer without ceasing.

We "continue to pray without ceasing" or persist, not because God is slow to respond or cannot hear our request. Persistence is required because we are not always open to His grace. This is all tied to the Ignatian idea that prayer, reflection, and meditation are all part of opening ourselves to the sound of God's voice.

Monday, September 26 *(Psalm 139)*

"Search Me God, and Know My Heart." It is harder for me to imagine the Old Testament scenes, and to put myself there. However, I love the poetry of the Psalms, and I especially like hymns based on Psalms. So I imagine myself as the Cantor, singing praise to God in front of a congregation.

Psalm 139 is a great psalm. As I reflect on the idea that God knows my heart, that He knew me before I was born, I am reminded of something Ian Weldon said at one of our CRHP meetings. Ian was the Lay Director of the CRHP team presenting to my CRHP team. He was talking about God's infinite being, infinite knowledge, and infinite love. Ian talked about the mathematics of infinity. Dividing infinity by two does not result in two halves of divinity. Infinity divided by two is still infinity; just as infinity divided by 7 billion (the population of the planet expected by early next year) is still infinity. What this means is that God can love me completely, and, at the same time, love every other human being on the planet just as completely. God knows my heart, and the hearts of every other person on earth. While this may seem obvious to a lot of people, I struggle with the idea that God has the time or interest to care about me as one of the billions of people alive now or ever having lived.

---

theran and many Anglican provinces commemorate him on the traditional Eastern feast day of 27 January. The Coptic Orthodox Church of Alexandria also recognizes John Chrysostom as a saint (with feast days on 16 Thout and 17 Hathor). John is known in Christianity chiefly as a preacher, theologian and liturgist. Among his homilies, eight directed against Judaizing Christians remain controversial for their impact on the development of Christian antisemitism."

Sure, He can deal with global things, but how can He deal with so many individual things? Well, the answer has to do with God's infinity.

Tuesday, September 27 *(Prayer of My Dossier)*

In the notebook [journal], I jot down all the vital statistics of my life. As I note each piece of data, I raise my mind to God my Maker, and praise and thank the Creator for this detail in my life history and in myself.

I have prayed the following prayer each morning this week:

> *Oh, Lord my God,*
> *You called me from the sleep of nothingness*
> *merely because in Your tremendous love*
> *You want to make good and beautiful beings.*
> *You have called me by my name in my mother's womb.*
> *You have given me breath and light and movement,*
> *and walked with me every moment of my existence.*
> *I am amazed, Lord God of the universe,*
> *that you attend to me and, more, cherish me.*
> *Create in me the faithfulness that moves You,*
> *and I will trust You and yearn for You all my days. Amen*

This wonderful prayer, obviously a continuation of Psalm 139, forced me to work out and think through a thorough description of myself, including the things I like and the things I do not like. I have gone over my dossier in my mind many times.

> *"But I remember that God did not finish making me once, long ago, when I was conceived or born. I remember that God continues making me and has hopes for me and desires that I keep growing in love until I love as completely as God loves."*

What I have not done with rigorous regularity is end each section of my mental dossier by praising and thanking God. I am reminded more each day how little of who I am, what I have done, and what I have accumulated is my doing. Everything is a gift from God. I will return to this prayer, soon and often.

This, then, is my dossier. It is an accurate and truthful summary of my life story. It is not intended as a complete, detailed memoir. Nor have I attempted anything close to full disclosure. It is not my confession. I believe I have provided enough details to convey an accurate picture of my faith journey.

My Dossier

Family

My father's name was Glen Robert Hart. Dad was born in Buhl, Idaho, in 1921. He died in 2009 in Salt Lake City, Utah. Dad was the third of five children. His oldest sister, Miriam, is in her late 90s, and, as of April, 2012, alive and well in Payette, Idaho. Ralph, one of his younger brothers, is also still alive, and living in Oregon. The youngest child in his family, a brother named Warren, died in a farming accident several years ago, and an older sister, Belle, has also passed away. The family was originally Presbyterian. They were regular church goers, but not at all born again. Over the years, they all left the Presbyterian Church, each going in a different direction. Dad converted to Mormonism in the early 1950s.

Dad was extremely quiet. I suppose partly due to that, he always seemed rather content. It might be a little too much to suggest that he was happy, but he was certainly not sad.

My mother, Gwendolyn Irene Hoopes, was born in Tetonia, Idaho, in 1920. Tetonia is a small farming town (the population is still less than 250) on the western slope of the Grand Teton Mountains. The dry mountain desert around Tetonia, which includes Rexburg, was settled by the Mormons in the 1880s. To the best of my knowledge, it remains more than 90 percent Mormon. Mom died in 2003 in Terre Haute, Indiana. Mom was the only girl in a family of five children. Her four brothers were all very active in the Democratic Party, and in various political activities related to agriculture. Both her oldest brother and her youngest brother committed suicide. Another brother died in a farming accident. The final brother died from complications associated with his heart. Mom died following double knee surgery, a somewhat elective procedure that I have often thought seemed much like suicide.

Unlike my father, Mom was inclined to talk quite a lot. She was not at all content with her lot in life, and was anxious for the rest of us to know that. I remember her as being depressed a lot, and prone to various physical issues that kept her either in bed or in a wheelchair the last couple years of her life.

My parents were married in Rexburg, Idaho, in 1943. It was the first and only marriage for both of them.

I have two brothers: Leonard, born in February, 1944, and

Sitting: Nancy, Leonard, Connie. Standing: Terry, Bob, Sallie Ann, Debbie, Wayne, Shirley, Kirt.

Wayne, born in 1950. I have two sisters: Connie, born in 1954, and Nancy, born in 1955. Leonard and I left home to go to college when the other three children were quite young. We therefore had relatively little time together to form much in the way of sibling bonds. Wayne, Connie, and Nancy are close friends.

Leonard and I have a difficult relationship. He was older, and should have been entitled to the normal perquisites available to first-born children. I would not allow that to happen. I competed with him in most areas, and almost certainly enjoyed more recognition from our parents than a second child should. This was especially so with respect to my mother. Sadly, Leonard and I have never developed a close friendship. He has been married more than once, and has two sons from his first wife. He is not active in the Mormon Church. I would say that he has not had a very happy life, largely due to a variety of health problems. I admire his attitude in the face of these challenges.

Wayne is just six years younger than me. Our mother used to tell us that he was the smartest of all the children. He is clearly unique and lives a life consistent with his values. I have enormous respect for him. Wayne has also had marriage problems. He recently married for the third time. He has a daughter from his second wife. He is not active in the Mormon Church. On balance, I would say that Wayne is well-adjusted and happy.

Connie and Nancy are devoted Mormons, superb mothers, and fabulous sisters. They were the best daughters our parents could ever have hoped for. Both girls are still married to their first husbands. Connie has seven children. Nancy has four children. To the best of my knowledge, both of my sisters, and every member of their large families, are very active in the Mormon Church. They are both "steel magnolias" and seem to be quite happy.

As I write these observations about the relative happiness of my siblings, I realize just how far away from them I have been all my life. The distance has been physical and personal. The simple fact is that I have no basis for any of my opinions about their contentedness. I have seen them fewer than a dozen times in the last forty-five years. I hope they will for forgive me if I have it all wrong.

My family moved several times before I was seven, always within the state of Idaho. First, we moved from Rexburg, where I was born, to Moscow, when dad returned from World War II and went to the University of Idaho on the GI bill. From Moscow, we moved to Filer, which was a small town near dad's birthplace. In 1950, when I was just six years old, we moved to a farm about seven miles west of Blackfoot, where we lived until I left for college in 1963.

Growing Up on the Farm

I was born in Rexburg, Idaho, on December 28, 1944, barely ten months after my brother Leonard. I began life a healthy Caucasian male, with brown hair and hazel eyes. Except for my hair, which is snow white, I am still pretty much the same. I grew to be six feet tall, and have struggled with weight all my life, fluctuating between 180 and 220 pounds.

God chose all of this for me, and for this, I praise and thank Him.

It is sometimes hard to separate the force of nature from that of nurture, especially when trying to describe my mental and psychological characteristics. As a child, I was curious and remain so to this day. I read from as long ago as I can remember, devouring everything from the back of cereal boxes to every book in the house.

I was alone a great deal from the age of about nine, often as a result of being assigned farm tasks that were performed in fields a long way from the house. My memory of that time alone is not unpleasant. I gave speeches to various audiences, none of which were human, often trying to repeat what I had heard on the radio or from my uncles on my mother's side.

Although I was only eight years old at the time, I considered myself a Stevenson supporter in the 1952 election. I gave speeches to my horse and my dog Tippy, who was a little black dog about the same size as Maggie. I explained to both of them why the Democrats should win the election. Over the next few years, I addressed some of my speeches to President Eisenhower, and others to the then-Secretary of Agriculture, Ezra Taft Benson. Benson was a Mormon. In 1956, when I was twelve, I idolized Frank Church, working as a volunteer in his successful campaign for the US Senate.

By the time I was 14, I had developed a couple of standard speeches that I can almost give today. One was a "peace" speech, arguing that the cold war was distorting priorities. Another, my favorite, was a "poverty" speech that argued for an agriculture policy that would bring farmers into the mainstream American economy. For the record, however, I want to re-emphasize the fact that there were no human audiences for those early orations! However, when I entered high school at the age of 15, I rather quickly immersed myself in school politics. I found an audience for my by then well-rehearsed tirades! When I could finally do so, I joined the debate team and competed regularly in various competitions.

One of the saddest memories from those early years had to do with bed wetting, something that plagued me well into junior high school. It explains some of the solitude. It was also the cause of the worst experience I can remember from my youth. While having the best of intentions, one night my parents forced me outside with no clothes, making me sleep with the farm animals. I cried all night, and then walked two miles to my assigned irrigation field. I stayed out there all the next day, naked and ashamed. To say that this experience was traumatic is an understatement. I was nine years old at the time.

All this, God chose for me, both the good and the bad, and all this He chose for me in order to make me an instrument of His will. And for this, I praise and thank Him.

I ran the half-mile in high school, and was on both the basketball and football teams. Note, however, that Snake River High School was so small that virtually every male able to walk made the teams. I played the trombone in the band and I led the debate team. I was class president my sophomore year, Student Body Vice President my junior year, and Student Body President my senior year. I had good grades, finishing second in my class. I attended both Boy's State and Boy's Nation.

When John F. Kennedy was elected President in 1960, I learned that he was a graduate of Harvard, an eastern school with a good reputation. So impressed was I that I sent a letter to Harvard College, New York, New York, stating my intention of going on to college after graduation from Snake River High School and my belief that Harvard would be a fine place to do so. As I would later learn, Harvard is located in Cambridge, Massachusetts, not New York. The letter found its way to the Harvard Club in New York, and from there it got to the Dean of Admissions in Cambridge, who eventually arranged a "boot strap" scholarship for this rhubarb from the Idaho sticks.

College and Mission

In the early part of August 1963, I boarded a Union Pacific passenger train in Pocatello, Idaho, bound for Cambridge, Massachusetts. I was about to begin my freshman year in the Class of 1967 at Harvard College. I arrived lonely, tired, and suddenly very uncertain about what I had gotten myself into.

To say the least, Harvard was a huge shock for me. I lived in Lionel Hall with two roommates, both from Idaho. One of them was Lou Dobbs, the very conservative commentator on CNN and Fox. My grades as a freshman were mediocre.[23]

Most of my friends were Mormons. Almost all of them were graduate students who were studying law or business after having graduated from BYU or some other university in the west. They had all served missions for the Mormon Church in a foreign country. I had Sunday lunch with their families after church, and the talk all during that year was about missions.

So I left Harvard after one year, and joined a group of earnest young Mormons on bicycles in Germany. We did our best to convince good Lutherans and Catholics to change their lives and join the quintessential American faith, founded on the claim of a visit from Christ to upstate New York two thousand years ago. As young missionaries (most of us were 19 and 20 year-olds), we were pastors of congregations. We performed the normal pastoral duties: we married people, buried people, blessed their newborns, and counseled them in times of distress.

---

[23] My transcript shows that I earned two B+s and one C+ in the fall (the C+ was in Government 1a, not a good indication for my future concentration in Government). All spring grades were some shade of B (a B+, a B-, and a simple B). While this does not sound very impressive, it was actually quite good for a "bootstrap" student that had not even been predicted to make it through the first year!

At some point during the first of my nearly two years in Germany, I had some "white light" religious experiences. As I recall it, the first occurred when I was blessing the sick child of one our parishioners. The baby got better. Both parents and I were so moved by the energy in the room that we wept with joy. Something similar happened once when I was able to end a bitter argument among a group of parishioners. As I prayed, it seemed as though a presence filled the room. The shouting subsided and, again, everyone wept with a quiet joy.

I came to believe deeply in God. I accepted Christ as my Savior. While I never grew to like the idea of proselytizing, I was a leader in the West German Mission.

And then it all collapsed. I was wrongly accused of violating my oath of celibacy. I was held under house-arrest in the basement of the mission headquarters in Frankfurt for three weeks, then convicted in a Bishop's Court, excommunicated from the Mormon Church, and sent home from my mission. Custom required my parents to send a black-bordered card to all their friends, neighbors, and the church community, announcing my spiritual death. My mother never forgave me for this.

Harvard was gracious enough to accept me back into the sophomore class in the middle of November of 1965. I appealed my excommunication in Salt Lake City, but to no avail. So I returned to Cambridge (hitch-hiking all the way), leaving the Mormon Church behind forever. For the next forty years, I did my best to forget that I believed in God.

While my faith life was suspended (at least that part of it associated with any institutional religion), I busied myself with what the Franciscan friar Richard Rohr[24] describes as "building my life container." In his book, Falling Upwards, Rohr maintains that we devote ourselves to this task, i.e., building the container, in the first half of life. In the second and more important half of life, Rohr suggests we decide what to put into that container, and then set about filling it. Obviously, these halves of our lives are not measured in years. Some people may never reach the second half. I assume they die with empty life containers.

Like that of many others, my life container consisted largely of various facades – degrees and pedigrees, personas, and images I wanted the world to see. I finished Harvard with some distinction (Magna Cum Laude in Government and Phi Beta Kappa), married the daughter of a respected intellectual and political family, and fully immersed myself in my first career, which was to build and operate low-income housing

---

[24] According to Wikipedia, "Richard Rohr, O.F.M. (born in 1943 in Kansas) is a Franciscan friar ordained to the priesthood in the Roman Catholic Church in 1970. He is an internationally known inspirational speaker and has published numerous recorded talks and books. Rohr was the founder of the New Jerusalem Community in Cincinnati, Ohio in 1971 and the Center for Action and Contemplation in Albuquerque, New Mexico in 1986 where he currently serves as the Founding Director." Sallie Ann and I both subscribe to his daily meditation.

projects throughout the country. We had two wonderful daughters, lived in five cities, and lasted two years together.

My daughters, Melissa Hart and Jennifer Hart Love, are extraordinary women. Melissa was born in Boise, Idaho, in 1969, has two children and teaches at the University of Colorado Law School. Jennifer was born in Denver, Colorado, in 1971, has one child and teaches at the Sylvan Learning Center in Asheville, North Carolina.

Low Income Housing

My first career, developing low-income housing, began as a result of some misguided missionary fervor. When I returned to Harvard in 1965, I volunteered, along with most of my classmates, to work in some of the poorest neighborhoods in Boston. My particular cause was organizing rent strikes against slumlords. One night, at a celebration of our success in causing the housing authorities to condemn a building, I was asked a question by an older lady who, up until that day, had been living in the building. "Where am I supposed to sleep tonight, Mr. Hart? We were living in that building because it was the best available place to live."

The room was suddenly quiet. It slowly dawned on me that the problem of substandard housing could not be solved by simply condemning the dangerous buildings. Somehow, there needed to be new housing built that was affordable and of acceptable quality. Over the five years following graduation in 1968, I developed, owned and operated low-income housing. I worked the first year for Boise Cascade Corporation, but left when I concluded it would be more satisfying to develop real estate in my own company. The decision to strike out on my own, to start a new company; to raise capital and to put together a staff would be repeated seven times before I finally retired.

Coal Mining

Throughout the 1970s, my life was long on excitement and painfully short on meaning and substance. In the middle of the decade, I moved out of real estate and into coal mining, building my first mine with a book about coal propped between the steering levers of a bulldozer. I loved the coal business, in spite of the fact that I lived alone in a trailer located at the mouth of a hollow on Hell's Creek in Delbarton, West Virginia. Seven years of that Spartan lifestyle allowed me to learn a lot about energy, and to commence a life-long love affair with architecture.

We had two fatal accidents during the period that I owned the mines. I was underground when the second man died, and joined the futile effort to revive him during the three mile trip to the surface. I had to talk to the families of the miners after the accidents. Most of the people in those West Virginia hollows were deeply religious. They faced death regularly, but struggled nonetheless with the fairness of sons and husbands dying so young in the mines. I spoke as the owner of the mine, but, more important, as someone who might console them at a particularly difficult time. What little I help I could provide was only due to the relationship with God that I had developed in Germany a decade earlier.

The coal business was truly insane in those days. Most independent miners were bankrupt most of the time, but didn't know it or couldn't do anything about it. Well, at least I knew it, but it was like having a tiger by the tail. C. S. Lewis[25] said it well:

Experience is a brutal teacher, but you learn. My God, do you learn.

However difficult, I look back on those days with very fond memories. Among other things, we sold our coal to the Japanese steel companies, which required that I learn how to conduct myself and my business in a foreign country, speaking through translators, and dealing with relatively complex currency transactions.

Marriage to Sallie Ann Robbins

Near the end of my coal mining career, I bought a house in the Washington, DC, area. It was there, on the night before my birthday in 1980, that a blind date was arranged with a beautiful, bright, enchanting and charming woman named Sallie Ann Robbins, an event that changed my life several times over. I fell in love with her that night, and my love has never wavered. She was Catholic, but wisely chose not to ask that I convert to her faith.

Sallie Ann was born in Washington, D.C., and lived there all her life until we moved to Houston in 1994. Her father's family lived in Upper Marlboro, Maryland, where they grew and marketed tobacco. Her father, a lawyer, worked most of his life on the staff of a congressman from New York. He died of a heart attack when Sallie Ann was only 19 years old. Her mother was a proud Southern lady, the daughter of Henry Steagall.[26] Sallie Ann graduated from Holton Arms, one of the most prestigious private girls' schools in the country. After her father's death, she had to leave Mary Washington College and join the work force, which for her meant returning to Holton Arms as a Drama teacher and housemother.

---

[25] According to Wikipedia, "C. S. Lewis (29 November 1898 – 22 November 1963),was a novelist, poet, academic, medievalist, literary critic, essayist, lay theologian and Christian apologist from Belfast, Ireland. He is known for both his fictional work, especially The Screwtape Letters, The Chronicles of Narnia and The Space Trilogy and his nonfiction, such as Mere Christianity, Miracles and The Problem of Pain. According to his memoir Surprised by Joy, Lewis had been baptised in the Church of Ireland (part of the Anglican Communion) at birth, but fell away from his faith during his adolescence. Owing to the influence of J.R. Tolkien and other friends, at the age of 32 Lewis returned to the Anglican Communion, becoming "a very ordinary layman of the Church of England." His faith had a profound effect on his work, and his wartime radio broadcasts on the subject of Christianity brought him wide acclaim. In 1956 he married the American writer Joy Davidman, 17 years his junior, who died four years later of cancer at the age of 45. "

[26] Henry Steagall was the co-sponsor of the famous Glass Steagall Act, the banking regulation that was repealed in 1999, leading, in the view of many (including me) to the financial collapse in 2008.

She married Sabin Robbins, a Yale graduate with a second degree from Oxford, who was working for National Geographic. They lived in Wesley Heights, one of the best neighborhoods in Washington. They had two sons: Rob, born in 1960, and Will, born in 1963. She wrote and published two travel books and proclaimed the word at Holy Trinity in Georgetown (the first female lector in the Washington diocese). She was a trainer in a human-potential program, and ran her own public relations firm. When she and I met, she was a real estate broker with a high-end firm in Georgetown.

Sallie Ann and I were married on Valentine's Day in 1982. We traveled the world together, occasionally for pleasure, but mostly on business trips as I tried to sell my coal in Asia and Europe. Sallie Ann was a great asset whenever she traveled with me on business trips. After I sold the coal mines, we lived part-time in Milan, Italy, where I had taken a job as CEO of the US operations of the Italian government coal company, Agip Carbone.

Sallie Ann's two sons were teenagers when she and I were married. Rob Robbins, her oldest, lives in Jacksonville, Florida, and works for a cellular telephone company. He has three children. Will Robbins, Sallie Ann's younger son, lives in Seattle, Washington, where he works for a small private equity firm.

Independent Electric Power

My coal career came to an end when I was trying to sell some of our coal production to a utility in Maine. They suggested that I sell them electricity rather than coal, something made possible by a new law enacted in 1978, which required US utilities to buy electricity from qualified independent producers. When I explained that I had never been inside a power plant and was not sure whether the turbine was meant to face the window or the door, my business partners countered that I had known even less than that about the coal business a decade earlier.

We launched US Energy in 1983, joining the handful of other pioneering independent power producers who offered an alternative to the investor-owned monopoly utilities that theretofore completely dominated the power industry in this country. Our first power plant was a wood-burning facility in Maine, one of three we commissioned before I sold my controlling interest to the rest of the employees.

International Electric Power

In 1988, I started another new power company, focused on the countries in Eastern Europe that were just beginning to break free from the Soviet Union. It was one of the most exciting periods of my life. Frankly, it was one of the most exciting periods for almost anyone to be alive, especially with the opportunity to work in Poland, Hungary, the Czech Republic and elsewhere in this newly-free part of the world. Our primary project was the privatization of the heat and power plants in Krakow, Poland. However, that project required that we, along with the World Bank and other international advisors, work with the various governments of the region to completely redesign the laws and regulations that governed their power sectors. The laws had to be changed to allow for the private ownership and operation of the electric power infra-structure, which had theretofore been a fundamental component of the Soviet-style centrally planned, command economy.

The whole process was as challenging as anything I have experienced. We were literally making up the rules as we went along. T. S. Eliot once asked:

If you aren't in over your head, how do you know how tall you are?

Ultimately, the French government won the bidding for the Krakow power plants, but not until our new company had become prominent enough to attract attention from several large energy companies. I became CEO of Coastal Power Company in 1994, folding my Washington-based staff into the power division of one of largest oil and gas companies in Houston, Texas.

Over the next five years, Coastal led a truly global explosion of private power. We – the international independent power companies - were the tip of the globalization spear. Each year from 1994 through 1999, we invested more private capital in developing country infrastructure than the total amount ever invested. Our message in every country was essentially the same, and it was the central message of what has become known as the Washington Consensus:[27]

If you, the countries around the world, will de-regulate, privatize, and adopt fiscal policies that protect our investment, there is no end to the amount of capital we will make available for your growth and development.

In country after country, our development teams helped the authorities to create legal and regulatory structures friendly to us, then built and began operating power generation facilities, distribution companies, and even transmission lines.

Coastal built new power plants in El Salvador, Nicaragua, the Dominican Republic, Jamaica, and Guatemala. We acquired the state generating systems in Panama and Peru. We built three power plants in Pakistan, one in Bangladesh, and five in China.

However, it was not my company. Moreover, by the end of 1998, the Coastal Board of Directors was losing interest in foreign countries with odd currencies and strange

---

[27] The term **Washington Consensus** was coined in 1989 by the economist John Williamson to describe a set of ten relatively spec`ific economic policy prescriptions that he considered constituted the "standard" reform package promoted for developing countries by Washington, D.C.-based institutions, such as the International Monetary Fund (IMF), World Bank, and the US Treasury Department. These economic reforms, popular from the late 1970's to mid 1990's, are generally described as a form of economic liberalism, which seeks to emphasize the efficiency of private enterprise, liberalized trade, and the opening of markets. The adoption of these policies was often a precondition to receiving aid from the World Bank and IMF.

people. So I left Coastal after five years to start a new company that would focus exclusively on the poorest countries in the world.

The strategy for Globeleq (the name was derived from Global Electric Equity), my new company, was to capitalize on the fact that many of the US companies that had invested so heavily during the nineties in Latin America, Africa, and Asia were now excited about opportunities here at home. We started buying before we had even fully organized the new company. At the end of 2001, when Enron filed for bankruptcy, the US and European power industries virtually imploded. Almost every power plant built or privatized in the nineties was on the block. In the poor countries, Globeleq was about the only buyer. Needless to say, we made some pretty good deals.

The only investor I could find was the British government.[28] They had more than a lot of very patient capital, half of which they ultimately invested in Globeleq, with extremely low yield requirements. Talk about the "perfect investor."

One of the only requirements the British government attached to its investment in my new company was that I acquire a map of Africa and spend some time there. I took this seriously, traveling to east Africa long before I could see any opportunities for investment.

In late 2001, one of the world's largest international energy companies agreed to sell its assets in South Africa, Tanzania, Nigeria, Zambia, and Uganda to Globeleq. We concluded the transactions in South Africa and Tanzania by the middle of 2002. We became the national distribution company for Uganda two years later, and completed our Africa acquisition program in 2004 with a plant in Egypt. Our final African portfolio included all of these, plus operating plants in Kenya and the Ivory Coast. We were also developing power plants in Nigeria and Kenya. We had exceeded the mandate to be serious about investment and operations in Africa.

Along the way, a classic dispute arose between my management team and our British investor. CDC, the government development agency, had converted itself into a private equity firm. The view of its leadership was that they had hired a management team for their company. Of course, I and my management team felt like we had found an investor for our company. It was a dispute destined for an unhappy ending.

---

[28] The actual investor was the Commonwealth Development Corporation (CDC), which was part of the British Department for International Development. CDC was formed in 1947, originally called the Colonial Development Corporation, as its purpose was to invest in the development of what were then British colonies.

To understand how important the electric power infrastructure is in Africa, look at this satellite map showing the world at night. Europe and North America are brightly lit. Much of Asia and the coastal parts of South America are lit, though not as brightly. Africa is a large, dark land mass, with virtually no electric power lighting even the larger cities. Our objective was to light up those dark places on the planet.

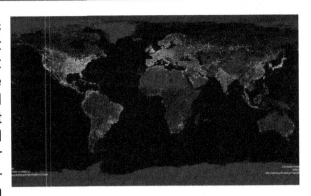

Our investment in Tanzania provided a wonderful opportunity to appreciate the significance of what we were doing. We acquired the right to complete the development and construction of an integrated gas project. Natural gas had been discovered off the coast of Songo Songo Island, which is located about 200 km south of Dar es Salaam. A small government-owned power plant in Dar used heavy fuel oil to make a relatively small and quite unreliable supply of electric power. Our project consisted of completing the gas field, building a pipe-line up to Dar, converting the old plant from dirty oil to clean natural gas, and, finally, building new gas-fired capacity. In the process of completing the gas field, we had to install a small power generating facility on the island, which facility I was privileged to dedicate early in the development of the project. There was a small school on the island, along with an equally small medical clinic. Both were provided electric power for the first time when we commissioned that small generator.

I cannot describe in words the level of emotion among the inhabitants of that little island off the east African coast when the lights were turned on. The students at the little school saw a computer for the first time. The staff at the clinic was finally able to refrigerate drug supplies. A year later, when we joined President Mkapa to dedicate the connection of the gas supply from Songo Songo to the power plant in the capital, I experienced a kind of joy that I had rarely experienced in my life.

I could go on from one country and project to the next, each time achieving a sense that I was finally realizing the potential of the gifts of grace I had been blessed with by God. I mean this. These were intensely spiritual experiences, even though I was still three or four years away from commencing the spiritual journey that would lead me to Rome.

Heart Problems and Depression

There is a wonderful Hasidic tale that goes something like this:

> *The pupil comes to the Master and asks, "Why does the Torah tell us to place these words upon your hearts'? Why does it not tell us to place these holy words in our hearts?" The Master answers, "It is because as we are, our hearts are closed, and we cannot place the holy words in our hearts. So, we*

place them on top of our hearts. And there they stay until, one day, the heart breaks, and the words fall in.

My doctors first diagnosed coronary artery disease in 2005, which led to a relatively simple and very safe angioplasty and a couple of stents in December of that year. I actually felt fine, but my British overlords pounced on my cardiac condition with enthusiasm. By the middle of 2006, I was forced to move from the position of CEO to that of Founding Partner, a position I described as "finding pasture." Globeleq was put up for sale. Since I had defined myself by my job, I suddenly found myself without the protection of a defining persona. I sank into a deep hole of depression.

On the evening of June 18, 2007, Sallie Ann and I celebrated both the sale of Globeleq and the welcome news that I had "aced" a stress test that morning. Four hours later, in the middle of the night, I had my first major heart attack. It hurt more than anything I have ever experienced. Another angioplasty and three more stents followed. A second heart attack hit less than a month later, resulting in yet another angioplasty. I learned the hard way that the physical damage done by cardiac events is almost always accompanied and, often, exceeded by mental anguish and depression. So the good news of the sale of Globeleq was entirely lost on me, as I spent that summer and early fall sinking deeper and deeper into what had become suicidal despair.

Then in October, while giving a speech in Arizona, I suffered the most severe of my three heart attacks. The doctors declared my stent system a complete failure and performed a triple bypass. Little did I know then just how life-saving that surgery would be. It is often said that there are no atheists in foxholes. Well, I can tell you that there are very few atheists in cardiac wards.

Faith Journey

The good news for me was that I had never completely lost faith in God. I prayed for a lot of things during the long convalescence period. I asked God to grant me the grace to discover what He wanted me to do. I asked Him for the strength to do it. I asked Him to extend His grace to those I had taken for granted that they might forgive me – particularly Sallie Ann, my daughters and her sons, and Buddy, my best friend of forty years. I was 62 years old when I began what Rohr describes as the primary task of the second half of my life – choosing what to put into my "life container."

Long before I realized that the ultimate destination was Rome, I embarked upon a journey of spiritual discovery. Buddy, who was a Southern Baptist, sent me a copy of the Catholic research doctor Francis Collins' book The Language of God,[29] which

[29] According to Wikipedia, "Francis Sellers Collins (born April 14, 1950), is an American physician-geneticist, noted for his discoveries of disease genes and his leadership of the Human Genome Project (HGP). He currently serves as Director of the National Institutes of Health in Bethesda, Maryland. Prior to being appointed Director, he founded and was president of the BioLogos Foundation. Collins

was based in no small part on C.S. Lewis's <u>Mere Christianity</u>. I read and read. Each day, I tried to put the most valuable things I learned into my life container, a process that goes on today and will continue, I hope, until I die.

Catholicism

Sallie Ann and I prayed together constantly. I often joined her at Mass, but only as a cautious visitor. The Pastor of St. Anne's parish in Houston, where we lived, was Father John Robbins, an incredible man who decided for some strange reason that I was worth saving, probably because I was married to Sallie Ann. We all became extremely close friends. After numerous dinner conversations, I finally expressed an interest in finding some kind of structure for my newly revived focus on spirituality. He suggested that I learn more about what it means to become a Catholic. I called the people in charge of the Rite of Christian Initiation for Adults (RCIA), a call I would never have made had I felt pressured to do so by others.

RCIA was not easy. I learned that my Mormon baptism didn't count, so I would have to complete two years of RCIA, instead of one. The diocese said not to worry, however; the annulment would take at least as long! Buddy said he could make me a Baptist in fifteen minutes, which included the driving time to find a river.

> If I were looking for God, every event and every moment would sow, in my will, grains of His life that would spring up one day in a tremendous harvest...If these seeds would take root in my liberty, and if His will would grow from my freedom, I would become the love that He is, and my harvest would be His glory and my own joy. [30]

Father John talked to me throughout the process. He once said to me that many of the things described in the Bible probably never happened, but that they are all true! I loved that. He said the two most important words in the Catholic faith were *forgiveness* and *inclusion*. I loved that too. He said I would know that becoming Catholic was the right thing for me to do when I came to love the Eucharist more than anything in my life. He was right.

My father died in the summer of 2009. I had been working in Asia six years earlier when my mother died. I was barely able to make it back for the funeral. However, I did fly out to Salt Lake City to visit with Dad a couple of times in the last few months of his life. He surprised me by actively supporting my exploration of Catholicism. He astonished me by telling me I had made him proud, in no small part because I seemed to get back up after each time that I fell. He said I had practiced that a lot.

---

has written a book, The Language of God, about his Christian faith, and Pope Benedict XVI appointed Francis Collins to the Pontifical Academy of Sciences"

[30] Merton, <u>New Seeds of Contemplation</u>, p. 42.

I told him how much I loved him.   Apparently, Dad would have agreed with C.S. Lewis:

>   *Failures are finger posts on the road to achievement.*

Then Father John and Buddy learned that their battles with prostate cancer were coming to an end.   I was still six months away from baptism.   Both of these remarkable men had been with me in moments of doubt and moments of joy.   I was completely unprepared for them to die.

Father John lived until December 2009, long enough for him to counsel me through yet another period of doubt.   In the month before his death, he asked that I be a pall bearer in his funeral, which felt like he was pulling me towards God with his shepheard's crook as he left this earth for heaven.

Buddy died in March of 2010, after spending January and February at M.D. Anderson in Houston.   I visited him every day, which did far more for me than it ever did for Buddy.   We prayed together and talked about all the years and all the deals and all the false paths we had gone down.   I kissed him on his balding head each day when I left the hospital.   For the second time in three months, I was a pall bearer.

>   *Death is someone you see very clearly with eyes in the center of your heart: eyes that see not by reacting to light, but by reacting to a kind of a chill from within the marrow of your own life.*[31]

My new life officially began a month later during Easter Vigil in the most powerful ceremony I have ever experienced.   After forty years in a spiritual desert, more than two years of intense searching at RCIA, and several months of mourning the deaths of my father and closest friends, I celebrated four sacraments in as many days. First, Sallie Ann and I were married in the Church.   Without ever pushing, she had held my hand every step along the journey to Rome.   I was baptized, confirmed, and received first communion.   I continue to this day to experience all of that spiritual excitement each time I take the Eucharist.   I am trying to fill my life container with actions as well as knowledge.

I think about that Hasidic tale frequently.   God's words were indeed placed on top of my heart, and there they stayed until the day my heart broke and the words fell in.

Reading the pages of my dossier notes, and reflecting on them, I can certainly see traits in the resulting man that I like.   I work hard.   I am driven to achieve.   I am sensitive to people at the margins of our society.   I am honest with others, though not always with myself.   The combination of high energy and a thirst for knowledge has resulted in some considerable accomplishments.

---

[31] Thomas Merton, *The Intimate Merton: His Life from His Journals*

I know these gifts came from God, and it is to God that any credit for the accomplishments is due. I praise and thank Him for the gifts and for what they have enabled me to achieve.

I can see many traits that I do not like. I am obsessive in much of what I do. I worked myself out of my first marriage. I allowed my workaholic nature to threaten my marriage to Sallie Ann. When I became depressed, I obsessively allowed the depression to go deeper and to cause more damage than would otherwise have been the case. I carry resentments for a long time. I carry shame for a long time.

Yet I know that these traits are part of the person God chose. They exist for me to overcome. I thank and praise God for giving me these opportunities to grow.

Wednesday, September 28   *(Matthew 6:25-34)*

While Jesus was born in Bethlehem, south of Jerusalem, He and His family returned to Nazareth (after a few years' exile in Egypt), far to the north above the Sea of Galilee. While traveling south to Judea, Jesus is baptized by John the Baptist in the Jordan River. Having returned from Hiss forty days in the Judean desert, Jesus begin His public ministry: first, briefly, in Judea, and then after traveling back to His home, in the north. It was here in the region around Capernaum that huge crowds gathered to hear the new gospel Jesus preached. In Chapters 5 through 7, Matthew tells the story of Christ delivering His incredible Sermon on the Mount. This sermon, the longest in the New Testament, takes place on Mount Eremos, a short distance northwest of Capernaum. Chapter 6 begins with Matthew's account of the Our Father, the version that we all pray. I imagine myself one of the crowd gathered around Christ throughout the entire sermon. It is a long sermon, but one packed with incredible meaning from beginning to end. Every verse requires careful study and quiet reflection. The verses assigned today are no exception.

The gist of this reading is that we should not be worried with silly things like food and clothing. Instead, we should be focused on the kingdom of God. Or, as verse 34 suggests, we should be in the present, not worry about tomorrow or, implicitly, regret yesterday. I like the idea of the Kingdom of God being the present; the "now." As I read this passage in the garden, I particularly love the reference to the "lilies of the field" that grow and thrive without "toil or spin." Commenting on this passage, Saint Jerome said:.[32]

What work of man has the red blush of the rose? The pure white of the lily?

---

[32] Saint Jerome was Presbyter and Monk of Bethlehem, A.D. 378.

Thursday, September 29   (The Lilies of the Field)

"How much of me is mine? How much is God's?" These are powerful questions. It is a commanding thought-piece:

Jesus called on His disciples to "consider" the lilies of the field, and we should do the same. The lily does not choose in which field it will stand. When it grows from seed or runner, it finds itself in this field, with this hard clay or soft loam. So do I find myself on a "field" - the twentieth century, America, a state, city, town, neighborhood? How much of my life world is my making; how much is God's?

The lily has no control over what grows around it. When it shoots up, it might have to fight for its life with thorns or clumps of crabgrass. Or it might be out-shone by great sunflowers. So have I very little control over what surrounds me. I live in corporate structures, in political processes. I am caught up in earning a living, buying insurance, preparing for illness and old age. I cannot change the stock market or banking practices or taxation. I cannot make the ghettos disappear, or dry up acid rain. How much of my life world is my making; how much is God's?

The lily of the field has absolutely no control over the weather - rain or drought, it must simply stand and endure. So have I no control over nations warring on one another, or over international cartels poisoning the air with pollutants. I cannot control whether people around me drug themselves and fill the atmosphere of my life world with fear and violence. I cannot control people feeling prejudice toward me and my kind. I cannot make male chauvinism or strident feminism go away, or stop people from aborting babies or abusing their children. How much of my life world is my making; how much is God's?

The lily came up a certain kind of lily of a certain color and shape, and its shapeliness an health depended on the spring and the summer, and whether grazing cattle let it grow. So did I come up a certain kind of person, of a certain color and shape. So were my psychic health and physical shape much influenced by the forces around me when I was coming up. And until now, all created things have let me live and even thrive, though many, many threatened and still threaten me. How much of my life growth is my making: how much is God's?

For all that, not even Solomon dressed up in gold-embroidered brocade was any more lovely than that lily. So for all that has shaped and misshaped me, for all that has given me health and inflicted ill health on me - I am precious in the eyes of God, and honored, and God loves me as I am. Otherwise, I would not be as I am, though God would be glad were I to slough off my selfish sins. But they are trash compared to God's creating love in me, whose love will burn them away like flakes on the bark of a flaming pine log. How much of me is mine; how much can be God's? [33]

I read it and re-read it many times this morning. It was a good time to read this message. Last night I spoke to the parish Men's Group at Our Lady Star of the Sea, delivering an account of my life in business and my journey of faith. Over and over again, I returned to the theme that I have tried to live my life with a focus on "making a difference." The message of this prayer is that we are who we are, and the world around us is as it is. I cannot change the world, or control other people. I am reminded of the wonderful prayer written by Reinhold Niebuhr.[34] The prayer is known throughout the world as the Serenity Prayer:

> *God, grant me the serenity to accept the things I cannot change, the courage to change the things I can, and the wisdom to know the difference.*

Niebuhr's actual prayer differed in some small, but very important ways. The emphasis is mine:

> *God, grant me the grace to accept with serenity the things I cannot change, the courage to change the things I **should**, and the wisdom to distinguish between the two.*

Throughout my life, I have tried to change the world around me, perhaps responding to the message in the actual Niebuhr prayer without knowing it. I built low-income housing. I built power plants in poor countries. I have tried to reduce hatred and bigotry. I worked in the civil rights movement, hoping to bring some reason and love to race relations in this country. I tried in every way possible to bridge the gap between Muslims and the rest of us, talking frequently to my many Muslim employees.

So this prayer flies a bit in the face of my life experience and effort. Yet, when combined with the verses we read yesterday from Matthew, there is another message here. Jesus counseled us not to be "anxious." not to worry obsessively. He did not

---

[33] Thought-piece from the Tetlow handbook.

[34] According to Wikipedia, "Karl Paul Reinhold Niebuhr (June 21, 1892 – June 1, 1971) was an American theologian and commentator on public affairs. Starting as a leftist minister in the 1920s indebted to theological liberalism, he shifted to the new Neo-Orthodox theology in the 1930s, explaining how the sin of pride created evil in the world. He attacked utopianism as ineffectual for dealing with reality, writing in The Children of Light and the Children of Darkness (1944): "Man's capacity for justice makes democracy possible; but man's inclination to injustice makes democracy necessary." His realism deepened after 1945 and led him to support United States' efforts to confront Soviet communism around the world. A powerful speaker, he was one of the most influential religious leaders of the 1940s and 1950s in American public affairs. Niebuhr battled with the religious liberals over what he called their naïve views of sin and the optimism of the Social Gospel, and battled with the religious conservatives over what he viewed as their naïve view of Scripture and their narrow definition of "true religion.""

say that we were to simply accept evil or to sit idly by in the face of wrong. I hope I am not simply trying to rationalize my life choices. John Chrysostom, commenting on the passage from Matthew, said, "We will be held to account not whether we were rich or poor. Rather we will be judged on whether we did well or ill." I like to think I tried to live in accordance with this guidance.

Friday, September 30 *(Isaiah 43:1-7)*

Because you are precious in my eyes, and honored, and I love you.

God is speaking to the people of Israel in this passage, but I read it to apply to any of us as individuals as well. The theme of all of the readings this week comes back to God's love for us, and His role in our individual lives.

In the long forty years I spent wandering in a spiritual desert, I rejected any thought that God cared for us as individuals, or that He acted in our lives. It was difficult enough for me to accept His existence. Even that, however, I chose to consider in a very general, theoretical sense. God was out there, way out there.

It was not until I reached the depths of depression that I began to appreciate that everything I was, everything I had ever done, was God's gift, His doing. When jotting down notes in my dossier earlier this week, I could see over and over again how much all of this was not mine, but His.

Why would He bother? Why give me so much, and then allow so much of it to be at risk? Why bless me with gifts, and then watch as I squandered those very gifts? Why pick me back up after I fell through my own selfishness or ambition or grandiosity? My whole life story could be entitled "Second Chance."

I love the meditation garden. It is just simple enough that I see little human touch. It is all about God's work, His beauty, His serenity. Its perfection is all a gift from God. The additions I have made – fountains and temples and rills – are all gifts of God resulting from whatever design talent God gave me, from the educational and travel opportunities God gave me, from the family and early surroundings God gave me. There is nothing in my life that is not a gift of God. Even this time to reflect and give Him praise and thanks is itself a gift of God.

Saturday, October 1 (Psalm 139, again)

I read Psalm 139 last Sunday and wrote in this journal after prayer and meditation. I read this Psalm again after the Prayer of the Dossier on Monday. So here I am again, reflecting on Psalm 139 for the third time in a week.

As I read it this morning, I smiled to myself about the audacity of writing my dossier. God knows all of this and so much more about me. It humbled me. I struggle to remember the names and places and dates of this tiny handful of events in my life, which has covered a span of 66 years – not even a grain of sand to God.   As I wrote before, God's omniscience and His omnipresence are but two aspects of His infinity.

Maggie and I took this passage with us to the meditation bench, reading it slowly.   It is important that I acknowledge Maggie's role in this first month of the Exercises in my life.   I did not intend for Maggie to be present with me in the library, where I begin my prayers and read the assignment next to a candle and a crucifix.   Nor was it my original plan to walk with Maggie down to the garden at least once during each morning "worship," often two or three times.   It had not occurred to me that my meditation and reflection would continue so much while walking on the beach, something I almost always do with Maggie.   Finally, thus far, Maggie has been with me when I have met with Sister Joan.

However, plans and intentions notwithstanding, Maggie has been a very real part of this phase of my spiritual journey.   I talk with her constantly, trying out ideas and observations about what is going on for me.   I pretend to hear her objections and to argue points of difference.   I find her presence comforting.   I imagine her with me in the biblical settings.   This may not last throughout the nine months.   Thus far, however, it feels right.   Her presence adds to my experience.

God is present in my meditation spaces.   He is in the library, listening as I read the passages for the first time, and as I think out loud about this journal.   His very presence is an answer to my prayers.   He is present in the meditation garden, in the roses and the citrus trees and the live oaks and the wonderful hollies and on the lagoon. I hear Him in the rustling leaves and in the cries from the great heron and the osprey. He walks with us on the beach, and whispers to us from the waves and in the wind.

As I reflect on Psalm 139, I marvel at the idea that He knows completely each "word on my tongue" before I say it.   When I am able to express my thoughts clearly, I grow more certain each day that He inspires the words.   Thinking back on the prayer of the dossier, it was God's gift that I learned to read and understand in the way that I do, which informs the way I speak and articulate thoughts.   So whether God inspires each sentence I speak, or "only" gave me the many gifts that allowed me to craft the sentence, He is a major part of it.

The same can be said about all of the travel in my life.   He was there to guide me on "the far side of the sea," either directly or in His gifts that made my international career possible.   He was there to "weave me together in the depths of the earth," and to "knit me together" in my mother's womb.   The more I contemplate His extraordinary role in every aspect of my life, the more I am humbled.   I can only thank and praise Him for all that I am, all that I have ever done, and all that I have.

Our CRHP team met this morning to begin preparations for the retreat that will be held next weekend.   Father Stephen heard confessions, including the second confession I have ever made.

After our CRHP meeting, I read from Michael Paul Gallagher's Faith Maps,[35] a series of wonderful descriptions of the faith journeys of several prominent theologians, including Pope Benedict. I read the chapter on John Henry Newman last night.[36] Newman advanced two concepts that appeal to me, though both were a little "dense."

First, he talks about "antecedent probability," which is a fancy term used to describe the notion that we must become spiritually ready to accept any intellectual evidence before we will truly accept that evidence. This really resonates for me. I have read more books and studied more thinkers than many people I know whose faith is much deeper than mine. As often and as hard as I tried, I could never get past the logic of intellectual alternatives. However, when I got sick, and then fell into deep depression, something changed. I became spiritually ready for conversion. While the journey had not yet begun, it was as though I was packing bags and tying loose ends, anticipating something important. Without this "opening of my heart," the messages of RCIA and the homilies of Father John and the lessons from the Bible would have fallen on deaf ears. Second, Newman introduced the idea of "existential interiority," by which he meant that faith and conversion occur on the inside, not the surface of our existence. He describes a faith "venture," constantly searching and changing. Newman coined the famous phrase "to live is to change, to be perfect is to change often." My faith has certainly been a journey, not a destination. Just reflecting on these past few weeks, I feel "re-born" each day, growing in my understanding and acceptance of God's role in my life.

Sunday, October 2

What a beautiful fall morning! It is clear, dry, cool, cloudless, and calm. Indeed, it is another day in paradise.

Maggie and I sat on the bench for a while, and then came into the library to listen to Vivaldi, meditate, and pray. Richard Rohr's meditation this morning was about St.

---

[35] According to Wikipedia, "Michael Paul Gallagher is an Irish Jesuit and Roman Catholic priest. He teaches fundamental theology at the Gregorian University, Rome where he was dean of the faculty of theology from 2005 to 2008. Before 1990 he taught literature for nearly 20 years at University College, Dublin."

[36] According to Wikipedia, "John Henry Newman, D.D., C.O. (21 February 1801 – 11 August 1890), also referred to as Cardinal Newman and Blessed John Henry Newman, was an important figure in the religious history of England in the 19th century. Originally an evangelical Oxford academic and priest in the Church of England, Newman was a leader in the Oxford Movement. This influential grouping of Anglicans wished to return the Church of England to many Catholic beliefs and forms of worship traditional in the medieval times to restore ritual expression. In 1845 Newman left the Church of England and was received into the Roman Catholic Church where he was eventually granted the rank of cardinal by Pope Leo XIII. He was instrumental in the founding of the Catholic University of Ireland, which evolved into University College, Dublin, today, the largest university in Ireland."

Francis:

> *The outer world began to name the inner experience and the nature of God for Francis. It all became a two-way mirror through which he could see God and also see His deepest soul.*

I relate so much to that here. Reflecting about my faith journey, it is no accident that I started thinking about God in the solitude of my lonely patch of the farm sixty years ago, surrounded by nature's beauty and the rhythm of the seasons.

I am troubled this morning with my continuing struggle with grandiosity. Near the end of a very pleasant dinner with a couple from the parish last night, I blurted out something about Phi Beta Kappa. In retrospect, it was out of context, added nothing to the conversation, and served only to call attention to something that would some-how burnish my image. Obviously, it had the opposite effect. I wish I could simply recall the comment, but that is not how it works.

I read the Bernard Lonergan[37] chapter in Faith Maps before going to sleep last night. This Canadian Jesuit will take a great deal of patient study to fully comprehend, but the taste of him provided by Gallagher is tantalizing. Lonergan wrote his first great book, Insight: A Study of Human Understanding, in 1957, in which he introduces a "ladder" of thought modes required for knowing or obtaining knowledge: attentive, intelligent, reflective, responsible, and active. I will come back to this as I understand it.

Gallagher's summary focuses heavily on Lonergan's notion that the faith journey is successful only when we achieve a state of "being in love" with God. He suggests that the love of God is not something we achieve; rather it is something we receive. I really like this. It ties into everything we read this week. The key to understanding and knowing God is not to master theology or scripture, it is to open our heart's enough to receive His grace. Lonergan, and Newman before him, make it clear that no amount of intellectual effort can succeed without an open heart. It is like my favorite story of God's words staying on top of our hearts until the heart finally breaks and the words fall in.

Lonergan had three lung surgeries for cancer in 1961, something he credits with opening his heart to the love of God. Ignatius was seriously wounded in battle before he found his way to Manresa and the spiritual searching that followed. Richard Rohr writes about "falling upward," how the redemption that comes after a fall "bounces" us higher than we were before the fall. Of course, I think of my own heart

---

[37] According to Wikipedia, "Fr. Bernard J.F. Lonergan, CC, SJ (17 December 1904 – 26 November 1984) was a Canadian Jesuit priest, philosopher, and theologian widely regarded as one of the most important Catholic thinkers of the twentieth century."

problems and depression. Only when I reached the bottom of that hell hole did I bounce back and up to my own spiritual journey.

3. I am constantly being created by God

Go back to those places where you felt discouragement, revulsion, anger, or simply nothing at all – places like the "black holes" in our universe from which no light or warmth comes. Go back also to those places where you felt great encouragement, love for God, and enthusiasm to go on – places like the volcanoes on our globe that throw up blazing rivers and that roar with energy.

Monday, October 3   *(Luke 4:16-30)*

Jesus has begun His public ministry by now, having recently traveled to Judea to be baptized by John the Baptist and tempted in the desert. He returns north to Galilee, making Capernaum His home base. In these verses, Luke describes the return of Christ to Nazareth, His birthplace. I imagine myself in the temple when Jesus is handed the scroll of Isaiah. Jesus reads the prophesy of Isaiah, and then tells the gathering that the prophesy is "being fulfilled in their hearing." Isaiah's prophesy is that he has been anointed by the spirit of the Lord to "proclaim good news to the poor, free the prisoners, recover sight for the blind, and free the oppressed." Shortly after this event, Christ will deliver the Sermon on the Mount, which is such a profound bit of good news for the poor. I am struck by the fact that the Old Testament prophet Isaiah so accurately foretold the fundamental messages of the New Testament gospel of Jesus Christ. The gospel message targets the poor, the prisoners, the oppressed, and the blind.

When Christ states that "no prophet is accepted in his hometown," the crowds drove Him out of town. He walked right through them when they tried to throw Him over a cliff.

Tuesday, October 4   *(The Way Things Are)*

I repeated this prayer several times - in the library, at the bench, and on the beach. What keeps coming back to me is the notion that God's creation of me is ongoing. As Cardinal Newman said, *"to live is to change, to become perfect is to change often."* The very fact that I am alive means that I am growing. This is hugely important.

Just as important is the idea that I am not doing this growing – God is. Everything I was yesterday was the work of God. Everything I am now is God's work. Everything I will be tomorrow will be God's work. God accomplishes His work with my participation. I love the phrase, without Him I can't; without me, He won't. He does this out of love.

Wednesday, October 5   *(Hosea 11:1-4)*

Today was one of the saddest days I can remember. Maggie is sick. She spent last night in the hospital with serious pancreatitis. I just left the veterinary hospital. Maggie was very much alive, wagging her stump of a tail, and obviously happy to see me. I could only weep. It would be such an understatement to say that Maggie has been hugely important to my progress through these preparatory days of the Exercises.

The last line of Verse 3 of Hosea,

> *[T]hey did not realize it was I who healed them. I led them with cords of human kindness, with ties of love. To them I was like one who lifts a little child to the cheek, and I bent down to feed them.*

The passage from Hosea is a powerful statement about God's love. One of my favorite stories came up as I reflected on this scripture. It is called <u>Footprints in the Sand</u>:[38]

> *One night I dreamed I was walking along the beach with the Lord. Many scenes from my life flashed across the sky. In each scene I noticed footprints in the sand. Sometimes there were two sets of footprints, other times there was one set of footprints. This bothered me because I noticed that during the low periods of my life, when I was suffering from anguish, sorrow or defeat, I could see only one set of footprints. So I said to the Lord, "You promised me Lord, that if I followed you, you would walk with me always. But I have noticed that during the most trying periods of my life there has only been one set of footprints in the sand. Why, when I needed you most, have you not been there for me?" The Lord replied, "**The times when you have seen only one set of footprints, were when I carried you.**"*

This is beautiful poetry. Walking on the beach, I repeated these lines. I was reminded of how often I "did not realize" it was God who gave me my success and my achievements. He gave me challenges to overcome.

Monday, October 10   *(Psalm 103)*

It is now Monday night. I have not written in this journal for five days, too long in spite of the relatively good reasons. Sister Joan and I were meant to meet last night, but we agreed to postpone the session due to the CRHP retreat for Team 11. I want to record the reasons for my absence from the exercises these past few days.

---

[38] Written by Mary Stevenson in 1936. The poem inspired the cover of this journal.

As on most Thursdays this fall, I taught my class at UNF last Thursday morning. On the way home, I took the unusual step of shopping for Sallie Ann, picking up some things required for a party we hosted for the MaliVai Washington Foundation[39] on Thursday evening. So instead of spending an hour or so in the library, in the meditation garden, and/or on the beach with Maggie (who was in the hospital anyway), I prepared to host a hundred people for a very good cause. It is important to report that the evening, the crowd, and the house were filled with the Holy Spirit. Mal's foundation provides after school activities for children from some of the poorest homes in Jacksonville.

I left Jacksonville early Friday morning to fly to Washington, DC, for a strategy committee meeting for the Woodstock Theological Center board.[40] I had hoped that I would be able to spend some time on the plane meditating on Psalm 103, which I had read Wednesday night, before going to bed. Unfortunately, after reading through the Woodstock material, I fell asleep. The Woodstock meeting involved a good discussion about some hard choices, blessed throughout by the Holy Spirit. It was close to midnight when I arrived back at home, too tired to write in this journal.

All day Saturday and most of Sunday were spent at the CRHP retreat at the parish. While I have not progressed through the readings as I intended, it seems to me that I have been living in the spirit of Ignatius. I have felt the strong presence of the Holy Spirit constantly since reading from Psalm 103. I have been talking to God. Many times during these four days, I have sensed that He was speaking to me.

Tuesday, October 11   (Job 1:21, 38, 39, 40:1-5)

I read from Job this morning before going to class, my first class since the CRHP weekend. I particularly liked the verse "Resentment kills a fool, and envy slays the simple." I have harbored resentment for way too long on several occasions.

Job is tough. I prayed both for an understanding of the challenge God put to Job, and for a similar degree of faith and persistence to that shown by Job. The story of

---

[39] MaliVai "Mal" Washington (born June 20, 1969, in Glen Cove, New York) is a former professional tennis player from the United States. He is best remembered for reaching the men's singles final at Wimbledon in 1996. The MaliVai Washington Kids Foundation promotes academic achievement and positive life skills in Jacksonville youth through the game of tennis.

[40] The Woodstock Theological Center is an independent, Jesuit-sponsored research institute located at Georgetown University that carries out theological and ethical reflection on the most pressing human issues of the day. Drawing on the Roman Catholic tradition, the Woodstock Center is ecumenically open, multi-disciplinary, and collaborative with, among othrs, the business community, government, religious groups, universities, other research centers, and the media.

Job is very Old Testament. I cannot imagine Jesus telling the story of such merciless testing.

It came as no surprise that I included a significant amount of religion in my lecture to the class at UNF. I am increasingly persuaded that the issue of achieving "the good" must be a paramount objective in all our pursuits – personal, familial, social, and business. So I put the question to my students, "What is 'the good' that is served by globalization?" Particularly for those of us actually responsible for the decisions and actions in the poor countries during all those years, what were our definitions of "the good?" Obviously, we owed our shareholders an acceptable return on their investment. I suspect that at the time, I would have described this as our "first order" duty. However, I tried to see this first task – satisfying the investors – as the cost of our "license to operate." In other words, return on investment was not "the good" we were trying to achieve. Rather, it was what had to be done in order to even have a chance at making a real difference. In my mind, "the good" involved several stakeholders. I owed my employees a safe and secure place to work, with fair compensation. I owed my customers reliable electric power at a reasonable cost. I owed the communities in which our power plants were located a safe and friendly operation, one that provided economic security for the community and supported schools and hospitals. I felt a strong sense of duty to "the planet" to be sensitive to the environment, controlling sulfur dioxide, nitric oxide, and dust pollution. We did not know about the negative impact of carbon dioxide on climate twenty years ago. As I explained all of this to the class, I tried to argue that the only acceptable reason to even be in business was to achieve some level of "the good.." No level of corporate profit or personal compensation could ever justify a life spent otherwise. I think the young students liked what they heard.

Wednesday, October 12   (Isaiah 45:7-13)

The reading, Isaiah 45:7-13, is a powerful restatement of the theme that has dominated much of these first few weeks. God made me and all that is now or has ever been around me. All of my possessions, all of my gifts, all of my successes – all of these are from God.

I am writing this on the way to New York, where I am going for a Woodstock board meeting. The board is made up of several Jesuits, along with both business and other religious men and women. Most of the board members teach at or attended one of the Jesuit colleges. Every minute of every meeting for more than two years has been an Ignatian experience, filled with the Holy Spirit. The very fact that I am a member of this board is such an incredible gift. My old friend Chris Dorment invited me to join the Arrupe Program advisory board, one of the activities of the Woodstock Center. I now Chair that advisory board and sit on the Woodstock Board, all because the initial gift of the Holy Spirit keeps on giving. I am sure that I would not be a Catholic today had I not benefited from the gentle instruction and powerful examples of these wonderful men.

Saturday, October 15   *(Luke 4:16-30)*

The board meeting in New York and the general hassle of travel kept me away from my reading, meditation, and this journal these past two days. I did pray often during the intensely spiritual board meeting. All of the meetings and presentations begin and end with prayer. Perhaps even better, though, is the sense that many of the incredible conversations that take place among the fellows and the directors are a form of prayer. We talk openly and honestly. We search for meaning and truth. We treat each other with a quality of respect that I did not often see in all the business meetings I attended or led over the years. There is a clear sense that our meetings are guided, or in some way graced by the Holy Spirit.

I once again had the wonderful experience of Mass at St. Patrick's Cathedral. I am deeply moved and humbled by celebrating the Eucharist in that extraordinary space. Somehow, I sense the Holy Spirit echoing in the soaring height of the columns and vaulted ceilings.

I returned this morning to the shores of Galilee with Jesus and His disciples, reading and reflecting again on Luke 4:16-30. It felt so very good to be home in the "altar" in my library with Maggie. We returned to all our habits: praying together on the bench in the meditation garden, and then walking along the beach, imagining Jesus and His followers ahead of us in the sand next to the ocean. No matter how much I enjoyed the spirituality of the Woodstock community in New York, I much prefer the communication I have with God in these spaces that have become so special.

4. God's project hidden deep in things: Save All

You are finishing a month of the Exercises that you wanted to go through. You might begin examining whether you are doing what you set out to do.

Monday, October 17   *(Ephesians 1:3-14)*

It is now after two in the afternoon and I have just finished my duties as Formation Director. I certainly hope this will take less time going forward.

Ephesians 1:3-14 introduces some concepts that have been debated throughout history. In verse 5, Paul tells the Ephesians:

> *In love He predestined us for adoption to son ship*

He is suggesting that all mankind is predestined for salvation. We were chosen "in God's love" to be His sons and daughters before the creation of the world. This is not the whole story. Paul is very clear later in Ephesians and elsewhere that our salvation is not something that will come to us without any effort or action on our part. The argument among theologians over the years has been predestination versus free will. That is not the primary message in this passage. What Paul is saying here is that it is God's intention that we all be saved, and that has always been God's plan. We are one with Him, loved by Him, and part of His family from the moment creation began..

This cosmically collective redemption is essentially God's grace. It is there for each of us to accept, but our acceptance must be active and intentional. Accepting grace requires an act of free will.

In the fall of 1996, I organized the first (and last) "annual" Coastal Power tennis tournament in Ephesus. We were trying to build a power plant in Izmir. Our local partner organized a villa in Selcuk that looked down the mountain toward the Ephesus theatre and, beyond that, to the sea. My memories of the area are sadly very faint, but I know that Paul is meant to have preached to crowds in the theatre and around the Roman town that is today only ruins. Sitting on the bench with Maggie, I tried to imagine Paul speaking to a small group of Christians in an upper-room in Ephesus. I listened to Paul's description of God's saving grace. Even in this quiet garden paradise, I could sense the spiritual excitement, mixed with a certain level of fear (which must have been present whenever and wherever those first Christians met). More than anything, however, I could feel God's grace – always and everywhere. Later, when our little community received the letter from Paul calling our attention to His message, I sensed the excitement (and fear) as we gathered to discuss our new faith.

Maggie and I walked for more than two hours on the beach this afternoon. We imagined we were walking along the beach west of the amphitheater in Ephesus, down the slope from the military town built by the Roman soldiers. We walked in small groups, trying not to draw too much attention to that which distinguished us from the others – our new faith. We talked in hushed voices about grace and God's plan.

Tuesday, October 18   (2 Corinthians 5:14-18)

Before going to class this morning, Maggie and I knelt next to the crucifix in the library and read through 2 Corinthians 5:14-18. I had used verse 17 from this fifth chapter of Second Corinthians in my witness at CRHP:

> Therefore, if anyone is in Christ, he is a new creation. The old has passed away; behold, the new has come.

We spent the morning lecture period discussing income inequality, particularly in the context of the "Occupy" movement currently going on throughout this country and even in Europe. I am so caught up in these exercises that I cannot avoid bringing them into my classes. This morning, I suggested that all of us who have come out of the financial crisis of 2008 and the elections of 2008 and 2010 must accept the fact that "the new has come." Old formulas employing hackneyed prescriptions for tired diagnoses simply do not work. I came perilously close to quoting Paul!

Back on the bench, I am overwhelmed by the peace and beauty of this place, even on an overcast day, with hints of fall in the air. I reflected on the fact that Paul generally wrote his letters to groups of believers, advising them on behaviors that would deepen their faith. He was not addressing nonbelievers.

After about half an hour in the garden, I spent some time in the library, trying to sort out Paul's various journeys, his visits to Ephesus and Corinth, and the timing of his letters. Paul met Christ in a vision on the road to Damascus in 37 CE, only five years after the crucifixion. He lived for another thirty years, teaching and preaching the gospel of Jesus Christ. His audience was largely Gentile - i.e., not Jewish - and they lived in various cities at the eastern end of the Mediterranean.[41] We know all this because Paul was kind enough to send letters to many of the churches in the cities he visited.

---

[41] For much of the next eight years, Paul lived in Antioch in Syria, where he learned from Barnabus (who "called" Paul to come to Antioch to preach) and other apostles. Paul had met both Peter and James in Jerusalem some time earlier. It was in Antioch that converts to the new faith were first called Christians. He journeyed three times around the eastern Mediterranean between 44 CE and 58 CE. The first journey appears to have begun after 44 CE and ended before 50 CE. Paul, Barnabus, and Mark travel from Antioch to Cyprus and southern Turkey. Mark leaves the trip to return to Jerusalem, while Paul and Barnabus continue on for some time, eventually returning to Antioch. Apparently, Paul wrote none of his letters during this first journey. In the spring of 51 CE, Paul and Silas leave Antioch together, traveling through northern Syria and southern Turkey. They are joined by Timothy in Lystra, and I think Luke joins them in Philippi. Paul leaves his companions to travel to Athens, where he spends the winter of 51-52 CE, before traveling down to Corinth. It appears that Paul spent a year and a half in Corinth, from the spring of 52 CE until the fall of 53 CE. Silas and Timothy rejoin him in Corinth. It is here in Corinth that Paul wrote 1 Thessalonians and, quite possibly, Galatians. Scholars now believe 2 Thessalonians to have been written by someone other than Paul, and at a later time, perhaps even after Paul's death. It was in Corinth that Paul met Priscilla and Aquila, a Jewish Christian couple who had recently been banished from Rome by Claudius Caesar. The couple joins Paul to sail to Ephesus, after which Paul returns to Antioch, ending his second journey. Paul's third journey apparently begins in the spring of 54 CE in Galatia. Paul had traveled to Galatia in the late 40s, founding the churches there early in his ministry. Paul's time spent in Galatia was not considered part of his great "missionary journeys." From the fall of 54 CE until the early fall of 57 CE, Paul lives and preaches in Ephesus. He wrote 1 Corinthians near the end of this stay in Ephesus, apparently without the help of his scribe and companion Timothy. Paul left Ephesus, traveling north to Macedonia, where he rejoins Timothy and, eventually, Titus. Apparently, 2 Corinthians was written somewhere in northern Greece, possibly in Philippi, in anticipation of his pending trip to Corinth. It was during the winter of 57-58 CE, while residing in Corinth, that Paul wrote his epistle to the Romans. It was his intention to eventually travel to Rome (but only stopping on his way to Spain, not to preach or form churches), but this would not occur on this third journey. Paul ends this trip in Jerusalem in 58 CE, after sailing to the south of Cyprus. From sometime in 58 CE until the fall of 60 CE, Paul is imprisoned by the Sanhedrin (the Jewish leaders), first in Caesarea, and then while traveling to Rome. From 61 CE until 63 CE, Paul was a prisoner of the Roman authorities. It was during this long period of imprisonment that Paul wrote his letters to the Ephesians, Philippians, Colossians, and Philemon. Paul was martyred sometime between 64 CE and 67 CE in Rome. It is clear that he traveled extensively in the last years of his life, though the record is not clear as to where he went. He also wrote extensively, completing Hebrews, First and Second Timothy, and Titus.

The reading today is from 2 Corinthians, a letter written by Paul in northern Greece, somewhere in Macedonia. It seems clear to me that Paul sees conversion as an ongoing process. He is urging those new in the faith (and, frankly, everyone was new to the faith at that time) to continue on their journeys. I am overwhelmed by the notion that Paul wrote his letters to the Corinthians at least a few years before Mark wrote the first of the four gospels!

Maggie and I are back in the library. I am trying to imagine myself traveling with Paul through northern Greece. We left the relative warmth and comfort of Ephesus to travel west and south to Athens and Corinth. I imagine the travel arrangements to be difficult at best.

Paul may have been born into a family of Pharisees, arguably "middle-class" at the time, but after his conversion, he lived as an indigent. He worked as a tent maker, assiduously avoiding the practice of seeking handouts from his followers. He was considered a troublemaker by traditional Jews, the Jewish Christians, and the Romans, all of whom frequently punished him for his ministry. He was beaten, imprisoned, and cast out of communities. Walking with Paul was a dangerous thing to do!

I imagine that Paul and I continue to invite families to gather in their upper-rooms to hear the story of Jesus Christ, so recently crucified for nothing more than proclaiming a new gospel. In Paul's teaching, the central message of Christ is self-giving. His messages of love and the power of the Holy Spirit stand in contrast to the traditional Jewish insistence upon the law (including, particularly, circumcision). Now, after eating and listening to Paul preach, the rest of us try to sleep as Paul and Timothy hover together in the corner to work on yet another letter. I imagine that we are occasionally asked to listen to some verses. Paul asks us whether what he has written is clear. I am humbled by this request. It becomes a part of my continuing conversion.

I alternately sit and kneel, listening for the Holy Spirit. There is no question that I am a new creation. I am a different man from the wretch I was four years ago when I began this journey. Now, as I imagine myself traveling with Paul, walking with Jesus Christ, or meeting with other new Christians, it is no exaggeration to say that the *"old has passed away; behold the new has come."*

Wednesday, October 19   *(Romans 8:14-27)*

I imagine Paul in a corner in the home of one of the believers in Corinth. It is winter. Paul intends to travel to Rome, not necessarily to preach, but only to stop on the way west to Spain. Little does he know that he will eventually travel to Rome in chains, and spend most of his time there imprisoned. Nor can he know that it will be in Rome where his life ends.

Paul writes to the Romans that their "present suffering" is like the "groaning of childbirth" as we are guided by the Holy Spirit to "son ship" in the kingdom of God. I am struck by the fact that once we say yes to Jesus Christ, the Holy Spirit guides us with enormous power. Each day, I feel more surrounded by the Holy Spirit, more propelled by the Holy Spirit to move forward on this journey. I once lamented the feeling of being a pebble in a stream, not able to control where the force of the water moved me. This feeling today that a force greater than me is pushing me in a direction that feels like "the will of God . . . good and acceptable and perfect" – this is a truly wonderful feeling. I want to simply sit back and let it happen.

Thursday, October 20 *(Luke 15:11-32)*

It is hard to believe that I read this passage almost a month ago, in the second preparatory week of these exercises. This journey with Ignatius is well begun.

After reading the passage through again and again, I walked down to the garden. I prayed for understanding and clarity. Sometimes, I feel overwhelmed by all that I am learning. I have been here before, when learning about other, less important things. All of the information seems to cloud my vision until all at once there is clarity. We often say that it is as if someone finally turned on the light. I prefer a different mental concept, which is that somehow everything slows down, coming almost to a stop. At first, all the bits and pieces of information are coming at me so fast that I cannot see them, much less understand them. Then, suddenly, everything stops. I see everything. I have time to wrap my head around each individual fact, bringing it into some kind of relationship with every other individual fact.

Now, I have to say that this experience of clarity and understanding comes comparatively easy when the subject matter is coal mining or electric power generation. Clarity is far more elusive in the present case. Just as I begin to appreciate the messages of the synoptic gospels, the focus shifts to Paul's letters, or to the mysticism of John. Even the Pauline teachings fall into the category of those letters universally acknowledged to have been written by Paul, and the category of those letters generally ascribed to others. When I read the comments of the early church fathers in the Catena Aurea, a whole new flood of information and perspective adds to the clouds of my confusion.

So I pray for clarity, understanding, and, often, just for enough memory to retain a little of what I am learning. I am helped in all this by imagining that I am not alone on this journey. Father John is next to me, repeating his favorite bit of wisdom that the most important concepts in our faith are inclusion and forgiveness. This is so appropriate to these verses from Luke. Buddy Tudor is also "in the house." He approached everything in life as if it were another engineering problem. Slow it down. Break it down. Put it in logical order. He would say, for heaven's sake, get out of your head! Let the simple patterns speak to you. Buddy would love my growing understanding of Paul - which is that the whole of the gospel is about loving self-giving.

Ambrose[42] wrote in the fourth century that the three parables in Luke (the lost sheep, the lost coin, and, now, the prodigal son) represent God as the shepherd who bears us on His own body, God as the woman seeking us as lost coins, and God as the father who receives us. In the first parable, God acts through pity. In the second, God acts through intercession. Finally, God acts through reconciliation.

Richard Rohr was particularly good this morning (Sallie Ann and I have been receiving his daily meditation for some time now):

The gospel cannot happen in your head alone. You never think yourself into a new way of living. You invariably live yourself into a new way of thinking. The gospel is about relationship. Unless there is someplace on this earth where it's happening between you and another person, I don't believe you have any criterion to judge whether it's happening at all. Unless you're in right relationship with at least one other person on this earth, unless there is some place you can give and receive love, I don't think you have any reason to think you're living the gospel

Sallie Ann wrote to me that I have become that "other person" in her life. In ways far too numerous to mention she has always been that person to me. I have not always been in a "right relationship" with her, but, like the prodigal son, I now recognize how wrong I have been and have returned to reconcile that fact, and to love her in the fullest sense of the word.

Friday, October 21   *(Luke 13:10-17)*

As I currently understand the history, Luke traveled with Paul through parts of Paul's ministry to the Gentiles.[43] So much of the Pauline gospel is the simple admonition to "give of self in love" as opposed to strictly adhering to the laws of the Pharisees and Sadducees. Much of this emphasis arose in connection with preaching to Gentiles, for whom adherence to the laws of Judaism would mean adult circumcision. While both the Gospel of Luke and the Book of Acts were written after Paul's imprisonment (and, probably, his death), most scholars agree that Luke (or his source, "L") had not read Paul's letters. Nonetheless, it seems clear that the emphasis in Luke reflects the teaching of Paul.

The passage today, Luke 13:10-17, involves just such a simple, yet stark contrast between doing the right thing (self-giving love) and using a technicality to ignore the suffering women (strict adherence to the law of the Sabbath). After prayer and medita-

---

[42] Saint Ambrose was Bishop of Milan in the late fourth century. He famously inspired St. Augustine to be baptized.

[43] I now understand this particular Luke to be a physician. He is almost certainly not the author of either the Gospel or the Book of Acts.

tion in the library, Maggie and I braved the chilly morning to walk down to the garden. I imagined the south pavilion to be the synagogue. Jesus and the crippled woman were just inside the columns facing east toward the lagoon. I listened to the exchange between the woman and Christ, and watched as the woman straightened up.

As I reflect on this story, I am struck by how much I have allowed the concept of "putting the right thing ahead of the law (or rule or regulation)" to govern my thoughts and actions throughout my life. I confess that I often did so believing simply that "I knew better," only to learn later, with the passage of time and a little experience, that I was only putting myself first. The essential part of the gospel message is selflessness, not civil disobedience.

The fall air is incredible, as is the morning light on the lagoon. I am surrounded by the Holy Spirit, and at the same time, I am filled by the Holy Spirit. I am more excited each day as I rush down to the library to begin these times of prayer, reflection, and meditation.

Paul pushed the idea that grace trumped works specifically in regard to three particular "laws" of Judaism – circumcision, dietary rules, and the Sabbath. Over the past two decades, a growing consensus of Biblical scholars has formed around what is called a "new perspective on Paul," which is that Luther, among others, way overstated the "grace over works" argument. The better reading, they argue, is that grace trumps strict observance of these three, highly visible, Jewish laws (and maybe some others), but not self-giving good works. God's grace – unearned favor – is available to all of us, but we need to not only say yes to His grace, but follow up with good works.

Saturday, October 22   *(The Way Things Are)*

The assignment was to read The Way Things Are, again this morning. Among other things, I was struck with the notion that "God planted deep inside me an original purpose," and that my life goal is "to discover in myself that original purpose – what my concrete self adds up to – and to live it out."

Some months ago, Sallie Ann and I read together Richard Rohr's book Falling Upwards. In this book, Rohr advances the idea that each of us spends the first half of life "building life's container," and then spends the second half of life choosing what to put in that container and filling it. This is very much the same idea as that expressed in the reading this morning. When building my life container, I am merely discovering the original purpose that God planted deep inside me. I live out that purpose by choosing the contents of my container and filling it.

It is a truly glorious day today. I have just come back from tennis, and Maggie and I are about to take a walk. I have been ruminating about my "extra" reading this morning.

Before playing tennis this morning, I read about Marcion,[44] a second-century Christian, whose efforts to clarify the gospels led the early church figures Tertullian,[45] a prolific writer from Carthage, and Saint Irenaeus,[46] Bishop of Lyon, to label him a heretic. The story is fascinating for several reasons, not least of which is the way Marcion glorified the apostle Paul. The second century after Christ was crucified must have been a rather wild and crazy time. Several gospels were produced in somewhat frantic efforts to collect and put in writing the oral history of Christ and His ministry. The leadership of the early church was fractured, at best.

The major divide in the first century following the death of Christ appears to have been between Jewish Christians and Gentile Christians. Even though Paul was a Jew (a zealous Pharisee, no less), he considered his calling to be the conversion of Gentiles to Christianity. This certainly led to some distance between Paul on one side, and James, the first Bishop of Jerusalem,[47] on the other. James died in Jeru-

---

[44] According to Wikipedia, "Marcion of Sinope (ca. 85-160) was a bishop in early Christianity. His theology, which rejected the deity described in the Jewish Scriptures as inferior or subjugated to the God proclaimed in the Christian gospel, was denounced by the Church Fathers and he was excommunicated. His rejection of many books contemporarily considered Scripture in the catholic part of the church prompted this church to develop a Catholic canon of Scriptures. In the second century, both Marcion and Valentinius, an early leader of the gnostic heresy, attracted the attention of the early fathers of the church. But they were clearly not the only "Christians" preaching variations of the faith. Only toward the end of the second century did Ireneaus prevail in his efforts to limit the number of gospels to four. Origin of Alexandria, one of the Church Fathers, considered the New Testament to be complete with twenty-seven books by around 240 CE. However, it was not until 325 CE that Constantine convened the first council in Nicaea, which more or less forced the early church into conformity."

[45] According to Wikipedia, "Tertullian (c. 160 – c. 225 CE), was a prolific early Christian author from Carthage in the Roman province of Africa. He is the first Christian author to produce an extensive corpus of Latin Christian literature. He also was a notable early Christian apologist and a polemicist against heresy. Tertullian has been called "the father of Latin Christianity" and "the founder of Western theology." Though conservative, he did originate and advance new theology to the early Church. He is perhaps most famous for being the oldest extant Latin writer to use the term Trinity (Latin trinitas), and giving the oldest extant formal exposition of a Trinitarian theology. Other Latin formulations that first appear in his work are "three Persons, one Substance" as the Latin "tres Personae, una Substantia" (itself from the Koine Greek "treis Hypostases, Homoousios")."

[46] According to Wikipedia, "St. Irenaeus, (2nd centuryCE – c. 202) was Bishop of Lugdunum in Gaul, then a part of the Roman Empire (now Lyon, France). He was an early church father and apologist, and his writings were formative in the early development of Christian theology. He was a hearer of Polycarp,[1] who in turn was a disciple of John the Evangelist."

[47] According to Wikipedia, "James, first Bishop of Jerusalem, who died in 62 or 69, was an important figure in Early Christianity. He is distinguished from the Apostle James by various epithets; he is called James the brother of the Lord by Paul (Galatians 1:19), James the brother of the Lord, surnamed the Just by Hegesippus and others, "James the Righteous," "James of Jerusalem," "James Adelphotheos," and so on. James became the leader of the Christian movement in Jerusalem in the decades after Jesus' death, but information about his life is scarce and ambiguous. Apart from a handful of references in the Gospels, the main sources for his life are the Acts of the Apostles, the

salem in 62 CE, close to the time that Paul died in Rome.   James lived through the ministry of Paul, whose teachings seemed often to have been directed negatively toward the Jewish Christian community in Jerusalem.   While Paul was certainly not living a happy, comfortable life, James must have often felt as though he was under siege from the prolific author Paul, and his rapidly growing Gentile Christian community.

Jewish Christians began to lose in the competition with Gentile Christians with the decision of the Council of Jerusalem in 50 CE, in which it was decided that circumcision was not required for Gentiles to become Christian.   Then the sack of Jerusalem by the Romans in 70 CE dealt further blows to Jewish Christians.

I find the history of the early church fascinating.   Particularly when walking on the beach, I mull these questions over again and again, and then revert to my biblical library to search for answers.   I read from the Cambridge Companion series on both St. Paul and The Gospels this morning.[48]

Walking on the beach with Maggie was almost painful today.   I imagined the lives and deaths of the various men named James, about whom I read so much this morning.

James, son of Zebedee,[49] was beheaded by Herod in Judaea about ten years after the crucifixion.   He died the year that Paul began his first missionary journey.   As I

Pauline epistles, the historian Josephus, and St. Jerome, who also quotes the early Christian author Hegesippus.   The Epistle of James in the New Testament is traditionally attributed to him, and he is a principal author of the Apostolic Decree of Acts 15.   In the extant lists of Hippolytus of Rome, Dorotheus of Tyre, the Chronicon Paschale, and Dimitry of Rostov, he is the first of the Seventy Apostles, though some sources, such as the Catholic Encyclopedia, draw the conclusion that "these lists are unfortunately worthless."   Hegesippus in his fifth book of his Commentaries, writing of James, says "After the apostles, James the brother of the Lord surnamed the Just was made head of the Church at Jerusalem."

48 In the second century, both Marcion and Valentinius, an early leader of the gnostic heresy, attracted the attention of the early fathers of the church.   But they were clearly not the only "Christians" preaching variations of the faith.   Only toward the end of the second century did Irenaeus prevail in his efforts to limit the number of gospels to four.   Origin of Alexandria, one of the Church Fathers, considered the New Testament to be complete with 27 books by around 240 CE.   However, it was not until 325 CE that Constantine convened the first council in Nicaea, which more or less forced the early church into conformity.

[49] According to Wikipedia, "James, son of Zebedee (died 44 CE) was one of the Twelve Apostles of Jesus. He was a son of Zebedee and Salome, and brother of John the Apostle. He is also called James the Greater to distinguish him from James, son of Alphaeus, who is also known as James the Lesser.   Saint James is the Patron Saint of Spain and according to legend, his remains are held in Santiago de Compostela in Galicia (Spain). The traditional pilgrimage to the grave of the saint, known as the "Way of St. James," has been the most popular pilgrimage for Western European Catholics from the early Middle Ages onwards."

understand it, James went to Spain – the western end of the known world – to preach the gospel. When Sallie Ann and I were in Santiago de Campostela several years ago, we heard the traditional story about the body of James being returned to Galicia by his disciples. In my imagination this morning, we were walking on the beach on the Bay of Biscay, which runs along the northern coast of Galicia. I felt the loneliness of the Apostle following the death of Jesus. He traveled all the way across the Mediterranean in solitude, and then traveled back to his death at the hands of Herod in even greater solitude. Walking along the windswept beach, making that lonely journey with James, I suddenly felt alone and cold and sad.

Later, I felt a different kind of solitude as I considered the life and death of the other James, son of Alphaeus,[50] also one of the twelve. James of Alphaeus is mentioned only four times in the Gospels, and then only in the lists of the apostles. I suspect this James lived the solitude of non-recognition.

Sunday, October 23

The assignment this morning was to repeat one of the scriptural passages from earlier in the week. Luke 13:10-17 was my choice, largely because I am so intrigued by Saint Paul. My understanding of his letters is evolving daily.

I freely confess to having gone a bit overboard on the idea of "grace without works." This may be a consequence of my sense that the Holy Spirit is currently working in my life. I feel grace all around me, particularly in the library, at the bench, and on the beach. So Paul's writing truly touched me.

However, the more I understand the particular issues that bothered Paul – circumcision, dietary rules, and the Sabbath – the more I can understand the more limited sense in which Paul spoke of "the law." Gentiles would have had enormous problems accepting a faith that required adult circumcision or wholesale changes in eating and dining practices. Moreover, it seems clear to me that Paul often evangelized at "agape meals," using table fellowship as part of the message about Jesus. As is so clear in these verses from Luke 13, refusing to help someone in need simply because it was the Sabbath made no sense.

Paul clearly walked the walk as much as he talked the talk. His whole life was filled with self-giving, loving, and work. He did not let grace wash over him, and then sit back and wait for salvation. He said yes to Jesus Christ, then devoted his whole life

---

[50] Saint James, son of Alphaeus, was one of the Twelve Apostles of Jesus Christ, appearing under this name in all three of the Synoptic Gospels' lists of the apostles. He is often identified with James the Less and commonly known by that name in church tradition. He is also labelled "the minor," "the little," "the lesser," or "the younger," according to translation. James, the son of Alphaeus, is rarely mentioned in the New Testament. He is distinguished from James the Lord's brother (Gal.1:19), an important leader in the New Testament church, and James, son of Zebedee, another one of the Twelve Apostles.

and being to evangelizing, forming new Christian communities, and supporting those communities he had already formed. He raised money for the support of the poor Christian community in Jerusalem. He worked to support his own needs, choosing not to rely upon those to whom he was preaching to feed and clothe him.

As I understand it, this "new perspective on Paul" has always been the Catholic view of Paul's message. It was Luther and his followers who first got carried away with the idea of salvation through grace alone. I spent much of this morning learning about and reflecting on the Epistle of James.

First, it seems clear that James, son of Zebedee, was clearly not the author, in that his early death (ca. 44 CE) precluded him from knowing Paul's teaching on "faith alone." Second, it is highly unlikely that either James, son of Alphaeus, or James, the Bishop of Jerusalem, was the author. Raymond Brown,[51] whose commentary on the New Testament is one of my favorite sources, suggests that the author was a fan of Bishop James. He agreed with the generally more conservative and pro-Old Testament views of the Bishop of Jerusalem. Brown concludes that this author probably wrote the letter in the final third of the first century.

"Faith without works is dead" is perhaps the most frequently quoted line from the Epistle of James. It is somewhat ironic that the strongest argument for a "new perspective on Paul" was written prior to the date that the letters of Paul were even collected and canonized. Brown points out, correctly I think, that Paul stressed faith and grace over ritual works prescribed by the Old Testament law, but always emphasized behavior that reflects love. The author of James repeats much of the message of the beatitudes found in Matthew.

---

[51] According to Wikipedia, "The Reverend Raymond Edward Brown, S.S. (May 22, 1928 - August 8, 1998), was an American Roman Catholic priest, a member of the Sulpician Fathers and a major Biblical scholar of his era. He was regarded as a specialist concerning the hypothetical 'Johannine community', which he speculated contributed to the authorship of the Gospel of John, and he also wrote influential studies on the birth and death of Jesus. Brown was professor emeritus at the Protestant Union Theological Seminary (UTS) in New York, where he taught for 29 years. He was the first Roman Catholic professor to gain tenure there, where he earned a reputation as a superior lecturer. Brown was one of the first Roman Catholic scholars to apply historical-critical analysis to the Bible. As Biblical criticism developed in the 19th century, the Roman Catholic Church opposed this scholarship and essentially forbade it in 1893. In 1943, however, the Church issued guidelines by which Catholic scholars could investigate the Bible historically. Brown called this encyclical the "Magna Carta of biblical progress." Vatican II further supported higher criticism, which, Brown felt, vindicated his approach. Brown remains controversial among traditionalist Catholics because of their claim that he denied the inerrancy of the whole of Scripture and cast doubt on the historical accuracy of numerous articles of the Catholic faith. His centrist views especially angered conservatives when he questioned whether the virginal conception of Jesus could be proven historically. He was regarded as occupying the center ground in the field of biblical studies, opposing the literalism found among many fundamentalist Christians while not carrying his conclusions as far as many other scholars."

Bernard Lonergan developed a five-level hierarchy of decision making that he suggests should be the basis of all knowing.[52] My Jesuit friends at Woodstock advocate the Lonergan hierarchy as the basis of Ignatian learning.

So my focus this morning is to intentionally follow this Ignatian approach as I read, reflect, pray, meditate, and, hopefully, learn from this experience. Reading the passage from Luke 13 led me back to Paul's strong reaction to using observance of the Sabbath as a reason not to "behave in a manner reflecting love." The thought process flowed from Paul's emphasis of "grace not works" to James and his famous "faith without works." I tried to attentively inform myself by reading about the context within which these various scriptures were written, when, and by whom.

I prayed for clarity, understanding, and insight. I reflected, repeating over and over again various parts of what I had read and what I understood. My reflection continued in the garden and while walking on the beach.

Discernment is ongoing. For me, it involves repeating the process several times: inform, reflect, pray, judge, decide. It is only after I leave the library (with no fewer than six books, including the Bible and the Catena Aurea, opened to passages from or about Luke, Paul, and James) that I can turn inward, seeking clarity from the Holy Spirit.

In the quiet by the fountain, among the roses in the garden, walking on the beach in the imagined company of the saints and disciples, and while discoursing with learned theologians, I finally, faintly, and, sometimes, intermittently hear the Holy Spirit affirm my search and confirm my understanding.

5. God continually calls me by my name

God creates you in concrete circumstances and with definite gifts and charisms. Without tyranny, God our Creator and Lord plants in you not only gifts and limitations that add up to some definite choices in your life, but also the desires leading to those definite choices. Your task as a creature is to find what God desires in you, down at the root of yourself, and freely to enact your own deepest desires. When we do this, we are godlike. This is our profoundest joy and happiness.

Monday, October 24   *(Ephesians 2:1-10)*

Sister Joan asked yesterday that I restrict myself to the assigned reading during my

---

[52] First, we must be attentive to and inform ourselves about data. Second, we must experience the data at the level of perception. Third, through reflective insight, we must understand the implications of our perception. Fourth, through prayer and discernment, we make a judgment about the data. Finally, on the basis of this judgment, we make a decision with respect to what action is required.

exercise time each day this week. I know that I have been "over thinking" and "over researching" my assignments over the past couple of weeks. I am so excited about learning all that is out there to learn about this gospel. My thirst is hard to quench, but I will endeavor to be obedient.

It is almost ironic that the first reading this week takes me right back to the theological dispute between Paul and James on the subject of salvation by grace alone or through grace and works together. Today, though, I am experiencing something closer to pain as I reflect on the reading.

Before I embarked on this incredible journey four years ago, I was indeed "dead in my transgressions and sin." I followed the "ruler of the kingdom of the air." I want to be clear about this. Most of my career I chose courses of action that at least held out hope of helping others. However, in the crucial months following my first cardiac event, I made choices that repeatedly distanced me from my value system. My god was resentment. I wished ill for my imagined enemies and worse for myself. In fact, I wished nothing more than to be dead.

I did not recover from this terrible place through any act of my own. God's grace acted powerfully in my life. His grace was not quiet, nor hidden from view. He used the proverbial "two by four up 'side the head" to get my attention. He supported me in the difficult task of finding and following the path that would lead to the start of this great journey. Not just once, in that single grand gesture, but over and over again, in subtle, quiet ways, His grace lit the path I needed to take. It was not always pleasant, and certainly not easy. I lost my way a few times. Only through His grace am I here today, searching for meaning, seeking answers and trying to be a better man.

Tuesday, October 25   (The Way Things Can Be)

This long meditation requires reading, re-reading, and more reflection than is possible in a single morning. I have been working on a speech that I have to give in February (this, by the way, is a unique concept for me – preparing months in advance!). My current idea is to talk about what it means to "seek and serve the good" in our business choices and management decisions. What is "the good"?

Ethics philosophers have kicked this question around since the time of Socrates. Three themes have survived the millennia of discussion.

> **First**, "the good" is hedonism; it is whatever makes us happy. Good things give us pleasure. Bad things give us pain.

> **Second**, "the good" is that which we desire. Desire satisfaction allows for the possibility that we might desire something painful in the short term in order to achieve some hoped for long term goal.

Third, "the good" can be found on an Objective List, which is assembled by reasonable men and women with Full Knowledge. It is neither necessary nor sufficient that something on the Objective List give me pleasure (though it is possible). Nor is it necessary or sufficient for everything on the Objective List to be desirable to me (though, again, I might desire some or much of what is on that list).

In all the hundreds and thousands of words written on this subject by the great thinkers of the ages, I have not yet come across a definition of "the good" that is as simple as "the good is what God wants from me." I may not desire it, but if God wants it for and from me, it is good, regardless of whether it gives me pleasure or pain, and regardless of whether I desire it. So, in this sense, a God-centered definition of "the good" is closer to the Objective List theory. However, what is missing from the discussion of the Objective List is that one "expert's opinion" as to what goes on the List trumps all others. If God wants it, it matters not one bit what all the men and women with Full Knowledge have to say.

As I read through this initial journal entry again, I am struck with how I allowed my head to interfere with the process of listening for God or of hearing His words. I returned to the meditation reading. The operative word is balance. Yes, it seems to me that it is possible to list several activities or achievements or states of being that are objectively good. A balanced view of "the good" must stipulate that the surest way of compiling that list is to listen to God.

Wednesday, October 26 *(Genesis 22:1-19)*

This wonderful story about Abraham, and the request of God that he sacrifice his son Isaac, is a classic "obedience" lesson. As I reflect on the reading, I obviously ask myself the question, "What would I do in Abraham's situation?" Obedience has always been difficult for me, and I have never had to face such an unthinkable challenge as sacrificing my own child.

I look around me and reflect on my life today. I am making every effort to live as I understand God wants me to live. Everything I have done these past four years is "pushing against an open door." My life is better and gives me more pleasure and joy, even as I obey what I understand God is asking me to do. Doing the right thing is not difficult. It does not require sacrifice. It is not even close to the idea of Abraham facing the excruciating pain that must have been involved in sacrificing Isaac.

Thursday, October 27 **(Black holes and volcanoes)**

The assignment today is to look back on the "black holes" in my life, where nothing happened, or ugly things happened. I am to also look back on the "volcanoes" in my life, where I found "love of God" and light and insight.

Well, the black holes are those times when I was "dead in my transgressions and sins." Ugly things happened. I continue to feel guilt and shame for my sins "through my own fault, in my thoughts, in my words, in what I have done and what I have failed to do." For me, these were truly black holes. There was no light of faith at the end of a long tunnel to show me a way out of my misery. It was all darkness and death.

Happily, the volcanic events of God's grace are even more memorable than the black holes. Two volcanic events occurred more than forty years ago, when Melissa and Jennifer were born. The world was very different in that period when the 1960s turned into the 1970s. Men were not yet allowed into delivery rooms. The roles of men and women in the parenting process were still defined by norms that seem antediluvian compared with the standards today.

I was very different as well. I never tried to do more as a father (or husband) than the minimum requirement of that unfortunate era. Focusing on my role at the time will lead to a "black hole" reflection, not one involving "volcanic joy." The daughters themselves were the volcanoes, and they gave rise to many volcanic moments over the years.

There were many challenges and ups and downs in my business life. In retrospect, however, it all runs together as one long volcanic experience! I have loved my work from the earliest days of multifamily housing to coal mining to international electric power. I loved most of the people who joined the companies I organized. I loved my architectural efforts, including particularly the houses I built for Sallie Ann and me to live in. I loved the creative effort required to conceive of the designs, and I loved the experience of living in a house and garden environment knowing that I created it.

There have been so many "volcanic days" in my life that I could fill half of this journal describing them. Perhaps a time will come later in the exercises for that. At this stage, when the focus is on sin, it is difficult for me to talk much about the good times.

However, I remember so well coming out of the recovery room in Arizona to see Sallie Ann. That was volcanic. While I did not know the details of my journey, I knew at that moment that there was light, insight, and beauty in front of me. God's love shone brightly at dinner with Father John, when my daughters and grandchildren were with me, at RCIA lectures, and, particularly, when sitting next to Sallie Ann during Mass. During this past year and a half, each time I take the Eucharist is a major volcano event.

Friday, October 28 *(Isaiah 6:1-13)*

So what does it mean when Isaiah says that we are:

Hearing, but never understanding; seeing, but never perceiving?

Is this the state of sin? It is only through God's grace that we are able to understand what we hear or perceive what we see. Are we cut off from God's grace when we are in a state of sin?   Or is it only through God's grace that we leave that state, truly repent, and finally understand and perceive?

The more I reflect on this, the more certain I am of the phrase:

Without Him, I can't; without me, He won't.

It is our acceptance of God's freely-given grace that allows us to leave the state of sin. We cannot do it alone, but God will not do it without our participation. I am persuaded that saying yes to God is only the first step in that participation. We have to live righteously, love completely, and, in all things, get beyond ourselves.

Saturday, October 29   *(Romans 8:28-39)*

Paul once again confuses us with predestination:

And those he predestined, he also called; those he called, he also justified; those he justified, he also glorified.

This is heavy stuff. Paul does not suggest in this passage that there is much of a role for us. Nothing can separate us from the love of God. We were chosen before we were born, and everything after that is in God's hands.   So I pray for understanding.   I listen for God's voice.

Maggie and I just visited the bench. It seems the whole Ponte Vedra Beach community is inside somewhere watching the Florida/Georgia football game. The only sounds in the garden were the ocean, the birds, and the rustle of the branches where Maggie was looking for lizards. I arranged a cushion as a kneeler, and used the quiet moment to humble myself on my knees in hopes of hearing a whisper of insight.

It all comes down to surrender. Am I in charge or is God? The free will versus predestination debate cannot be resolved in a way that leaves me unaccountable for my actions. I have been called by God. There is no way that I can initiate that call. I can only answer the call. God will hold me to account for actions not consistent with loving Him.

When Paul says that nothing can separate us from the love of God, I believe that he means God will stand by us in the face of any opposition. The idea is that God is there at our side, not in our stead. We have been predestined to succeed, and no force outside of us can prevent that success **provided only that we answer God's call, and act out of love for God and for others**. With God's grace and His help, we are indeed "more than conquerors." We accomplish nothing without Him. We are nothing without Him. All that we have and all that we are, we have and have become as gifts from God. However, we had to say yes. We had to surrender, and, in that surrender, we had to accept God's grace and His commands. Again, He is there at our side, not in our stead.

Sunday, October 30   (Black holes and Volcanoes)

Again today, I am meant to look back on the black holes and the volcanoes in my life. I read from Thessalonians this morning at Mass. Maggie and I then walked on the beach, reflecting on this past week, the exercises thus far, and the idea of black holes and volcanoes.

Back in the library, I read the thought-piece on centering. It was very helpful. As I reflect on some of the ideas contained in the thought-piece, I am reminded of Lonergan's "attentive listening." Years ago, I developed the unfortunate habit of listening to cable news in the background, both at the office and in a thousand hotel rooms around the world. "Hearing" background noise is just about as opposed to attentive listening as it gets. Attentive listening involves what the centering piece referred to as growing aware of what one listens to, and becoming conscious of each separate sound.

So I started the session this afternoon listening to the sounds of silence in the library. I opened the door to the garden. The wind was still blowing hard outside by the fountain. Water trickled from the upper spouts into the fountain, and from the lower spout into the rill. In the distant background, I could hear the surf hitting the beach. Three different bird sounds broke the stillness. Maggie made noise dashing out to chase a lizard into the hedge.

I prayed the Jesus prayer, "Jesus Christ" in and "Have Mercy" out. The grace I am praying for this week is knowledge of God's desire for me. What are the gifts and charisms God has given me that inform my life purpose? How have I used those gifs in the past sixty-seven years? More important, what is God's desire for me now? What is He asking me to do with the rest of my life?

In the stillness of the garden, I seek to close out the extraneous sounds of wind, surf, and various creatures. As Meister Eckhart said almost five hundred years ago:

Nothing in all creation is so like God as stillness.

I try to be attentive, to focus on focus. I don't hear words, but I sense a presence. It is as though I can touch a "knowing" or certainty. This strange sensation of knowing is very short term or immediate.

I know that I am doing God's will leading the CRHP team as Formation Director. That is right now. It was this week, is today, and it will be something for the next nine weeks.

This certainty extends to my role as grandfather and husband. It was right to be next to Sallie Ann at Mass. It is God's will that I live in and honor the state of love that exists between us. Rob and the twins are part of this "right thing."

I am much less clear about the middle and distant future. This is not troubling. It seems acceptable that I do "the next right thing"; that I do what God wants me to do today and tomorrow. I question the utility, and the necessity, of knowing what I should be doing next year, much less a decade from now.

6. My life is God's gift to me and my response to God

You will find that human activity swings back and forth between delightful and tedious. These exercises are very likely sometimes to console you tremendously, and sometimes to seem like the most desolate wasteland you ever chose to wander through. When these swings happen, take them patiently; you can learn a lot about yourself and your world.

Monday, October 31   *(Romans 7:14-25)*

The reading this morning is one of the most studied, most written about, and, for many, most confusing passages in all of Paul's works. Generally, even after a day of prayer, I can be counted among the confused. Paul's words are harsh:

> *We know that the law is spiritual; but I am unspiritual, sold as a slave to sin. I do not understand what I do. For what I want to do I do not do, but what I hate I do. And if I do what I do not want to do, I agree that the law is good. As it is, it is no longer I myself who do it, but it is sin living in me. For I know that good itself does not dwell in me, that is, in my sinful nature. For I have the desire to do what is good, but I cannot carry it out. For I do not do the good I want to do, but the evil I do not want to do—this I keep on doing. Now if I do what I do not want to do, it is no longer I who do it, but it is sin living in me that does it.*

> *So I find this law at work: Although I want to do good, evil is right there with me. For in my inner being I delight in God's law; but I see another law at work in me, waging war against the law of my mind and making me a prisoner of the law of sin at work within me. What a wretched man I am! Who will rescue me from this body that is subject to death? Thanks be to God, who delivers me through Jesus Christ our Lord! So then, I myself in my mind am a slave to God's law, but in my sinful nature, a slave to the law of sin.*

I think I have come to the understanding that Paul is saying that we are all, by nature, subject to temptation, and that we generally yield to that temptation. Paul seems to be describing this temptation to sin (which he refers to as sin itself) in terms that anticipate Carl Jung's[53] "shadow aspect." In this passage, Paul suggests that there is

---

[53] According to Wikipedia, "Carl Jung (26 July 1875 – 6 June 1961) was a Swiss psychiatrist, the founder of analytical psychology. Jung is considered the first modern psychiatrist to view the human

an ongoing battle between "what we want to do" and "what we hate." Ultimately, it is only through God's grace that we can ever be saved from yielding to this temptation.

It seems to me that it matters little whether the sin or evil is inside of me or simply all around me in the world. The fact is that sin, in myriad forms, is always an option. It is always presented, in one way or another, as an enticing and attractive option. In fact, sin, even in the most benign form, is a very bad option.

Maggie and I knelt at the bench again (we have to arrange the cushion due to the "sensitivity" of my knees!), praying for clarity. Reflecting more on the reading, I think there are many varieties of sin. Some are clearly proscribed in the laws that have come down over the millennia. The Ten Commandments, various "natural laws," and many sectarian or political laws or rules come to mind. Some are simply part of being courteous and respectful of others.

To me, however, the most difficult "sin" is the sin of self. Self-interest, self-centeredness, self-righteousness, simple selfishness – these are the evils inside each and every one of us. While I have committed some other sins (I divorced the mother of my daughters for example), my greatest difficulty is getting past self. It could even be argued that these exercises are selfish.

Tuesday, November 1   *(Romans 7:14-25, again)*

The assignment today is to repeat reflection and prayer on Romans 7. The general instruction for the week is that I read and reflect on the Principle and Foundation, which open the Ignatian Spiritual Exercises.

Every person in the world is so put together that by praising, revering, and living according to the will of God our Lord he or she will safely reach the reign of God. This is the original purpose of each human life.

Every other thing on the face of the earth is meant for humankind, to help each person come to the original purpose God has put in each of us.

---

psyche as "by nature religious" and make it the focus of exploration. Jung is one of the best known researchers in the field of dream analysis and symbolization. While he was a fully involved and practicing clinician, much of his life's work was spent exploring tangential areas, including Eastern and Western philosophy, alchemy, astrology, and sociology, as well as literature and the arts. Jung considered individuation, a psychological process of integrating the opposites including the conscious with the unconscious while still maintaining their relative autonomy, necessary for a person to become whole. Individuation is the central concept of analytical psychology. Many psychological concepts were first proposed by Jung, including the archetype, the collective unconscious, the complex, and synchronicity. Popular psychometric instruments like the Myers-Briggs Type Indicator (MBTI), have been principally developed from Jung's theories. His interest in philosophy and the occult led many to view him as a mystic although Jung's ambition was to be seen as a man of science."

The only thing that makes sense in the use of all other things, then, is that a person uses everything that helps realize that original purpose deep in the self, and turn away from everything that alienates him or her from the original purpose.

We can push this a little further: When we are under no obligations in conscience, we ought to keep ourselves free of any fixed preference for one or other created thing. Instead, we ought to keep ourselves at balance before anything. What does this entail? It means that before we ever face any decision we do not determine to do everything that will keep us healthy and nothing that might make us sick, to be rich rather than poor, to be considered somebody important rather than a nobody, to live to a very old age rather than to die younger. In that way, we would keep a balance before any created thing when the times come for decision.

We set ourselves to live in careful balance, to want to choose solely on the grounds of what leads more directly and more certainly to our original purpose.

Original purpose and balance – these are at the heart of the exercises. Ignatius discovered his original purpose during his meditation and prayer in Manresa. As the Principle states, Ignatius believes that his original purpose is to "safely reach the reign of God." This is the purpose of every human life.

We achieve that purpose by praising and revering God, and by living in accordance with His will. The only sensible conclusion is that we pursue everything that contributes to the purpose, and turn away from everything that alienates us from the purpose. This is pretty straight-forward.

Just as the Principle of the Exercises is the simple discovery and pursuit of our original purpose, the Foundation of the Exercises is balance. Living in careful balance makes remarkably good sense.

Now, I immediately question whether this makes good sense to me because it allows me to pray for humility in an extremely comfortable library, meditate on getting beyond self at a bench in a luxurious garden, and seek simplicity walking on the exclusive beach of a resort community. On reflection, it seems pretty clear that this balance is somewhat favorable to me!

Wednesday, November 2   (Hebrews 2:5-13)

It was my intention not to read anything outside of the assigned readings this week. However, as I read the passage from Hebrews this morning, I realized how little I knew about this book in the New Testament.

So I turned to the Anchor Bible Commentary for some background. The general consensus of biblical scholars today, including Catholics, is that Hebrews was written late in the first century, probably in Rome, probably by a follower of Paul, and probably to one of the Jewish Christian house-churches in Rome. The timing has been reasonably certain since both Clement and Origen[54] made reference to Hebrews in their writings around the turn of the first century.

For centuries, scholars assumed Paul was the author of this letter, due largely to the agreement between Hebrews and the rest of the established Pauline letters. However, modern biblical scholars have been essentially unanimous in concluding that linguistic differences rule Paul out as the author, and equally unanimous in concluding that Barnabus, Apollos, Pricilla, or another associate of Paul did write this letter.

References to various Old Testament passages and to the relationship between the old and new testaments lead to the conclusion that the intended audience was Jewish Christians, not Gentile Christians.

After all that study, I find myself no closer to a clear understanding of this passage, or, for that matter, much else in Hebrews. I guess I am meant to better understand the idea that Jesus Christ became human, and then, through the grace of God, died on behalf of all other human beings, including me.

Thursday, November 3   (Hebrews 2:5-13, again)

Sallie Ann and I saw the movie The Way this afternoon.[55] What a wonderful story about the thousand-year-old pilgrimage from France through the foothills of the Pyrenees down to Santiago de Compostela - in Galicia, the northwest province of Spain. We went to a wedding in Santiago many years ago, spending a week in the hotel across the square from the cathedral. The cornerstone of the hotel was laid in 1492, the year Columbus arrived in America and also the year both the Moors and the Jews were expelled from Spain!

This fictional story of the pilgrimage of St. James appeals to me so much because it is a journey of discovery. That is one of the beautiful things about these exercises so far. Each day, I have moved a little further along my own journey, discovering both more about my faith and myself. It seems that the more I learn, the more I realize there is to learn.

---

[54] According to Wikipedia, "Clement, 150-215, taught at the Catechetical School in Alexandria, and has been designated a Church Father. Origen, 184-254, was a scholar and theologian , also in Alexandria. Like Clement, his early writing earned him designation as a Church Father."

[55] According to the film's promotional material, "THE WAY is a powerful and inspirational story about family, friends and the challenges we face while navigating this ever-changing and complicated world. Martin Sheen plays Tom, an irascible American doctor who comes to France to deal with the tragic loss of his son (played by Emilio Estevez). Rather than return home, Tom decides to embark on the historical pilgrimage "The Way of St. James" to honor his son's desire to finish the journey. What Tom doesn't plan on is the profound impact this trip will have on him. Through unexpected and oftentimes amusing experiences along "The Way," Tom discovers the difference between "the life we live and the life we choose."

Friday, November 4   *(John 1:1-18)*

John is the name I chose for my confirmation name, thinking of John the Evangelist. As it happened, somewhat bizarrely, John was to play a larger role in our lives. Father John was my mentor throughout my conversion to Catholicism. We live on San Juan Drive in St. John's County. In spite of all that, I have some trouble understanding John's gospel, even though I find readings from John to be the most interesting and inspiring of the four gospels.

So I referred to Raymond Brown's commentary, and to the Catena Aurea of Thomas Aquinas, for a little background understanding. After centuries of disagreement about the authenticity and importance of John's gospel, scholars now generally agree that this Gospel was written in the late first century, between around 90 CE and 100 CE.

There is growing support for the idea that the Apostle John, son of Zebedee, was the principle author, and that he wrote most of the Gospel in Ephesus, with some work having been done in Antioch. John is considered a brilliant theologian, substantially the most intellectually gifted among the various gospel writers.

John 1:1-18 is the Prologue to the Gospel. It is one of the most beautiful pieces of poetry in either the Old or New Testaments. As I mentioned, John is commonly thought to have lived past the turn of the first century, making him a very old man at the time of his death – at least well past 85 (I assume he must have been born by 10 CE, putting him in his early twenties when he sat with Jesus at the Last Supper). Just imagine having been present at the time of Christ's crucifixion, then living another 65 years. Imagine living most of those nearly seven decades in considerable fear and hardship.

While there are no complete records of his travels from the time of the Pentecost until his death, he must have been teaching and preaching throughout the eastern Mediterranean the entire time. Only because he doesn't mention Paul anywhere in the Gospel, I assume he did not come to Ephesus until Paul was long gone. However, even at that, John could have spent 30 to 35 years in Ephesus after Paul and Paul's closest friends had moved on.

Anyway, I can imagine John teaching the gospel in the house-churches of Antioch and Ephesus. I can imagine John and his parishioners opening their services with hymns.

So I put myself in one of those upper-rooms, gathered together with both Gentile Christians, who were converted by Paul, and Jewish Christians, who fled Jerusalem following the Roman conquest of 70 CE. We begin singing a favorite hymn of the Apostle John, son of Zebedee, member of the "Twelve," beloved disciple of Jesus.

> *In the beginning was the Word, and the Word was with God, and the Word was God.*

He was with God in the beginning. Through him all things were made; without him nothing was made that has been made.

In him was life, and that life was the light of all mankind.

The light shines in the darkness, and the darkness has not overcome it.

As we sing these opening verses, candles are lit, and their light fills the room. The Holy Spirit was with us in the room, filling our hearts and opening our eyes to the meaning of the hymn we were singing.

There was a man sent from God whose name was John. He came as a witness to testify concerning that light, so that through him all might believe. He himself was not the light; he came only as a witness to the light.

This verse does not fit the poetic style of the verses we have just sung, nor the verses we are about to sing. Someone in the room whispers that John added it earlier in the week to distinguish our meeting from that of the Gnostics, a Jewish sect that was formed by followers of John the Baptist. Our John wanted to make it clear that Jesus was "the light," and that John the Baptist came only to announce Jesus. While the whispered explanation interrupted the flow of the music, we understood its purpose.

The true light that gives light to everyone was coming into the world.

He was in the world, and though the world was made through him, the world did not recognize him.

He came to that which was His own, but His own did not receive him.

Yet to all who did receive him, to those who believed in His name, he gave the right to become children of God— children born not of natural descent, nor of human decision or a husband's will, but born of God.

The Word became flesh and made His dwelling among us. We have seen His glory, the glory of the one and only Son, who came from the Father, full of grace and truth.

As I sang the words "born of God," I trembled with joy. All around me, I could feel the strength of God's grace and truth ripple through our small group. Again, our singing was interrupted by further reference to John the Baptist.

John testified concerning him. He cried out, saying, "This is the one I spoke about when I said, 'He who comes after me has surpassed me because he was before me.'"

This short interruption took nothing away from the beauty of the words we were singing. For some of us, it was the first time we heard the word grace while at the same time experiencing the indwelling of that grace.

Out of His fullness we have all received grace in place of grace already given.

For the law was given through Moses; grace and truth came through Jesus Christ.

No one has ever seen God, but the one and only Son, who is himself God and is in closest relationship with the Father, has made him known.

In my mind, all of us gathered in that upper-room in Ephesus kneel when the singing ends. In fact, I kneel in the library as Maggie watches in fascination. I pray the Our Father. I thank God for this incredible experience, and for the Holy Spirit that fills this library and my heart.

Saturday, November 5   (Deuteronomy 30:15-20)

I dreamt of Buddy Tudor last night. It was one of those serial dreams, interrupted from time to time to answer the call of nature, after which I hurriedly returned to the bed to pick up the story. We were debating these exercises in the context of his wishes and concerns for me after his death. Among other things, I listened to him tell Patsy, his wife, that she should check up on me from time to time.

This was fascinating because the conventional wisdom is that those of us who were Buddy's good friends should take care of his widow after he died. But Buddy seemed more concerned with me, urging Patsy to confirm that I was still on the right path. Of course, I had given him about forty years' worth of good reasons to worry.

He constantly talked to me last night about keeping things simple. He did it in that engineering way: outline the problem, list the alternatives, make a decision, implement the solution, and check the work. At each step, Buddy learned enough (or knew enough from experience) about the situation to be able to concisely state the problem, the alternative solutions, the basis for decision, and the process of implementation.

I kept explaining that I was trying to compress a lifetime of learning into just a few months. So the argument proceeded until early this morning, when I told Sallie Ann about the dream-filled night.

The reading this morning from Deuteronomy is appropriate.

"Now choose life, so that you and your children may live and that you may love the Lord your God, listen to His voice, and hold fast to Him."

This is an Old Testament version of the Ignatian principle, but without much room for the foundational balance. The reading does underscore my strong belief in the idea that God extends His grace, but we must say yes — we must make the clear choice to accept His grace and surrender to and obey His commandments.

Sunday, November 6   (Black holes and Volcanoes)

There has been a great deal of reflection and reading over the past six weeks. I sometimes find it difficult to back far enough away from the trees to see the forest. Much of what this preparation process has been about is a rather simple message: I cannot even begin to know myself until and unless I know with a certainty that God made me and that He did so with a purpose.

As the Principle states, we are all here with the same Original Purpose, which is to safely reach the Reign of God. We are meant to pursue that which moves us closer to that Purpose, and avoid that which moves us away from that Purpose. The Foundational premise of these exercises is that we are to do all of this in a balanced way.

God created me and all that is around me, and He has given me all that I am and all that I have, with an additional, unique, and personal purpose. His unique purpose for me is entirely consistent with the universal Original Purpose of all mankind, and each of us individually, which is the safe arrival in God's Kingdom. My purpose must be achieved in conformance with the two great commandments: Love God and love my fellow man.

Reflecting on these statements, it is emphatically clear that this Ignatian method requires, more than anything else, getting beyond self. God made me. I had nothing to do with it. God did so for His purpose, not mine. His unique purpose for me is that I achieve the Original Purpose – getting back to Him – by following the path He chose for me. I must follow that path in a state of being "in love" with Him, and with my fellow man.

I ended the day reading the Ignatian prayer for the First Principle and Foundation:

> The Goal of our life is to live with God forever.
> God, who loves us, gave us life.
> Our own response of love allows God's life
> to flow into us without limit.
>
> All the things in this world are gifts from God,
> Presented to us so that we can know God more easily
> and make a return of love more readily.
> As a result, we appreciate and use all these gifts of God
> Insofar as they help us to develop as loving persons.
> But if any of these gifts become the center of our lives,

They displace God
And so hinder our growth toward our goal.

In everyday life, then, we must hold ourselves in balance
Before all of these created gifts insofar as we have a choice
And are not bound by some obligation.
We should not fix our desires on health or sickness,
Wealth or poverty, success or failure, a long life or a short one.
For everything has the potential of calling forth in us
A deeper response to our life in God.

Our only desire and our one choice should be this:
I want and I choose what better leads
To God's deepening his life in me. [56]

---

[56] St. Ignatius of Loyola, as paraphrased by David L. Fleming, S.J.

First Week

(Four Weeks)

1. The negative force of sin in the world

I want to feel the power of sin in my human nature and to be confused that I have sinned and not suffered so much for it.

Monday, November 7   (The Sin of the Angels)

Sister Joan and I met last night, as usual, to review progress for the past week and to discuss the assignments for the week to come. This time, however, the assignment is meant to cover two calendar weeks, allowing Sister Joan to lead another group of parishioners to the Holy Land. As a result of my intensive study of the New Testament these past few weeks, I feel close to that trip and to that part of the world. I look forward to someday going back to Israel and to the other New Testament locations now that I have become a Catholic. I am sure everything will have deeper meaning than it did when I was last there. I doubt it will ever happen.

The general purpose of the exercises for the next two weeks (in fact, for this month-long period, which is called the First Week of the exercises) is to understand and reflect upon the role of sin in the world, and in my life particularly. In some ways, it is meant to be the hardest part of the Ignatian exercises. Each day for most of the next 30 days, the objective will be to deepen my sorrow and shame for the many sins I have committed in my life.

The reading this morning was a thought-piece entitled The Sin of the Angels. Among other things, it is suggested that I consider the sins out in the world, especially those that trouble me. For several reasons, this is a relatively easy task to complete, though it is a particularly uncomfortable process. I am a news junkie, watching, listening to, and reading about current events at least ten to twelve hours every single day. I have only recently become aware of how unusual this is, especially after teaching the class at UNF. I mention this "news addiction" here because the overwhelming majority of the stories reported each day describe "sins" in the world. Most of these stories are deeply troubling to me.

Where to begin? I am teaching the course at UNF because I was so troubled by the great and growing disparity between the rich and the rest, both here in the United States and around the world. There are countless sins involved in that disparity. Almost uniformly, those at the top of the wealth distribution are guilty of self-centered gluttony, engaged in what seems to be a never-ending quest for more. This alone is a major sin. Imagine a man like John Paulsen, whose 2010 income was $4.7 billion!

However, the sin is enormously compounded by the fact that most of those at the top care little or not at all about everyone else. In fact, the extraordinary generosity of people like Bill Gates and Warren Buffet, each of whom have given close to 90 percent of their enormous wealth to philanthropy, serves only to highlight the selfishness of most of the others.

As I reflect on the reading, the sins of the world grow in number and abhorrence. I become more and more depressed about the little that I can do about it.

Friday, November 11   (The Sin of Adam and Eve)

For some reason, I have had some difficulty writing in this journal this week. We have had a house guest, I have struggled a little with my UNF class, and I have otherwise been distracted. Maybe I have been avoiding the subject.

More reflection on sin led me to a long examination of old feelings. In the fall of 1965, I was the District Leader of the Mormon missionaries in Wurzburg, Germany. I remember the fortress high on a hill above the river that ran through the town. I remember teaching English to a group of Germans, hoping to hook them through English lessons to the idea of learning more about Mormonism. I remember a young girl named Petra, and her East German mother. East Germans were quite rare in West Germany back then (the Wall really worked rather well).

I knew about sin. In fact, I thought about sinning almost hourly, throughout every single day. We were celibate, and we were 20 years old, and the German girls were both quite beautiful and very much aware of our missionary vows. So I did a fair amount of sinning in my mind on a more or less constant basis.

We have been "imagining" scenes from the scriptures, putting ourselves in the place of disciples or Jewish law givers. This morning, I remember vividly the scenes from that long summer of 1965 in Germany. By then, my German was quite fluent, and I was a veteran of the baptismal font, having converted and baptized several German families during my first year as a missionary. So the little Mormon community in Wurzburg looked up to me, and so did my fellow missionaries. I remember a lot of laughter, and a few fun-filled social events, where friendships certainly approached the line between pastoral distance and too much familiarity.

Petra and her mother were regulars at both our religious services and the social functions. It is easy now to create in my mind the intense feelings of torment and temptation I experienced almost daily. All of the testosterone-generated desires were as present in me (and, I assume, the other missionaries) as they were in any normal young men in their early twenties. So we never left our companions, and we often prayed for God's help in our efforts to honor our vows.

While I know with comfortable certainty that I did not act out my sexual fantasies, I know with equal certainty just how vivid those fantasies were. During July and August, I allowed those sinful thoughts to entertain me at every opportunity. I knew the thoughts themselves were sinful. I became increasingly aware of the dance I allowed, even encouraged, to take place in my mind.

It became clear that I had gone too far when I started talking about my excitement with Petra. I asked the Mission President to move me from Wurzburg to Sachsenhausen, a suburb of Frankfurt, sometime toward the end of October, only partially disclosing that I had grown uncomfortably close to some of the students in our English classes.

So I would be lying if I said that I was a completely surprised that fall night. I was at the podium in a large meeting room. I had just begun the evening sermon. Two missionaries approached me, one from each side. The escorted me to the basement of the mission headquarters, where I was to stay for nearly three weeks.

I knew about sin. I knew then that sin would separate me from God and from all that I believed God represented in my life. My anguish in that basement reflected the coming together of a monumental religious crisis on one hand, and, on the other hand, the worst possible reaction to my coming of age sexually. The rather normal shame and embarrassment associated with sexual fantasies was about to be judged in the white-hot cauldron of religious exposure.

There was a trial, but the charges were not sinful thoughts, which I had expected. Nor were they too much familiarity with potential converts, or any of the other sins I had been praying about. I was charged with violating my oath of celibacy, of "going all the way" with the young lady in Wurzburg. Petra never confronted me with that charge, nor did I hear any other evidence of my sins. The trial lasted only an hour or so. The guilty verdict, along with my excommunication from the church and immediate departure from Germany, were announced to me later that night.

I knew about sin. The flight back to the United States, sitting between two "guards" on a Lufthansa flight from Frankfurt to Boston, seems fresh in my mind today. It is as though it happened last week, not forty-five years ago. I was completely overcome by shame, more shame than I had ever experienced before. That shame did not release me until after I lost an appeal of my conviction several months later. Even then, I went nearly two years before attempting my first date.

I knew about sin. After hitchhiking across the country from Salt Lake City, I moved into a small one-room apartment at the foot of William James Hall. It was mid-November. It was bitter cold. There was dirty snow on the sides of the walkways and roads. I knew a grand total of no one in the Cambridge to which I had returned.

The memories of walking around the Harvard campus over that Christmas holiday are as fresh in my mind as my actions last week. I was extremely lonely, and deeply depressed. Thoughts of suicide were always present.

The shame I felt for leaving the mission field in disgrace was made infinitely worse by the impact it had on my family. My parents drove from Moreland, Idaho down to Salt Lake City to witness my official "drumming out." My mother could not stop crying. She wanted nothing more than to never show her face again in our little community in Snake River. She called me a failure, and told me she would never forgive me for the shame I brought down on the family. Even Dad, who quietly supported me in everything, wept in silence. Oh yes, I knew about sin.

My relationship with God slowly entered a strange twilight zone. How could I say that God did not exist when I spent several hours each day talking to Him? My communication was clouded by my humiliation and my anger. I was separated from God by my shameful sense of sin.

So sitting on the bench this afternoon, I finally moved past the purely cerebral contemplation of some universal sense of sin – the sins of the very rich as they selfishly ignore the poor. My contemplation of sin involves one person – me – sinning through thought and deed, through what I did and what I did not do, and wallowing in the shame of that sin for decades.

The words in the assigned readings make more sense to me now. I am truly confounded by the glaring fact that I have been blessed with so much in spite of my life of sin. I am like the world – caught up in sin, but saved nonetheless by the grace of God. Saved for what, I ask. The answer is right there: Saved for the Original Purpose, which is to safely return to the Reign of God.

However, these words offer little solace tonight. I know about sin. After forty years in a religious desert, I finally said yes to the grace offered by God. Through baptism, I accepted salvation. I am now making every effort to put my faith into works.

Sunday, November 13   *(The Sin of One Person)*

Maggie and I walked today for the first time in several days. I read last night at Mass, and again this morning. It felt very good to lector again, although it has only been a couple of weeks since I last did so. Each time I do so now, I feel more like I am indeed proclaiming the word. The reason for that is tied directly to these exercises. I now routinely imagine myself in the place and with the people involved in the reading. I attempt to speak with the voice of Paul, addressing a small group in the upper-room of a house-church. It clearly adds something to my reading.

So I have thus far written in this journal about the global sins of the nameless rich, and about some very specific sins of one man, me, almost half a century ago. I find that the reading material somewhat encourages this avoidance. What I mean by avoidance is failing to focus on my sins for the last forty-plus years.

The fact is that sin is part of my life today, eighteen months after my baptism, four years after I began my journey of faith, and forty-five years after I came to terms with what happened in Germany. At various times during most days I am thoughtless, lazy, selfish, envious, gluttonous, and simply not in harmony with God. Even when working through my prayer and meditation hour, I allow all manner of distractions to pull me away from the clear focus I so sincerely want to achieve.

I am excited about CRHP tonight. Two more brothers will share their HGFS.[57] I have heard from several of the Team 11 guys this week, all of whom seemed to be really pleased with the extent to which the Holy Spirit is present in our meetings. At least the time I spend in formation with this group of men seems to be "sin free."

Friday, November 19   (Sin in My Life)

A long week has passed since I last wrote in this journal. I prayed each day, and I reflected on the grace I am seeking this week. I allowed extraneous thoughts to keep me from writing.

Maggie and I started the day together with a renewed spirit of commitment. We walked down to the bench and nearly froze to death in the cold wind. So we rushed back to the library and prayed this week's prayer:

> I ask to feel in human affairs and all through my own life world how subtly and virulently sin flourishes.

We have spent a great deal of time over the past three years at Woodstock talking about "steward leadership." The idea is that everything in our lives is "on loan" from God. We are meant to take care of it, increase its value, and return it to God better than we found it. Sin, from the perspective of steward leadership, is any action or failure to act that detracts from this objective.

So I once again face sin in my life. I profess to be an environmentalist. I supposedly care about energy efficiency and waste. Yet the list of my shortcomings in this area is as long as my arm. I drive a wasteful and inefficient V-8, even though I have installed a charging station for an electric car in my garage. Whom do I think I am kidding? I do not recycle waste, even though I have an expensive and elaborate rainwater harvesting system designed to conserve water.

I profess to be extremely troubled by inequality. Yet I live a luxurious life and enjoy numerous profligate habits. It has been many years since I allowed the cost of an activity or a thing to interfere with my desire satisfaction. I sin each time I yield to my

---

[57] History Giving and Faith Sharing (HGFS) is a core element of the CRHP process. Each participant in the retreat takes a turn sharing as much or as little of their life story in front of the other members of their team. It is through this process that long-lasting, close bonds are created between and among the participants.

obsession to have or do whatever I want whenever I want. Imagine what would happen if I diverted each of these impulsive, obsessive expenditures to the poor or to my family. I am able to live with myself only because I am relatively less profligate than many others with similar levels of career success. I know something about sin. We are commanded to be selfless, not relatively selfless.

So what about the Ignatian concept of balance? I can certainly make an argument that I am doing some things for others, which provides some balance for the good life I enjoy. This is a slippery slope. The voice I hear when I pray and meditate on this issue today suggests that my life-scales are weighted way over toward selfishness.

Saturday, November 20   *(More Sin in My Life)*

Both last night and this morning, I prayed for a better understanding regarding the sin in my life. As I read through the journal entries I have made since beginning this focus on sin, my sense is that I continue to avoid the most important battles I have had with sin during my life. Certainly, the experience in Germany in 1965 was huge, both in terms of the power that sin had in my life and the damage done by my sins. To say that there were consequences is to drastically understate what happened to me and to my family.

The sin did not stop during those years that I came to terms with my excommunication from the Mormon Church. I started dating in 1967, two years after I left the basement of the mission home in Frankfurt. My efforts to meet women were extremely cautious. In fact, for the most part, I limited my actual dating to Phyllis Cox, the woman I would marry in June of 1968.

We met as like-minded idealists, working together to bring peace and love to the world. The furthest thing from my mind was the very thought of getting a job in the business world, climbing the ladder of corporate success, or negotiating terms with a compensation consultant. In the end, I did take a job with a for-profit company, Boise Cascade, but my job was initially equal employment opportunity (assuring compliance with Lyndon Johnson's civil rights acts), followed by low-income housing and community development. Phyllis worked as a community organizer in the Anti-Poverty Program.

As far as sinning goes, I managed pretty well from 1965 until 1972. My work was focused on helping others. I was paid very little, and would have worked for less. I had begun to travel, but nothing like what was to come. I took full advantage of the then-current notion that mothers were meant to perform the parental functions, with fathers charged with bringing home enough to pay the rent.

The marriage ended in 1972 with no rancor and hardly any notice. It was not until the order of divorce was mailed to me a year after we separated and filed the petition that I can remember feeling any remorse. I did feel badly then, and my mother was quick to get on the phone with some pretty strong reminders of the extent of my failure. She pointed out that this was my second major life failure and I was not even 26 years old!

As I reflect on the first ten years after my divorce, it is obvious that the seeds of sin had been sown on fertile ground. The first observation about that period is the obvious and well-documented sea change that took place in the cultural norms of most parts of the United States. I lived and worked at the cutting edge of this Cultural Revolution. So I truly applied myself to the task of making up for all the years that I had only cautiously explored women. Oh yes, I knew about sin.

Those single years of the 1970s allowed me to develop what I consider to be one of my greatest sins. I am a workaholic. Now, I know this might sound like the answer some politicians give when asked to name their greatest weakness. "I care too much," they say. It is not meant to. There is an enormous difference between working hard and addictively working. Hard work very seldom hurts others. Addictive work almost always does.

My addiction to my career had already emerged during my brief marriage to Phyllis. I think back now on those days, nights, and weekends that I went back to the office or, worse, went to the airport to fly to yet another deal opportunity. It shocked no one that Phyllis wanted something more than that from a husband. She deserved more.

However, compared to the wild decade that followed, my years of marriage to Phyllis were a scene from *Father Knows Best*. The trailer house at the coal mine in a hollow next to Hell's Creek was not a place for a wife and small children. I was never content with one mine or a comfortable market niche for my coal. As soon as one piece of equipment was in place, I bought another, which meant finding new markets, selling more coal, borrowing money against that new production, and on and on and on.

Over the 45 years that I was active in business, I can see several brief interludes when a tiny bit of sanity would emerge. The year before I married Sallie Ann, for example, I sold the coal mine and promised her that my life would change. We went to Europe that year, where I suggested to Sallie Ann that we commit to never sleeping apart (meaning that I would never travel without her) and that we devote time each day to each other and to the enjoyment of our blessings (although I almost certainly used some other word than blessings!).

We had not been married three months before I started a new company, which required that I search out and develop deal after deal. Each deal required major financing and obsessive hours of hard work to develop, build, and commission. I know about sin.

Sunday, November 21   *(More Sin in My Life)*

What a glorious, magical day in paradise! Maggie and I started the day in the library with prayer. We then walked down to the bench and prayed again. How is it possible that this Thanksgiving week could begin with such an incredibly wonderful day of blessings? Richard Rohr's daily meditation was particularly good this morning:

> *Give me your failure, God says, and I will make life out of it. Give me your broken, disfigured, rejected, betrayed lives, like the body you see hanging on the cross, and I will make life out of it. This is the divine pattern of promise and transformation which gives such hope to history. It is probably the central Gospel message.*
>
> *We are all still handicapped and terribly aware of our wounds, but as St. Augustine (354-430) says in his Confessions, "In my deepest wound I saw Your glory and it dazzled me." He seems to be saying that against all expectations our very failures can be our way through to God and to ourselves. That utterly levels the playing field. Even Julian of Norwich (1342-1416) says,*
>
> *God sees our wounds, and sees them not as scars but as honors. For God holds sin as a sorrow and pain to us. He does not blame us for them.*
>
> *If the Gospel is true, we might eventually thank God for our very weaknesses and failures.*[58]

It was hard to focus on sin while sitting on the bench in the beauty of the garden and this day, so we walked down to the beach. I was so moved by the enormousness of God's presence that I started to weep. This has not happened to me on the beach before. Frankly, it seemed like a perfect Amen to a morning of prayer.

Back in the library, I reflected about sin in my life. There was a long descent into hell at the end of my active career, the details of which I will not describe in this journal. Suffice it to say that my decision to embark upon a journey of faith was prompted by a trifecta of near-death experiences. First, several heart attacks forced me to confront my *physical* mortality. Second, a losing battle with intense resentment and blinding hatred brought me face to face with my *mental* death. Finally, when I reached the bottom of that painful descent into darkness, I realized that I had lost all contact with my *spiritual* core. Yes, I know about sin.

---

[58] Throughout this journal, I will frequently refer to or quote from the Daily Meditation published electronically by Richard Rohr. The Daily Meditations are copyrighted by the Center for Action and Contemplation, 1705 Five Points Rd SW, Albuquerque, NM 87105. I have requested and obtained verbal consent to use them in this journal.

Monday, November 28   (Sin of One Person)

Gap and I met last night to discuss Woodstock.[59] However, we spent all of our time together reviewing my progress in these exercises. His honest feedback was not easy to hear.

So before reviewing my prayer this morning, I want to reflect on what has been happening over the past two months as I began these exercises.

First and foremost, I have tenaciously held on to the controls. Sadly, I must confess that I have only scanned the instructions given to me each week, assuming that I could forego most of what was written. I chose to begin these exercises my way; not the way Ignatius Loyola prescribed more than 450 years ago; not the way Sister Joan suggested on a regular basis; and not the way Father Joseph Tetlow instructed in the weekly handouts. I now realize how mistaken I have been. Happily, I do not think it is too late to change.

Second, in spite of my stubborn refusal to accept and follow the guidance of others, I believe I have been regularly blessed by the presence of the Holy Spirit in my morning sessions, my garden meditations, and my walks on the beach. That is the good news. The bad news is that I have not experienced the growth in my understanding of God and my approach to prayer that Ignatius intended. I am still at the beginning of that process.

As it happened, I found it difficult to separate myself from all the family visiting for Thanksgiving last week, and, therefore, did not write in this journal each day. Looking back on my entries over the past month, it seems that irregularity has become my normal fashion. I did read hurriedly through the handout sheets, and I did pray about and reflect on sin throughout the week. However, I did not read the words with my mind and heart open to understanding what those words were saying.

So I start this week with a new approach. I intend to follow the instructions.

I began this morning sitting in the chair in the corner of the library. I lit the candle and positioned the cross and the bible on the table next to me. I opened my notebook to the thought-piece entitled The Sin of One Person. This was the reading for the Thursday of the week before Thanksgiving, one that I only hurriedly read. I in-

---

[59] Father Gasper (Gap) Lo Biondo is a Jesuit priest from Rosenhayn, New Jersey. He was ordained in 1968, and trained as an economist. He currently serves as Director of the Woodstock Theological Center, a Jesuit center for theological reflection on the human problems of today, located at Georgetown University. Prior to becoming Director, he was a Senior Research Fellow at Woodstock, and directed the Center's Global Economy and Cultures project. His areas of expertise include economic globalization and grass-roots research in developing countries, based on his seven years' experience in Chile.

tend to move forward from that point, which means that I will have to read more than one daily assignment at each prayer and meditation period for a few days.

For the first time in many weeks, I began my prayer by acknowledging God's presence. I thanked Him and praised Him. I asked that He accept me into this place and this space where His presence is so powerful. That power seemed to grow through my simple acknowledgement.

In my own words, I offered myself to Him and to His service. I wanted other words. I made a note to myself to find prayers and readings that conveyed my desire to give to God my heart and soul in an effort to understand His will for me and to carry it out today.

Then I composed myself in a place where I could understand and appreciate the discussion about sin, having read in advance that I would go in my mind to some other places during the discussion. First, though, I contemplated this place I am in. God has given me a great deal of comfort, security, warmth, and peace at this stage in my life.

I prayed for the grace to understand my sin. I asked Him to let me feel shame. He must have been listening carefully, because I was immediately overcome with shame. I flashed back on what I had thought about so much over the past two weeks, and even how poorly I feel I have been doing these exercises.

I asked Him to allow me to be confounded by the fact that I am surrounded by so many blessings in spite of all of my sins. This was easy to do in the library, where God's blessings are so obvious and so abundant. Simply being able to pray in this room increased both my confusion and my shame.

Then I read again the reflection paragraphs on the page about the Sin of One Person, of which there are five. Each reflection will require a new composition of place.

Luke 16:19-31 requires that I compose myself in Hades, listening to Dives, the rich man, talk with Abraham about his situation. Dives enjoyed many blessings prior to his death, while Lazarus was poor and homeless. As a result of this huge disparity, a chasm was created between the two men, one which cannot be crossed. I am struck with the great income disparity in the world today. The sin of Dives was not his richness; it was his lack of concern and caring for Lazarus.

The second reflection involves a central teaching of Christ and the Church. Selfishness and love of self may be such serious sins that they will result in a solitary life of self-love forever. I am saddened by this prospect.

Dictators, selfish and acquisitive rich men, and indolent hedonists are the subjects of the third paragraph. In answer to the thought questions, I am not clear what I think happens to these people when they die, or where they are now. I am not sure whether I fully embrace the idea of a "hell down below," or whether I generally believe there to be a virtual place where evil people go, one that feels like hell due to the way these people have lived.

The fourth paragraph takes me to Vietnam, where I imagine a village attacked by American troops. One soldier wantonly kills an old man and some children. I am sad and angry when I put myself in that place. Whatever else this soldier may have done in his life, this single horrific act defines his life. He must be with the others in that place once called hell.

Finally, I reflect on my own life of sin. God's grace has saved me thus far, but it will only be through His continued blessing that I do not find myself in the company of the sinners in today's reflections. My primary sin has been self-love, so, in my mind, I stand somewhat above the dictators and the soldiers who needlessly destroy the lives of others. However, the prospect of a life after my death consisting of solitary confinement in my own selfish being is real.

Matthew 26:24. Still in God's presence, I again offered myself fully to Him and to His service. I prayed for the grace to feel the power of sin in my human nature. I prayed to be confused at how little I have suffered as a result of my sins. After composing myself in the upper-room with Jesus and His apostles at the Last Supper, I read Matthew 26:24 for the second time before reflecting on its meaning.

"It would have been better for that man if he had not been born," said Christ referring to Judas. When Judas asked "Is it I, Master?" Christ said simply, "You have said so." I am saddened by this, and a little angry. What greater sin can there be than betraying Jesus Christ, the Son of God? What greater shame could any man feel than that felt by Judas? As I pondered these questions, I felt the shame of Judas.

Black holes and volcanoes. The tangible presence of God powerfully fills the space all around me. The reflection on the black holes of my sin and shame produced the same emotions of sadness, shame, guilt, frustration, and discomfort that I have felt all day. Once again, I found myself vividly surrounded by the real presence of people, places and things that were there during the periods of my worst sin. Someday, perhaps, I will write about those times; however, not now and not here. This is a journal about prayer and meditation, not a general confession.

Meditation on Hell. The place in which I next composed myself this morning was Hell itself, alien, lonely, frustrating, and absurd.

The meditation on Hell reminded me of those times in my life when I visited Hell. I remembered when my selfish and sinful behavior took me to a place exactly like the one described in the reading. Isolation was my antidote for depression. Loneliness and frustration were my medicines. I felt truly awful during this meditation period, sick that I had risked so much and sick with the prospect that turning from God in the future could come at such an incredible price.

For perhaps twenty minutes, I talked comfortably with God about these reflections. We talked about my commitment to honor the structure created by Ignatius for these spiritual exercises. Now, after writing several pages instead of just a few paragraphs, I need to re-visit that commitment! I hope this lack of brevity is just a reflection of the challenges involved in transition.

2. A meditation on our sins

I want a sharp sense of how I have really sinned, and how much. I want the Lord to open me to a deep sorrow for and shame at what I have done. I wish I could weep like Simon Peter.

Tuesday November 29   (Remembering my Sins)

It is extremely painful to remember my sins. More than anything, I remember feeling deep in my soul the sense of alienation, isolation, and separation from everyone that I loved. It was mindless, selfish, uncaring, blind pursuit of ephemeral pleasure. More than anything, I remember having had certain knowledge that I was sinning. Still, however, I persisted, insanely following a course of action that I knew to be disastrous.

Thank God for His grace and love. I look around this library, this garden, this place along the lagoon, and I pinch myself over and over again. How is it possible to have been so lost and still to be blessed with this? It is confounding, to say the least.

John 21:17. This is a short, simple, and very powerful passage. The shame that Peter must have felt is painful to imagine. Denial and betrayal are among the sins that I know.

God answered my prayer with tears. I wept as I reflected on the thoughtless, selfish, and uncaring state into which I descended during those dark moments of 2006 and 2007. We have guests coming to dinner tonight. I don't know how I will be able to face our guests. Worse, I don't know how I will be able to face myself in the mirror when I dress for the dinner party.

As I prepared for this review of my prayer, I looked at a list of human feelings. The meditation this evening brought back memories of times when my behavior evoked sadness, disgust, and anger. Ultimately, I was angry at myself then for risking my whole life; risking whatever legacy of trust and respect I had built up over the years. I am angry at myself now that I risked hurting so many friends and family members.

Wednesday, November 30   (Weighing my Sins)

Maggie and I sat together in the pavilion at the end of the rill. The warm sun felt good on our backs on this rather cold morning. The presence of God was evident all around us, and in us. I was humbled as I offered myself to His service and prayed for the grace to feel my sin and be confounded by the blessings around me.

The reflection today was to weigh my sins, building on the remembrance of my sins yesterday. In the daily Examen, we are meant to look at various parts of the day, remembering where we were and what we did. As I reflected on the task of weighing my sins, I sought to remember them again by looking at various periods during my life. I have written autobiographical entries in this journal, going into greatest detail concerning the period 45 years ago in Germany.

This morning, I examined several periods in the long interval between my mission experience in Germany and my rapid descent into hell at the end of my business career. There were so many sins, both of commission and omission. How do I weigh them? Against what do I weigh those sins? Should I compare them to other sins in my life? Or should the comparison be against the sins I know others in the world are committing?

In the end, I conclude that my sins have been heavy, regardless of how they are weighed. I did many things that took me away from God, and failed to do many things that could have brought me closer to God. I did this with clear knowledge. While I was not a Catholic, and did not openly profess faith in God, I knew God and I knew what brought me closer to Him, and what pushed me away from Him.

I wept as I thought about those times in my life. I wanted to reach out to those I hurt, but the events are so far in the past. As I sat in the pavilion in my garden, I was deeply moved by the shame of so many blessings, in spite of my life of sin.

Luke 9:25. It was chilly outside, so I returned to the library. It seems more each day as though God is present throughout the house and garden. Simply coming down stairs is entering into His presence. I felt this very strongly last night at dinner, when we invited Monsignor Logan, Father Stephen, Sister Joan, and Deacon Dan to honor Father Gap LoBiondo at a small "agape dinner." Rolf, Jenny, Terry, and Carol were also with us. The dining room was heavy with God's presence.

Luke 9:25.is a very short passage:

> What gain, then, is it for a man to have won the whole world and to have lost or ruined his very self?

I could not help thinking about the whole idea of the Synoptic gospels, those written from a similar viewpoint. Three different passages in the gospels repeat this question in very much the same language. My earlier research into the origins of the Gospels suggested that Mark was the first written, and that Matthew and Luke used either Mark or another common source as a reference. This common source takes its name from the German word for source, "quelle," and is referred to as "Q." The language in Luke 9:25, Mark 7:34 and Matthew 16:24 is so close that it is hard not to agree with those scholars.

So I break away from the intellectual questions and focus on the essence of Christ's question. What good is it for me to have all the success in the world, all the money I could ever want, all of the "things" money can buy, a wonderful house and a beautiful garden – to have all of this, if I then throw it away in choosing a life of sin? In answer, frequent occasions come very vividly to mind when I danced to the music of that risk; when I casually, thoughtlessly, and wantonly put everything at risk for nothing more than a fleeting moment of pleasure. We are not talking about a life of sin. We are talking about a tiny, insignificant moment when a tiny, insignificant decision puts a life of good works, an abundance of blessings, and some irreplaceable relationships at risk. God has answered my prayer. I can feel the shame of my sins. I offer myself to Him and to His will. I seek the grace of sorrow and His permission to weep in shame.

These days are long. When I am not in prayer, I am lost in thought about the themes of my sin and the sins of the world. I have survived this life of sin, but only at the cost of a huge debt to all those I have injured, ignored, or neglected in the process of surviving. God blessed me, and continues to bless me, in spite of my sins. I pray more than anything for clarity. I seek guidance in what He wants me to do and how He wants me to do it.

Thursday, December 1   (Black holes and Volcanoes)

Again this morning, Maggie and I enter into God's presence in the pavilion. How glorious is this presence? God is here in the clear blue sky, the brilliant green of the living plants, the very quality of the air, and the crispness of the chill of morning. As I offer myself to Him, I also thank Him for that presence. I thank Him for allowing me to enter it.

Again, I ask for the grace to feel the sharp edges of my sin. I want to feel the pain of those I have hurt. I want to feel shame for all that I have received in spite of my sin.

Frankly, this corner of paradise is not the perfect place to meditate on the black holes in my life. I can certainly bring to mind those moments when I have put all these blessings at greatest risk. I shudder with these thoughts. They are cold, solitary, and deeply depressing.

As I contemplate the volcanoes, however, I see that my traditional remedy for depression, which was isolation, is precisely the wrong choice. Community, fellowship, the love and support of Sallie Ann, and even the shadow-like devotion of Maggie pull me away from sin and toward God. Like beacons, they show the way. Like magnets, they exert a force for good.

In my colloquy with God, I express my gratitude to Him for the people in my life. I read a line from Meister Eckhart this morning:

If the only prayer you said in your whole life was, "thank you," that would suffice.

I talk about St. Anne's parish in Houston and Father John and the RCIA team and Sister Kim. I talk about OLSS, CRHP, Sister Joan, and my fellow lectors. I talk about Woodstock and Father Gap. I talk about Buddy Tudor. Suddenly I look around and see such a large and wonderful community that I joke with God about fishes and loaves.

It is a good morning to be alive, even though I am not at all well.

Meditation on Hell. I interrupted my prayers to see a doctor. I was not well enough to attend my board meeting in Washington.

God's presence is so welcoming. I like to think I never leave it, but it is with special intention that I enter His presence for the specific purpose of these exercises. As I offer myself to Him, I compose myself in a space where I can meditate again on Hell.

Tetlow describes four characteristics of Hell:

> *Selfishness and self-orientation, isolation and loneliness, frustration, and absurdity.*

It is quite easy to slip into self in times of physical distress. Even though I am only suffering from a winter cold, I wallow in as much self-pity as I can muster. I invite everyone I see to recognize my plight. Of course, this leaves me more alone, which gives me yet greater reason to feel sorry for myself.

In Matthew 11:23, Christ seems to suggest that Capernaum was just as sinful as Sodom. Only due to the numerous miracles performed by Christ along the shores of Galilee does Capernaum continue to exist. This resonates in my mind. I have sinned in so many ways and on so many occasions. I am only alive and in the place that I am because of God. He has wrought miracles in my life. He continues to do so every day.

3. Faced with my sin and sinfulness I call on the Holy Ones

I ask God for a deepening and more intense sorrow for my sins. I ask to weep over them.

Friday, December 2   (Triple Colloquy)

Before beginning to pray this morning, I walked outside in the garden. It was still dark at first, and then the southeastern sky began to lighten with golden rose hues behind the dark grey clouds. God's presence was thick throughout the garden. I talked to Him about all that has happened this week, noting especially the fellowship with Gap and the dinner party on Tuesday evening. I thanked Him for my relationship with each individual and for the glorious blessing of this community of disciples.

Sitting on the bench at the north end of the garden, behind the dock, I tried to remember the steps of the Examen. Expressing gratitude for all His blessings, both for me and for the world, was easy in the beautiful, chilly morning as I listened to the waves and the wind. I asked for enlightenment regarding my sins. I thought about my thoughts, words, and deeds this week, both those done and those undone. There is still so much in my life that takes me away from Him, and I ask His help to avoid it. I ask that He guide me and give me strength to do those things that take me closer to Him. I prayed for His help throughout this day, and tomorrow, especially as I lead the CRHP formation. I prayed the Our Father.

Back in the library, I had to smile when I thought about entering into God's presence. That presence had been all around me, and inside me, all morning.

After meditating on all manner of sin (of the Angels, Adam and Eve, and my own), I proceeded to the Triple Colloquy. It was the first time I had ever really talked to Mary. Unlike Sallie Ann (and, I assume, most other cradle Catholics), adoration of Mary has not been a significant part of my Catholic experience. I prayed the Hail Mary for the first time when praying the rosary (also for the first time) at the CRHP candlelight session in May. I remember feeling very clumsy and ignorant.

It was easier this morning. I imagined myself sitting with Mary, talking to her as I would talk to the mother of a good friend. I asked for her help. I asked her to talk to Christ, her son, asking on my behalf that He grant me greater knowledge of my sins, deeper revulsion from my own sinful life and disgust with the sins of the world.

The transition from my conversation with Mary to a similar conversation with Christ Himself seemed natural. It was as though Jesus simply entered the space and joined the discussion. I told Him that I felt truly miserable about my sins. I told Him that I had felt depressed and unhappy for the past few weeks as the daily contemplation of my sins seemed to be having a cumulative effect.

Saturday, December 3   (Meditate on my own death)

I composed myself in the hospital, where I was dying. The imagined scene came easy to me. It was a scene I experienced in real life several times during the past five years.

I first reflected on my memory of what I actually experienced during the moments when I was near death (or thought that I was near death). The strongest recollection from the early hospital visits – during the first half of 2007 – was that I did not particularly care whether I lived or died. In fact, there was probably even a bias in favor of death. I even remember thinking, while in the hospital bed, that there were all manner of incomplete, even embarrassing things in my life, but that I did not care.

As I think about it now, I must have been somewhat numb to even the idea of sin, or of sin's consequences. The company I had created was no longer mine. The promises I had made to my employees and to the government officials in the countries where we worked had long since been broken.[60] I entered the hospital bitter, depressed, and drowning in self-pity. So death was simply a way out; an end to the misery. God was not yet at the front of my conscious existence. I was too self-centered to even feel guilt.

These memories are accurate with respect to the hospital stays in January, June, and July of 2007. Something very different began to emerge in September, and it had become dominant by the middle of October. When I went into the hospital in September, I remember a much higher level of pain than I had felt at any earlier time, even during the major heart attack in June. As I literally writhed in pain during the September attack, I vividly remember wanting to spend more time with Sallie Ann, and wanting God to forgive me for all that I had done. I can list now some of the things I wanted to complete before dying.

I left the hospital the next day with what turned out to be a very inaccurate diagnosis of good health. After two more weeks of moderate chest pain, all of which the doctors and I thought to be indigestion, the serious pain returned, along with several other indications of a major heart attack.

I was awakened some hours later. I had to sign a consent form. The surgeon asked me about calling Sallie Ann before commencing the bypass. I clearly wanted life. I wanted the chance to undo as much as possible some of what I had done during the most selfish periods of my life. I had a very clear idea about renewing my quest to make a difference in the world. I was not yet thinking in spiritual terms.

It was the next day when I scribbled a note to Sallie Ann in the recovery room. She reminded me again just the other night that I had written three words on a scrap of paper. "I am sorry." Even thinking about it now brings me to tears.

There was a lot of fog during the next several days. I emerged from that drug-induced fog determined to resolve the massive spiritual dilemma that had trapped me for the forty years since my excommunication in Germany. I asked Sallie Ann to pray with me several times. I talked to her a lot about being so close to death and wanting so much to live.

So, getting back to the library in real time, I found it easy to think about my own death. The difficulty came in distinguishing between a new fantasy and the old

---

[60] Each time that I sought permission from a government of a developing country to invest in their electric power industry, I took great pains to stress that Globeleq was a very long-term investor. I promised them that we would not "flip" any assets we built or acquired. I said we were there to be a permanent part of the solution to their energy problems. The sale of the Globeleq assets in 2007, after less than five years of ownership, directly violated my solemn promise.

memories. The difference, of course, is that I obviously did not die in 2007. Rather, I lived to renew my relationship with God, go through RCIA, become a Catholic, and begin a fruitful and increasingly fulfilling spiritual journey.

Meditating on the fantasy of my death, I could certainly appreciate the continued existence of sin in my life. Largely as a result of the exercises during the past several weeks, I felt shame as I contemplated my sins. I was anguished to consider the inequity of my rich blessings in spite of that sin.

Happily, however, I did not feel the same self-pity that seemed to dominate my whole being five years ago. In spite of my sins, I did not want to die. As the Anima Christi says, "I choose to breathe the breath of Christ..." While I can list several people I want to talk to, and things I wish I had said (and not said), I can think of no embarrassing discoveries that would be found after I am gone.

There is so much that I want to do before I die. In fact, there is much that I am excited about doing. However, I feel like I would be leaving behind a fairly decent legacy, in my professional life, my personal life, and my religious life. There may not be a huge crowd at my funeral, but those who did show up would generally be happy to have known me.

I ended with the Triple Colloquy. After talking with Mary, Christ, and the Father so many times earlier today, I thought the conversations were comfortable. I shared with them my pride in the progress I have made over the past five years. I prayed for forgiveness for all that I have left undone.

Maggie and I walked out in the garden, eventually reaching the meditation bench. I reflected on the whole concept of the Holy Spirit and the almost tangible presence of God. Often during the past three months, I have noted in this journal that I felt the presence of God enter into a space, whether that space was the library, the bench, or the beach. I sometimes remark at CRHP meetings that the Holy Spirit seemed to enter the room after someone shared, or while we were praying.

What occurred to me this afternoon was that I had it just backwards. God is always present. He does not enter our space. He is already there. We become aware of His presences. He is present always, in all places and spaces on earth, and in our very beings.

One of the primary tasks of my spiritual journey is to humble myself enough to enter God's presence. So instead of saying that I feel God enter a place, I should actually say that I have opened myself to feel the presence of God. That openness involves forgetting or humbling myself enough to acknowledge the existence of the other. My prayer is not that He visit me. Rather, I pray that I can quiet myself enough to hear God's whisper, to feel God's touch, and to sense God's love.

Once again, I composed myself in an upper-room, surrounded by new Christians, all innocent and curious and excited. Paul and Timothy were in the room, working on a letter. As he had on other occasions, Paul turned to our small group and asked our comments on his turn of phrase. I felt incredibly happy. In that moment, I forgot about black holes and experienced only a small volcanic moment of joy.

Sunday, December 4 *(Luke 16:19-31)*

Before praying this afternoon, I reflected on this wonderful Sunday. The RCIA candidates and catechumens were presented today at Mass. I relived my own experience, bursting with joy and pride. Sallie Ann and I squeezed each other's hand, and both said how much Father John meant to us and to my faith.

One last time for this week, I prepared the bench in the garden for prayer. God's presence was palpable. I offered myself to Him. The place I composed for my meditation was a small gathering of disciples listening to Jesus on the bank of a river. We listened to Him tell the story about the rich man and Lazarus.

As is so often the case, the message seemed directly applicable to me. My blessings are so great, and they have come to me in spite of a multitude of sins. Is the only end for me eternal life in Hades? Is every moment of joy and comfort here simply a down payment on punishment after death?

Once again, I chose to focus on the chasm that the rich man allowed to develop between himself and Lazarus. His wealth alone was not the problem. Rather, it was the fact that he did not care about or give to those less fortunate.

I had conversations again with Mary, Jesus, and God. I told them how happy I felt at Mass, and how much I respected the RCIA program. I asked each of them to guide me in giving back the rich blessings that surround me. I shared with them my shame for sinning. I talked about Their presence and the humility I needed to experience that presence. I ended with a Hail Mary, the Jesus Prayer, and an Our Father.

4. I consider my sinfulness before God

I ask God to reveal to me the mystery of sin in myself, more and more fully, and to give to me the gift of repentance and of weeping for my sins

Monday, December 5 *(Triple Colloquy)*

My prayer period this morning was brief, and not consoling. Chest pains continued all of Sunday, leading Sallie Ann to a high degree of stress and both of us to the now all too familiar state of cardiac depression. Shortly after a brief effort to think through the past three weeks, we left the house for the hospital for a long day of tests. As usual, the pain seemed to be the result of micro-vascular angina.

Tuesday, December 6   *(Triple Colloquy)*

God's presence was heavy throughout the house and library today. By heavy, I mean that it was both palpable and depressing. Again today, I thought about the past three weeks. My sins feel heavy. My life feels sinful. I am desolate.

Wednesday, December 7   *(My Own Death)*

The heaviness grows worse. I prayed about my own sins again, ending with reflection on my own death. For the first time in many months, I welcomed the idea.

Thursday, December 8   *(Triple Colloquy)*

The desolation began to lift this morning.[61] I played tennis with my group. Because of my teaching schedule, today was the first weekday morning since August 15 that I have played with my group. The laughter and the physical exercise acted on my spirits, even though the game began in 40 degree semi-darkness.

Back in the library, my assignment was a summary review of all that I have prayed about over the past several weeks. Much of my journal reflects the consoling influence of prayer, with some entries going off in odd intellectual directions and other entries celebrating the wonderful presence of the Holy Spirit. My sins were clearly in evidence, as was the irony of my blessings. However, the Triple Colloquy did not sink me into depression as it has since Sunday. Maggie and I will walk on the beach later today. I will read tonight at Mass celebrating the Immaculate Conception. I am ready for some consolation.

Friday, December 9   *(The Last Judgment)*

Praying through the various scriptures on the Last Judgment was not easy. After several passes, I came back to a few key words from each passage, and then engaged in conversation with Jesus about these concepts.

---

[61] In her 1999 book <u>Inner Compass</u> , Margaret Silf provides a nice bullet point summary of the Ignatian concepts of desolation and consolation.): "Desolation: (1) Turns us in on ourselves, (2) Drives us down the spiral ever deeper into our own negative feelings, (3) Cuts us off from community, (4) Makes us want to give up on the things that used to be important to us, (5) Takes over our whole consciousness and crowds out our distant vision, (6) Covers up all our landmarks, and (7) Drains us of energy Consolation: (1) Directs our focus outside and beyond ourselves, (2) Lifts our hearts so that we can see the joys and sorrows of other people, (3) Bonds us more closely to our human community, (4) Generates new inspiration and ideas, (5) Restores balance and refreshes our inner vision, (6) Shows us where God is active in our lives and where he is leading us, and (7) Releases new energy in us."

From Matthew, I especially like what was said to the people sitting on the right hand of Christ:

> *For I was hungry and you gave me something to eat, I was thirsty and you gave me something to drink, I was a stranger and you invited me in, I needed clothes and you clothed me, I was sick and you looked after me, I was in prison and you came to visit me…*
>
> *Truly I tell you, whatever you did for one of the least of these brothers and sisters of mine, you did for me.*

These words represent the core of my faith, even though I have not lived them as much as I would like.

From Daniel, I was struck by the suggestion that the wicked will continue to be wicked:

> *Many will be purified, made spotless and refined, but the wicked will continue to be wicked. None of the wicked will understand, but those who are wise will understand.*

The Book of Revelation remains a little difficult for me. John, presumably the author, uses words and phrases that speak to me, although I am never sure whether the concepts are metaphor or literal:

> *[T]he new Jerusalem, coming down out of heaven from God, prepared as a bride beautifully dressed for her husband….He will wipe every tear from their eyes. There will be no more death or mourning or crying or pain, for the old order of things has passed away…*
>
> *It is done. I am the Alpha and the Omega, the Beginning and the End. To the thirsty I will give water without cost from the spring of the water of life. Those who are victorious will inherit all this, and I will be their God and they will be my children. But the cowardly, the unbelieving, the vile, the murderers, the sexually immoral, those who practice magic arts, the idolaters and all liars— they will be consigned to the fiery lake of burning sulfur. This is the second death."*

Considering my own self in connection with these passages, I am consoled by the idea that I could be seated on the right side of Christ, provided only that I do enough good things for the people in the margins of life. Not surprisingly, the New Covenant described by Matthew offers hope.

Both Daniel and the Book of Revelation suggest a different possibility at my own judgment day. The wicked will still be wicked. Those guilty of cowardice, murder, sexual immorality, idolatry, and lying seem to clearly be among the wicked. If I am among them, I can only look forward to a second death in the "fiery lake of burning sulfur."

Saturday, December 10   *(Triple Colloquy)*

My consideration of a summary of all that I have prayed about and reflected on since the beginning of these exercises resulted in more desolation than consolation.[62] The past three weeks of focusing so much on sin, particularly my own sins, have been tough. I found it hard to compose myself in some of the spiritually wonderful places that I had found on the beach, or sitting on the bench in the garden. When I did imagine myself in an upper-room gathering of early Christians, I could no longer hear Paul speaking to me.

Overall, however, two of the concepts emphasized so much at the beginning stand out. First, God made me and all that is around me. Everything I am and all that I have are gifts from Him. Second, He is not finished. I am made anew each day. I receive new blessings and new gifts each day. He has something in mind for me.

Sunday, December 11

After coming into God's presence and offering myself to Him this morning, I composed myself in Hell, once again talking to fellow inmates. Selfishness and self-centeredness characterized all of us, so much so that I think we were all really just talking to ourselves. I described my condition in an earlier meditation as self-love. It does not seem like that at all today. Rather, it is self-loathing. I love nothing about myself. This does not mean that I love anyone else, or think about anyone else. I still act only out of selfishness and self-interest. I detest myself for being this way.

Dante Alighieri wrote the epic poem <u>The Divine Comedy</u> in the first quarter of the fourteenth century. As he passes through the gate of Hell, he sees an inscription above the portal, which ends with the famous phrase:

Abandon all hope, ye who enter here

---

[62] Vinita Hampton Wright describes consolation and desolation as "states of the soul that, if we pay attention to them, can guide our steps and aid our prayer. When in consolation, we are growing in love and grace, moving toward God and God's desires for us. When in desolation, we are moving away from God, and we experience a diminishment of peace and other marks of spiritual growth and health. It's important to understand that consolation does not always feel good, and desolation does not always feel bad. False consolation can give us feelings of pleasure and satisfaction in situations and activities that are not enhancing our spiritual growth. And sometimes when we are moving in the right direction, we can experience emotional turmoil, even deep sadness." As we learn to recognize when we are in desolation and consolation, we can respond accordingly—changing course (through prayer, community, discernment, spiritual direction) when in desolation, and staying the course when in consolation."

In my self-loathing, I stand in front of that portal.   I can honestly say that I feel hope-less.

It is reported that Vincent van Gogh, the great Dutch painter, was depressed much of the time throughout his life.   He once said that:

> It always strikes me, and it is very peculiar, that when we see the image of in-describable and unutterable desolation - of loneliness, of poverty and misery, the end of all things, or their extreme - then rises in our mind the thought of God.

As hopeful as that sounds, I remain desolate today.   It is important that I distinguish my current desolation from the depression I experienced in 2006 and 2007.   At the depth of my present hopelessness, I want to live.   This was not the case five years ago.   Thoughts of God did not rise in my mind during those dark periods. Now, how-ever, I spend most of every waking day in conscious awareness of God's presence.

Second Week

(Fourteen Weeks)

1. Praying about the Kingdom of Christ

I want to hear Jesus' call.   I want to feel how great His project is, and how tremendous His desires for it.   And I want to be right there, working for Him.

Monday, December 12   *(The Kingdom)*

Maggie and I walked on the beach for almost an hour as I worked through the fantasies suggested for today's prayer.   The thought-piece begins by restating the grace we are seeking:

> *I remember Jesus accepting God's loving gaze on Him, as He moved around His homeland.   I let my imagination move me into the little towns He was in; the synagogues, the roads He walked.   Now I am ready to ask God for what I want: Here, I want to be the kind of person who will hear when Jesus Christ the King summons me, and not be shy or hang back, but quick and persevering in following His lead.*

Tetlow asks us to first imagine a charismatic new leader for a tremendous people. That new leader has proposed a fabulous program to address a long list of problems faced by the people.   The leader asks me to join his intimate circle of followers.

As anyone who knows me can certainly imagine, the fantasy involving a secular leader was very easy for me.   Walking along the beach, I trying to repeat the words I remember from Senator Frank Church, Congressman Ralph Harding, President John Kennedy, Candidate Gene McCarthy, Senator Bobby Kennedy, or President Barack Obama.   At times, these different heroes of my past (and present) merged together into one great leader, speaking to only a handful of excited campaign workers.   I sat right in front, as full of joy and belief as anyone in the room.   While I never sat in that small room with Presidents Kennedy and Obama, I did have that extraordinary experience with the others.

Tetlow asks several questions at the end of the first part of the thought-piece:

What kind of person could reject such an invitation? What kind of person could accept it? Would I accept that invitation? Would I want to work with that kind of leader?

Well, I did accept the invitation, and it was magical. In fact, I remember wondering how anyone could ever reject an invitation from such powerful and charismatic leaders.

The second part of the thought-piece requires that I apply the questions in my fantasy to Jesus Christ. I had become so caught up in my speeches on behalf of my political heroes that I kept shifting back to them. I was talking out loud, sometimes even shouting, as we walked along. When people stopped to look at me as though I was slightly addled, I tried to pretend I was simply talking to Maggie!

Tuesday, December 13   *(The Kingdom)*

Since I spent most of yesterday focused on the secular part of the leadership fantasy, I decided this morning to omit the political leaders and spend all my time on the hill with Jesus. Shifting from the secular, political leaders to Jesus Christ worked well, due largely to the way the exercise was set up.

Maggie and I sat quietly on the bench throughout the prayer. Sitting around us in the garden, on the grass, and on the steps leading up to the pavilion were all the other disciples. Jesus walked back and forth along the path in the garden and on the bulkhead walkway. He was delivering an invitation to serve:

> *It is my will to win over the whole of humankind. No enemy can defeat me or finally interfere with my Kingdom. I will draw all to myself. I will stay with my friends and we will labor and struggle, watch and pray. No one will have to go through anything that I do not myself go through. Whoever works with me and suffers with me will also share the glory of the Kingdom with me. I assure you, I will see my project crowned with total success*

His call to us was much more compelling than the call from the politicians I chose to follow over the years. I found myself filled with gratitude and extremely happy. I wanted with all my heart to say yes to His call and to honor it with my very best effort. I ended the contemplation with the prayer suggested by Tetlow:

> *Eternal Lord of All Things! I feel Your gaze on me.*

> *I sense that Your Mother stands near, watching, and that with You are all the great beings of heaven, angels and powers and martyrs and saints. Lord Jesus, I think You have put a desire in me. If You will help me, please, I would like to make my offering: I want it to be my desire, and my choice, provided that You want it, too, to live my life as You lived Yours. I know that You lived an insignificant person in a little, despised town; I know that You rarely tasted luxury and never, privilege, and that You resolutely refused to accept power.*

I know that You suffered rejection by leaders, abandonment by friends, and failure. I know. I can hardly bear the thought of it all. But it seems a toweringly wonderful thing that You might call me to follow You and stand with You. I will labor with You to bring God's reign, if You will give me the gift to do it. Amen.

Wednesday, December 14   *(Ephesians 1:3-14)*

What a glorious morning to be alive! In my contemplation, I am back in Ephesus, the little town I have come to love, nestled in the hills on the eastern shore of the Aegean Sea. A small group of fellow Christians are gathered to hear one of our leaders read to us from a letter recently received from the Apostle Paul. There are rumors that Paul has been imprisoned in Rome, and that he is writing to us, among others, in some final way. He lived among us almost ten years ago, introducing us to Jesus Christ and forming us into a fellowship of disciples.

Now, in his letter, Paul is praising God for His gift of His Son Jesus Christ to us, and to the rest of the world. What a gift! What grace! God has given us nothing less than redemption from our sins:

> *For he chose us in Him before the creation of the world to be holy and blameless in His sight. In love he predestined us for adoption to sonship through Jesus Christ, in accordance with His pleasure and will— to the praise of His glorious grace, which he has freely given us in the One he loves.*

> *In Him we were also chosen, having been predestined according to the plan of Him who works out everything in conformity with the purpose of His will, in order that we, who were the first to put our hope in Christ, might be for the praise of His glory.*

When I converse with God about this amazing gift of grace, I am almost overpowered with a sense of gratitude. I am moved to tears more powerfully than I was last week when I was brought so low in the contemplation of my sin. For today, at least, I choose not to allow the conflict between predestination and free will to cloud my joy. Paul's message in these verses is about as optimistic and positive a communication as anyone could ever imagine.

Thursday, December 15   (Hebrews 2:5-13)

Maggie and I sat in the library this morning, revisiting the fantasies about charismatic leaders and their calls to disciples. Again, this exercise comfortably appeals to my history, and my inclination to answer challenges from leaders I respect. I smiled as I said to myself, "Well, here we go again!"

Friday, December 16   *(Matthew 4:18-25)*

In my contemplation, I have been fishing in the Sea of Galilee with Simon Peter and Andrew, two brothers. Jesus saw us fishing and called out to Peter and Andrew, telling them to follow Him. Without protest or question or hesitation, my fishing buddies simply dropped their poles and nets and followed Jesus. They were not even out of sight when I saw Jesus approach two other brothers, James and John, and make the same request. The suddenness of their departure left me alone on the shore with Zebedee, the father of the second pair of brothers.

I reflect on the times in my life when I have been asked to do something that required a quick decision about a major disruption in my living arrangements and plans. There were many times when I resisted the call, putting forward all of the perfectly logical reasons why I needed to give "reasonable thought" to the question. In most of those instances, I missed a major opportunity. There were other times when I immediately jumped on the opportunity. Right now, I can think of no time when I regretted that instant acceptance of the opportunity or challenge.

However, those were all business or career decisions. I have never been faced with a call to abandon all of the comforts in my life to follow God's direction in the service of others. I pray that I will act as decisively and with as much faith as these four apostles.

Saturday, December 17   **(1 Corinthians 15:20-28)**

My contemplation takes place in Corinth, listening to the leader of our house-church read a letter from Paul, who has written to us from Ephesus. Maggie and I walk down to the bench with some of our fellow Christians, talking about the content of Paul's letter. How is it possible that we, sinners all, will have new life in Christ? What must we do to truly belong to Christ? How can we not be counted among His enemies?

We continue this discussion over a meal sitting around the table in the pavilion. We, a handful of early first century Christians in Corinth, imagine both Paul and Jesus joining us in that *agape meal*. In our table conversation, Jesus makes it clear that He will reign over all God's creation. I am almost overcome by the power of prayer.

2. How it happened that God became human

I want to know, to love and to follow Jesus my Lord.

Monday, December 19   (Contemplating the Incarnation)

We begin this second part of week two by contemplating the Incarnation. There are three parts to the exercise. First, we remember the history. Second, we compose ourselves in the real world. Finally, we pray for such a clear knowledge of Christ and such unconditional love for Him, that we follow Him.

Christ became man at a time when things were bad on this planet for sure. My limited understanding of the history leads me to believe we have made it much worse in the two thousand years since Christ died. Perhaps that is the reason God chose that time to make Jesus human. Knowing that mankind would make such a mess of things, God may have determined that we would need the gospel of salvation to get through it all.

I compose myself in Nazareth. Mary is pregnant with Jesus, having heard and answered the call. I pray for the courage and the faith to do now what God wants me to do, knowing that it will be so little when compared to what Mary did.

Tuesday, December 20   (Contemplating the Incarnation)

In once again contemplating the Incarnation, I reflect on how important it has been throughout the centuries that Christ became man, proclaimed the new gospel, and was sacrificed for all of us[63]. While human history since the Incarnation of Christ seems like more than two thousand years to me, it is but the blink of an eye to God. So all of the speeding, fighting, playing, laughing, weeping, creating and destroying done by man over all this time has occurred in the same brief moment in God's time that He initiated and accomplished the Incarnation. In that instant, God saved all of mankind, knowing just how desperately we would need that salvation.

Wednesday, December 21   (Luke 1:26-38)

I compose myself in Nazareth, where Joseph and Mary were living prior to the birth of Jesus. There are only two hundred residents of this little town. The town itself is situated in the center of a bowl at the top of a ridge on the north side of the Jezreel valley. The town of Cana is located about nine miles to the north, and the Sea of Galilee is another seven miles further to the northeast. So the families of Joseph and Mary are substantially isolated, seldom coming into contact with the traders and wandering tribes living in the valleys to the south and north of them.

---

[63] My understanding of the role of sacrifice in our faith is growing. Many religions once believed that sacrifices were required to please the angry gods. Of course, that belief system begins with the concept of an angry or un-loving god. Early Christians believed that the death of Jesus was a sacrifice paid to Satan. In that belief, God demanded payment of this sacrifice as penance for the Original Sin, which was the sin of Adam and Eve. Sometime later, the belief changed slightly. The sacrifice of Jesus on the cross was payment to God, whose love for mankind was destroyed by the Original Sin and could only be gained by this ultimate sacrifice of His only begotten son. My faith begins with a God who loves us. The sacrifice He requires of us is the death of our own false self. Jesus taught us to love God and serve others. His death was part of incarnate life. He suffered terribly and was crucified because He was the good person that he was in the midst of many people making precisely the wrong use of their free will. His resurrection shows us the ascent that can follow descent.

Mary is only fifteen years old. This is absolutely astonishing to me. As is the custom, the two families have agreed that she and Joseph will marry, but the marriage is still some time distant and Mary is very much a virgin.

In my contemplation, I am present when the angel Gabriel appears to Mary and makes the amazing announcement. It was quite apparent that angels were not in the habit of approaching young girls with greetings from God. Mary is nervous, and a little afraid. She cannot believe what Gabriel tells her about conceiving and giving birth to a son. However, when Gabriel provides the incredible and amazing explanation that the Holy Spirit will "overshadow" her, thus making this miracle possible, Mary simply said, "I am the Lord's servant."

There can be no better example of a call from God being answered with so much simple courage and faith. We prayed about the call of Jesus to His various apostles earlier this week. Those apostles were indeed brave and faithful in their immediate decision to "drop their nets and follow." That does not even approach the call and response involved in this fifteen-year-old girl saying yes to Gabriel.

I prayed for the simple faith required to know Jesus. I prayed for the simple courage to say yes.

Thursday, December 22   *(Luke 1:26-38, again)*

I returned from tennis to find that Maggie was off having her Christmas haircut. The library was quiet. The presence of God was again palpable. We conversed easily about the passage from Luke, and moved rather quickly to this week and the celebration of the birth of Christ. I lament the fact that this week has lost so much meaning for so many people. For years, I numbered myself among the non-believers. At best, I considered the story told in the bible as allegory, communicating important moral principles through metaphor. However, J.R.R. Tolkien may be on to something when he writes:

Of course, Allegory and Story converge, meeting somewhere in Truth.

These verses from Luke, for example, provide powerful allegorical support for acceptance, commitment, humility, and faith. Even now, I am not totally convinced about angels appearing to teenagers. I do not need to completely accept the literal statement in Luke to believe that Mary learned she was to become the mother of Jesus and that she courageously accepted that challenge with great humility.

I took a break from writing in this journal to walk down to the bench, where I prayed for greater faith. What a wonderful morning! What a fabulous place to converse with God about Mary and her call from Him two thousand years ago. I feel strongly this morning that I am being called. God has graced me with extraordinary gifts, which surround me. In a sense, these gifts are simply part of His call. I answer that call each time I undertake a new task that benefits others in any way. I answer it even more when I complete those tasks!

Friday, December 23   *(John 1:1-18)*

The prologue to John's gospel is one of my favorite bible passages. I have written before in this journal about my fantasy involving the singing of the prologue in a meeting with John and a handful of other Christians in Ephesus late in the first century. I used it one night in the CRHP Team 11 formation meeting, inviting all of my CRHP brothers to join me in that upper-room to sing this opening hymn. It was magical.

The Incarnation of Jesus Christ is the core foundation of our faith. The Incarnation introduces Christ to our lives and to this earth. The Incarnation represents the "fall" of Jesus, merely by becoming human. In John's words, His death and resurrection represent:

> *The true light that gives light to everyone was coming into the world... Yet to all who did receive him, to those who believed in His name, he gave the right to become children of God...*

In his meditation this morning, Richard Rohr wrote this very pithy and quite relevant observation in reference to Isaiah 7:

> *To put it even more plainly, Yahweh says I am going to be with you whether you know it or not, ask for it or not, or enjoy it or not. God is GIVEN once, and for all, and forever, to the human species and to the whole created world! That is the meaning of Incarnation, the meaning of Emmanuel, and the first and final meaning of Christmas.*

Tomorrow is Christmas Eve. As has become our pattern, we will have a quiet family gathering that includes Sallie Ann's first husband. Everyone agrees that Christmas is one of the most stress-filled holidays of the year. That is true in our household, even without my husband-in-law!

Saturday, December 24   *(Philippians 2:6-11)*

Writing to the church in Philippi from his prison cell in Rome, Paul describes in this passage an extremely humble Jesus Christ. Jesus was not incarnated in the form of the conventional expectation of someone who was "king of the Jews." He was not rich. He was not outwardly perceived as the most powerful person in the community, much less the world. Over and over again, Christ chose to emphasize His humanity, showing, in fact, more humility in that human condition than all of the rest of us.

This passage adds something very important to my consideration of the Incarnation. Christ was so humble that he was not a King, but just a man. Moreover, he was not an ordinary man, but just a servant. He allowed death to take Him in a particularly brutal, painful, even humiliating way. This is heavy stuff.

I compose myself in the Roman prison cell with Paul. Timothy is also in the cell. Perhaps sensing that something very important is underway, the guards have given Timothy papyrus, pen and ink. Paul has announced that letters are to be written to several local churches. What strikes me this morning is how humble Paul is in this cell, even as he writes about the humility of Jesus Christ. It is as though Paul is exhorting those who read his epistle to be more like Christ, even as he, Paul, is a living example of that humility. I ask Paul about the passage in Matthew about a rich man getting into heaven, realizing only after I have put the question that the gospels have not yet been written. We talk about the idea anyway.

As happy as I am to have received so many gifts throughout my life, I realize that such great bounty imposes a heavy obligation of humility. It is clear that many others have received more, and have nonetheless managed to live humble lives of service. It is equally clear that I have not achieved either the necessary level of humility, or performed the required amount of service to others. I pray for God's help. It is Christmas Eve, my second Christmas as a Catholic. I will lector tonight at the midnight Mass. Sallie Ann will sing in the choir at the six o'clock Mass. This will be her first time singing in the praise choir, and I know she is excited about it.

Sunday, December 25   (Summary)

As I think back on this week, and review my journal entries, I am struck with what appears to be a "second wind" of consolation. I am happier than I have been in a month. I am excited about coming down to the library each morning.

Is it odd, or is it God? What an interesting coincidence that we would be focusing on the Incarnation during Christmas week.

Today I composed myself high above the earth, maybe in some kind of space vehicle or super-high-flying airplane. I could not only see the whole earth, but also all time, past and present. This strange time and space travel allowed me to see man's history of bedlam and pandemonium. Throughout all time prior to the Incarnation, mankind kept getting things wrong. War and disease and suffering - all existed beyond anything I have ever imagined. There were periods of brilliance, when great art, architecture, literature, and philosophy managed to find a foothold. Many of these brief periods of light occurred under the rule of tyrants and fools.

Even during the infinitesimal moment in time that Christ was human (33 years is a short time period, even measured in human scale), mankind was generally making a good mess of things. Christianity survived against odds that are hard to imagine. Despotic kings and corrupt popes did their utmost to destroy the message of the gospel, but could not do so.

I saw the beginning of the modern age, with incomes and living conditions improving rapidly. The wealthy lived lifestyles that would embarrass even the rich man described in the gospel as challenged with respect to salvation. However, even now, two thousand years after the birth of Christ, most of the people on the planet live in the same squalor and poverty as the poorest among us during the time of Christ. Most of those with the greatest wealth are perfect examples of rich men following camels towards needles.

As desolate as the world and its history look from my strange viewpoint, I can also see threads of man's goodness woven into the massive tapestry. Art, music, architecture, and literature are joined by science, medicine, physics, and mathematics to bring flashes of light to the otherwise dark picture. From my perspective, I can see that these sparks are gifts of God, freely given to all mankind. The only reason the flashes are so few in number is that so few men and women say yes to the gift.

The contemplation ends and I am happy again. I am left with the impression that the light cast by those few who accept God's gifts is sufficient to illuminate the whole of our planet and our history. I have sinned and I have sought reconciliation. I am aware that my blessings are many, vastly exceeding what I deserve. I am pained to see how many others, whose sins are not as many and as great as mine, suffer so much.

It is Christmas morning! We will entertain Sallie Ann's first husband again today. Maggie and I just returned from the garden bench. We are listening to Gregorian chants in front of the fire. After my long fantasy prayer this morning, I used the time in the garden to meditate. The Incarnation is overwhelmingly powerful. As John tells us in the prologue to his gospel:

> *The Word became flesh and made His dwelling among us. We have seen His glory, the glory of the one and only Son, who came from the Father, full of grace and truth.*

Today is the day we celebrate by contemplating the significance of God becoming flesh.

Raymond Brown noted in one of his most famous lectures how bizarre it is that the Catholic Church, one of the world's most successful institutions – the largest and longest in duration – is the extension of the Incarnation. He asks us to contemplate how this one man, Jesus Christ, living among us for such a short time, and teaching a gospel that is so counter-intuitive, could give birth to this institutional giant.

The logic of institutional survival demands managers to manage expediently, making decisions that preserve the institution first and regard the plight of the individual, if at all, last. Christ incarnate taught us precisely the opposite. This wonderful institution continues to exist due solely to the courageous people down through the ages who have resisted institutional logic; who have led the church and lived lives devoted to the least among us.

This may not be coming out right. Paraphrasing Thomas Merton, I am not sure that what I am doing is what God wants me to do. I am not certain that I am among the few who are lighting the world. I do know that I now want to do God's will. It is my fervent desire to accept His gifts and serve mankind. I believe that God knows what it is that I desire. I believe that the very fact that I am now trying to do the right thing must please God.

3. Jesus is born

I ask to enter into the mind of the One who chose to be born as I was born. I ask to love this little Infant so that my life will fall into His life's pattern.

Monday, December 26   *(The Birth of Jesus)*

The theme for contemplation this morning was the birth of Jesus. I composed myself in the cave down the hill from Bethlehem. Like the Holy Family, I have come to this place to pay the Roman Emperor his tax.

Caesar Augustus had ruled the Roman Empire for nearly three decades, and was to do so for another 14 years. He was the adopted son of Julius Caesar (a posthumous adoption, achieved through the written will of the first Caesar). He was born relatively humbly. He only came into his inheritance by seizing power and funds after the assassination of his adopted father. Augustus was good for the Empire, reforming the tax system, building roads, and establishing a peace, the "Pax Romana," which would last for centuries.

In my contemplation, I know all of this, and am able to converse with the handful of others waiting, like I am, for the birth of Christ. All of us in the cave, including Joseph and Mary, share the strange burden of answering to a distant overlord. When Caesar issues orders from far away Rome, the commands filter down through his military ranks to the ends of the Empire, where we must subserviently "render unto Caesar."

I obviously think about King George's tea tax and the long battle for representative taxation waged throughout history. In the course of our conversation during the long night, I hear the resentment of the others regarding this Emperor's tax. Everyone feels bitter about the oppression of the occupying army of Roman legions.

There is great excitement in the group about the rumor that a new king is about to be born. Anticipation is building that this new king will free us from the yoke of the distant Roman emperor and his puppet, the client-king Herod. How could it possibly be true that the new King of the Jews would be born so humbly in this manger in a cave?

I repeated to all who would listen what I had learned about the humble birth of Augustus. If the first Caesar could make Octavian his heir through a last will and testament opened only after his death, I argued, it should be completely possible for the one God to anoint this child of humble birth King of the Jews. Of course, none of us during that long night had any idea what we were eventually to learn about the Kingdom of Heaven.

I thought about the times in my life when I have resented authority. I reflected on the enormous blessing that we live in a place where and at a time when we can be involved in so many of the decisions that impact our lives. Our democracy is far from perfect, but it is far and away the best approach to secular government ever achieved.

Tuesday, December 27   *(Luke 2:1-7)*

I love the way the story of the birth of Christ is told In Luke 2:1-7. Phrases like "it came to pass" and "the days were accomplished" are the purest form of poetry in our language.

Deacon Dan and Peggy entertained us last night, along with Sister Joan and the Goodells, the couple providing leadership and direction for the music ministry in our parish. It was a perfect night to follow Christmas. Most of the morning, however, I reflected on the beautiful prayer Father Tetlow wrote for this week. This prayer is also a pure form of poetry:

> *Lord Jesus, right from the moment of your birth, you lived with both the little and the great.*

In this world of increasing income inequality, the exhortation of Christ that we "do unto others" and "to the least of these" is more important than ever.

> *You charmed and challenged and won them all.*

The alliteration in this verse is beautiful, but so is the thought. In the very moment when Christ charms us with His love, He challenges us with His call to service. The combination wins us to Him.

> *Lord, let me feel your charismatic warmth, that tremendous welcoming grace that made the simple love you, and their leaders seek you in the night.*

I love the idea of "charismatic warmth." There have been many charismatic people in my life, and, while I have never thought about it this way before, I have felt warm and safe in their presence. How about the idea that Christ *"made the simple love [Him] the leaders seek [Him] in the night?"* The leaders sought Christ out in the night because they were afraid to be seen doing so in the light of day. Their fear arose in direct response to the love they could see among all the people for Christ.

> *Teach me to rest easy where you select, as easy as hairy shepherd and smooth shaven savant, easy as the Lady Mary who bore you gently, your abba!*

I am asking Jesus to teach me to rest easy, which means to me that I am to rest with a clear conscience and quiet soul. The sentence continues with the suggestion that my "easy rest" equal that of the "hairy shepherd and smooth shaven savant." The reference to the shepherds and wise men gathered at the birth of Christ is obvious, but it calls forth an acceptance of each of these very different kinds of people by the other. Acceptance is a part of resting easily.

My "easy rest" should resemble that of Mary, "who bore [Him] gently." Mary's acceptance of her role as the mother of Jesus Christ is the key, not any idea that she was comfortable giving birth.

Tetlow ends this verse comparing the easy rest I am seeking from Christ to that of "[His] abba." Abba is an Aramaic word normally translated as father. Paul uses it in Galatians when referring to Christ addressing His heavenly father. However, in this prayer, I think we can consider both to be abba: Joseph, resting easily at the birth of his wife's child that night in the cave, and God, the Father, resting easily at the birth of His great gift to mankind. Finally, I pray that Jesus will:

> *Accept the homage of my heart along with the shepherds' adoring gaze and the gifts of the worshipful kings!*

Once again, the poetry is powerful. I read that the concept of homage originated in connection with the medieval relationship between a commoner and his feudal lord. So, in this phrase, I am asking Jesus to accept my heart into this special relationship of vassal and lord. It is a relationship that can only exist as a result of my acceptance of Jesus as my lord. True homage cannot be forced. I am asking that Christ consider my acceptance of Him as comparable to the "adoring gaze" of the shepherds and the gifts of the "worshipful kings." This wonderful prayer is one of the most moving poems I have ever read. It is a hymn I will sing often and with great pleasure.

Wednesday, December 28 *(Luke 2:8-20)*

I read the passage from Luke last night, and again this morning, beginning with the first verse of the chapter. Again, I am struck by the poetry of these verses. I reflect on the incredible process through which an oral tradition was passed from one generation to the next for roughly sixty years before being written down in *koine* or common Greek. Along the way, the oral tradition was augmented by several written versions of Christ's life, also used as sources by Luke. Luke, who may have been Paul's good friend, presumably had access to early versions of Mark's gospel, along with the so-called Q document, a collection of Christ's sayings written by a source (*quelle* in German, thus q) common to both Mark and Luke. Using these sources, Luke, perhaps with assistance from scribes, wrote and transcribed his gospel. Many years later, near the end of the fourth century, the *koine* Greek version of Luke was translated into vulgate Latin by St. Jerome. John Wycliffe translated this vulgate Latin translation into English at the end of the fourteenth century. The King James Version was produced in 1611, translated from original Hebrew and Greek manuscripts.

So through this arduous and lengthy process, it is amazing to me that phrases like "good news" and "great joy" are contained in the same passage as "Glory to God in the highest heaven, and on earth peace to those on whom His favor rests." Would this sound like beautiful poetry to me had I not learned what beautiful poetry sounded like by listening to phrases like this? Which came first, the chicken or the egg?

What is true is that I find myself overjoyed this morning. Maggie and I went down to the bench, wrapped tightly against a clear but briskly cold day. I repeated the verses from the reading. Then I started singing them.

Today I am sixty-seven years old. I have been blessed beyond my wildest dreams. My granddaughters, Alexis and Alison, came into the library to wish me happy birthday with hugs and big smiles. My 96-year-old aunt called to wish me well. I awakened to both Sallie Ann and Maggie kissing me with wet good wishes.

Thursday, December 29   *(Luke 2:8-20, again)*

I played tennis this morning, returning afterwards to shower and begin praying in contemplation of the passage in Luke again. The account of Christ's birth moves from the first family to the shepherds in the field, who were visited first by one angel, and then by "a great company of the heavenly host." I composed myself in a rocky field in the hills outside of the little town of Bethlehem. I imagined the shock among the rest of the shepherds when the angel first appears, along with a level of fear that did not lessen with the arrival of a whole company of angels only a few minutes later.

After we had seen the holy family in their cave, we began telling everyone we met about the angels and the newborn king. In my contemplation, it became almost immediately clear that we were creating a potential problem for the infant Christ and His parents. Some of those we told were happy, jumping at once to the conclusion that a prophecy had been fulfilled. Most, however, were both skeptical and alarmed. On one hand, they doubted our veracity. On the other hand, they considered this announcement as a clear sign of rebellion against both the Jewish establishment and the Roman occupation. I thought about the game of gossip, when a story is retold several times and comes out much different after the retelling. I imagined how alarming our reports of angels making an announcement and a new king being born would be after the third or fourth retelling. It was no wonder that the client-king Herod called for the killing of all newborn children.

I wondered how different things might have been had we not been so anxious to spread the word. As it happened, the holy family would leave Judaea, fleeing to Egypt to allow things to cool down for a while. Even after their return, the young man Jesus led what must have appeared to be a rather normal life for almost three decades. By the time His ministry began, I suppose all the fuss made at His birth would have been long forgotten by most people. Herod the Great died only a few years after the birth of Christ, replaced by his sons, Herod Antipas and Herod Archelaus. Historians suggest that the holy family returned from their Egyptian exile to Galilee instead of Judea because Archelaus, considered to be the crueler brother by far, had succeeded his father in the south. Antipas, who succeeded Herod the Great in the north, played a crucial role in the passion of Christ, refusing to judge him, but instead turning the case back to Pontius Pilate. The Jewish hierarchy was presumably more upset by the early actions of Christ in His actual ministry, than by the events surrounding His birth.

I reflect on the foolishness of "what if" games, especially in regard to the life and ministry of Jesus Christ. He did what He was meant to do, and it worked. End of game.

Friday, December 30   *(Matthew 2:1-12)*

Matthew only confirms some of the conclusions I reached yesterday, while contemplating Luke's story of the shepherds. Matthew shifts the focus from the shepherds to the wise men or magi. While they were not visited by an angel and a company of angels, they were first informed about the birth, and then led to the newborn Christ by a star. Matthew explicitly describes the reaction of Herod to the news of a new king.

I wonder how the world would react today to an announcement of the second coming of Christ. I contemplate this question by composing myself in Rome at the time of Christ's birth. Significantly, there was no mention of the birth anywhere in Rome; at least none recorded in our history books. Herod, the Roman client-king in Judaea, heard the news and was alarmed, but Judaea was not only distant from Rome, but relatively unimportant in the empire. I can imagine hundreds of thousands of places in the world today where Christ could begin His ministry, and none of us would know about it, even with 24-hour news. Christ could be born of a virgin mother in some remote village. He could teach and work miracles in the area near where He was born. Most of the rest of the world would know nothing about the momentous event.

What is most incredible about the first century following the birth, life, and death of Christ is not how isolated and limited the knowledge of the events was at the time, but rather how universal both knowledge about and faith in those events became over the next several centuries. Estimates of global population at that time are at best tentative, but reasonably reliable sources suggest roughly 50 million in Europe, another 50 million in Asia, and another 50 million in the Americas, for a total global population of around 150 million. Historians estimate there to have been 25,000 Christians at the end of the first century after the death of Christ, which amounts to roughly 16 one-thousandths of a percent of the world population! Compare that with the 2.1 billion Christians on the planet today, which is 30 percent of the 7 billion people on earth.

All of this is to say that the events surrounding the birth, life and death of Christ were known to an infinitesimal percentage of the world's population at that time. As much as it has mattered to almost everyone on earth over the millennia since then, it would not have registered on even the most sensitive scale when it actually occurred.

Saturday, December 31   (Matthew 2:1-12, again)

It is a beautiful morning. Maggie and I began in the library, and then moved down to the garden bench. I composed myself again in Bethlehem. The area around the manger in the cave was crowded with those who have been told that something hugely important is happening. The infant Jesus was by now several days old, yet people continued to arrive each day. Most impressive were the Magi who had arrived after traveling from somewhere far to the east, possibly Persia or even further east. I think about modern Iran and Afghanistan, and the unlikely journey of wise men or kings from these distant lands to witness a newborn foretold by long-dead prophets.

Perhaps Matthew's account of these wise men from the east should be read as an allegory. I quoted Tolkien a couple of weeks ago. This additional comment on the importance of allegory, particularly in this case, speaks to me:

> So the only perfectly consistent allegory is a real life; and the only intelligible story is an allegory…. the better and more consistent an allegory is the more easily it can be read 'just as a story'.

The idea is that the Incarnation was foretold and that it was extremely important. Clearly, anyone believing what was prophesied in the Old Testament would have been anxiously following rumors of fulfillment. There may have been some kind of obligation for some of these visitors from the east to come to Judaea to pay taxes to the Romans. Could they have been descendants of David?

Certainly, any special attention paid to the birth of this child would have increased the level of suspicion in the mind of Herod. No ordinary birth could attract wise or royal visitors, even if they had come as part of the requirement for increased Roman revenue.

2012

Sunday, January 1   (Summary)

This wonderful week began on Christmas day, when Sister Joan gave me my assignment. My prayers all week have been reflections on the events surrounding the birth of Christ. I have walked in the fields with the shepherds and talked during the week with wise men from Persia. I listened this morning to the music of Taize,[64] an

---

[64] According to Wikipedia, "The Taizé Community is an ecumenical monastic order in Taizé, Saône-et-Loire, Burgundy, France. It is composed of about one hundred brothers, from Protestant and Catholic

ecumenical community in France whose singing I admired while at dinner with Deacon Dan. I prayed for the peace and humility required for me to fully grasp the meaning of the birth, life, and death of Jesus.

Sallie Ann sent me a quotation from C. S. Lewis, which seemed particularly apt as I reviewed the week:

> *At the end of things, the Blessed will say, 'We have never lived anywhere except in Heaven.' And the lost will say, 'We were always in Hell.' And both will speak truly.*

I have been blessed. Not only do I awake each day in paradise, I am increasingly able to recognize and celebrate it. I became a Catholic almost two years ago (yes, Easter Vigil is fast approaching!), but I am becoming more Christian each day. In another week, I will mark the end of the fourth month that I have been engaged each day in these spiritual exercises. It seems as though I have always begun each day this way. It seems like I began to do so only yesterday.

The baby in the manger was, in fact, a baby in a manger. He was a child like any other child, probably crying and burping and doing all the other things infants do. The miracle of the Incarnation is that Jesus Christ our Lord became human. Richard Rohr's meditation this morning was spot on, as it is so many mornings:

> *The human journey is not about becoming spiritual beings nearly as much as becoming fully human beings, which is actually much harder. We are already spiritual beings from the moment of our conception; we just don't know it yet. The Bible tries to let you in on the secret, by revealing God in the ordinary. ...We have created a terrible kind of dualism between the spiritual and the so-called non-spiritual. The principle of Incarnation proclaims that matter and spirit, sacred and secular have never been separate. Jesus came to tell us that these two seemingly different worlds are and always have been one. We just couldn't see it until God put them together in one body that we call Jesus.*

On this first day of 2012, I return again to that cave in the rocky hills of Judaea outside Bethlehem. I stand silently. I listen to the shepherds describing their encounter with angels. I watch the wise men from Persia dismount from camels, weary from a long journey. I am in awe as I see such commotion surrounding this incredibly tiny, very ordinary, and quite normal baby.

I back away from the cave and see the span of two thousand years of human history. I see the whole earth. That normal little child has changed the lives of billions of human beings, more than two billion of whom are still alive on the planet. The quiet

---

traditions, who originate from about thirty countries across the world. The monastic order has a strong devotion to peace and justice through prayer and meditation. It was founded in 1940 by Brother Roger Schutz, a Protestant."

birth in an isolated cave outside a small town in an unimportant part of the then-known world has now reached out to every corner of the earth. Great thinkers, powerful leaders, terrible scoundrels, the richest and the poorest of men and women, healers and the sick – all of these and more have played roles in the development of the religions that were spawned by that simple birth. It is simply too much to contemplate.

4. Jesus comes into our exile

I want to know, to love, and to follow Jesus Christ.

Monday, January 2   *(Luke 2:22-28)*

The scriptural passage today is inspiring. It is inspirational to contemplate the infant Jesus being circumcised in the cave and named by His father, Joseph. I am also inspired by the presentation in the temple after the required "purification period." Jewish tradition required an infant son to be circumcised on the eighth day after birth, which presumably meant that Joseph circumcised Jesus in the cave outside Bethlehem. However, that same tradition prevented entry into the temple until 40 days after the birth for males, and a full 80 days for females. Commentators speculate that Joseph took his family back to Nazareth to pass the time of purification.

I compose myself in the cave, joining a handful of others to celebrate the *brit milah* or *bris* of the infant Christ. I am humbled and honored to play the role of *kvatter* or godfather, taking the child from Mary and handing Him to Joseph, who will play the role of *mohel,* actually performing the circumcision. Joseph leads us in the traditional prayer:

> *Praised are you, Adonai our God, King of the Universe, who has sanctified us with Your commandments and commanded us in the ritual of circumcision. Blessed are You, Adonai our God, King of the Universe, who has sanctified us with Your commandments and commanded us to make him enter into the covenant of Abraham our father.*

Wine is poured for everyone in our small group. Joseph names the child with this prayer:

> *Creator of the universe: May it be your will to regard and accept this circumcision, as if I had brought this baby before Your glorious throne. And in Your abundant mercy, through your holy angels, give a pure and holy heart to Jesus, the son of Mary and Joseph, who was just now circumcised in honor of your great Name. May his heart be wide open to comprehend Your holy Law, that he may learn and teach, keep and fulfill Your laws.*

We sit together for a celebratory meal, consisting of the simple food available to us in this humble cave in a land far from home. I am moved to tears, both in my fantasy in the cave two thousand years ago, and here in the library on the second day of 2012. How more incarnate can it be than to be circumcised?

Tuesday, January 3 *(Luke 2:22-28, again)*

Today I am to pray again about Luke's account of the circumcision of Christ and His presentation in the temple.

Before coming downstairs this morning to pray, I read from the Catena Aurea, reading all of the commentary recorded by Aquinas for these verses from Luke. It was a troubling experience. Some of what had initially bothered me yesterday was the idea of juxtaposing the very human and real-world experience of a *bris* with the miraculous nature of Christ's conception and birth. The early Christian commentators literally tied themselves in knots as they attempted to explain these events.

I prayed for clarity and faith.

Significantly, I attended a baptism at the parish this past Saturday. I loved the obvious pride of the parents and the love of family and close friends.

I chose to compose myself in the temple in Jerusalem. As I watched the small group entering the temple, presumably having walked all the way from Nazareth, I was struck by how proud Joseph and Mary are of this baby son. Imagine how Joseph might have felt. His betrothed just bore a son of whom he was not the biological father. It would have been entirely understandable for him to have abandoned Mary from the moment he first learned of her pregnancy. Instead, he enters the temple with his head held high, presenting his son to the priests for full recognition. Mary is simply beautiful. She has fully recovered from giving birth under difficult circumstances.

As I watched the ceremony, I was struck with how normal it seemed that the Holy Family was about to engage in the same ritual that countless other Jewish families went through in towns throughout Israel.

A child was born in Bethlehem. Like all other children born anywhere and at any time, this child was a child of God, infused with the spirit of life as beautifully and miraculously as any other. As I have come to understand and believe about the Incarnation, however, this child, while incarnate, was something more. This child was both the son of God and God Himself.

For me, believing literally that angels appeared individually and in groups or that the Holy Spirit "overcame" the fifteen-year-old Mary is not the central foundation of my faith. Unlike those early church fathers, I do not need to hypothesize various explanations for how all this happened. As Father John used to say, "Much of what is written in the Bible probably never happened, but it is all true."

Richard Rohr spoke to this earlier in the week:

A human woman is the Mother of God, and God is the Son of a human mother! Do we have any idea what this sentence is saying, what it means, or what it might imply?! Is it really true? If it is, then we are living in an entirely different universe than we imagine, or even can imagine. If the major division between Creator and creature can be overcome, then all others can be overcome too.

To paraphrase Oswald Chambers:

[T]his is a truth that dumbly struggles in us for utterance! It is too much to be true and too good to be true. So we can only resort to metaphors, images, poets, music, and artists of every stripe. Five days after Christmas, we are still struggling for utterance. What most of us do, myself included, is to stop thinking about it. Divine Incarnation is not what you think! In fact, you can't think it at all. You can only fall into it and give thanks in all directions.

What is true for me is that Jesus Christ is the son of God. He became man for the very specific and crucial purpose of delivering the good news of salvation. He loved and was loved by the people at the margins of life, and He exhorted all of us to do that as well. I love Him for that. He died for our sins. I love Him for that as well.

Wednesday, January 4 *(Matthew 2:13-18)*

As I read Matthew last night, my first thought was that the Jews must have been desperate for a new king after the repeated atrocities of the Roman client-king Herod. When Herod the Great ordered the killing of all males in and around Bethlehem under the age of two years, he was already 70 years old, and would only live another four years. He had murdered several members of his own family and many others, including several rabbis.

What a family. Herod the Great married several times, notably to the two Mariamnes and Malthace, the Samaritan. Four of his heirs play prominent villainous roles in the early history of the Church.

The first Mariamne was the mother of Herod Agrippa and Herodias, among others. We remember Herodias primarily because she was married to both Herod II (son of the second Mariamne) and Herod Antipas (son of Malthace). John the Baptist criticized Herodias' divorce of her still-living husband in order to marry his cousin. It was her daughter, Salome, who so tantalized Herod Antipas with her dancing that he agreed to give Herodias the head of John the Baptist.

This first Mariamne was also the mother of Aristabulus, father of Herod Agrippa. History's treatment of Agrippa depends entirely upon the viewpoint of the historian. Agrippa was proud of his Jewishness. He was generally admired by the Jewish historians who described his brief reign as King of the Jews from CE 41 to CE 44. Luke, however, the presumed author of Acts, reports that Agrippa was a cruel and heartless king ultimately struck down and eaten by worms.

The two sons of Malthace were Herod Antipas and Herod Archelaus. We remember Antipas due to his role in the death of John the Baptist and his decision not to deal with the trial of Christ, turning it over to Pontius Pilate instead. It was due to the murderous reign of Archelaus in Judaea that Joseph was warned not to return to Bethlehem when he returned from Egypt. He took Mary and Jesus to Nazareth to live in the client-kingdom of Antipas.

I composed myself in Jerusalem, outside the temple where Jesus has just been formally presented. Note that there seems to be a bit of confusion regarding place and time. Matthew tells us that Joseph was warned to flee Israel for Egypt directly after the wise men visited the Holy Family in Bethlehem. However, Luke makes it clear that Jesus was presented at the temple in Jerusalem after the period of purification, which would have been a minimum of 40 days (if Mary remained outside the temple), and would have been at least 80 days if Mary entered the temple. The encounter with Simeon and Anna reported by Luke certainly suggests Mary was with the family inside the temple. Egypt does not figure at all in the account of Luke. Instead of exile in Egypt, Luke has the Holy Family returning directly to Nazareth.

I resolve this discrepancy in my contemplation by inserting Matthew's period of exile in Egypt into a four-year period between the presentation at the temple and the return to Nazareth. In my version, there is a tiny amount of dark logic to Herod's instruction that all infant sons under the age of two years be killed. Herod must have heard that there had been a presentation at the temple, which would mean the child was at least two or three months old. As I said, it is only a tiny amount of logic, and it is very dark.

The bottom line is that the Jewish client-kings of Herod's family were the archetype of despotic subcontractors. Throughout history, the "trustees" in prisons and "kapos" among slave populations were often more brutal than the leaders who appointed them. Compared to Herod and his sons, the emperors back in Rome were benevolent leaders. In fact, however, many of those who followed Augustus, particularly Nero, Caligula and Claudius, were some of the worst leaders in all of history.

So we are off to Egypt, fleeing Israel with virtually nothing but the clothes on our backs. Since the purpose of our departure was to escape the evil Herod, it was crucial that no one know where we were going or what we would be doing when we arrived. Egypt had been a Roman colony since 30 BC, when Octavian, the future Caesar Augustus, defeated one of his rivals, Mark Antony, and deposed Cleopatra. Roman rule of Egypt was reasonably benign throughout the period. In 70 CE, many years after the Holy Family was in exile in the country, Alexandria became the most important Jewish center in the world, as most of the leadership fled Jerusalem following its destruction by the soldiers of the Roman Emperor Claudius.

As a carpenter, Joseph would have found work with relative ease. In my contemplation, he learned important skills, which he would introduce back in Nazareth when it was safe to return to his native land. I see Joseph as a good father, but not some kind of "stay at home dad." Mary was the primary care-giver in the family.

Jesus was just an ordinary toddler, learning to walk and talk, just like any other human being. I am a little tempted to envision the boy Christ as someone very special, showing wisdom and skill far greater than others around Him. That is simply not the Gospel. God incarnate was human like us, probably struggling with the normal difficulties associated with growing up. The important message in this is that each of us can be as good and decent and Christian as Christ Himself.

Thursday, January 5   (Matthew 2:13-18, again)

I thought a great deal about the impact of this sudden move on Joseph and Mary. Consider the situation:

- There was no notice of the flight into exile.
- The reason to flee Judaea was the danger involved in remaining under the jurisdiction of the Roman client-king Herod.
- They presumably had few, if any, of their belongings with them.
- Whatever they were able to take from Bethlehem would not be sufficient for a stay abroad for years.
- They were presumably not allowed to tell their family and friends where they were going and why.
- Mary had only recently given birth.

If Sallie Ann and I were to receive such an instruction, I have to honestly say that we would be challenged. Of course, we would never leave Maggie!

Once again, I composed myself in the place of a fellow traveler with the Holy Family. We traveled at night in order to avoid detection by Herod's spies. We slept during the day in caves, where we were hidden from view. Joseph begged for food in the towns near our route, correctly assuming that no one would be looking for a man alone.

Egypt was a safer place than Judaea, but not a safe place. Walking across the Sinai Peninsula was dangerous, even without Herod's search for the newborn king. Once inside Egypt, we hugged the coast, joining other travelers to avoid being identified as a three-person family. Our goal was Alexandria, a town friendly to Jews. It was also a city undergoing rapid growth, which meant excellent work opportunities for Joseph.

As has been the case in some of my earlier contemplations, I had the advantage of some personal experience with the area. One of our largest power plants was located in Sidi Krir, a coastal village outside of Alexandria. I walked along that coast for exercise one morning in 2005. So the path followed by the Holy Family in my contemplation was familiar to me. I advised Joseph to make this area to the west of Alexandria his home base. He and I walked together each morning into town, to work on the construction of new projects for the growing population, one of which was the great library. Just as I would fantasize during my college days, I was confident that we were learning from all those books from mere proximity. Actual reading was not required.

Joseph and I talked about going home, and wondered when that would be possible. We also questioned where "home" would be. Our ancestral home was, of course, Judaea, where we were registered and had paid our taxes. However, the arid, rugged terrain of Judaea compared quite poorly to the hills above and shores along the coast of Galilee. Joseph became a comfortable companion. His humility was inspiring.

Friday, January 6   *(Matthew 2:19-23)*

As Matthew 2, verses 19-23 report, our exile came to an end with the death of Herod the Great, a little more than four years after we had left the land of the Jews in such haste. I walked on the beach this morning with Maggie, composing myself back on the shore of the Sea of Galilee. Joseph was walking with me. We were both extremely pleased to be back in the north, above Jerusalem and among our friends from what seemed like such a long time ago.

We talked as we walked about the amazing events that had transpired. Mary and her cousin Elizabeth had both been visited by angels. Both had given birth to sons. Mary had humbly and completely accepted the honor and the challenge of giving birth to the Son of God. Joseph commented how normal his young son was, particularly when viewed in the context of all the momentous signs and celebrations that surrounded His birth.

Walking on the beach with Maggie is a magical experience. I cannot imagine a more beautiful place to converse with God. The union of so much physical beauty and peace with the contemplative, spiritual place I am reaching in my fantasies is simply amazing.

Saturday, January 7   (Matthew 2:19-23, again)

Maggie and I sat on the bench this morning after a foggy, drizzly, and cold game of tennis. It was a bad choice. Actually, both playing tennis in the wet cold and then sitting on the bench shivering with Maggie were bad choices. The garden, however, was a perfect place to contemplate again the return of the Holy Family from Egypt. I imagined a conversation with the young boy Jesus. His intelligence was obvious from the moment He could form sentences out of sounds. He asked questions, but did so in a way that respected me, while at the same time demonstrating how shallow my initial answers were. In my fantasy, I envied the incredible depth of His young, humble mind. It was with considerable regret that I left the fantasy and the bench to come in out of the chill.

Sunday, January 8 (Summary)

I awakened this morning singing a wonderful song over and over again. Sallie Ann sang it with the choir last night at Mass.

Mary did you know that your baby boy would someday walk on water?
Mary did you know that your baby boy would save our sons and daughters?
Did you know that your baby boy has come to make you new?
This Child that you delivered will soon deliver you.

Rob and the twins joined me in the pew to listen and celebrate the Epiphany. We had dinner afterwards at an Italian restaurant, where we all joined with Sallie Ann in singing this song. It was a great way to cap off a very good week.

Maggie and I walked on the beach again this morning. The day may have been the most beautiful of all the truly beautiful days I have experienced living here in Ponte Vedra Beach. We continued to sing "Mary did you know" as we walked. Once on the beach, we were transported at once to Galilee. There we found our friends - Joseph, Mary, and the energetic young boy, Jesus. He played with Maggie, throwing sticks and teaching her to fetch. Since I have been totally incapable of conveying the concept of fetching things to Maggie, I was hugely impressed!

Conversing with God, I remarked on this very human quality of Jesus and His parents. We had developed a bit of a relationship over the past three weeks. While I was still very much in awe of who they were and what they had done and, even more, what I knew they would do, I addressed them by their first names. They called me Bob or, in Jesus' case, Popeye. God spoke to me in the gentle waves of low tide and the calls of all the birds. I heard those sounds, and with them, the powerful urging of God to learn from my new friendships. He asked me to consider their complete acceptance of His commands. He asked me to reflect on their humility in the face of angels, wise men, and proclamations of kingship. He asked me to embrace their courage in the face of danger and adversity. He asked me to consider their gratitude for the kindness showed them by all the simple people along the way and in the background in Judaea and Egypt.

Through it all, He asked me to get my life right by loving my family, accepting the challenges of my new faith, and showing true gratitude for all that I have been given. I asked what He wanted me to do next. He whispered "be patient, stay on this path, and walk on."

5. Jesus waits to serve the God of Israel

Jesus of Nazareth lived out of a very deep and definite mind-set. He loved in wonderful ways. I want to know all that, and to stand under His Standard, and live out of His value system.

Monday, January 9   *(Luke 2:39-40, 51-52)*

The passage for today from Luke is an account of certain events in the life of the boy Jesus. I read it through this morning in the library. I left the room, and my exercises, for a few minutes. When I returned, I decided to pray and contemplate in the garden. Maggie, of course, was with me. We walked along the rill, then down the steps, along the lagoon, back up the steps, and back along the rill to the fireplace. While walking, I composed myself in the company of the twelve-year-old Jesus, walking from Nazareth to Jerusalem.

My research into the history and geography of Israel had produced a few facts. The distance between Nazareth and Jerusalem is about 100 miles. Assuming that we walk at a pace equal to about three miles an hour, it would take more than a day and a half to walk that distance.

So, in my contemplation, Jesus, His parents, and many others from Nazareth traveled together to the Passover Festival. We allowed two weeks for this annual event. The festival itself normally lasted for seven days, sometimes even ten. We allowed three days for the journey, both to and from Jerusalem. We walked close to twelve hours each day and slept two nights in travelers' camps along the way. It was while walking next to Jesus on the way down to Jerusalem that I was able to see how intelligent and articulate He had become. We talked a little about the political situation. Jesus and His family had returned to Nazareth from Egypt some eight years earlier, when Herod the Great died. Herod's kingdom had been divided into two parts, the northern one of which, including Nazareth, was now under the rule of Herod Antipas.

Jesus was familiar with all of this political history. He knew that it was Herod the Great whose threats against the Holy Family caused their flight into Egypt. He knew that His father Joseph had hoped to return from Egypt to Judaea, but was warned to go instead to Galilee in order to avoid the rule of Herod Archelaus. Jesus described the reign of Antipas at the time of our journey to Jerusalem for Passover as reasonably benign. I loved it that Jesus knew I liked politics and wanted to learn as much as possible.

So intrigued was I by this well-informed young man that I stayed with Him when His parents and the rest of the Nazarenes left for the journey back to the north. It was the custom then for the brightest students to enter into Socratic discussion with the scholars and teachers. Only the very best of the young boys ever had the opportunity to engage the teachers connected with the temple in Jerusalem. Jesus, the young Nazarene, created quite a stir with His display of learning, so much so that we simply lost track of all time.   I was in awe.

Tuesday, January 10   (Luke 2:39-40, 51-52, again)

I repeated the reading of Luke this morning.   I chose to compose myself in the company of Joseph and Mary as they walked north out of Jerusalem following the Passover Festival.   There were many Nazarenes in our group, all of us happy to be going home after so much joy and excitement in the capital city.   We walked all day before stopping to organize our sleeping arrangements for the night.   It was only then that we realized Jesus was not among us.

Joseph and Mary were both panicked.   Life as parents had begun in a state of near emergency, complete with a hasty flight into Egypt to live in exile for more than four years.   The danger was still very much in evidence even after the death of Herod the Great.   They had made Galilee home instead of Judaea when the warning came that Herod Archelaus had succeeded his father.   Yet here we were, just leaving Jerusalem, the capital of Judaea, after a week-long festival.   Mary was particularly concerned that someone had told the authorities that Jesus was back in town, and that He was the very person whose birth had caused the deaths of so many young male children more than a decade earlier.

Joseph insisted that we sleep for a few hours before returning to Jerusalem in search of Jesus.   We made good time covering the thirty miles back into the city, heading straight to the temple to inquire as to any reports of the lost young man.   It was with angry relief that Joseph and Mary greeted their son among the teachers in the temple.   I talked to them about a couple of occasions when my own parents were similarly torn between wanting to hug me for being safe and punish me for causing them concern.

All of the conversations with the Holy Family during these two days of contemplation had the powerful feeling of reality.   The conversations were very much like conversations I have had (and thoroughly enjoyed) with my grandson, Tyler.   The emotional responses of the various participants in my fantasies were as normal and understandable as those same responses have been in situations involving me or my brothers.

I prayed for knowledge and understanding of Jesus and His family.   My prayers were answered.

Wednesday, January 11   (Luke 2:41-50)

Again today, the scriptural passage was from the second chapter of Luke.   I composed myself again in the temple in Jerusalem with Jesus and His parents.   They had just expressed angry frustration that Jesus had not informed them that He wanted to stay longer in the temple to talk with the teachers.   It was an anger softened by their joy that Jesus was safe.

I listened again and again to Jesus respond that He could not understand why His parents were searching for Him. After all, Jesus said, didn't they know that He had to be in His Father's house? When Joseph and Mary seemed not to understand, it was Jesus who seemed to be frustrated.

My feelings were somewhat complex. It seemed that right before my eyes something very natural was taking place. A child was becoming a man. As is so often the case, the wisdom and intelligence of the young child was not apparent until, suddenly, He was a man. His parents were simply incapable of getting their heads around this apparently sudden change.

Yet this time, the appearance of the man emerging from the child was complicated, to say the least, by the identity of His Father. When the child-become-man Jesus announced that He had to be in His Father's house, He was giving just a small hint of what was to come almost two decades in the future. Even though Joseph and Mary had been told who Jesus was, even before His birth, they must have come to love Him as a normal, incarnate son. I can imagine their irritation at being reminded that He was far from normal.

Thursday, January 12   (Luke 2:41-50, again)

Again today, I prayed about the young Jesus. I played tennis before coming home to contemplate and pray. My contemplation was crowded with images from the tennis court. Seagulls and pelicans were added to the scene with Jesus and His family. We were walking together along the shore of the Sea of Galilee, having returned from Jerusalem and the momentary tension resulting from the disagreement at the temple.

I read from John Meier's A Marginal Jew last night.[65] Part of the first of this four volume study is devoted to the early years of the life of Jesus. While admitting that there is precious little information about the "missing years" in the Gospels, Meier provides a good summary of what is known about the culture, education, and economic system of the Nazarene region of Palestine in the first century. Joseph was a "woodworker" in Nazareth, a community of around 2,000 people located in the fertile farming area on the western side of the Sea of Galilee. Like more than 99% of the population in the world at that time, Joseph and his family were poor, living a subsistence-level lifestyle as peasants in a remote part of the Roman Empire. Nazareth was actually an isolated community in the "client-tetrarchy" of Galilee and Perea,

---

[65] According to Wikipedia, "John Paul Meier (born 1942) is a Biblical scholar and Catholic priest. He attended St. Joseph's Seminary and College (B.A., 1964), Gregorian University Rome (S.T.L, 1968), and the Biblical Institute Rome (S.S.D., 1976). He is author of the series A Marginal Jew: Rethinking the Historical Jesus (4 v.), six other books, and more than 60 scholarly articles. Meier is professor of New Testament and holder of the William K. Warren Foundation Chair in the Department of Theology at the University of Notre Dame. Before coming to Notre Dame, he was professor of New Testament at The Catholic University of America."

which was formerly included in the client-Kingdom of Judea. The native language of the area, which Jesus would have learned from childhood, was Aramaic, though some Hebrew and some Greek were spoken. Less than one percent of the population could read and write, though the Gospels suggest that Jesus was capable of reading some of the Old Testament scriptures, which were written in either Hebrew or Greek, requiring some knowledge of both.

Jesus probably did not go to any formal school. Joseph would have taught Him the trade of woodworking. That trade would include enough reading and writing to be able to negotiate transactions, so-called "tradesmen literacy." Anything beyond that would have been taught in the synagogue by the scribes with whom Jesus would ultimately argue.

Back again in my fantasy, walking with Jesus and His father along the shore, I related to them with this somewhat greater knowledge of the context in which they lived. Jesus was once again merely a young man, intent upon learning His earthly father's trade and contributing to the family. Joseph explained the basics of carpentry as we walked along the rocky shore. Jesus was a quick study, taking in everything Joseph said. While I enjoyed listening to the two of them talk, I loved even more the freedom and joy of walking next to the sea on a sunny morning. I felt their presence as much as I imagined it.

How could it be, I wondered, that Jesus would not begin His ministry for another 20 years? Knowing in advance how important His message would be, I was anxious that it be shared. As I contemplated this question, it occurred to me that these years living a "normal" life might be part of His message. Perhaps Jesus was saying something about how the Truth could be found in the daily task of living, learning, and loving one's family and friends. I let this thought stay with me until I ended the morning with the Our Father.

Friday, January 13 *(Two Standards/Two Value Systems)*

This morning I first read and then prayed about the meditation entitled "two standards and two value systems." This meditation brought to mind the wonderful C.S. Lewis book The Screwtape Letters, which is about instructions given by Screwtape, a senior devil, to Wormwood, an under-devil. Screwtape is advising Wormwood how to tempt his British "patient" away from God and toward sin. It is an amusing approach to the two standards.

I prayed for more than understanding today. Some of the sins involved in the wrong value system are incredibly tempting, at times seeming entirely justified. Having things my way, or taking credit for my accomplishments, or feeling entitled to success – all of these are very clearly not the values we are taught by Jesus Christ. Yet I yield to these temptations all the time. So my prayers are for more than understanding. I need help in acting on the knowledge I have, and I need forgiveness.

Saturday, January 14 *(Two Standards/Two Value Systems)*

Our assignment today is to repeat the meditation on two standards and two value systems. My exercises started late in the day, which was so filled with wonder and joy that I could only talk to God about my gratitude for the first several minutes. Sallie Ann, Rob, and I took the grand twins to the White Oak Conservation Center for the day. The sun was out, though the temperature was quite cold. We were with other children and their parents, all from the elementary school the twins attend. We were there to learn about conservation of nature and wild animals, and to celebrate the joy of family. Today was a day devoted to the right standard and the right value system.

I went to Mass before writing this journal entry. Sallie Ann was singing in the choir. Rob sat next to me in the pew in front of the choir. We were filled with joy from a day outside with the girls, and we joined in singing every song as loudly (but not as well) as the members of the choir.

Sunday, January 15 **(Summary)**

The assignment on this beautiful, clear, cold morning is to repeat or review the exercises for the week. Maggie and I came downstairs early, walked down to the bench in the garden, and hurriedly returned to sit by the fire to pray and meditate in warmth.

It was only natural to compose myself at the eastern end of the Mediterranean two thousand years ago. I wanted to join the Holy Family. Having reread the relevant passages from both Luke and Matthew, I knew we would travel from Galilee to Judaea to Egypt and back to Galilee. I knew we would live the first third of the twelve-year journey in constant fear in a strange land.

Using my historical atlas, I traced the route from Nazareth, near Galilee, to Alexandria, Egypt. The total distance is more than 500 miles. I assumed a walking pace equal to that of camels, which is roughly 25 miles a day. Assuming no stops along the way, the journey would have taken about 21 days. In fact, however, we know that the travelers stopped in Jerusalem long enough for the young Jesus to be presented in the temple. It was only after this that Joseph was warned to flee into exile in Egypt.

In my contemplation, we left Jerusalem immediately, not waiting to join other travelers or otherwise organize a journey. We did have the donkey that had accompanied us on our trip from Nazareth. Mary rode on the donkey, carrying the two-month-old Jesus. We walked only at night, hiding as best we could during the day. We arrived in Beersheba five days after leaving Jerusalem. It was in Beersheba that we were finally able to join a camel caravan for the treacherous journey across the Sinai desert. The caravan plodded steadily from Beersheba to what is now Port Said, stopping every third day to rest. We arrived at the western edge of the desert two weeks after leaving Judaea. We parted company with the camel caravan, found a donkey (we had to barter away our donkey for the trip across the desert), and began the week-long walk across the fertile delta plain of the Nile.

In my contemplation, much of this month was pure misery. Walking in fear next to a donkey during the night was certainly not an experience to repeat. The blowing sand and blinding sun and stifling heat of the Sinai did little to enhance the smell and nastiness of the camels. It was only after arriving in Egypt that we could begin to relax our vigil.

What I experienced in my contemplation, and repeated today in the library, was a powerful feeling of humility. We left Nazareth a poor peasant family, walking next to our donkey to celebrate the presentation of Jesus at the temple. While we were not rich in any material sense of the word, we did have family, friends, and faith. Suddenly, we were plunged into fear, running and hiding, uncertain where we would sleep each night or find our next meal. How low can one go? How much more vivid can the idea of incarnate be?

While in Egypt, we had to learn new languages in order to communicate. The camel train across the desert communicated in Berber, an ancient nomadic language. Once in Egypt, Coptic was the language on the street, required in order for Joseph and me to ply our woodworker trade. Fortunately, the *koine* dialect of Greek was the teaching language in Galilee, Judaea, and Egypt. The child Jesus learned to speak Aramaic from His parents, and a mixture of Coptic and Greek from His friends in the streets. This linguistic capability would stand Him in good stead later in life.

When word finally arrived that we could return to our home in Galilee, our lives took a major turn for the better. Joseph had learned some important and valuable new skills in Alexandria. His improved language skills would prove valuable in Nazareth, as well as in the journey back to Galilee. The young Jesus could now walk alongside the donkey part of each day. So we re-traced our journey of fright and flight, now hopeful and unafraid. Jesus began His transition from childhood to manhood in a surge of good news. I loved this feeling as I contemplated the reunion of the Holy Family with their family and friends.

In truth, we know very little about the next eight years of Jesus' life. It is safe to assume that He was a normal child, growing up the son of a tradesman in a rural community. I have learned that woodworkers at the time of Christ were not just house builders. In fact, houses were not made of wood, but rather of stone and a stucco-like substance. The skills of the woodworker were required for furniture inside the house, and for tools for use outside the house and in the fields. There was probably very little work for Joseph in the little town of Nazareth. He almost certainly worked in the farming areas outside of Nazareth and in other small towns along the western side of the Sea of Galilee. Jesus presumably worked with His father from the very moment He was able to walk and carry tools or supplies.

As I understand Catholic theology, Jesus did not have any birth brothers or sisters. Mary would not have been immaculate if she had other children. However, John 7 and Matthew 13 strongly suggest that He did have siblings.

For me, the presence of a larger immediate family takes nothing away from my belief in the divinity of Jesus Christ. It does support my appreciation of His normalcy, and the powerful message of His Incarnation. So my contemplations about the early life of Christ generally include His brothers (though, for some reason, not His sisters).

My experience of Jesus helping His father has greater reality for me due to my own experience working alongside my brothers as we helped our father build the house we lived in and maintain the equipment we used at our farm. After about my ninth or tenth year, I was assigned chores and regular farm duties that took me away from my brothers. However, until then, my concept of "doing my chores" always involved my brothers. We worked, but we also managed to engage in a bit of mischief and fun.

I see Jesus in the same way. I imagine that He learned much of what it means to "love one's brother" by quite literally loving His brothers. Luke's account of Jesus' visit to the Passover Festival when He was in His twelfth year supports my growing sense of what we mean by the Incarnation. Jesus lost track of time, and neglected to tell His parents where He was for three full days. That is at least as bad as anything I did when I was that age, and I did a few pretty bad things. I have to say, explaining simply that He was in His Father's house seems to me to be a pretty lame explanation. What was unusual, particularly for the son of a rural peasant, was the idea of a young man engaging in heavy spiritual conversation with the teachers at the temple. Jesus was a normal young man, but He had great curiosity and an easy ability to converse with and question His elders.

It is a pity that we do not know any more of what happened during the long period of almost twenty years between the temple visit and the beginning of His public ministry.

6. Jesus begins the life He chose

What ideas and images filled Jesus' mind in the desert? In the Jordan? I want to know them, and to love the One who entertained them. I would then follow Him.

Monday, January 16   (Matthew 3:13-17)

I fell asleep last night following the Discernment meeting of CRHP Team 11. My prayers this morning would not be complete without talking with God about CRHP, and the role I was blessed to play for the past three months. I have not researched the origin of this incredible program, but I feel certain the results have exceeded the expectations of those who created it. CRHP uses many of the tried and true concepts and tools of the human potential movement, with a little group therapy thrown into the mix. What distinguishes it so much from my experience with those two disciplines is the spiritual setting of the parish and the constant invocation of the Holy Spirit.

Part of its success derives from the fact that almost everyone in the room believes in the personal presence of the Holy Spirit. In my two CRHP team experiences, two or three men in each group of about twenty-five were non-Catholic. However, they were married to Catholics, and they regularly attend Mass. So the "buy in" to both a common belief system and the powerful and personal role of the Holy Spirit is very high. It is significant, however, that most of the men were very nearly strangers at the beginning of the retreat weekend, in spite of this powerful shared religious faith and regular participation in the same parish. CRHP taps into two of the most dominant characteristics of modern society: on one hand, "modern man" feels isolated and alone on an ever more crowded planet, on the other hand, we have an incredibly strong desire to belong, to be part of a group. Remember the theme song from the old TV series Cheers:

> *Sometimes you want to go where everybody knows your name, and they're always glad you came.*
> *You wanna be where you can see, our troubles are all the same*
> *You wanna be where everybody knows your name.*

CRHP provides a spiritual place where "everybody knows your name." Everybody offers a hug with meaning. Last night, the Team 10 guys sat silently in the background as Team 11 discerned for the various roles to be played at the retreat they will present to a Team 12 that they will form. After discernment, the men from each team who had played and will play the same role found each other, knitting the two groups together in the growing CRHP community of our parish.

My own role has been particularly rewarding to me. Each Sunday night since May of last year, I have met with a group of about twenty-five men. From May until October, I was part of the bonding and formation process of Team 10. I listened to their stories, and I told them my story. We prayed and listened to spiritual music and learned more about faith. We then prepared ourselves to work as a presentation team at the October retreat, where a new group of men, invited by us, would become Team 11. As Formation Director from October onwards, I met with Team 11 every Sunday night, guiding them through what is called the History Giving and Faith Sharing process. Over a three month period, nearly total strangers told each other the stories of their lives and their journeys of faith. I began these exercises about midway through the nine months that I have been involved with CRHP. These two powerful processes are incredibly symbiotic; each is made better by the other.

Sallie Ann and I attended the Interfaith Service in honor of Martin Luther King at St. Joseph's before the CRHP meeting started. A phrase quoted from Dr. King by Bishop Felipe stayed with me:

> *Injustice anywhere is a threat to justice everywhere. We are caught in an inescapable network of mutuality, tied in a single garment of destiny. Whatever affects one directly, affects all indirectly.* [66]

Dr. King is responsible for many powerful phrases in our language. Just as I have repeatedly used the phrase "bend the arc of history," I hope to incorporate "a single garment of destiny" into my language. I loved meeting Imam Joe Bradford, Rabbi Joshua Lief, and Bishop Felipe Estevez.[67] The service prepared me well for CRHP discernment.

The scripture this morning is Matthew 3:13-17, a brief passage describing the baptism of Jesus by John the Baptist. I spent part of the morning attempting to understand how Jesus could be baptized into the Christian faith before that faith existed. What little I had a chance to read last night leads me to believe that John the Baptist had created a messianic movement among the Jews along the Jordan River. The rite of baptism was intended for purification. It was a penance or repentance for sin, not a forgiveness of sins.

I composed myself on the east bank of the Jordan River, watching and listening to the event that would begin the public ministry of Jesus. It was a beginning and an end. The long period of quiet normalcy that passed between His three-day discussion with the teachers in the temple and His baptism by John the Baptist was now over. As the heavens opened and the Spirit of God descended like a dove, Jesus Christ effectively said "game on." All of us standing on that river bank were over-

---

[66] Martin Luther King, in a letter from the jail in Birmingham, Alabama, on April 16, 1963.

[67] These biographical sketches were taken from the published materials from each of the organizations represented by Messrs. Bradford, Lief, and Estevez. **Joe Bradford** embraced Islam as his personal faith and began religious studies at the Islamic Center of North East Florida in 1991. In 1999 he was awarded a scholarship to the prestigious Islamic University of Medina, was awarded a Master's in Islamic Law in 2009, earning a mark of distinction with honors for his research in contemporary issues. He worked for several years in the private sector before coming on with ICNEF. Joe is active in community and interfaith events, building bridges of understanding for various communities, congregations and organizations on the topics of Islam, Islamic Law, Faith, and community relations. Rabbi **Joshua B. Lief** is the Senior Rabbi of historic Congregation Ahavath Chesed. He attended Princeton University, where he swam on the varsity squad, competed on the debate team, and graduated with a degree in History. After Princeton, Rabbi Lief attended the Hebrew Union College-Jewish Institute of Religion. After living in Jerusalem for the first year of the seminary, he completed his studies at HUC-JIR's campus in Cincinnati, Ohio where he was ordained as a Rabbi in May of 2003. **Felipe de Jesús Estévez** (born on February 5, 1946) is the Bishop of the Roman Catholic Diocese of St. Augustine in Florida beginning Tuesday, June 1, 2011. He was formerly the Auxiliary Bishop of the Roman Catholic Archdiocese of Miami. Estévez was born in Pedro Betancourt, Matanzas, Cuba. He fled to the United States as a young man under Operation Peter Pan. He studied at Montreal University in Montreal, Canada, and received a Licentiate in Theology in 1970. In 1977, he received a Master in Arts from Barry University, Miami Shores, Florida (1977) and in 1980, a Doctorate in Sacred Theology from the Pontifical Gregorian University in Rome, Italy.

---

whelmed by the significance of the event. I, for one, was uncertain what would happen next. Yet I knew that it was a ride I wanted to take.

Tuesday, January 17 *(Matthew 3:13-17, again)*

Tennis this morning was a joy. I sat on the bench with Maggie and reflected again on the baptism of Jesus Christ. My strong feeling this morning is that the baptism of Jesus was like almost everything else in the Incarnation. That is, God did not have to become man. He did not have to be born, suffer childhood, and finally die. Yet that is what He did. Everything about the Incarnation is a message to us, including His baptism. It is as though He is saying, "Yes, I meant you. You must be baptized."

Wednesday, January 18 *(Matthew 4:1-11)*

I read the passage from Matthew last night. This morning, I woke up thinking about the significance of the number 40 in the bible and in my life. There are numerous occurrences in both the Old and New Testaments where it rained for 40 days and 40 nights or Moses was on the mountain for 40 days and nights or the Israelites wandered in the desert for 40 years. In this passage, Jesus fasts in the desert 40 days. It seems that the number 40 is generally connected to a period of trial or testing.

In my own life, I was drummed out of the Mormon Church 40 years before I began my journey of faith leading to my baptism as a Catholic. For me, those 40 years were certainly a period of trial. I did not do as well as Jesus Christ. On more occasions than I want to admit, I yielded to all manner of temptations. Remembering this led me to more of the desolation I felt several weeks ago.

Thursday, January 19 *(Two Standards, Two Value Systems)*

The desolation continued today. I composed myself in the desert with Jesus Christ. I was cold. I was hungry. I wanted nothing more than to leave that place and return to the warmth of the fire in the family room. I sought inspiration from the manner in which Christ resisted temptation. Instead, I felt weak and unworthy. I finally left that place by praying the Our Father.

Friday, January 20 (Two Standards, Two Value Systems)

Our assignment today is to read again the thought-piece "Two Standards and Two Value Systems." This morning I also read the thought-piece "Thoughts about Making Choices." The contrast between the value systems is enormous. I am particularly struck with the thought that we should begin each day, each decision process, and each action with one thought: I intend first to serve God and to love God. That opening commitment will inevitably improve whatever decision or action we take next.

Sunday, January 22   (Summary)

Most of yesterday was spent in bed with some kind stomach virus. After close to 24 hours of solid sleep, I am awake and anxious to be back at these exercises. The assignment today is to review the week. I began reflecting Monday morning about my final evening as Formation Director last Sunday night. Now I am reflecting on the fact that there is no CRHP meeting tonight! It seems very strange. I loved the experience.

Last Sunday also included the inspiring service in honor of Martin Luther King. While I was disappointed that so few (only one) of our fellow parishioners were there, the speeches and the actions of the Holy Spirit in the room were fabulous. It inspired my whole week.

From the standpoint of these exercises, the week was largely spent in the company of Jesus Christ at the beginning of His public ministry. My thoughts range from curiosity regarding most of the nearly thirty years of His life about which so little is known, to great anticipation for what would fill the next three years of His life. Beginning the ministry with His baptism and His trial in the desert seems entirely appropriate. In a sense, He was baptized by John the Baptist with water and by Satan with fire. The Holy Spirit led Him to both baptisms. He emerged from both of them stronger and better prepared for His ministry.

My own feelings regarding my baptism and various trials allow me to relate to the experience of Jesus. I clearly emerged from the baptismal font two years ago a stronger person, better prepared for whatever I would encounter during the rest of my life. The trials have strengthened me, even those I failed. On the occasions when I yielded to the temptation to veer away from my value system, I descended into dark places. Fortunately, as Richard Rohr suggests in the title of his book, I "fell upward." It is as though the depth of the fall increased the bounce upward to infinitely better places. I certainly yielded to some future temptation, but I think I can trace an upward trajectory to my journey. That is, I descend less and bounce a little higher each time.

As I review my feelings during this past week, I cannot help but consider the impact of these exercises since September 4 of last year. Assuming the normal duration of the Annotation 19 program is nine months, I am half-way through. Conceivably, I will be finished in early May, possibly even before Sallie Ann and I travel to Italy for our "Eucharistic celebration" and the Franciscan retreat. If that is the case, I will be happy, but I will be just as happy to return from Italy for more contemplation in all my spiritual hideouts with Maggie.

The exercises are definitely working for me. Over the years, I have occasionally thought that I prayed regularly. There have certainly been spiritual periods in my life, particularly since I began the serious search for meaning after my heart surgery. However, the past four and a half months have moved my spiritual experience to a whole new level. I find that I regularly talk casually with God throughout the day, discussing challenges, disappointments, people problems, and moments of joy. I smile when I think how much my relationship with Maggie has improved. The exercises clearly helped me in my leadership role in the CRHP community at OLSS. They provided foundational value for my teaching efforts at UNF.

I think about the admonition in the reading this week to begin each day knowing that I am being created by God momently. That is heavy stuff. Right now, He is giving me new gifts, new challenges, and new opportunities to grow. The intention that must be paramount in what I think, say, and do today and every day is to love and serve God. He has made it clear that I do so when I love and serve the people at the margins of life, the "least of us." I do so when I love and serve my family. I do so each time I make the choice to do the next right thing, and reject the choice to put myself first. I am clearly far away from what I know God wants, but I am continually making progress. That is also heavy stuff.

7. Jesus gathers His close friends

What kind of friend was Jesus of Nazareth? How did He think and feel about His friends, and about His mission? I want to love Him more, and to follow Him in His way.

Monday, January 23   *(John 1:35-42)*

We start the week with the passage from John, in which Jesus begins to build His team of disciples. After reading and reflecting on the scripture, I thought back on the numerous times I have built new companies from scratch. I thought about the difficulty involved in evaluating total strangers in just a few minutes of conversation. I thought about the risks of incompatibility that always exist when new employees come to work in a company. There are risks in the relationship between the boss and the new employee. There are also risks between the new employee and all the other employees.

As far as I can tell, the Gospels tell us very little about the selection process. We do not know what criteria Jesus used in selecting each of His disciples, nor do we know any details about the conversation He had with each of them before calling them to follow Him.

Now of course it is easy to conclude that Jesus used His greater powers to see into each of His disciples, and each of those disciples knew from first sight that Jesus was the Messiah and that they were to follow Him. In my contemplation, I saw it differently. Jesus engaged each of His potential disciples in the standard give-and-take that almost always takes place between a CEO and his first team of senior managers. Again, as in the normal manner, while Jesus was interviewing them, each of them was assessing Him. Each sought to inform the other, while at the same time, tried to court the other. In my fantasy, I saw the incarnate side of Jesus.

Tuesday, January 24 (John 1:35-42, again)

My focus this morning returned again to the contemplation of Jesus building His team. Today, however, I was interviewed by Jesus. I wanted desperately to be called as one of His key leaders. I tried to be casual in my conversation, but pushed my capabilities hard. I did not get the call. It was incredibly desolating.

Wednesday, January 25 (Mark 1:16-20)

Our reading this morning was the account of Jesus calling His first disciples reported in Mark. There were a few differences from the account in John. For one thing, Mark does not mention that John the Baptist played a role in the call of the first two disciples (simply by referring to Jesus as the Lamb of God). Nor does John place the initial call along the shore of Galilee. Mark uses the wonderful language so often associated with the call of the disciples: "Come follow me and I will send you out to fish for people." This is essentially the language of Matthew 4:18-20, though I prefer the translation "I will make you fishers of men."

My fantasy took me back to my interview with Jesus. After the interview, I waited with anticipation for Jesus to say, "Come, follow me." I watched Him interview others. Over the course of the morning, He called one after another to follow Him. As much as I wanted it, however, he did not call me. I came out of the meditation forlorn. What had He seen that caused Him to pass over me? What should I do next?

Thursday, January 26 (Mark 1:16-20, again)

The morning began more or less where I left off yesterday. I was on the shore of the Sea of Galilee, alone in my sadness. I kept going over the interview with Jesus. Could He see the dark side of me with such clarity that He realized there was simply no hope? Or was His message to me that I was to be a foot soldier in His army, not one of the twelve leaders? Assuming that was the case, could I serve faithfully and with humility? I ended the day in a long conversation with God about my struggle to be humble.

Friday, January 27 (Three Couple)

The assignment this morning was the thought-piece about three couples and a million dollars.[68] I spent most of the meditation trying to fully understand the three dif-

---

[68] The Tetlow thought-piece Three Couples. "Three good and deeply faith-filled couples happen to pull off a business deal that nets each of them a million dollars. Now, these three couples are good people, with strong consciences, and they did nothing wrong in the business deal. After a few weeks, at one of their regular get-togethers, they rather shyly begin to mention a feeling that they have each noticed. They do not feel entirely comfortable about having that money. This is a spiritual matter, for their consciences remain clear and firm. But they notice changes in their spirits. They are no longer

ferent reactions. The first couple was brought to inaction by their disquiet. They gave none of their new wealth to the poor. The second couple acted, but for the wrong reasons. They helped the poor to curry favor with God and others. The third couple simply asked to know God's will. I made the assumption that this third couple eventually came to a knowledge of God's will and acted on it to use the money wisely, and in service to others. I was reminded of the Merton prayer:

My Lord God I have no idea where I am going. I do not see the road ahead of me. I cannot know for certain where it will end. Nor do I really know myself, and the fact that I think I am following your will does not mean that I am actually doing so.

But I believe that my desire to please you does in fact please you. And I hope that I have that desire in all that I am doing. I hope that I will never do anything apart from that desire. And I know that if I do this you will lead me by the right road though I may know nothing about it.

My meditation ended after I focused for what seemed like a very long time on how to know God's desire for me. Have I finally come to appreciate what it is? Am I acting on that knowledge? Am I even making enough of an effort to qualify for Merton's suggestion that the effort to please is itself pleasing?

Saturday, January 28   *(John 2:1-11)*

As I repeated the reading about the three couples this morning, I thought about the second couple. While they acted for questionable reasons, and they achieved little comfort for doing so, the poor and others who benefited from their efforts probably

---

eager for Sunday Mass (and the homilies vex them as never before). They feel differently about the bishops' pastoral on the American economy and the Pope's letter about communism and capitalism. They no longer feel in harmony with the Church, somehow. They admit feeling exultant that they made the deal and got the million dollars. They like having the money and are doing great things with it. Still ... maybe they want it too much or something? It seems to be tainting their lives.

The first couple really wants to get rid of the disquiet. They talk a lot about it, at least in the beginning. But years later when they die - still rich they have done nothing at all about it.   The next couple can't sit still in the disquiet. They want to keep the money and can't figure why they ought to get rid of it. Still, they do not want to live with uneasy spirits, a little tentative with God. So they take some steps. Systematically, they give money to the poor and the dispossessed and the underprivileged, mostly through the Church. In this way, they try to bargain with God: "If we give this to the poor, You ought to give us peace." When they come to die, they have done good things, but they have not reached solid inner peace.   The final couple considered keeping the money and they also considered just giving the money away. But they had to admit that they did not really know whether either one would solve their uneasiness. Why would they keep it? Why would they give it away? So this is how they acted: They decided that they would not determine definitely to keep the money or definitely to get rid of it. They would wait to see what this disquiet really signified. Then when they knew, they would act. In this way, they generously said to God: "Either way. Show us and we'll do it. "

cared little or none at all about the reasons behind those efforts. The fact is that the recipients received benefit. It was not colored by the motives of those who gave. It seems clear to me that the second couple acted far better than the first couple. I am reminded of the phrase, "fake it till you make it" or "act your way into faith." The second couple may eventually have a true faith conversion as a result of witnessing the results of their gifts. Obviously, the first couple will never have that opportunity.

John tells the story about the wedding in Cana to open the second chapter of his gospel. When His mother mentions to Him that there is no more wine, Jesus seems to suggest that it is not His problem. Ignoring Him, His mother tells the servants to "Do whatever He tells you." It is as though she is speaking from some kind of prior knowledge. Whatever she knew, Jesus chose to use this wedding need for additional wine to "reveal His glory" through a sign. John tells us this is Jesus' first sign. My spiritual hero, Chris Dorment, and his wife are traveling to Cana soon to renew their vows. It is spiritually uplifting to me just to know that.

Sunday, January 29 *(Summary)*

I began the morning reading and reflecting on what I wrote in this journal this past week. As I read again about my sadness after my failed interview with Jesus, I considered that some of that sadness may have been similar to the feelings of the second couple in the note on couples. The fact that I put my case to Jesus for becoming one of the twelve was not a bad thing. I was not chosen, I believe, because I was not humble. My reasons for doing the good thing were not pure. Again, this morning, therefore, I felt the sadness of rejection.

I thought again about each of the companies I formed over my lifetime. Each time, at a key point, I gathered around me the men and women who would lead the new effort. I looked for creativity and initiative. In the end, however, I think loyalty may have been at the top on the list of qualities I looked for in my key leadership team. To some extent, this explains why more and more of the key players in each successive team were veterans of previous efforts. After Globeleq was sold and I had recovered from heart surgery, the most loyal members of my leadership teams, going all the way back to the first power plant in Maine, approached me with various plans to "sing a final song."

So, could Jesus see into my heart and know that I would be loyal to my own ambition instead of to Him? I suspect He would not have had to look very hard. I wear my ambition and desire for personal attainment pretty openly. Sallie Ann sent me a brief email message on the subject of trust:

Question: What is the nature of the trust between God and disciple?

Answer: A relationship of surrender and acceptance. If there is no trust, there can't be surrender and acceptance.

It occurs to me that each party in a relationship must trust the other, which means that each must surrender and accept the other. Jesus surrendered to, and accepted each of His chosen twelve, knowing their faults. He trusted them to work through these faults, and to serve Him well. Of course, each of them trusted Him implicitly, surrendering to Him with clear knowledge of the dangers inherent in doing so. By picking up His cross, they were picking up their own.

8. Jesus begins to announce Good News

I want to know Jesus of Nazareth, and to love Him, and to follow Him in His way.

Monday, January 30 (Luke 4:14-22)

This morning I read Luke 4:14-22, an account of Christ's return from the temptation in the desert to begin His public ministry. In Luke's account, the first thing Jesus read was a passage from Isaiah. Isaiah announced that:

> *He [presumably Jesus] had been anointed to proclaim good news to the poor... freedom for the prisoners ...recovery of sight for the blind... and freedom for the oppressed.*

Isaiah lived and preached during the period of the four kings of Judah, roughly 792-732 BC. Until I began these exercises, I was quite unaware of the extent to which the New Testament gospel was foretold in the Old Testament, particularly by Isaiah. Obviously, Jesus used the sacred beliefs and traditions of the Jews when preaching to them. It only made sense. Christ was not promoting a rejection of all that the Jews held sacred. Rather, He was building on what had come before, adding particular emphasis to some key elements of that faith.

Tuesday, January 31 (Luke 4:14-22, again)

When reading the passage from Luke again, I focused on the last line of the passage, when those who heard Jesus asked, "Isn't He the son of Joseph?" They were really asking how it could be that this son of a simple carpenter could be preaching with such knowledge and authority. It occurs to me that many of us often pre-judge each other. In the ordinary course of a day, we make judgments about people based on the clothes they wear, the color of their skin, the shape of their bodies, and the company they keep. We ask them what their fathers did for a living. We are all "profiling."

Wednesday, February 1 (Matthew 4:23-5:12)

Our assignment this morning was to read the introduction to the Sermon on the Mount from Matthew 4, commonly referred to as the Beatitudes. This may be the most frequently read, and referenced, passage from the whole bible. My immediate thought, as I reflect on the passage, is that it is one of the finest bits of poetry I have ever read. Each sentence builds on the one before it, creating a whole that deserves the status it enjoys. Christ builds on what He read from Isaiah as reported in the passage from Luke earlier this week.

I composed myself among the crowd listening to Christ that morning. I looked around at the others who had come from many places far away from Galilee. It was one of the most beautiful mornings I can ever remember. I walked down to the bench with Maggie, still in my fantasy. There were people on the grass next to me, and even more across the lagoon. The words of Jesus were in the air, as if He had been speaking on some kind of loudspeaker. We all started to repeat the words, saying them in unison with Jesus.

When I left the garden, I looked back on the multitudes listening to Jesus. He continued to talk to them in small groups or individually. He answered questions and offered suggestions. It was with some reluctance that I left all of them there and picked up the computer to write in this journal.

Thursday, February 2   *(Matthew 4:23-5:12, again)*

Again today, I read and reflected on the passage from Matthew. Like yesterday, I composed myself among the crowd, sitting at the feet of Jesus on the gentle slope of Mount Eremos. Like the others sitting near me, I had been taught the Mosaic laws, most of which told me what not to do. Now I listened to Jesus talk to me about what I am meant to do. It was beautifully different. I stayed in that place all morning, both in the library and at the garden bench.

As I write this journal entry, I am reflecting on the fact that Jesus promised a reward for all the good things we were meant to do, but it was a reward that would come only after this life ended. That thought was disconcerting. Is this world so mean that humility, love, patience, and good works are seldom, if ever, celebrated? Are the blessings for following Jesus only available in the life after this one? I hope not. I hope that part of being Christian is recognizing the good works and humility and love of others.

Or do I have it all wrong? Is it possible that the Kingdom of Heaven promised in the Beatitudes is actually here now? Is it a state of being that the faithful achieve through a combination of faith and works?

Friday, February 3   *(Three Phases of Humility)*

I prayed and reflected this morning on the thought-piece describing three phases of humility.[69] I read it through earlier this week and again last night. I love the idea

---

[69] **THE FIRST PHASE**. I see the world as it is. I see myself, first of all, desiring certain things. I might, for example, want a certain job or to live in a certain city. However, I understand that I do not determine which of my desires lead to my authentic life and to my deep happiness; I depend on God for that. God the Creator and Lord has created certain values for and in me, so when I evaluate any thing or any action, I cannot make up the rules on my own. So, if I value very highly writing a certain letter in order to get the job I want, and then realize that writing this letter would violate my own conscience very gravely - then I do not write the letter. God sets my values. To use language we once used: I want and value certain things very highly, but I would not under any circumstances choose to place a desire or a value that I have in front of the desires and values that God writes into my own conscience. I depend on God for my conscience. I am gifted by God with a conscience - this concrete conscience, with its own dictates. I acquiesce in the concrete dictates of the conscience, I am glad to depend on God and to acquiesce.

To put it succinctly: I live to obey God who speaks in my spirit. For I know this: God has placed deepest in me a desire for Himself and I have chosen to enact my desire to belong to God before I enact any other desire, and I will enact no desire that would separate me from God. This is the first phase of humility. **THE SECOND PHASE**   I begin to find in myself the desire to find God and to grow to love God. I do not spend my time "avoiding sin"; rather, I spend my time finding God. In this mind-set, I would not go against my own conscience deliberately even in relatively unimportant things. It is not so much that I want to keep from offending God and violating my own honesty and integrity. I have changed in this, that I have chosen to love God, and not just to obey God. Of course, I still want career, and job, and very much else, and in the pursuit of these things I often discover that I can attain a very important objective by just the mildest violation of my own conscience. I generally manage not to do that. I fear God, of course, and I dread acting unauthenticated. One thing helps a good deal: I see how vain and empty much of the world is. I see how futilely I would live, for example, were I to give myself entirely to the job I love. I would be a fool to count on earthly things to give me lasting happiness - they don't last. So, I see and perceive from within my own creature hood. I have happily accepted the wisdom of the prophets and the wise of old: The Lord's is the earth and all that is in it. But the fact is that I would find it impossible to follow my conscience so carefully except that a great love is growing in my life. **THE THIRD PHASE**   In this phase, I come to see the earth and all that is in it through other eyes: the human eyes of Jesus of Nazareth. Jesus came into a culture utterly unlike my own except in certain essentials: people then wanted wealth, power, fame, and pleasure just as people today want them. Jesus went against culture and human inclinations, by choosing to be born poor and to live poor, by electing to join the powerless and the outcast. I do not find it so easy to go against culture. I take my culture into myself and then contribute to it in my turn; and following that culture, I want to know a lot and to be known as wise, to have many skills and to be known as an accomplished person, to have wealth and to be known as a solid citizen. But along comes my Lord Jesus Christ. I am seized by His Spirit, and filled with His love. I come to love Him to this extent, that I really want to see as He saw, evaluate as He evaluated, appreciate as He appreciated, and simply to live the way He lived. He so humbled Himself that He poured Himself out, living like the lower classes, making the simplest and most outcast welcome in His company, always serving. He kept on His course even when the choices He made under the Spirit led to great suffering and to a cruel death. I find to my astonishment that I want very much to follow along after Him in all that. I deliberately suppress any desire to be famous, powerful, wealthy, and known to be wise. I want to live as He lived. However, I do not demand that specific kind of life from God my Creator. I accept with my whole heart that the choice does not finally rest with me; and humility means precisely that I acquiesce in what God our Lord creates in me.

In this phase of humility, some find themselves in this state of mind: I know that I am a sinful person,

that humility is an active concept, "the **enacting** of a relationship." Just like so much of what I am learning through these exercises, achieving true humility is an **ongoing** gift that is **momently unfolding** in each of us, provided only that we say yes to that gift.

The three phases of humility are given brief names at the end of the piece. The first phase is **obedience.** While still acting as I desire to act, I am to also obey the commandment to be humble. It could be thought of as humility in name only, or as acting our way toward true humility. I do not mean to suggest that achieving this first phase of humility is easy or unimportant. Just reaching a place where I know what God wants from me, and choose to do everything I can to honor His wishes is a major achievement. I cannot claim to have spent much of my life acting with this much humility.

The second phase is **active indifference.** When I read this, I was prompted to go back to the thought-piece about active indifference, which I read in October. I still struggle to understand the concept.

When applied to the phases of humility, I understand that the first phase is choosing not to disobey God. The second phase requires that I act out of a desire to actively please God, not to avoid displeasing Him. The active indifference concept seems to focus on allowing space in our consideration of options to learn God's desires. It is being quiet long enough to hear His whisper.

It is not inactive silence, but involves prayer, contemplation, and increasing openness to His communication. I still see the world through my own eyes, including all the choices available to me for what to have and what to do in my life. However, I create enough humility in me – I allow enough space – so that I can hear God communicate His wishes to me.

The third phase requires that I see the world through the **eyes of Jesus Christ**. As I understand it, it is not a higher or better phase of humility than the first two phases. However, just as it is a very powerful exercise to compose oneself in the place and time one is reading about in the Bible, it is extremely powerful to compose oneself as Jesus when considering life's choices. From time to time, I see those bumper stickers that say "what would Jesus do?" Well, imagine asking that question about every choice or situation that is encountered every single day. Imagine being humble enough to hear the answer.

---

and I find it astonishing that I feel summoned to intimate friendship with Jesus Christ. I know that His way leads to dying to the self. I know His way leads to the crown. While I do not feel impelled to go looking for suffering or invited to inflict suffering on myself, I do feel perfectly ready to take whatever suffering comes along, and I will accept it as from the hand of God because then I will be following Jesus.

One of the major challenges for me is choosing poverty. My life has been filled with material gifts for a long time, even before I could even vaguely appreciate the source of those gifts. So I wander around this house or out in the garden, reflecting on the idea of seeing all that is around me through the eyes of Jesus. I am simply embarrassed.

How is it possible that I have been given all of this when so many others are hungry or cold or alone? If I give it all away, how many more will be lifted out of hunger or solitude? Is that what Jesus would do? If I make the choice not to abandon all of this, a choice I am almost certain to make now and for some time to come, what am I achieving through these exercises? Is my faith journey nothing more than an effort to make me feel better about my good fortune?

So I return to the phases of humility humbled by my own weakness. I have not found much comfort this morning.

Saturday, February 4 *(Three Phases of Humility)*

It has been an unsettled twenty-four hours since I last sat in this chair. I dreamt of the disquietudes, not the beatitudes. I read again about humility.

Humility is the enactment of a relationship.

It is an active unfolding, not a state of being. There are always two or more parties to the relationship. I must be humble *vis-a-vis* the other party in the relationship. I understand these words, but I am not sure they square with some of the other statements about humility in the thought-piece. The primary relationship is between the would-be humble person and God.

The humble person accepts creature-hood. So humility is also about acceptance and surrender and gratitude. It is embracing limits and ceding control. It is self-knowledge. Is all of this only in respect to the other party to the relationship? Perhaps it is so.

As I read again about the three phases of humility, I take some comfort from the belief that I am making an effort to seek out and understand God's will for me. I pray each day for the knowledge of His will and the strength to act accordingly. So I only intermittently achieve the first phase of humility in respect to God. I am even more erratic in humbly enacting many of my other relationships.

There are many mornings when I converse with God so comfortably, especially walking on the beach with Maggie, that I can honestly say I love Him. My relationship with Him is like no other relationship. It is filled with hope and joy and warmth and honesty. During those conversations, I do not think about any of my other desires, though I am sure I still have them. I hope to do well in my teaching or in some other aspect of life, but I do not think about it when I fully abandon myself to my love for God. That must be the key - abandonment of self.

Again coming back to the third phase, I may be close to understanding how "losing self" is so fundamental to squaring the circle. Yes, I begin to see some things, some of the time, briefly through the eyes of Jesus. I want to be like Him. First and foremost, I must accept that He made me and gave me everything in my life. I am nothing without Him. I must fully surrender to that fact and accept my life on those terms. Humility, however, involves leaving all of that behind. I cannot be stuck worrying about what I have or do not have when I am truly thinking about or caring about the other. Jesus taught us to do unto others and to love one another. We can only do so by losing ourselves completely in that "other love." Giving away or tossing out God's gifts to me keeps the focus on me and mine, not on the other.

Sunday, February 5   *(Summary)*

Reading over the entries in my journal this week, I marveled at the range of feelings that have been engendered in just these seven days. As I wrote one morning, there have been beatitudes and disquietudes. I have struggled mightily with the three phases of humility, no doubt reflecting my lifelong daily struggle with humility in any form. Richard Rohr's daily meditation yesterday spoke to me regarding the first phase of humility:

> *God did not create us to obey laws, but to attend a banquet. Jesus makes that absolutely clear.*

As I prayed for insight and understanding this morning, my thoughts drifted back to the two large political battles that captured so much attention this week. I talked comfortably with God about my reactions to these issues. At some point, my eyes were opened to aspects of the arguments I had not seen.

Deacon Dan raised the first issue with me almost ten days ago, a few days before a letter from the Bishop was read from the pulpit at Mass. Part of the health insurance reform law passed almost three years ago involves a requirement that insurance providers cover the full cost of certain services which are opposed by our Catholic faith. At the time the regulations were being written, a one-year delay was agreed for organizations with conscience objections to these services.

That one year ended last week, when the Obama administration decided that the services must be included in the insurance that is provided by employers, including those with religious objections. While there is still another year of delay available to certain organizations, including some Catholic employers, the decision clearly requires Catholic employers – hospitals, clinics, schools, and so on – to act contrary to their belief. When Deacon Dan first asked my views, I said that I thought it seemed to be more about providing poor people the same rights as wealthy people (the services were available for a co-payment). As I talked it through in my long conversation with God this morning, it became increasingly clear to me that Obama's decision was wrong. The right of conscientious objection is well established in this country.

The government should not be able to force an employer to offer insurance coverage to employees for services that are objectionable as a matter of religious faith.[70]

I do not conclude as a result of this enlightenment that I should abandon the Democratic Party, or my support for Obama's reelection. I do conclude that I should join the effort to reverse the objectionable part of this recent decision. In fact, I believe my position as a recent convert to Catholicism and, at the same time, life-long Democrat adds to my credibility in advocating this change.

The second issue is the Susan G. Komen decision to abandon and then not to abandon Planned Parenthood.[71] For as long as I can remember, I have been a supporter of both of these organizations. This support continues today, even after my becoming Catholic and re-examining my position on abortion. I never promoted abortion, even though I supported legalizing the right of a woman to choose. My view was that everything should be done to reduce the number of abortions, particularly education and contraception. I generally agreed with the concept that abortions should be legal, safe, and rare. Somehow during my two years of RCIA, I remained quite unaware of the central importance of the abortion issue for Catholics.

---

[70] On February 10, Obama announced a compromise, essentially relieving the employers with conscientious objections from the obligation to pay for the offending services. Instead, insurance companies must offer these services at no additional cost to the insured. The Catholic Bishops rejected the compromise, but several Catholic organizations accepted it. I am satisfied with the compromise.

[71] According to Wikipedia, "Susan G. Komen for the Cure, formerly known as The Susan G. Komen Breast Cancer Foundation, often referred to as simply Komen, is the most widely known, largest and best-funded breast cancer organization in the United States. Since its inception in 1982, Komen has invested nearly $2 billion for breast cancer research, education, advocacy, health services and social support programs in the U.S., and through partnerships in more than 50 countries. Today, Komen has more than 100,000 volunteers working in a network of 124 affiliates worldwide. As of March 2011, Komen is listed on Charity Navigator with the site's highest rating of four stars. According to the Harris Interactive 2010 EquiTrend annual brand equity poll, Komen is one of the most trusted nonprofit organizations in America. Planned Parenthood Federation of America (PPFA), commonly shortened to Planned Parenthood, is the U.S. affiliate of the International Planned Parenthood Federation (IPPF) and one of its larger members. PPFA is a non-profit organization providing reproductive health and maternal and child health services. The Planned Parenthood Action Fund, Inc. (PPAF) is a related organization which lobbies for pro-choice legislation, comprehensive sex education, and access to affordable health care in the United States. Planned Parenthood is the largest provider of reproductive health services in the United States, which include contraceptives and abortions, among other services. Contraception accounts for 35% of PPFA's total services and abortions account for 3%; PPFA conducts roughly 300,000 abortions each year, among 3 million people served. The organization has its roots in Brooklyn, New York, where Margaret Sanger opened the country's first birth-control clinic. Sanger founded the American Birth Control League in 1921, which in 1942 became part of the Planned Parenthood Federation of America. Since then, Planned Parenthood has grown to have over 820 clinic locations in the U.S., with a total budget of US $1 billion. PPFA provides an array of services to over three million people in the United States, and supports services for over one million clients outside the United States. Many Catholics consider Planned Parenthood to be an "evil" organization due to its promotion of contraception and abortion, both of which are forbidden by the Catholic Church.

It came as somewhat of a shock to learn just how powerful and fundamental this single issue is in our faith community. Most of my friends here in Florida are Catholic, and almost every one of them is a very conservative Republican. While abortion is largely the decisive issue, their views on everything from tax policy to immigration to ecumenism to education to voter registration to foreign aid to military force and on and on and on, are all about as far right as I have ever seen. I would like to say that this is all unimportant background noise. Sadly, it has not been possible for me find much peace.

So I pray about it almost every day. I talk to God about it, particularly during these periods when the most divisive issues are on the front page of the paper. Most of the time, I choose to push this political noise to the side, focusing instead on my own sins, my own pride, and my own need and desire to deepen my personal relationship with God. Trust me, there is enough there to occupy the rest of my life. However, this journal would be neither complete nor honest were I not to occasionally mention the pain and disquiet caused by the extent to which I am such a political misfit, in my local parish and in much of my new faith.

9. Jesus continues His public life

I want to know Jesus better, to love Him more, and to follow Him wholeheartedly.

Monday, February 6   (Mark 10:46-52)

I read this morning's assigned passage last night, after meeting with Sister Joan. However, I think I lost most of my connection to Mark during the Super Bowl that followed! It seems that I watch a great deal more TV in retirement than I have ever watched before in my life. This is particularly true of sporting events.

After reading the passage again this morning, I began my conversation with God in the library, and then walked with Maggie down to the bench in the garden. Jericho is located not far from the north end of the Dead Sea. Our conversation moved easily to the idea of a blind man asking Jesus for sight. I said I could identify with Bartimaeus in the sense that I have been spiritually blind most of my life, and struggle to this day to maintain the gift of sight that I have received. Bartimaeus spoke for me. I imagined myself on that road outside of Jericho next to Bartimaeus. Bartimaeus said, "Rabbi, **we** want to see."

Tuesday, February 7   (Mark 10:46-52, again)

I began the exercises late this morning. After playing tennis for the first time in a couple of weeks due to a bruised left arm, I talked with Sallie Ann about the speech I gave last night at UNF. The fact is that I had become extremely anxious about the speech for what turned out to be no reason. I had allowed my concern about the speech to interfere with my serenity.

After our conversation, I read the passage from Mark again. Again I identified with the blind man on the road, even more powerfully than I had yesterday. I think I allow many unimportant things to cloud my vision. Sometimes, it is an impending obligation, like the speech last night. Sometimes, it is a desire to acquire a thing that is both unnecessary and unhealthy. I prayed for clear vision.

Wednesday, February 8 *(Luke 8:26-39)*

The passage this morning from Luke gives an account of a man from Gerasenes who asks Jesus to rid him of evil spirits. Jesus does so, sending the evil spirits into a herd of pigs that is promptly drowned. The man, now in his right mind, is told to go back to his people and report how God has helped him.

I composed myself in that small town near the Sea of Galilee, listening to the healed man report his experience with Jesus. All of the people in the crowd were comfortable with the concept of evil spirits, and with the idea that a man could be possessed by those evil spirits. So the suggestion that a man of God could command those evil spirits to depart was easily accepted by the people around me.

I found myself in the strange position of trying to talk them out of that comfortable belief. The "evil spirits" were not actual entities, physical or spiritual, I said. They were more like thoughts or temptations. Jesus did not actually cause these entities to possess the pigs. That was just a way of saying that He caused the man to abandon evil and resist temptation.

I asked God for help in making my point, and the conversation shifted to my blindness! Evil is real, He said. He can help me conquer the evil in my life. However, I will never be able to accept His help if I continue to scoff at the reality of evil. I said I could understand that, but I thought the idea of the pigs was going too far. Once again, God suggested that I focus on the important things.

Thursday, February 9 (Luke 8:26-39, again)

After a brief prayer seeking clarity, I composed myself once again along the shore of the Sea of Galilee in a conversation with Jesus. We picked up immediately where we left off yesterday. How real is evil in this world and in our lives?

I began the conversation by reporting that I felt a little misunderstood yesterday. I know evil is present in the world. I know that evil has been present in my life and continues to tempt me every day. I know that it is only my awareness of and surrender to the power of the Holy Spirit that allows me to resist evil. It is not necessary for me to see this evil in an anthropomorphic form to fully accept its existence. Jesus did not argue the point, which often means that He is not happy that I persist in my view.

We left the issue to focus on the political storm brewing around the recent Obama decision regarding birth control. It is clear to me that the Pope will not change the position of the Church regarding birth control and other reproductive issues.

I asked God if He could see the validity of the argument that women of all income levels should have equal rights (and funding) to make their own choices. He answered that all men and all women have free will, and can, therefore make any and all choices freely. Some of these choices, however, are against the law of the state (harming others), against the rules of an employer or contract (even issues as small as dress code), or against the rules of faith (dietary restrictions, conduct during holy days). So the question is what happens when the state attempts to interfere with the rules of faith, which is the question involved in the current argument over contraception coverage by religious insurers. That made sense to me. I prayed for peace and acceptance.

Friday, February 10 (Luke 19:1-10)

After reading the passage from Luke last night, I turned again to the Catena Aurea of Aquinas for additional perspective. Ambrose commented that simply by climbing the tree in order to see Him, Zaccheus pleased Jesus enough to earn recognition. This reminds me again of the Merton prayer. Ambrose also commented about the implications of Zaccheus being a wealthy tax collector:

> Let the rich learn that guilt attaches not to the goods themselves, but to those who know not how to use them. For riches, as they are hindrances to virtue in the unworthy, so are they means of advancing it in the good.

So I began to pray, somewhat enlightened. I composed myself in the crowd that was blocking the ability of Zaccheus to see Jesus. I watched the tax collector climb the tree and heard Christ acknowledge him, and then go so much further by announcing that He would speak to this sinner privately in the sinner's house.

Then, as now, it was a great honor to be visited at home by someone important. All of us in the crowd could only dream of Christ Himself choosing to come into our homes to honor us before the whole community. So watching this short tax collector receive such an honor was somewhat disturbing. I walked with Maggie down to the garden bench and wanted desperately for Jesus to visit us here in our house and in our garden. Then I smiled as I realized that He was sitting on the bench next to me.

Saturday, February 11 (Luke 19:1-10, again)

As I prayed this morning, my thoughts returned to the beauty of God's presence. Richard Rohr wrote yesterday:

> You cannot earn this God. You cannot prove yourself worthy of this God. Feeling God's presence is simply a matter of awareness, of fully allowing and en-

joying the present moment. There are moments when it happens naturally, **when we are out of the way**. *Then life makes sense.*

When we are out of the way! When I cannot see God or experience His presence, it is invariably because I am in the way. My ego consumes all of my awareness. My desires crowd out the presence and love of God. Getting out of the way should be easy, but, for me at least, it is not.

Zaccheus was able to get around himself and his riches by giving half away to the poor, and making fourfold reparation to those he had defrauded. These are good precedents for today. On the one hand, literally giving a significant portion of our blessings away to those in the margins of life reduces the size of the blockage standing in the way of our awareness of God's presence.

As I have commented before, the recipients of those gifts have the gifts. They do not care much about the motives of the giver.

Zaccheus takes the additional step of making direct reparations to those he has harmed. Fortunately, my gains in life were obtained by excessive zeal and obsessive drive, but they were not ill gotten. I have amends to make to Sallie Ann and my children, but to some extent, they are just the opposite of monetary damages. All too often, I gave things purchased with money instead of actions inspired by love. That is the imbalance I am now addressing.

Sunday, February 12   (Summary)

It has been a wonderful week from the standpoint of these exercises. The conversations with God were lively. He corrected me without scolding. He comforted me with challenges. I began this morning filled with quiet joy.

Sallie Ann and I watched the movie *Evelyn* early this morning.[72] It was about the effort of an Irish family, separated by the mother's desertion, to reunite. Evelyn, the young daughter in the family, gave the winning testimony in the successful court case, using a wonderful prayer to do so. I recount it here because the final scenes in the movie were watched from our bed by Sallie Ann, Maggie, our two granddaughters and me, all laughing and crying and loving the moment. The experience stayed with me during my review of the week.

---

[72] According to the film's publicity release, Evelyn is a 2002 drama film, loosely based on the true story of Desmond Doyle and his fight against the Irish courts to be reunited with his children. The film stars Sophie Vavasseur in the title role, Pierce Brosnan as her father and Aidan Quinn, Julianna Margulies and Stephen Rea as supporters to Doyle's case. The film had a limited release in the United States, starting on December 13, 2002 and was later followed by the United Kingdom release on March 21, 2003. The film was produced by, with others, Brosnan's own production company, Irish DreamTime. It opened to generally favourable reviews.

We read three scriptural passages this week, all reporting miracles performed by Jesus in and around Jericho, a town located east of Jerusalem, not far from the Dead Sea. As I understand the chronology of Christ's ministry, these events occurred late in the three-plus years of His public life.

We have skipped around a bit. We read the introduction to the Sermon on the Mount last week. Jesus delivered this wonderful sermon shortly after beginning His three-year ministry. I can only surmise that Ignatius had something important to say by the order of these readings (assuming, I think correctly, that Tetlow followed the order first set forth in 1540).

I composed myself with Jesus in Jericho. We talked about the three miracles, and the messages He wanted to convey.

Mark's account of Bartimeus receiving sight was more about "ask and you shall receive" than it was about any special power of Jesus. In my own case, there was never really any doubt that my blindness could be removed by God. I only had to ask.

However, just like the man in Gerasenes described by Luke, I had yielded to so much temptation that it was fair to say I was possessed. I was no longer able to make intelligent decisions, even the obvious ones like "help me to see." Jesus could, however, take that temptation away. I had to be willing, but He had to rid me of the compulsions that controlled my life. I could not do it. He could and would, if I only asked.

Finally, the story of Zaccheus makes a very simple point: there are two sides to a bargain. Yes, God can and will make us see, even going so far as removing the obstacles that prevent us from asking for sight. However, God can and does ask us to do something in return. He wants to come into our house and into our lives. He wants us to give up ourselves and give of our blessings to others.

These three stories hang together nicely. When I said this to Jesus, He looked at me with that quiet smile that said, "What did you expect?"

This whole thing is so very simple. We do not need to search for God. He is always right there in front of us. We only need to open our eyes and our hearts to His presence. He is sitting on the bench next to us.

10. Jesus continues His public ministry

I want to know Jesus better, to love Him more, and to follow Him wholeheartedly.

Monday, February 13   **(John 6:1-15)**

Another week and another seven assignments begin today.   I like Monday mornings!   I begin by organizing my material for the week, generally reading the scripture assignments and reflecting a bit about how they support the grace for the week.

Richard Rohr's meditation is particularly suitable today:

> Everything exposed to the light itself becomes light," says Ephesians 5:13. In prayer, we merely keep returning the divine gaze and we become its reflection, almost in spite of ourselves (2 Corinthians 3:18). The word "prayer" has often been trivialized by making it into a way of getting what we want. But I use "prayer" as the umbrella word for any interior journeys or practices that allow you to experience faith, hope, and love within yourself. It is not a technique for getting things, a pious exercise that somehow makes God happy, or a requirement for entry into heaven. It is much more like practicing heaven now.
>
> Such prayer, such seeing, takes away your anxiety for figuring it all out fully for yourself, or needing to be right about your formulations. At this point, God becomes more a verb than a noun, more a process than a conclusion, more an experience than a dogma, more a personal relationship than an idea. There is Someone dancing with you, and you are not afraid of making mistakes."

I am especially struck by the suggestion that "God becomes more a personal relationship than an idea…Someone dancing with you, and you are not afraid of making mistakes."   That clearly describes my appreciation of God, not just during my daily conversation, but throughout the day.   He is, more than anything else, my friend.

Maggie and I went into the library and prepared ourselves for prayer.   It was bitterly cold outside, but the sun was shining and the sky was a beautiful clear blue.   I read the passage in the Gospel of John again.

The wondrous and special acts of Jesus, generally referred to as miracles, are called signs by John.   John describes eight signs, one of which is the feeding of the multitudes reported in John 6.   This is the only such act (miracle or sign) that is common to all four of the Gospels.   Matthew, Mark, and Luke all report that Jesus feeds the five thousand shortly after learning that Herod has beheaded John the Baptist.

I composed myself in the crowd gathered to hear more from Jesus.   He was sitting a little higher up the side of the hill from us, talking quietly to His disciples.   I imagined Him somewhat sad for some reason.   Then a rumor stared making its way through the crowd, a crowd that included many who had been baptized by John the Baptist. It was said that John had been beheaded by Herod.

I, for one, expected Jesus to decry this tragedy, and to ask all of us to join Him in mourning the loss. To my surprise, and to the surprise of all around me, the disciples were suddenly walking toward us with baskets of bread and fish. We were to eat as much as we wanted. It became a celebration of life, not a mourning of death.

I managed to get close enough to Jesus to thank Him for the food and to ask about His friend John. He said the only gratitude that mattered was to live according to His gospel. He said I should celebrate John's life in the same way, by living life in the right way. Then Jesus left.

For some time now, as I work my way through these exercises, God has been my friend. I look forward to talking to Him, not only about the daily reading and the grace I have prayed for, but also about whatever else is on my mind at the particular moment. He is an easy friend to talk to, and to be with. He allows silence to deepen our relationship. He encourages me to see more, hear more, and understand more. He smiles when I get carried away with unimportant things. He hugs me when I hurt.

I want to be clear about this friendship. There are evangelical Christians who live so much in their friendship with God that they make a cup of coffee for Him when they sit down for a conversation. This is not the case for me. I have never seen God. I have never heard His voice. I know that it is not His arm that I feel around me.

I believe that the conversations I have with God are taking place inside me. I believe these exercises have opened me *interiorly* to the presence of something greater than I am. I believe that this "something greater than I am," this Higher Power, this presence, is God. God created me through the long process of evolution.

I believe He gave me the many gifts that I have used to accomplish all that I have accomplished and obtain all that I have obtained.

I believe that by surrendering my ego to the existence and power of God, of "the other," I come into contact with His presence. When I pray, meditate, and contemplate regularly and sincerely, I can achieve a meaningful dialogue with Him. I am not "creating" God through my prayers. I am humbling myself enough to recognize His presence.

Contemplative prayer, as I have come to understand it, involves engaging my imagination, along with all my senses and my greatest rational efforts, to create a mental composition. This composition is three-dimensional and it is active. It involves people, places and events in a different time and space. The more I know about that different time and space, the more real my composition will be. Thus, when I read Biblical commentators and historians, I increase my knowledge and understanding of the physical and cultural space surrounding the reports of events in the time of Jesus

Christ. Doing so enables me to compose my participation in those events more realistically. As a result of this, I gain more insight from my contemplation of the things that are said and done in that time and place.

I am seeking a grace or gift in each day's period of prayer and meditation. I want to know and love Jesus Christ more. I want to choose to follow Him. Contemplative prayer – composing myself in His presence and at His time – dramatically increases my knowledge and love of Jesus Christ. The more regularly, persistently, and sincerely I pursue contemplative prayer, the closer I come to Him. He becomes my Friend, and I believe I become His friend as well.

Tuesday, February 14 *(John 6:1-15, again)*

I played tennis again this morning, ending what seems like another long sabbatical. I enjoy the company of my tennis friends. It is clear that the physical exercise sharpens my awareness. Maggie was beside herself when I returned to the house, jumping, running and kissing me with what must be dog joy. Whatever it is, it elicited a great deal of human joy in me.

We prayed in the library, reflecting more on the reading from John's gospel. We had dinner with close friends last night, including Deacon Dan and Sister Joan. Dan and I talked about my view of Jesus feeding the five thousand as a wake honoring the life of John the Baptist. Dan was not convinced, suggesting, among other things, that I may be assuming too much in concluding that the news of John's death was only made known to Jesus when he came down from His prayers and encountered the large crowd.

Dan emphasized the Eucharistic references that can be found in the story of feeding the five thousand. As I thought about it this morning, it seemed that the conversation with Dan was just another component of the grace I have been praying for, which is to better know and understand Christ.

Today is the thirtieth anniversary of my marriage to Sallie Ann. It began badly when, after saying good night to our guests, I fell asleep without helping Sallie Ann clean up after dinner and close up the house for the night. I had been inconsiderate and selfish. Sallie Ann was hurt. It was a sad way to begin this special day.

Wednesday, February 15 *(Mark 8:27-30)*

Maggie and I came down to the library very early this morning. Happily, Sallie Ann and I resolved our differences last night. She will give me my ten thousandth second chance to be more considerate in the future.

I have a plane to catch at noon, one that will take me to Washington for the Woodstock board meeting. I am excited about the trip. I know it will be another three days of spiritual growth.

In the scriptural passage assigned for this morning, Mark 8:27-30, Jesus asks His disciples who people say that He is, and then asks them who they think He is.

I composed myself among the disciples. I heard the questions, and thought I would say something. Before I could, however, Peter said that we all thought Jesus was the Messiah. I felt two things.

First, I was consoled by the idea that Peter considered me one of the group he represented. I was among the "we" that included the small handful of men called personally by Jesus to follow Him. I reflected on how disappointed I had been after my interview with Jesus on the shore of Galilee, when I was not invited into the select few. So today, I belong. It is a wonderful feeling.

Second, I am struck with how human Christ seems when He asks this question "What do the people think about me?" Somehow, I cannot imagine Christ asking this except while He was incarnate.

Thursday, February 16   (Mark 8:27-30, again)

It is now early afternoon. I spent the morning with Gap, and will see him again later today in a committee meeting and tonight at the board dinner. Before turning to a repetition of the prayer and meditation from yesterday, I want to record some thoughts about the long and wonderful morning with Gap.

I shared the first three months of journaling with Gap before he and I met just after Thanksgiving. Gap helped me understand more clearly what Sister Joan had been saying with respect to the way Ignatius intended these exercises were to be done each day. Knowing we would have an opportunity to discuss my progress, I sent Gap my journal entries for November and December.

Among the many helpful comments and suggestions he made this morning, the one that stands out in my mind is Gap's emphasis on my need for humility. Gap believes that these exercises are helping me find it, albeit slowly and often, it seems, in fits and starts. Some of what Gap said was hard for me to hear, just as it is hard for me to live in the way I know I should, and act in the way my conversations with God make clear I should act. As I rode the elevator upstairs after our long breakfast, I was almost overcome by the presence of the Holy Spirit. Gap makes me aware of God's reality in my life.

I prayed for the grace of knowing Christ more, and in a more personal way. I prayed to know how I would answer His questions. The gift of that grace comes through more and more each day during my prayers and meditations.

Friday, February 17   (Mark 8:31-33)

I attended Mass this morning at the Ignatian chapel at Holy Trinity Church in Georgetown. The celebrant quoted a wonderful poem or prayer from Pedro Arrupe, the former head of the Jesuits:[73]

> *Nothing is more practical than finding God, than*
> *falling in Love in a quite absolute, final way.*
> *What you are in love with,*
> *what seizes your imagination, will affect everything.*
> *It will decide what will get you out of bed in the morning,*
> *what you do with your evenings,*
> *how you spend your weekends,*
> *what you read, whom you know,*
> *what breaks your heart,*
> *and what amazes you with joy and gratitude.*
> *Fall in Love, stay in love,*
> *and it will decide everything.*

This truly spoke to me during Mass, and does so even more now as I read it again after several hours of meetings with my fellow directors on the Board of Woodstock. I am on the plane, flying back to Jacksonville. It feels as though the Holy Spirit has been deep within me every minute of every day since I left for Washington three days ago. I am exhausted from joy.

I used the first hour of the flight to pray and meditate on the passage from Mark 8:31-33. With some difficulty, I composed myself standing next to Peter when Jesus rebuked him, saying "Get behind me, Satan!" Just hearing those words hurt me. I saw how much it hurt Peter. I experienced some of the sting, embarrassment, and humiliation that Peter felt. Then I thought of how remarkable it is that Peter only emerged from this (and his other difficult moments with Jesus) stronger and more committed.

What a remarkable blessing it is to have these periodic encounters with the Jesuit community at Georgetown. I am in the "pink cloud" that often follows me around after either the Arrupe or the Woodstock board meetings. This week, the experience began Wednesday afternoon, when Gap and I discussed the possibility of bringing the Ignatian tradition into the Georgetown Executive MBA program.

This meeting was followed by Mass in the basement of Jesuit House, and a fabulous conversation during dinner with six amazing Jesuit fellows from all around the world. The ride continued Thursday in the morning meeting with Gap, followed by the ad-

[73] According to Wikipedia, "Fr. Pedro Arrupe, S.J. (November 14, 1907 – February 5, 1991) was the twenty eighth Superior General (1965–83) of the Society of Jesus. He was born in Bilbao, Spain."

vancement committee meeting, and ending with the board dinner and a wonderful speech from Father Tom Michel about interfaith efforts.

Mass this morning and the discussion about strategy at the board meeting simply tied the whole experience together with a bow.   Thank you, God, for all of this.

Saturday, February 18   *(Mark 8:31-33, again)*

Sallie Ann asked that I sit with her in the family room to watch the Whitney Houston funeral this morning.   Maggie and I had a wonderful reunion when I came home last night.   With the exception of tennis this morning, she has not left my side since morning.   We prayed together in the library first, and then at the garden bench.   The morning was absolutely perfect.   We brought the computer from the library into the family room, where I am sitting with the family, writing in this journal while listening to an incredibly moving religious service take place in Newark.   We have been moved to tears more than once.

Earlier, while still in the library, I composed myself once again standing with Peter. When Peter first called Jesus aside to speak to Him about all He would suffer, ending in such a tragic death, Mark describes Peter's words as a "rebuke" of Christ.   It was clear to me that this is not what Peter intended.   I thought about Joseph and Mary returning to the temple in Jerusalem after Jesus had been missing for three days. Their scolding of Jesus, while real, was only evidence of the deeper reality of their profound love for their Son.

Peter's words may have sounded somewhat like a rebuke, but behind the words was a profound and loving concern for the safety and well-being of Christ.   Likewise, Jesus loved Peter.   His statement "Get behind me, Satan" was not directed at the man He loved.   I think Jesus was referring to the temptation of some relief from pain and suffering.   Jesus was, after all, incarnate.   He could be tempted.   In snapping as He did at Peter, He achieved three things:

- First, He spoke to Satan, the ultimate tempter in the story.
- Second, He buttressed His own strength in resisting temptation.
- Third, He taught Peter (and all of us) the important lesson that we will be tempted, and that we must resist that temptation.

I prayed for the grace of greater love and understanding of Jesus.   As always, the gift of that grace was present.   It was available to me.   I felt some tangible inner peace as I accepted the gift.   Gratitude slipped easily into my conversation with God.

Sunday, February 19   (Summary)

Maggie and I came down early this morning to sit in front of the fire in the family room to pray.   God's presence was palpable.   I started the morning by thanking Him for the many gifts I have received this week, all of which added to the grace of greater knowledge and understanding of Jesus.   I read through my journal entries for the week, and came away with a deeper appreciation of my friendship with God. We walked outside to talk. Maggie, as always, was delighted.

I told Him about Mass last night, about how proud I am of Sallie Ann in the choir and how happy I felt greeting and being greeted by my many CRHP friends. I hugged Sister Joan, Deacon Dan, and Father Steven. God smiled in that way He does when He already knows what I am telling Him.

I reviewed my week with Him, excitedly pointing out the high points. I told Him about the chapel in the basement of Jesuit House; Dahlgren chapel, located behind Healy Hall; the chapel in the crypt under Copley Hall; and Ignatian chapel, on the hill behind Holy Trinity. I described the architecture of each of these wonderful places. I told Him how excited I am about the spiritual spaces and places we will be visiting in Idaho and Italy. I told Him about my love for the Jesuits. I told Him my body was beginning to feel full of joy. I said that I could, at any moment, lift off the board walk and float above the garden and the lagoon.

When we came back inside to pray and to write these thoughts in this journal, I knew that no words could sufficiently describe my feelings. I feel renewed. I taste the Eucharist from last night and Friday morning and Wednesday night. Thank you, God, for all of this.

11. Jesus continues His public ministry

I want to know Jesus better, to love Him more, and to follow Him wholeheartedly.

Monday, February 20   (Matthew 8:23-27)

It took a long time to organize my material this morning, primarily because Sister Joan gave me assignments for two weeks. As has become my custom, I read through all the scriptural passages for the period. The grace I am seeking is to better know Jesus and to deepen my relationship with Him.

The prayer reading today is from Matthew 8:23-27, in which the evangelist gives us an account of a storm sweeping over Jesus and His disciples while they are out on the lake in a boat. In response to the fear expressed by His disciples, Jesus famously asks them "You of little faith, why are you so afraid?" Christ then calms the wind and waves, causing His disciples to ask in amazement "What kind of man is this?"

We then walked down to the bench. Maggie and I opened our session with a prayer both praising God and asking for the grace of greater knowledge and understanding of Jesus and His ministry. It was bitter cold, more than thirty degrees colder than yesterday! As I walked along the bulkhead, it was easy to compose myself among the disciples on the lake in the cold wind and whitecaps.

I became afraid, even as I sensed their fear. I felt the rebuke of Jesus when He be-littled my fear with the phrase I have heard hundreds of times in my life, "You of little faith." I walked back to the library embarrassed by my weakness.

Most often, my absence of faith has shown through when I am overly anxious about something I have to do, like the speech last week at UNF. Often, I walk into a room of strangers feeling so insecure that I hide behind arrogance. As I reflect on those occasions, it occurs to me that in virtually every one of these instances, my entire fo-cus was on myself. I was not interested in or thinking about others. I was certainly not immersed in gratitude for the numerous gifts that created the very opportunity to speak to or even walk into a room of people. The question might just as easily have been, "You of little **humility**, why are you so afraid?"

Tuesday, February 21   (Matthew 8:23-27, again)

Standing in the tennis court earlier this morning, I was once again overcome with the grace of this place. Beautiful clear skies, the waves breaking loudly all along the beach, birds sweeping across the sky, both alone and in groups, and fun tennis with happy friends – all of these wonderful gifts given for no reason whatsoever. I am alive again for another day in paradise!

Maggie is with me now in front of the fire in the family room. I prayed again for greater knowledge and understanding of Christ and His ministry. As I reflected for a second time on the passage from Matthew, I recalled the many times I have heard the phrase "ye of little faith." It is used at least twice more in the Gospels (Luke 12 and Matthew 14), and it was one of our favorite phrases in the business world. We used it whenever we accomplished something even slightly difficult in the face of doubt. Of course, most of the time, the doubt was our own!

I composed myself on the boat with the disciples. It was cold. The wind was blow-ing. In my fear, I was tempted to jump out of the boat, but I hesitate. Hesitation is another way to think about doubt. When I hesitate to take a leap of faith, I do so be-cause I am in doubt. When I hesitate to declare innocence or guilt, it is because the decision is not clear beyond all reasonable doubt. The dictionary defines doubt as a status between belief and disbelief.

How much of my long journey in the desert of unbelief was the result of doubt? What happened in 2007 to remove that doubt? As I reflect on these questions now, it is clear that I surrendered something four years ago. I overcame doubt just enough to be open to answers when I asked the big questions.

I did not take a leap toward faith. Rather, I chose to take a small step away from unbelief. I had to first accept the possibility of Christ, and only then could I whittle away at the doubt that had ensnared me during the forty years since my excommuni-cation. For me, the big challenge was acceptance. It was becoming open to a pos-sibility. It was not a bold leap of faith or an act involving great effort.

I did not make my faith happen.   I let it happen.

Ash Wednesday, February 22   (Luke 5:17-26)

I read the assigned passage from Luke 5:17-26 when I returned from teaching my class at UNF late last night.   I want it on the record that a three-hour class at night is a bridge too far for this 67-year-old!

Maggie and I are back in the library, which is a better place to pray.   It is substantially more isolated than the family room.   The south garden, with its fountain and rill, are just outside the door.   It is the place where we have prayed most mornings for the last five months.

I composed myself in the room with the Pharisees and teachers of the law.   We had a chance to talk among ourselves before Jesus arrived.   These men were very knowledgeable about the laws of our Jewish faith.   They were meticulous about the fine points of strict observance, including precisely what to wear, what to eat, when to pray and fast, and when and how to end each period of prayer and fasting.

I have been around people like this many times in my life, both in various religious settings and in the business world.   I have to confess that I chafed against strict observance of rules and regulations for as long as I can remember.   This is in stark contrast to Sallie Ann, who meticulously follows instructions and directions, much less rules and laws.   Sometimes I argue that my independence is based on a desire to focus on the big things, and not to bother with the small details.   In fact, I acknowledge that my problem with authority is just another manifestation of my lack of humility.   It is a challenge.

Back in the room with the Pharisees, Jesus has begun to preach.   I love it that the first thing Jesus did was forgive the paralytic his sins.   This same passage was assigned on September 20.   I want to repeat part of my journal entry that day:

> It occurs to me that forgiveness is perhaps the first crucial step in the healing process.   While I have never considered the possibility that physical ailments could be helped by forgiveness, I am now persuaded that mental anguish and depression require forgiveness.   Not only is it critical to let go of resentment by forgiving others, but it is even more important that we forgive ourselves for our own wrong-doing.   The adage that we are to "hate the sin, but love the sinner," is perhaps most important when applied to our own actions.   This may have something to do with the distinction between shame and guilt, though I am not sure.
>
> I am also reminded again and again that our faith requires us to get outside ourselves.   It is not a faith governed by rules, regulations, and restrictions.   The Pharisees and law givers said that Jesus did not have the authority to forgive.   They said that tax collectors were to be avoided.   They said that lepers were unclean.   Yet Christ acted in defiance of all of that, not simply to chal-

lenge the old system, but to demonstrate that the new gospel of "loving thy neighbor" was the key to salvation. We cannot be Christians without a core commitment to help the poor, sick, and outcast.

These thoughts accurately reflect my thinking today. Before ending my prayers with an Our Father, I talked to my Friend about the beginning of Lent. I will Lector at Mass tonight. I asked for His grace that I do a good job. For a variety of reasons, this Lenten season feels different to me. I am much closer to God and to my spiritual core.

Thursday, February 23   (Luke 5:17-26, again)

Maggie and I prayed in the library after tennis. I entered easily into conversation with my Friend. We talked about forgiveness.

Luke tells us that Jesus forgave the paralytic after seeing that he had faith. This is a very simple bargain. We believe. He forgives.

Stated differently, the gift is given. We only need to accept it. We need to say yes. God said He stands behind His decision about free will, but He is amazed at the number of people who choose not to say yes. When I reminded Him that it had taken a long time for me to accept Him, He reminded me that He knew.

At the end of our prayers, I said to Maggie that, like the people in the passage, we had seen remarkable things today!

Friday, February 24   (Matthew 14:22-33)

God was very present in the library this morning. In fact, His presence was intense throughout the house. It may be more accurate to say that we were much more aware of that presence simply because all the furniture had been removed from the family room in anticipation of setting up theatre seating for a presentation by Father Steven tonight. Whatever the cause, we began prayer this morning mindful of the Holy Spirit.

After reading Matthew 14:22-33 again, I composed myself in the boat with the disciples, out on the lake as the storm violently rocked the boat back and forth. We were already frightened, long before we saw Jesus walking toward us on the water.

Several times during the past several months, I have walked along the beach after reading various passages involving the Sea of Galilee. My compositions of those scenes took on a remarkable level of reality. The images I formed in my mind this morning drew from those on the beach. Rain blew against my face, and a cold wind whipped the surface of the sea into roiling lather. The people walking along the shore were moving in and out of visibility, lost in the driving rain and low clouds.

So I was also alarmed to see one of these people walk out on the water toward our boat. The closer the figure came to us, the more it looked like Jesus. As Matthew reports, we were all terrified. Peter, by now often assuming the role of our leader, called out to Jesus, asking that He prove Himself by causing Peter to walk on water as well. Peter started out well, but began to sink when the wind frightened him. Christ proved Himself to all of us in the boat by lifting Peter up. As He did so, we heard Him say again, "You of little faith, why did you doubt?"

It requires little reflection for me to admit that I have too little faith to get out of the boat in a stormy sea. I suspect I would even be afraid to grab a life preserver.

Saturday, February 25   *(Matthew 14:22-33, again)*

Last night, Sallie Ann and I hosted Father Steven's speech for my CRHP brothers and their wives. He showed us a movie about confession. It was a great evening, filled with both the Holy Spirit and the joy of genuine fellowship. I did come away reconciled to the idea that I need to seek reconciliation more frequently.

After tennis, I returned to the library with Maggie. I had barely begun my conversation with God before I was once again in the boat on that stormy sea. We talked about faith and courage. I brought up the times when I failed to "walk my talk"; times when I made bad choices.

Is weakness in the face of temptation the same thing as the absence of courage? Is it evidence of little faith? It feels different to me. I recognize the role that ego and self-interest play in sin. It requires strength to get past self, but I am not persuaded that courage or faith is involved.

My bad choices were not made out of ignorance. I knew what I was doing. I did not choose self because of something I did not understand. It was weakness, not ignorance that caused my failure.

So what about faith? Would I be stronger in my determination not to sin if I had greater faith?

What is clear to me is that I sin less when I am close to God. It is as though self seeks to drive a wedge between my faith and my actions. Selfishness finds any crack or space that I leave, regardless of whether that space is created by the passage of time between prayers or by the distance I allow to develop between me and those who love me in my faith-life.

Sunday, February 26   (Summary)

The assignment today, as has become customary, is to review and repeat the week. I am sitting in the library alone, as Maggie is still upstairs with Sallie Ann and the rest of the family. I have just returned from the 7:30 Mass, where I read the first reading, a passage from Genesis.

This has been a Lector-filled week, including the first reading at the 7 PM Mass on Ash Wednesday (from Joel) and the second reading last night (from Peter). I credit these exercises with what feels like continued improvement in my proclamation of the Word. My daily conversations with God provide a solid foundation for reading the scriptures aloud to the congregation.

The grace I prayed for this week was greater knowledge, love, and understanding of Jesus Christ. I believe my prayers have been answered. We began and ended the week with readings from Matthew, both of which involved storms in the Sea of Galilee and the admonition from Jesus to His disciples, "You of little faith." Between these bookends from Matthew, we read the passage from Luke about the paralytic passed down to the presence of Jesus through a hole in the roof. Jesus healed the man by forgiving his sins.

It occurred to me this morning that accepting forgiveness requires strong faith. My new faith teaches me that I was forgiven when I was baptized, and I have been forgiven each time I confessed my sins since then. Father Steven talked at length about forgiveness during our evening together Friday night. Yet I sometimes feel something very different from the cleanliness that "forgiven" implies. I feel shame and guilt and unworthiness. When I mentioned this during my conversation with God this morning, He smiled and said, "You of little faith."

12. Jesus continues His public ministry

I want to know Jesus better, to love Him more, and to follow Him wholeheartedly.

Monday, February 27   (Matthew 10:1-16)

We read the passage in Matthew 10:1-16 describing the call of the twelve apostles by Jesus. In this passage, Jesus makes it very clear to the apostles that they are called to preach to Jews, not Gentiles or Samaritans. Jesus instructs them to go out without provisions, including any cash to pay for food and shelter. If the people to whom they are preaching will not feed and shelter them, the apostles are meant to move on to another house or town.

I composed myself among the twelve and reflected on these instructions. I had not been praying long before I found myself in a little town on the western border of Germany, with France on the other side of the valley. It was 1965, not the first century. The task at hand, however, was very much the same. Especially during those first several months, before I learned enough German to get around, I felt like a sheep among wolves.

Matthew ends the passage quoting Jesus telling the apostles to be as "shrewd as snakes and as innocent as doves." On more than one occasion in Idar Oberstein and Neustadt, I *shrewdly* worked my way into an apartment or house, overcoming the resistance of the hausfrau by feigning innocence!

It is uncanny how vivid these memories of Germany were this morning. I have not thought about this aspect of my mission experience in decades, yet once the recollections were triggered by the scripture, I was able to see the faces of some of the first people I met almost fifty years ago. Our instructions as Mormon missionaries were very much the same as those Christ gave His apostles.

Specifically, we were told not to waste time with people who did not show a keen interest in accepting the Mormon message during the very first meeting. The leaders of the mission referred to the process of befriending people and establishing bonds with them as "fellowshipping." They correctly assumed that we were so lonely and afraid that we would use repeated meetings with friends as excuses not to do the hard part of proselytizing. We were told not to have meals with those who had not yet committed to baptism.

Later, I would learn that our pastoral duties required us to spend quite a bit of time with the members of our congregations, most of whom were recent converts. Assuming we met with three or four families a week, it was still not possible to get around to everyone even once a year. Now, to be truthful, there were members of the congregation we wanted to visit, and there were members we tried rather hard to avoid.

By instructing His apostles to preach to the "lost sheep of Israel," Jesus was giving them a very difficult task. Presumably, many of the Jews the apostles needed to reach were quite serious about their Jewish identity and beliefs. They did not consider themselves "lost."

Moreover, conversion to this revolutionary new movement brought with it banishment from family and from the familiar social structure of the community. I assume everyone in most communities in Judaea and Galilee at that time knew everyone else. They knew when visitors called on neighbors. They would certainly know when someone in the community became involved in a religious reform movement.

In contrast, most of the people we encountered in Germany in the mid-1960s lived very isolated lives. Much of this certainly had to do with the dislocations both during and after the war. I am sure that some of my impressions at that time were based on too little real contact with the German families.

As I think back on the experience, most of my "friendships" had to be at the most superficial level possible. That was certainly the case among those who chose not to listen to our message. Both because of the mission admonition against fellowshipping, and because we were Americans, most people showed us very little of their lives.

Being American cut both ways. On the one hand, we were the occupiers. Literally, American troops occupied the part of Germany where I worked. Our tanks and jeeps and troop carriers rumbled through the streets every day. Deep down, the Germans regarded us the same way we or any people would regard the victorious occupation forces after a war.

On the other hand, many Germans wanted nothing more than to go to America. In every possible way, they wanted to be like the Americans. What little success we had converting Germans must have been at least partially the result of this love for America.

Tuesday, February 28   (Matthew 10:1-16, again)

As I prayed this morning, I found myself moving around among several spiritual places. Part of the morning, I was with the apostles in Israel, two thousand years ago. Then I would be proclaiming the word as a Lector right here at Our Lady Star of the Sea, five days ago. Then I was trudging behind my mission companion as we walked up the five floors of one apartment building after another, fifty years ago. In all three of these "mental environments," I was proclaiming the gospel of Jesus Christ. There were numerous similarities in these settings, one imagined and the other two quite real.

One of the strong commonalties was my strong desire to "do a good job," maybe even to outperform others. I sought the approval of both my superiors and my colleagues, and in every case, I struggled with my ego. At times, I was proclaiming for my glory, not His. I did not (and do not) want pride and self-promotion to corrupt my work.

Wednesday, February 29   (John 2:13-22)

As usual, I read the assigned passage from John's gospel last night when I came home from teaching at UNF. The idea of Jesus making a whip and driving people and animals from the temple is powerful.

Prayer began in the library, and moved outside to the bench where the day was as warm and sunny as any we have had all winter. I composed myself in the temple among those selling animals for sacrifice. The words of Jesus were stinging. I felt humiliated and guilty at the same time. In my mind, the temple market became a metaphor for the commercialism of modern life. We have been given stewardship of the earth as a gift and a responsibility. We have been given numerous other gifts to help us steward the earth and its resources. Yet we have turned this extraordinary gift into a market where everything is bought and sold with the objective of maximizing short term gain.

Thursday, March 1   (John 2:13-22, again)

Sallie Ann and I went to Grandparents Day at Discovery School, where Alexis and Alison Robbins, our granddaughters, are in the second grade. I am late, therefore, in writing in this journal. Before turning again to Jesus in the temple, I want to note how good it feels to be a grandparent. What a gift! I cannot exaggerate the happiness that I felt when each of these wonderful young girls hugged me and literally jumped for joy when we entered the room. The feelings are precisely opposite of those evoked by the mental picture of Jesus condemning me for my avarice and disrespect in the temple.

Friday, March 2   (Luke 6:6-11)

It was very early when I prayed this morning. Sallie Ann and I are flying most of the day, from Jacksonville to Chicago and then on to Seattle. We have traveled very little together in the past four years, which makes me somewhat sad.

For the first 25 years of our marriage, we traveled extensively all around the world. Of course, for most of my career, my business required that I travel. Sallie Ann tried to come with me whenever possible, particularly when the itinerary included the great cities of Europe and North America. At one time or another, we had apartments in New York, London, and Milan.

All of that came to a sudden stop when I got sick in 2007. Since then, we have traveled to New York and Washington a couple of times together, but never for more than two or three days. She very seldom comes with me when I go to Woodstock board meetings. Part of this agoraphobia is the result of my cardiac condition, or, at least, Sallie Ann's fear that I will have some kind of cardiac event. Part of it must have something to do with a certain amount of travel exhaustion. Frankly, we have become so involved in our new community that we have neither the time nor the desire to be away for long.

The reading this morning from the gospel of Luke involves Jesus healing a man at the synagogue on the Sabbath. I composed myself in the synagogue with the Pharisees and teachers of the law. We had been called together for the specific purpose of trapping Jesus in a violation of the law. I suppose one could call it "Biblical entrapment." Jesus put the questions to us:

> [W]hich is lawful on the Sabbath: to do good, or to do evil, to save life, or to destroy it?

These questions answered themselves. I looked around at the group of pious religious leaders. I was amazed at how unimportant the questions were to them. They had already decided that Jesus was a threat and that they would find any excuse get rid of Him.

How often do we see that today? Almost all of our public debate on truly important issues is useless precisely because each side has made up their mind. They will not, or cannot, even consider obvious logic presented by the other side. How often do I listen without hearing, or look without seeing?

Jesus put it so simply. Do good, or do evil. Save life, or destroy it. These are not difficult choices.

Saturday, March 3 (Luke 6:6-11, again)

We arrived in Seattle last night exhausted. I read this morning what I wrote yesterday, lamenting the fact that we travel so little any more. Well, one of the reasons is that much of travel is simply not fun! In fact, it is awful. I was repeatedly reminded yesterday how much I detest long lines and crowded places. I had forgotten how hard it is to sleep, or even sit, comfortably in three-across coach seats that do not recline and have very little room for knees. I could go on.

I had also forgotten how beautiful Sallie Ann is when she is in the company of her sons. We had not seen Will for a long time, and the reunion was, therefore, especially sweet. To a large extent, I guess, travel is just the opposite of falling off a high building. In that case, the trite line is that the fall is not so bad, but the arrival hurts. In the case of travel, the journey is painful, but the arrival is a joy.

I prayed this morning after reading the passage from Luke again. I put myself in the place of the man with the shriveled hand. I was frightened when Jesus told me to "get up and stand in front of everyone." All my life, people had stared at my hand and mocked me for it. Most of the time, I hid my deformed hand.

Now this strange man asked me stand in front of the leaders of my synagogue and let them see how disfigured I was. I could see that the Pharisees and lawgivers were not interested in the simple questions put to them by Jesus. They were angry and intent upon doing Him harm. Then Jesus told me to stretch out my hand. It was completely healed. I could not have cared less that Jesus healed my hand on a Sabbath. My hand was restored!

The people at the margins of life do not care about the motives of those who help them, or the day of the week that they are helped. The important thing is that good is done, not evil. A life is saved, not destroyed.

I prayed this morning for the grace of greater knowledge of and love for Jesus Christ. The power of His presence is all around me as I reflect on the simple message of His gospel. Do good, not evil.

Sunday, March 4 (Summary)

Sallie Ann and I are in Seattle. We have just returned to the hotel following Mass at St. James Cathedral. The service was one of the best spiritual experiences I can remember, and is worth describing here.

In the first place, the Cathedral itself was architecturally wonderful. On the outside, the architect chose an unfortunate light-brown brick for the skin of a building that, aside from two dramatic bell towers, shows little sign of majesty.

However, the interior spaces were fabulous, beginning with a central altar placed under a glass-topped dome that literally lit the altar from heaven. The east-to-west axis consisted of two barrel vaulted naves of equal length. The vaults were coffered. At the end of each nave, organ pipes rose all the way to the top of the vault. The north-to-south axis consisted of identical apses, each ending with wonderful stained glass windows.

We sat in the second row back from the altar in the west nave, right behind chairs reserved for the readers and the cantor. Behind us, against the organ wall, sat a 70-person choir wearing simple white robes. When the Eucharistic ministers, the readers, and the cantor proceeded into the altar space, we saw that they too were wearing simple white robes.

Obviously, I watched and listened to the readers with great interest. They both read with strong voices and clear passion. I liked the use of music and long silences. For example, after saying "The word of the Lord," each reader bowed his head and waited in silence for about 15 seconds. Then the music would start again, and the reader would leave the ambo. Even though there were two priests and a deacon, the second reader read the petitions. Again, he read with passion and clarity.

I have saved the best for last. From the very first note sung at the beginning of the procession, the choir was simply magical. Their voices filled the large cathedral, both during several solo performances and when all 70 sang as one. When the celebrants proceeded out at the end of Mass, hand bells were rung by two men bringing up the rear. Sallie Ann and I, along with our son Will, were left in a state of awe.

What a way to end a wonderful week! I am writing in this journal after a somewhat frustrating effort to pray in the way I have grown accustomed to praying each morning. The hotel offered few opportunities for quiet solitude. When I did finally find a place to sit down, I nodded off, in spite of the commotion around me. I hope I can find better alternatives during the rest of this week, not to mention our trip in May.

13. Jesus continues His public life

I want to know Jesus better, to love Him more, and to follow Him wholeheartedly.

Monday, March 5   **(John 11:1-44)**

Sallie Ann and Will left the hotel to do what mothers and sons do. I took advantage of the time alone to read the passage from John 11 and to pray. In my fantasy, Jesus walked with me from the hotel down to the fish market looking out on Puget Sound. It was cold and windy, but a clear day with blue skies and an incredible sense of the divine. We talked about friendship and family, using the siblings Mary, Martha, and Lazarus as a starting point. The sisters feature rather prominently in the gospels of both Luke and John.

I told Jesus about the close bonds of friendship that exist between Sallie Ann and her sister, Mary Lou. I said these two sisters had passed the concept and practice of friendship on to their children. Sallie Ann's sons, Rob and Will, have an easy, comfortable friendship that has survived decades of distant physical separation. Likewise, Mary Lou's children, Michael and Sallie Ann (named after her aunt), are close to each other.

Sadly, I do not have this close friendship with any of my siblings. Jesus said the gift of friendship had been given to me and my brothers and sisters. Perhaps we felt that gift at our sibling reunion two years ago.

I have always regarded the story told by John about the three siblings from Bethany to be an account of the miracle of Jesus raising Lazarus from the dead. That is certainly a major part of the story. Our conversation walking up and down the hilly streets of Seattle this morning was about friendship and love, and the new life in faith that comes from saying yes. The faith of the two sisters in the story was an outgrowth of the love that they felt for Jesus. He gave them that grace. They said yes, accepting His love and offering Him all the love they could give in return.

When our conversation ended, I left Jesus at the fish market. I was overcome with gratitude. I walked back to the hotel in a state of bliss.

Tuesday, March 6   **(John 11:1-44, again)**

Last night, our last in Seattle, was filled with more than a little drama. We rushed Sallie Ann to the emergency room at Swedish Hospital after she developed symptoms that might have been the result of any number of frightening conditions. It ended well, but only after hours of tests and trauma.

We are now in Boise, Idaho, where we will have lunch with my extended family tomorrow. Sallie Ann is exploring the shops in what passes for the old part of downtown. I have just finished praying for the grace of acceptance. Specifically, I hope that tomorrow, I will be a better brother, nephew, and cousin to all of my relatives than I have been for the past half century. I will only do that by accepting them for who they are. I must accept the love and friendship they will be showing me, simply by their traveling to Boise to meet this long-distant relative.

Wednesday, March 7   (Luke 7:1-10)

When I read the passage from Luke this morning, I realized that the Centurion's message to Jesus was part of the prayer we say before taking communion at every Mass:

> *Lord, don't trouble yourself, for I do not deserve to have you come under my roof. That is why I did not even consider myself worthy to come to you. But say the word, and my servant will be healed.*

It is a statement of faith in the power of the Eucharist to heal our souls. Thomas Aquinas wrote a similar prayer:

> *Almighty and ever-living God, I approach the sacrament of your only-begotten Son, our Lord Jesus Christ.*

> *I come sick to the doctor of life, unclean to the fountain of mercy, blind to the radiance of eternal light, and poor and needy to the Lord of heaven and earth.*

> *Lord, in your great generosity, heal my sickness, wash away my defilement, enlighten my blindness, enrich my poverty, and clothe my nakedness.*

> *May I receive the Bread of angels, the King of kings and Lord of lords, with humble reverence, with the purity and faith, the repentance and love, and the determined purpose that will help to bring me to salvation. May I receive the sacrament of the Lord's body and blood, and its reality and power.*

> *Kind God, may I receive the body of your only-begotten Son, our Lord Jesus Christ, born from the womb of the Virgin Mary, and so be received into His mystical body and be numbered among His members.*

> *Loving Father, as on my earthly pilgrimage I now receive your beloved Son under the veil of a sacrament, may I one day see him face to face in glory, who lives and reigns with you for ever and ever. Amen.*

This powerful prayer moves me to a deep level of "connectedness." The Centurion had so much faith in Jesus that he did not even have to see Him to know that his servant would be healed simply by Jesus saying the word. Aquinas takes this further. We are not only unworthy to have Jesus enter our house, but we are also "sick…unclean… blind…poor and needy." But "only say the word," only offer the grace, and we will say yes and be healed. Why is it so hard to say yes? Why is my soul so often in pain?

Thursday, March 8   *(Luke 7:1-10, again)*

My prayers were unsettled this morning. Lunch with thirty distant relatives yesterday was both happy and sad. I battled less than successfully with my ego. Instead of getting outside of self, I tripped over my self-importance. I felt a genuine connection to my brother and sister, Wayne and Connie, as well as to dad's siblings, Ralph and Miriam. However, I had never met most of the cousins, and I treated them like strangers. Worse than that, I acted like a professor speaking to new students, or a guest speaker at a Rotary Club lunch.

The worst moment of the lunch occurred after I gave an incredibly long "brief introduction" of myself. I spoke last, after all of the other family members had said something like "I am married to so and so, we have four children, and we live in this town."

I talked at length about the importance of family. I told the story of my business career. I gave an account of my cardiac problems. Finally, I touched on a few of the major issues in the world today.

Then I announced that I was prepared to take questions!

I wish I were making this up. Even Aunt Miriam, who loves everyone in the family and was delighted that our visit caused the family to come together, was in a state of shock.

Sallie Ann and I had dinner last night with Wayne, Connie, and Wayne's daughter Veronica. It was difficult. Once again, I was distant and self-centered.

So I prayed this morning for forgiveness. I composed myself as the Centurion. Most of my life, I have been a "man under authority." I have ordered others to do my bidding. My image of myself is that of a kind and caring boss, interested in the common good or, even better, in the specific good of my subordinates. However, I doubt that image would be familiar to many others. Like my family yesterday, I suspect most of my subordinates saw me as an imperious, self-important man, one whose ambition had propelled him to positions of leadership.

I asked God to help me understand the limits of ambition. I asked for the grace of humility. I asked that He say the word, so that my soul would be healed and that I would know relief from this terrible pain of pride.

Friday, March 9   (Matthew 17:1-9)

I awakened this morning still talking to God about dinner last night with Sister Kim, her sister Debbie, and Sisters Janet and Margie from the monastery. The highlight of an amazing evening was Sister Kim giving each of us gifts, most of which were connected to Father John. My gifts included his favorite stole, a gold and silver crucifix he wore on a chain around his neck, a fossilized shell "heart" from the hill country of Texas, and an assortment of poems that he especially loved. I almost cried when Sister Kim gave these gifts to me at dinner, and I did cry when I read the poems while wearing the stole in my room last night.

I read the passage from Matthew 17 describing the transfiguration of Jesus. Mark's account of the same event was assigned six months ago (September 22), during the early days of preparation. I wrote then that I felt excluded when Jesus asked only Peter, James, and John to accompany Him on Mount Hermon.

This morning was much different. I composed myself with Jesus and His disciples walking on the mountain path. Father John was with me as we walked behind the others. I talked to him about the stole and the poems and Sister Kim. I told him all about these exercises and my baptism and proclaiming the word at Mass and the Jesuits. We talked about politics and the conservatives in our Florida parish. After a while, he said he did not recall me talking so much. He introduced me to Jesus, and Jesus said that He and I had been friends for some time.

This incredible conversation continued as I walked outside the hotel into a crisp, sunshiny, cold morning. In all of the amazing periods of contemplation that I have experienced over the past few months, I cannot remember anything quite like this morning. Father John and Jesus and I were comfortable together, laughing and crying and sharing each moment. I kept thanking them both. They both accepted my gratitude in a warm and easy way.

I came back to the hotel on a cloud, said the Our Father, and very reluctantly eased back into the present.

I am writing a second time today in this journal. After breakfast at the Bait Shop Café in Lewiston, we drove southeast, up onto the Camas Prairie that was once the land of the Nez Pierce Indians. Sister Kim explained that the little towns in this vast flat prairie were located precisely eight miles apart along the trail, which is now US Highway 95. Eight miles was the distance stage coach horses could travel between stops for water.

The first of these towns we encountered after turning south away from the Clearwater River was Lapwai, the present home of the Nez Pierce tribal council and casino. The town largely consisted of a depressing collection of run down trailer houses, a very sad reminder of the tragic fate of this proud tribe once led by Chief Joseph.

We continued on the highway, passing historic signs noting the sites of various events in the journey of Lewis and Clark. The highway climbed what is called the Winchester incline, rising from an elevation of 700 feet above sea level, in Lewiston, to 3,700 feet above sea level, at the top of the incline. When we reach the top, we drove through the town of Winchester, which marks the beginning of the prairie named after the camassia plant.

Cottonwood was the third small town after Winchester, 24 miles from the western edge of the grassy, flat prairie that stretches all the way from the Clearwater Range to the Salmon Range. Cottonwood itself is a tiny place with a population of less than 900 people. It is locally famous as the home of both a men's prison and our destination, the St. Gertrude Monastery.

I am writing this description of the trip to the Monastery in this journal because the presence of the Holy Spirit has been so strong all day. My morning fantasy continued. Father John came back down Mount Hermon with me to keep me company throughout the incredible day. Much of his presence was due to Sister Kim and her description of every town and turn as she saw it nine years ago with Father John. These memory-filled descriptions intensified as we approached the Monastery.

Father John donated the funds that were used to renovate the guest house where Sallie Ann and I stayed. He delivered a homily at the ambo in the chapel. He stood in front of the very picture of Jesus and the lamb that is behind the chapel today. He ate at our table, and walked along the paths leading from our room to the main building. He sat in the same stalls where we sat for evening prayer.

The spiritual celebration and contemplation reached a high point when Father Paul English arrived from Canada. Paul played an important role in my conversion. He gave one of the eulogies at Father John's funeral. He will preside over Sister Kim's final profession tomorrow night.

This whole day felt like a long contemplation, moving in and out of different time periods. I prayed throughout, and conversed easily with God and Father John. We talked early in the day about the transfiguration. We walked outside the Monastery after dinner, praying in gratitude for all these wonderful gifts.

The grace I am seeking this week in the exercises is to better know and more deeply love Jesus Christ. There are no words to describe how fully this grace has been given.

Saturday, March 10   (Matthew 17:1-9.again)

When I read the passage from Matthew again this morning, the words, "Get up, don't be afraid," called out to me. Jesus said this to the three disciples when they fell down after hearing God speak from the cloud.

I prayed this morning as I walked up the hill above the monastery. The Stations of the Cross had been set up along the path, which wound up to the cemetery where all of the deceased sisters are buried. My conversation with God started on the way up the hill. It continued as I walked to the edge of the meadow and looked across the prairie at the mountains far in the distance.

I told Him how amazing it felt to experience so much of the same spiritual connection to this physical space, so far away from home, as I experience at the bench in the garden. There is so much comfort in the sounds of birds and the chipmunks and the wind in the trees. Oddly, the big sky and the wide open prairie console me as though they were a warm sweater or blanket. I feel like snuggling up to the vastness.

So why am I afraid? And what do I fear?

I read something this morning about the need some of us have for more humility and less hubris. That is my challenge. There is something I fear about letting go of my image of myself, about which I am falsely proud.

God quietly reminded me of the simplicity of His gift. Give up yourself, He say, and He will give us everything. Love Him and love others and it all works. This is so simple and so not frightening.

I need to write in this journal Kim will make her final profession as a sister in the Benedictine order in less than an hour. We rehearsed the ceremony this afternoon.

After dinner with the community earlier this evening, I walked back up the hill above the monastery, conversing with Jesus as I walked. I felt light, as though I were floating above the path. Words flowed easily as I expressed gratitude for all the blessings I have received just today. It seemed as though each of these extraordinary sisters had a special message for me, a suggestion or encouragement supporting the graces I am seeking. I can imagine nothing more ideal than serving Sister Kim by playing my little role (bringing up the gifts) in her final profession. Her joy is my joy.

Jesus laughed when I told Him I would have to work very hard *not* to be close to Him in this environment.

Sunday, March 11   (Summary)

What a week! What a journey! If I were asked to recommend some activities that would support and enhance these Ignatian spiritual exercises, I can imagine nothing better than:

- First, celebrating Mass in a beautiful cathedral with an incredible choir,
- Second, reuniting with family,
- Third, staying a few days in a monastery, and
- Fourth, taking part in the profession of final vows and the sacrament of ordination for a close friend as she becomes a permanent part of a religious community.

Each day of this week has added to the spiritual high reached the previous day. I have been overflowing joy and love through it all.

We have just returned from morning prayers with the sisters in the chapel. I took the time between breakfast and prayers to walk alone in the garden for a conversation with God. He has been with me almost all day, every day this week. We have talked extensively about my contemplation of the scriptural passages, and about the extraordinary events taking place in real time. So this morning, I reviewed with Him the highlights of the week, beginning with the ceremony last night.

Sister Kim was radiant. Our small group (Father Paul, Kim's sister and her son and daughter, Keith and Richard from Austin, and Sallie Ann and I) gathered in the St. Scholastica room just outside the chapel for a last minute hug. Then all but Sister Kim and Father Paul went into the chapel and sat in silence for several minutes.

The entrance hymn was *The Summons*, the lyrics of which were simply perfect for the occasion:

> *Will you come and follow me if I but call your name?*
>
> *Will you go where you don't know and never be the same? Will you let my love be shown? Will you let my name be known, will you let my life be grown in you and you in me?*
>
> *Will you leave yourself behind if I but call your name?*
>
> *Will you care for cruel and kind and never be the same? Will you risk the hostile stare should your life attract or scare? Will you let me answer prayer in you and you in me?*
>
> *Will you let the blinded see if I but call your name?*
>
> *Will you set the prisoners free and never be the same? Will you kiss the leper clean and do such as this unseen, and admit to what I mean in you and you in me?*
>
> *Will you love the "you" you hide if I but call your name?*
>
> *Will you quell the fear inside and never be the same? Will you use the faith you've found to reshape the world around, through my sight and touch and sound in you and you in me?*
>
> *Lord your summons echoes true when you but call my name. Let me turn and follow you and never be the same. In Your company I'll go where Your love and footsteps show. Thus I'll move and live and grow in you and you in me.*

After a reading from Colossians, Father Paul read the gospel, which tonight was Matthew 5:1-10, the Beatitudes. We all stood and sang an invocation of the Holy Spirit in Latin.

Then Sister Kim and Sister Margie, her formation director, walked to the back of the chapel. They stood in silence for a few moments. Then they walked forward toward the altar, pausing three times, as the monastic community sang The Call:

Come, my daughter, I will teach you the fear of the Lord. Draw near to Him that you may be radiant with joy and your being will always be at peace.

I learned later that the only other time the call would be sung by the monastic community for this sister would be at her funeral. Hearing this gave me chills.

After making her act of profession, Sister Kim prostrated herself on the altar floor, and was covered by the Resurrection Pall, a beautifully embroidered silk blanket.

I struggle to find the right words to describe my feeling at that point in the ceremony. The symbolism of the Resurrection Pall was not lost on me. I could anticipate that when the blessings were finished, the Pall would be removed. Sister Kim would rise up from her prostrate position, restored to a new life. I felt very connected to her at that moment. My life was restored along with hers. My faith was renewed.

Sister Clarissa, the Prioress of the Monastery, then recited a Litany of Blessings. The Blessings opened with the line:

All Loving God, our desire to serve you is itself your gift.

This is a beautiful way to say what we worked on so hard in the first two months of these exercises. It is also Merton's prayer. The final blessing resonates in me still now, eighteen hours later:

When she comes at last to the throne of Christ, may she not fear him as her judge, but hear the voice of Jesus lovingly inviting her to the wedding feast of heaven.

With that, it was done. Sister Kim had perpetually professed her vocation. We applauded. We laughed. We cried. We hugged each other. Sallie Ann and I, along with Keith and Richard, presented the gifts in the Eucharistic service that followed. As I ate the bread, I felt refreshed and whole, fully renewed in my own commitment to this faith.

Looking back on this brief time at the monastery, I am truly amazed at the power and strength of these women. The readings, the prayers, the chanting, the silence, the meals, the walks up the hill and in the garden - all of these were beautifully led by women. Several of these women stand out as great leaders. Sister Janet orchestrated much of the weekend with quiet-but-firm control. Sister Margie and Sister Clarissa inspire me to follow them anywhere. I know that Sister Kim will take a prominent role in the leadership of this community. Again, her joy is my joy. Truly, I have been given great gifts and blessed with more grace than I deserve.

14. Jesus finishes what He came to accomplish

I want to know Jesus better, to love Him more, and to follow Him wholeheartedly.

Monday, March 12   (Luke 21:1-4)

We are on the plane, flying from Seattle to Atlanta, and then to Jacksonville. I read the passage from Luke earlier this morning, and again after we were more than an hour into the flight.   The widow's offering of two very small copper coins is a powerful reminder of the idea of real charity, of true philanthropy.

I composed myself at the temple, among the rich who were offering gifts. When Jesus remarked that the widow had put in more than all the rest of us, I felt the rebuke personally. Of course the meaning is clear. For a rich person, a large gift, even one amounting to a significant share of his or her wealth, is as nothing compared to a poor person giving everything, even the very necessities of life. I asked Jesus to help me understand what He wants from me now.

His response was that He has told me in numerous ways and on countless occasions. I am to give everything. It is that simple. I told Him I did not think I could bring myself to give up all of my material things – the house, the garden, my toys, my books, travel, and on and on. He urged me to keep talking.

I did so, repeating what I have said before about the extraordinary sacrifices of others. Sister Kim, for example, has given up all of her material belongings in order to join St. Gertrude's Monastery. I talked about Thomas Merton, and all that he gave up, even as he prayed that he did not know if that was enough. He hoped that it reflected his desire to please God, and expressed confidence that acting fully in that desire would, in fact, please Him. I regularly repeat Merton's prayer, and take great comfort from it, even though I steadfastly refuse to give up all that Merton or Sister Kim or any of my religious heroes and mentors has given up.

I asked Jesus again what I should do. I understood His answer to be that I should begin by giving up excessive pride, hubris, and all the other manifestations of self-centeredness. Perhaps when I have finally moved past the dominance of self, I will be more willing to let go of material things. We left it there, but I had the definite sense that we would return to this conversation.

Looking out the window of the plane, I felt a powerful sense of calm. I was reminded of the big space, both physical and emotional, that Idaho was, and is, for me. I left the state fifty years ago to go to college. Except for the year that I worked for Boise Cascade (part of 1968 and 1969), I can count the times I have been back in Idaho on one hand. Being there this weekend provoked a wide range of emotions in response to memories of family, faith, and forgotten dreams.

Several people we met said that most Idahoans were either Mormon or Catholic. Having grown up in southeastern Idaho, where close to 90 percent of the population was Mormon, I had only thought of the others there, and in the western and northern parts of the state, as not-Mormon. It feels strange to consider that I have switched from one of the two primary faiths to the other.

While I never considered myself a terribly serious Mormon while growing up in Idaho (that must have changed when I left Cambridge to serve a mission in Germany), most of what I can remember about the little town of Moreland, and even about the farm, relates to Mormonism. My social life was essentially limited to church on Sunday mornings and Thursday evenings. Even my participation in the Boy Scouts and the Explorers took place in the context of the local Mormon ward.

These memories of Mormonism are not bad. I remember virtually nothing about the doctrines of Mormonism, other than that we were simply one of the Protestant faiths. The only thing I can remember about Catholicism is that it was the faith against which we all protested, though for what reason, I was never certain.

The Mormons believed in and talked a lot about the importance of family and community. I never knew anyone who was divorced or the child of divorce. There were a few rushed marriages, but it never occurred to me that the haste had anything to do with pregnancy. I certainly remember becoming sexually active, but, for me, that meant some pretty wild fantasies, not anything I could convince the girls of Snake River High School to do. All of this innocence must have had something to do with the strong presence of faith in the community. In fact, I associated faith and religion with rural and agriculture. I remember thinking that bad girls were those who lived in Blackfoot or Pocatello, as though the difference between good and bad had something to do with living on a farm.

As I think back now on the solitude I experienced as a young boy and teenager, I associate it with the vast outdoors. I was a very little entity in a very big place, but that was not a bad thing. I romanticize as I stare out the window onto the enormous land mass of the Great Plains we are flying over. I am reminded of the line from Chris Hedges:

> The universe seems large and cavernous. I wonder if it knows or cares I am here.

There can be no question that the experiences of this past week leave me with a very warm and loving feeling about the places and people of my past. I want that feeling to last.

It is a long flight, so I have had time to walk around the plane a bit, which produced more prayer and meditation. I went back to my youth in Idaho, trying to remember when and why I first knew that I wanted out of that life and that place. It may seem something of a contradiction to think about this now, after recording such fond memories earlier during this flight. However, there can be no doubt that there came a time when I knew that life on a farm in southeastern Idaho was not for me.

Some people come to this realization as a result of perceived abuse of some kind, even a relatively mild version, like parents deemed to be too strict. That was not the case for me. At some point, I simply came to believe that, at least for me, there was more in this world than life on the farm. I would have followed in my parents' footsteps, studying vocational agriculture at the University of Idaho. I would have farmed with Dad for a while, and then struck off on my own. I simply wanted something else.

I have surmised from time to time that the election of JFK in 1960 triggered these ambitious fantasies. I think I knew much earlier, perhaps even when I was only nine or ten. It was not long after that that I spent so much time moving sprinkler pipe alone in a field a long way from the house. I remember the distance being too far to go back and forth during the day, so I would sit in the sun and continue to give speeches to myself and the crops.

I can certainly remember that some of those great discourses were aimed at large audiences in huge auditoriums, all figments of my active imagination. I talked about world peace, ending the Cold War and using our wheat to feed poor people in distant places. I know that Adlai Stevenson and Dwight Eisenhower talked about these issues during the presidential campaign of 1952. That campaign is probably the source of themes of my discourses.

I was only eight years old when Eisenhower won, but I remember listening to the news on the radio after dinner one night. (Oddly, I cannot remember praying before we ate that meal, or any other for that matter. We must have done so, but I cannot recall it.) After that dinner, just like all the others I can remember, Leonard and I washed the dishes in water we had heated on the stove. We dried the dishes and stacked them on a shelf next to the radio. Then we would join Dad and Mom at the Formica-topped table to listen to the news and, afterward, to Fibber McGee and Molly. Mom, not Dad, tried hard to answer question after question about politics.

From that election season until my excommunication from the Mormon Church a dozen years later, I never once doubted that I would be elected to high office someday in my life. That the end of my political career arrived before it even began was one of the consequences of that trial in Frankfurt, Germany, the first great failure in my life.

I know this journal is meant as a place to record my spiritual progress as I make my way through the Ignatian exercises, and for that purpose only. These wandering reflections on who I am and what made me this way seem to me to be connected to my experience of the exercises.

Jesus was with me last week in Idaho, and I have talked to Him continuously on this long flight. Only through His grace have I traveled the path that led from my Mormon youth in Idaho to the garden bench in Ponte Vedra. Only through His grace am I alive after teasing death four years ago. Only through His grace has Sallie Ann chosen to stay with me. Only through His grace am I able to celebrate with Him the sacrament of the Eucharist.

All of the stops along that winding path to Rome served a purpose in my continuing conversion. That is true about the beautiful flashes of the Divine. It is just as true about the dark moments of doubt and temptation. As Richard Rohr is fond of saying, everything belongs.

Tuesday, March 13   (Luke 21:1-4, again)

We are back at home. Maggie and I are in the library, where we have prayed and talked with God for more than an hour. My reunion with Maggie last night and this morning was simply as good as it gets. When I asked God if I had become a little carried away in my relationship with Maggie, He said my love of her is one of the purest things in my life. At least, that is what I heard Him say!

Among the gifts Sister Kim gave me last week were several poems that Father John saved over many years. I read them again this morning before coming downstairs. The wonderful, inclusive spirit of Father John was present in the poems he saved. One of them speaks to me when I reflect on the passage from Luke about the widow's offering. It is called *Dawn Without Darkness*, and was written by Anthony Padovano:[74]

> *We shall become Christians on that day when sunshine means more to us than a further acquisition.*
>
> *We shall become Christians on that day when the children of the world excite us at least as much as its rulers.*
>
> *We shall become Christians on that day when we use our hearts to measure the worth of a human being, on that day when greed or pride do not lead us to friendship but only love.*
>
> *We shall become Christians when we are joyful because so many people are in love rather than because so many people are affluent.*
>
> *We shall become Christians when we learn to make music and poetry, to make ourselves as human as He was.*

---

[74] According to Wikipedia, "Anthony Padovano is a laicized Priest and founder of Corpus. He is well known as a rare pro-choice Catholic. He is Pastor of the Inclusive Community, where Protestants and Catholics worship together."

We shall become Christians when the sight of the sea makes us dance more joyously than the purchase of a new car.

We shall become Christians on that morning when we laugh and sing for the right reasons and when we weep not because we have lost something but because we have been given so much.

I especially love the last line, "when we weep not because we have lost something but because we have been given so much." Sitting on the bench in the garden, I scratched Maggie's head as I composed myself with Jesus. I praised Him and thanked Him. I basked in His presence and gloried in His grace. I thought about the incredible love that binds me to Sallie Ann. I looked at all the beauty around me, and then closed my eyes and wept.

Wednesday, March 14   (Mark 11:1-11)

Nearing the end of His ministry on earth, Jesus is greeted by the crowds as a great man. Mark tells us that the people threw their cloaks on the road as Jesus rode the colt into Jerusalem. I composed myself among those in the crowd, but I could not feel elation. I knew what was to come. Even as I thought this, it occurred to me that Jesus knew what was about to happen as well. He had told us on numerous occasions. However, He also knew that it was important to His ministry that He be hailed as the king that He was.

I shouted out with the crowd, "Hosanna! Blessed is He who comes in the name of the Lord! Blessed is the coming kingdom of our father David!" I could not help but be excited, even though I was afraid.

Richard Rohr said it well (again) this morning:

We fear nothingness. That's why we fear death, of course, which feels like nothingness. Death is the shocking realization that everything I thought was me, everything I held onto so desperately, was finally nothing.

As John tells us, Jesus said:

I am the resurrection and the life. He who believes in me will live, even though he dies; and whoever lives and believes in me will never die.

His message, of course, is that when we give up self, which is nothing, we will have everything.

While sorting out a box of very old papers, I found a yellowed copy of a little poem I wrote at Snake River Junior High School. I was thirteen years old, but I was already fascinated, or worried, by death. The poem opens with some questions"

Will you be afraid to die, afraid to face your God?

How will you explain your life of sin and fraud?

Ignatius introduced the daily Examen early in the exercises. I first wrote about it in this journal in November. Sadly, I have not yet made it a daily habit. Sister Joan gave me a helpful summary of the five steps to follow each day, ideally each evening before retiring. I fell asleep last night reviewing the day. Suffice it to say that I have a long way to go.

Thursday, March 15   (Mark 11:1-11, again)

I went to Mass and had dinner with Gap and the Jesuits at their house in Georgetown again last night. I am in Washington for a meeting of the Arrupe board, which will take place later this morning. Tom Michel was at Jesuit House, so I told him about the opportunity to speak to a group in Boise. He expressed genuine interest. I talked to Gap about Michael Schultheis in Sudan.

The dinner conversation turned to my conversion experience, which seemed to interest the Jesuit brothers at the table. Leon Hooper, the Woodstock librarian who recently underwent open heart surgery, was obviously intrigued by the role my own surgery had in beginning my journey. They were all anxious to lend support to my efforts to complete these exercises.

Gap and I talked about the importance of continuing with the spiritual journey after completing the exercises. So I went to bed thinking about what a serendipitous turn my life has taken over the past four years. I conversed comfortably with God, praising Him, thanking Him, and seeking His forgiveness for my sins of pride and self-interest.

Reading the passage in Mark again, I am struck by the humanity of Jesus in His request for the colt. "The Lord needs it." This would be jarring at most other times during His ministry. Oddly, a great deal of the suspicion and animosity aroused by Jesus at the beginning of His ministry resulted precisely from His humility. The leaders in the Jewish community expected a "king" to make demands and to live large. They found it frustrating that Christ lived and preached a gospel of selflessness.

I read this week a painfully accurate description of the modern community:

They live only for mutual envy, for pleasure-seeking and self-display.

How else can I explain the great majority of my purchases over the past six decades? I only wanted what I saw others have, which is simply envy. In most cases (all that I can think of), I either wanted those things for my pleasure or so that I would look good.

Even as I write this, however, I know that I will continue to eat and dress well, play games that I enjoy, and take pride in my house. Especially after witnessing Sister

Kim give up all her material goods, I am reminded of how far my life is from the ideal described by almost every great religious figure down through the ages. I suppose I will continue to struggle with this fundamental dilemma for as long as I live.

I composed myself along the road again, part of the crowd watching Jesus ride the colt into Jerusalem. All around me, people were hailing Him as a king. They praised Him for bringing to them the kingdom of their father David. I understood His message to be both that the kingdom of God is here now, within each of us, and also that the kingdom of God will only be fully realized sometime in the future, when all men and women would live together in peace and love.

In the Brothers Karamazov, Dostoevsky asks "What is hell?" He answers it with "The suffering of being no longer able to love." Well, if hell is, in fact, no longer being able to love, then heaven must certainly be largely about love. Jesus taught us that the kingdom of God that is here now, inside each man and woman, is love. It is, first and foremost, love of God. It is love of others as we love ourselves.

Love is not easy. As C.S. Lewis tells us in The Four Loves:

> To love at all is to be vulnerable. Love anything, and your heart will certainly be wrung and possibly broken. If you want to make sure of keeping it intact, you must give your heart to no one, not even to an animal . . . The only place outside Heaven where you can be perfectly safe from all the dangers and perturbations of love is Hell.

I prayed for greater knowledge of Jesus Christ. Slowly, very slowly, I am gaining greater knowledge of Him. I have fallen in love with Him. He has become the friend I turn to most when I am frustrated, lost, and lonely.

This friendship does not diminish my friendship with and love for Sallie Ann. In fact, it exists inside my love for her. He is present in those moments when I am considerate, caring, and most alive. When I am closest to my new Friend, I am capable of a deeper connection with everyone else in my life.

My prayers are being answered with gifts of grace I did not know to ask for; with a transformation I did not know was possible.

Friday, March 16   (Matthew 26:6-13)

Twice this morning, I was reminded of how much I have been blessed. First, I awakened to find Maggie sleeping with her head nestled against my neck. To say that we have a special relationship simply understates too much. Second, the reading from Richard Rohr this morning seems to have been written for me:

> Soul knowledge sends you in the opposite direction from consumerism. It's not addition that makes one holy, but subtraction: stripping the illusions, letting go of the pretense, exposing the false self, breaking open the heart and the un-

derstanding, not taking one's private self too seriously. Conversion is more about unlearning than learning.

In a certain sense we are on the utterly wrong track. We are climbing while Jesus is descending, and in that we reflect the pride and the arrogance of Western civilization, always trying to accomplish, perform, and achieve. We transferred much of that to our version of Christianity and made the Gospel into spiritual consumerism. The ego is still in charge. There is not much room left for God when the false self takes itself and its private self-development that seriously.

All we can really do is get ourselves out of the way, and honestly we can't even do that. It is done to us through this terrible thing called suffering.

As has been the case every time I meet with the Woodstock or Arrupe board, I returned from Washington last night in a state of "spiritual bliss." Jim Nolan came to the Arrupe meeting. He preceded Gap as the director of Arrupe. His fight with cancer is nearing an end, which adds immeasurably to his aura of peace and spiritual strength. He discussed an article on Steward Leadership that he had written a couple of years ago. The discussion triggered another of those phenomenal discussions blessed with grace. That half hour alone made the rather long and inconvenient trip from Florida to Washington and back worthwhile.

I read the passage from Matthew last night. Jesus was in the home of Simon the Leper in Bethany when a woman anointed Him with expensive perfume. Responding to the indignant criticism by His disciples of the waste involved in the anointing, Jesus told them not to be bothered:

The poor you will always have with you, but you will not always have me. When she poured this perfume on my body, she did it to prepare me for burial.

I composed myself in the house with the disciples, watching the woman anoint Jesus. The woman looked familiar. Someone said it was Mary Magdalene. Another said no, it was Mary, sister of Lazarus and Martha. Whoever it was, I was moved by her adoration of Jesus. It was selfless and pure. I felt good for my friend Jesus, knowing that, while this kind of attention was not important to Him, He was nonetheless incarnate. Amid all the suspicion and unrest in the broader community, quiet moments of serene affection were rare.

Several of the disciples, however, were grumbling. To some extent, the criticism of the use of expensive perfume to anoint Jesus seemed perfectly logical to me. It was an expense that might have been avoided, allowing the money to be used for the poor. That was what Jesus had been talking about from the beginning of His ministry, so why this sudden departure? To be perfectly honest, I did not like the suggestion that we were not to bother ourselves about the expense because there would always be poor people. This certainly seems at odds with the dominant message of the Sermon on the Mount.

In John's version of this same event (in which the woman is identified as Martha's sister Mary), Judas Iscariot is named as the leader of those who were most critical. In his book *Palm Sunday*, Kurt Vonnegut reacts to the role of Judas, both here at the anointing and, implicitly, in the garden at Gethsemane:

> *If Jesus did in fact say that, it is a divine black joke, well suited to the occasion. It says everything about hypocrisy and nothing about the poor. It is a Christian joke, which allows Jesus to remain civil to Judas, but to chide him for his hypocrisy all the same. "Judas, don't worry about it. There will still be plenty of poor people left long after I'm gone."*

While I see the hypocrisy in the criticism by Judas, I am still a little confused by this statement by Jesus. I am as guilty as anyone with respect to profligate spending, particularly on luxuries for myself. I cannot imagine Jesus ever approving that profligacy.

When Jesus said that we would not always have Him, the room suddenly became completely silent. It was unthinkable that His death was imminent, even though He had hinted as much on several occasions. None of us wanted to think about the end of His life. A major reason for our concern was our inability to fully accept the idea of His resurrection. I am reminded of those times when He said, "You of little faith."

I have been richly blessed with the grace I am seeking this week, which is to know, love and follow Jesus more wholeheartedly. The Jesus I have come to know loved the brief moment when He was anointed in sweet smelling oil. It was a human moment. It was bitter-sweet in several ways:

- First, this anointing, like the cheering from the crowds as Jesus entered Jerusalem, took place in the general context of suspicion and rejection from the Jewish leadership,
- Second, even this short-lived respite from the strain of His public ministry was tarnished by complaints and criticism from His disciples, particularly, if John's account is accurate, from the traitor Judas, and
- Third, however pleasant the anointing was for Jesus "reclining at the table," it was a reminder of the anointing that would soon occur at His burial.

Being in that room with Him, I felt His pleasure and His pain. I loved Him more for both.

Saturday, March 17   (Matthew 26:6-13, again)

Maggie and I started this morning in the library as usual, and then walked outside into a truly wonderful morning. We sat on the bench, talking with Jesus about the bitter-sweet anointing in the leper's house in Bethany. I said that it seemed to me that the joy He felt during the anointing must have been even better than it would have been had He not suffered so much in the early part of His ministry.

I read yesterday the Chris Hedges line:

> *Insight in life comes through suffering, but suffering alone does not bring insight.*

This thought is similar to something I used to say often in business:

> *Good judgment comes from experience. Experience comes from bad judgment.*[75]

Sallie Ann is fond of saying that:

> *Experience is what you get when you don't get what you want.*

I am not sure that Jesus was enlightened by any of this. At some point, we all decided to walk down to the beach.

We continued to talk about the experience with the perfumed anointing oil. In John's account of the anointing, the perfume is identified as *nard.* I researched the term and learned that it refers to a sweet smelling essential oil produced by crushing the roots of a flowering plant. The plant itself might have been muskroot, a pink-flowered plant in the Valerian family. More likely, however, it was *lavender,* which the Greeks sometimes referred to as nard. Whether muskroot or lavender, it would have been expensive at that time.

I asked Jesus whether the quality of the anointing experience derived from the expense of precious oil, or from the simple fact that the woman, presumably Mary, cared enough for Jesus to anoint Him. In other words, was the argument about the cost of the oil almost irrelevant? Were the disciples, Judas in particular, simply envious of the attention being paid to Jesus?

He explained that it was very important that anyone preaching His gospel be able to relate stories about acts of kindness. It was equally important that God be praised, and that the leaders of the faith be respected. So beautiful places of worship would be built, and they would be decorated with beautiful things. All of this would be for the greater glory of God. While it may have seemed rather insignificant, what occurred that day in the home of Simon the Leper would be a precedent for similar anointing and celebrations.

The expense of the perfumed oil was not the essential part of the anointing. The expense or luxuriousness of the buildings, art and priestly robes surrounding the cel-

---

[75] I learned somewhere that this is attributed to the Sufi sage Mulla Nasrudin, who used the phrase in 1208.

ebration of the sacraments in the Church would never matter as much as the intentions of the participants and celebrants. However, beautiful music and beautiful surroundings do glorify God, and they do enhance the spiritual experience of the faithful. These were sentiments with which I easily agreed.

It is hard to deny the hypocrisy inherent in the enormous expense of the great religious art and architecture built over the ages, existing alongside the continuing poverty of so many. This is not an issue limited only to Catholicism. Islamic mosques, Hindu shrines, Buddhist temples, and even some of the headquarters of secular charities are all subject to the same criticism. While I absolutely love beautiful music, and am inspired by soaring religious architecture, I am brought just as close to God in the basement chapel at Jesuit House.

The significance of the conversation on the beach this morning was not any particular insight about the issues we discussed. It was the mere fact that the conversation took place. I have prayed for the grace of a deeper knowledge of and closer relationship to Jesus Christ. Putting myself in His time and place, walking with Him in the garden and on the beach, sitting with Him on the bench – all of these things are answers to my prayers. The genius of Ignatius was the concept of contemplative prayer. The more time I spend in contemplation, the more real my friendship with Jesus becomes. At the end of the day, it is only this friendship that might save my worthless soul.

Sunday, March 18   (Summary)

Maggie and I began our prayer period early this morning. I am to lector at both morning Masses today. I went to the evening Mass last night to listen to Sallie Ann sing in the choir. After Mass, Sallie Ann, Mary Lou, Rob and I went to the annual parish St. Patrick's celebration, where we saw many of our CRHP brothers and sisters. After that, we all stopped in at a party given by our neighbors Steve and Deborah Rogers, where we saw several other friends from the parish. It felt like a very full-immersion re-entry back into the life of the Our Lady Star of the Sea!

Like most recent Sundays, the assignment this morning was a review of the readings and contemplations of the week. We read from Luke 21 (the widow's coins), Mark 11 (the entry into Jerusalem), and Matthew 26 (the perfumed anointing). These events all took place in the last few weeks before the crucifixion of Jesus.

While still in the library this morning, I composed myself with Jesus in those final days of His ministry. We had begun what would be the last trip to Jerusalem. So much about this journey was different from all of the others. The Pharisees and senior bureaucrats of the synagogue were still hostile, but they stayed at the back of the crowds, silently and sullenly allowing Jesus to be cheered and praised. We celebrated the joyful entry into the city, but felt danger in the air. It was an uneasy feeling.

One of the nice things about contemplation is that I can move relatively easily through space and time. One moment, I can be a participant in the events of a distant time and place. In the next moment, I can observe that participation from a different time and place. Jesus moves back and forth with me.

So after walking out of the leper's house in Bethany into a crowd that was charged with dangerous excitement, I asked Jesus to join me two thousand years later to talk about what had just happened. Together in the library in Ponte Vedra, we watched ourselves moving through the crowd on the dusty road outside Jerusalem. Jesus agreed that danger was clearly present in the air, obviously foretelling what would happen after the feast of the Passover. He stressed to me the huge importance of the brief periods of praise and exaltation, not so much for Him as for the gospel He had introduced.

I fell asleep last night reading more of Chris Hedges, a line from which came to me as I began the review this morning:

> The themes and conflicts that define our lives are often not of our choosing. We cannot pick our demons or our angels. The fundamental questions, those formed within me by the church, would never change. And the questions, in the end, are what define us.

This resonates for me, particularly when I think about growing up in the Mormon faith. Being back in Idaho last weekend brought back many memories of the searching that I did fifty-odd years ago.

I asked then the same fundamental questions I struggled with for forty years in my own spiritual wilderness, and returned to when my faith journey began to move in the direction of Rome.

I do think these were, and are the right questions. I hope they define me. While I now have the answers to most of these big life-questions, I am far away from internalizing those answers.

I struggle daily with the most important and powerful "demon" in my life, which is ego and all its unfortunate manifestations. Grandiosity, selfishness, arrogance, and acquisitiveness are mighty adversaries.

The truly bad news is that when ego wins the battle, my defenses against other temptations are lowered.

The good news is that I have grown closer to the most powerful "angel" of all, my new Friend, Jesus Christ. The very good news is that when I am close to my Friend, my defenses against all temptations are stronger. They become impregnable.

I have been blessed with numerous "surrogate angels." In spite of all that I do to drive them away and how little I do to show my gratitude, they refuse to give up on me. The list of my surrogate angels is long and growing longer. Buddy Tudor and

Father John live still in my heart and in my daily life. Sallie Ann, Sister Kim, Gap LoBiondo, Chris Dorment, Sister Joan, Rob and Will and Melissa and Jennifer and all the grand-children and my godson Henry and my goddaughter Anna Grace – all of these are on the list. I could go on for a very long time!

Mark Twain once said:

An ethical man is a Christian holding four aces.

My angels are my aces, and I have many more than four! Truly, I have been richly blessed.

I found a prayer expressing gratitude to God for the angelic assistance of Christ. It speaks to me today:

Heavenly Father,

Your infinite love for us has chosen a blessed angel in heaven, and appointed him our guide during this earthly pilgrimage.

Accept our thanks for so great a blessing.

Grant that we may experience the assistance of our holy protector in all our necessities.

And you, holy, loving angel and guide, watch over us with all the tenderness of your angelic heart.

Keep us always on the way that leads to heaven, and cease not to pray for us until we have attained our final destiny, eternal salvation.

Then we shall love You for all eternity.

We shall praise and glorify You unceasingly for all the good You have done for us while here on earth.

Especially be a faithful and watchful protector of our children.

Take our place, and supply what may be wanting to us through human frailty, short-sightedness, or sinful neglect.

Lighten, O you perfect servants of God, our heavy task.

Guide our children, that they may become like unto Jesus, may imitate Him faithfully, and persevere till they attain eternal life.

Amen

Third Week

(Six Weeks)

1. The Last Supper

I want to feel sorrow at the wreckage, compassion with Jesus, and shame that He suffers because of our sins.

Monday, March 19 (Luke 22:1-13)

Luke's description of the temptation of the weak disciple, Judas, is chilling. "Then Satan entered Judas." What strikes me, as I reflect on this passage, is that Judas was not simply an innocent man, waiting in neutral for something to happen. He had to say yes to Satan, and it seems to me as though he had already shifted into gear to do just that.

I composed myself in the company of Judas, visiting the chief priests and officers of the temple. I watched as he approached them with a solution to their problem of getting rid of Jesus Christ. It was painful to be in that place, watching evil men dance. I left the temple and went to Jesus. We left that time and place together, meeting again on the bench in the garden.

I explained to Jesus my view that saying yes to any proposition requires preparation. Instead of focusing on Judas saying yes to evil, I described my own long journey to the place where I could say yes to the gospel of Jesus Christ. In the first place, the seeds of that decision had to be sown in fertile soil. I received several graces throughout my life, all conditioning me to ask the right questions. I was blessed with parents who stayed together, who honored the vow of until death do us part. They, and the faith they embraced, conveyed strong messages of fairness, justice, and action in support of the people at the margins of life. So the soil of my soul was fertile, and it had been conditioned for years to receive the seeds of faith.

The moral and physical crises in my life in 2006 and 2007 ushered in a planting season. I was broken. I was out of answers. I was willing to listen. However, I was still not ready to say yes. Father John, Buddy Tudor, Chris Dorment, Gap LoBiondo,

Barbara Munyak, and, first among equals, Sallie Ann were my angels. They planted the seeds that took another two years to sprout and grow into the faith that became a yes at my baptism. Frankly, my angels continue to support me when I have been tempted to back away from that yes.

So, I said to Jesus, consider Judas again. His decision to say yes to Satan must have had a similar back story. Somewhere along the way, Judas must have been exposed to the possibility of moral equivocation. His feelings of envy, jealousy, and avarice must have been developing for some time. I suggested, there must have been some precipitating event that opened the fertile soil of his soul to the seeds of sin. Those seeds grew in that soil to the point that Judas could and did say yes to Satan.

When, in the course of my conversations with Him, Jesus seems to quietly assent to my suggestions, it normally means that the suggestions came from Him. This morning, He nodded, as if to say that I seem to have finally understood what He has been saying.

Tuesday, March 20   (Luke 22:1-13, again)

As I read through the passage in Luke again last night, I was struck by the practical language used by Jesus when He instructed Peter and John to prepare for the Passover meal, the meal that would be the Last Supper. Jesus refers to Himself in the instructions as "the Teacher." I really like that.

I composed myself with Peter and John, walking into Jerusalem after hearing the instructions from Jesus. We were met by the man carrying a jar of water, just as we had been told. We followed him to his house, and were directed to the upstairs room where we would set the table for the Passover meal. Places were set for thirteen diners, which included Jesus and all twelve of the disciples. Ours was an odd task, mundane in one sense, and incredibly important in another. All three of us seemed to know that this would be a very different Passover seder.

I did some research on the seder, seeking to better understand the Jewish ritual that Jesus and the disciples would follow in the course of the Last Supper. All told, the celebrants would wash their hands twice, drink four cups of wine, and eat matzo three times (once in a sandwich with bitter herbs caller 'maror'). It is a ritual observed in much the same way by Jews today.[76]

---

[76] According to Wikipedia, the sequence goes as follows: "(1) Recital of Kiddush blessing and drinking the first cup of wine, (2) Washing of the hands, (3) Dipping the karpas in salt water, (4) Breaking the middle matzo; the larger piece of which becomes the dessert matzo, (5) Retelling the Passover story, including the recital of "the four questions" and drinking of the second cup of wine, (6) Second washing of the hands, (7) Blessing before eating matzo, and eating of the maror, and eating of a sandwich made of matzo and maror , (8) Serving or "setting the table for" the holiday meal, (9) Eating the dessert matzo, (10) Blessing after the meal and drinking the third cup of wine, (11) Recital of the

This particular Passover celebration would be deeply different from all the others, before or since. The betrayal and crucifixion of Christ would occur later that night. Of course, I had the advantage of moving easily between contemplation of the scene occurring 2000 years ago, and appreciating its implications as they unfolded throughout history. I experienced profound sadness.

Wednesday, March 21 *(Luke 22:14-20)*

During the past two years, since my baptism, I have come to truly love the Eucharist. It is the high point of every Sunday, so much so that I relish the opportunity to attend more than one Mass whenever I can. So it is a treat to read the passage from Luke that described the evening when the Eucharist began. I did it last night after my class at UNF, and again this morning as I began my prayers. We are experiencing truly extraordinary weather, so Maggie and I went immediately out to the garden. Sitting on the bench on this glorious morning, I composed myself in that upper-room with Jesus and His dinner party.

First of all, it was incredibly exciting to be in that room for that particular dinner. All my life, I have wanted to be counted among the few and the special. In fact, as I have written so often in this journal, I consider this desire for specialness to be too self-serving. It is something to get beyond as I grow spiritually. Nonetheless, I was gratified beyond words as I contemplated being present at the Last Supper.

Second, I was particularly moved by Jesus saying that He would not eat or drink again until the kingdom of God comes. It is not as though any of us knew precisely when the kingdom of God would come. In fact, the expectation at that time was that it would arrive very soon, certainly within our lifetimes. Still, there was finality to the words of Jesus.

Finally, I was almost overwhelmed by the words "take this, this is my body," or "this cup is the new covenant of my blood." It has become my practice to mouth these words along with the Priest celebrating Mass.

Sallie Ann celebrated another birthday today, the first day of spring. Several thoughts come to me as I reflect on her role in my conversion and the notion that spring is the season to plant seeds. Many of the seeds of faith that had been quietly growing in me, even as I wandered in the wilderness, were planted by Sallie Ann. I have no doubt that my ability to love Christ as I am beginning to love Him originated in my love for Sallie Ann.

Hallel, traditionally recited on festivals; drinking the fourth cup of wine, and (12) Say 'See you in Jerusalem again!'"

Thursday, March 22   (Luke 22:14-20, again)

When I returned from the tennis court this morning, the sun was shining on a very quiet, almost angelic garden.   Its serenity compelled me to spend the morning on the bench, praying and reflecting on that profound night in Jerusalem so long ago.   I composed myself in that room with Jesus and the other disciples.   We had followed the prescribed ritual of washing hands, reciting prayers, and eating matzo.   The seder was coming to an end when Jesus reclined in His chair and, very quietly and very peacefully, began to talk to us.   Ending the celebration this way – with bread and wine – was not our usual custom.   It was immediately apparent that Jesus was initiating something new.   I sensed that everyone present realized it was something vitally important.   I left that place very reluctantly to return to the bench in the garden. Maggie had returned from her morning walk with Caesar, and had come bounding into the garden to say hello.   It felt right that she join me in praying the Our Father to end our exercise.

Friday, March 23   (John 13:1-20)

As I read the passage from John about the washing of the feet, I composed myself not in Jerusalem 2000 years ago, but in the Browning Center at Our Lady Star of the Sea a few months ago.   My CRHP team was presenting the retreat to the new Team 11, and had reached that point in the weekend when it was our turn to wash their feet.   Just as that experience moved me at the time as much as anything else in the CRHP experience, contemplation of it today was moving.   There is so much about washing someone's feet that speaks to our faith.   It is humbling.   It requires love of others over love of self.   It is a form of praising God.   It is a powerful way to express love.

I returned to the place I have spent a considerable amount of time this week, the upper-room in Jerusalem with Jesus and His disciples.   We had just sat down to what would be known throughout history as the Last Supper.   As powerful as that supper and the sharing of bread and wine would be, it was this act of Jesus washing our feet that moved me the most.   I wept with joy.   After contemplating this passage in the garden, I walked down to the beach with Maggie.   Even though it was a beautiful day and many other people were on the beach, I could not leave the upper-room and the experience with Jesus.   I repeated over and over again my gratitude for the special grace of contemplation.

I am writing in this journal again today, moved to address some questions about what is happening as a result of these spiritual exercises.   These questions have been in my mind for some time now, partly due to what I suspect others may think about what I am doing, and partly due to some unease I am feeling about what, if anything, I am doing better in my life.   As I have frequently lamented in this journal, I am certainly still selfish and self-centered.

So I intend to devote some time each day for a few days to some prayerful reflection on these questions. I will start with the easier of the various questions: What must I look like to others as I devote so much time to a process that has me talking to imaginary friends, sometimes in the privacy of my library and sometimes on a public beach or walking down a city street? How is my behavior any different from that of a snake-handling, born again evangelical?

The first answer to that question that comes up for me is that it is related to the second question, which is about the extent to which I have begun to overcome self. Most people who even know about or notice any changes in my behavior are those who have been forced to listen to me talk about it. I am talking about it to call attention to myself. This is precisely what Jesus told us not to do. Matthew Chapter 6 says it clearly:

> *So when you give to the needy, do not announce it with trumpets, as the hypocrites do in the synagogues and on the streets, to be honored by others... But when you give to the needy, do not let your left hand know what your right hand is doing, so that your giving may be in secret. Then your Father, who sees what is done in secret, will reward you. And when you pray, do not be like the hypocrites, for they love to pray standing in the synagogues and on the street corners to be seen by others . . . But when you pray, go into your room, close the door and pray to your Father, who is unseen. Then your Father, who sees what is done in secret, will reward you. And when you pray, do not keep on babbling like pagans, for they think they will be heard because of their many words. Do not be like them, for your Father knows what you need before you ask Him.*

So whatever others may think, they think it because I chose to talk about the fact that I am doing these exercises. I have essentially forced them to listen to me talk about myself. I have asked them to listen to brief outtakes from my journal, not that it might make any difference to them in their own journeys, but that they might be impressed with me and my journey. There will be a time and a place to shout from the roof tops about this experience, and I am certainly not ashamed of the fact that I try to pray daily. That time is not yet and that place is not in the presence of everyone and anyone I can corner long enough to broach the subject.

As for the conversations with Jesus Christ, I can say without embarrassment or regret that they happen. I am not all together clear about what I used to think constituted prayer. I can now say with certainty that prayer, for me, is simply a conversation. That conversation is with a very real person, one that I talk to with ease. I know that others cannot see the person I am talking to, or hear what He says. That does not change the reality of my conversation.

Long before I first heard about the Ignatian Spiritual Exercises, I talked to people in their absence. At times I used these "imaginary" conversations to work something out, either something that troubled me or something that elated me. Contemplative prayer, to me at least, is not unlike that. I go to a place and time that has been described in a passage in scripture or in a thought-piece. I meet in that place the people that the passage tells me are present there. I join with them in talking about the events the passage tells me are unfolding. Many times, the people in that place and at that time are simply people like me, asking the kinds of questions I would ask and reacting to situations in very much the same way that I would react.

At other times, my conversation includes a divine presence. Over the course of the last few months, I have been seeking a greater knowledge of Jesus Christ, and closeness to Him. On one hand, He is God, a divine presence that exists for me through the grace of faith. On the other hand, however, I have come to know Jesus incarnate, a man with emotions and reactions very similar to my own. As I have written before in this journal, I have prayed for closeness and my prayers have been answered. Reading each day about this man Jesus and conversing with Him about the issues He confronted in His time and about the issues I am confronting today have indeed brought me closer to Him. I can say without embarrassment that I love Him.

Saturday, March 24   (John 13:1-20, again)

It is Saturday morning, and I have just returned to the library after playing tennis. I have not stopped thinking about the issues that troubled me yesterday afternoon. Before turning to the passage in John, I want to finish some thoughts about the progress, or lack thereof, I have made during the last seven months.

My decision to embark upon these exercises was only one of several decisions I have made since the summer of 2007 that can generally be described as efforts to become a better person. That broad objective required that I stop doing some things, and that I begin doing others. There has been some progress on both fronts. I continue to sin, but I do fewer bad things and do them less often. I have begun to do some good things, though, again, not as many good things and not nearly often enough.

I am sinning less now, in the sense that I no longer do some of the things I had been doing. I worked hard to change the way I eat. I cut back on ice cream. I have stopped drinking. I have essentially ended my various resentment campaigns.

I devoted myself to two years of Catholic instruction, and chose baptism. I am very seldom away from home, family, and, particularly Sallie Ann. We go to church together and celebrate the Eucharist together. We both chose to be very active in CRHP, and have volunteered for various parish ministries. I have given of time, talent, and treasure to Woodstock and Arrupe.

Becoming a better person requires that I *be* different, as well as *do* different things. My greatest sin of being has always been selfishness and self-centeredness. Sallie Ann describes it as being "self-conscious" as opposed to "other conscious." Based on all that I read in the Bible and all sorts of spiritual improvement books, this is the essential sin of the human condition. Nonetheless, it is that condition I have wanted most to change. It is that condition that most resists change. I do not think that I naively assumed that these exercises would somehow magically transform my selfishness into love of God and others. However, I am disappointed with what often feels like meager progress.

Maggie and I walked down to the beach after I wrote that last bit. As we walked, I explained to her how Jesus was betrayed by Judas. In the course of that explanation, it occurred to me that any of us who has seen the clear beauty of His gospel, but nonetheless chooses to live outside His value system has "turned against Him." We betray Him when we live in a way contrary to what He has taught us, and, far too often, we do so for a bag of coins.

The grace we are seeking in this phase of the exercises is essentially the same as the grace we seek each year during this Lenten season. We want to experience the pain and suffering of Christ. We want to understand how and why He was misunderstood. Somehow through this understanding, we want to reach that place where we will live our lives in accordance with His gospel. All I can say at this point is "progress, not perfection."

Sunday, March 25 (Summary)

It has been a week filled with family at home. Sallie Ann's sister, Mary Lou, and her children and grandchildren have begun a "spring break" tradition. Various groupings of these truly nice people have been with us for two weeks. Among the visitors was my Godson Henry. The day his parents asked me to be his godfather was one of those extremely important days in the course of my conversion experience. It cemented my decision to continue on the path to Rome. Seeing young Henry become a delightful boy adds to my determination to become the godfather he deserves.

Deacon Dan delivered the homily last night at Mass, speaking to the death of self. It was pitch-perfect for my greatest challenge. He has promised to get me a copy. Sallie Ann sang in the choir, which sounded incredibly good. I read the first reading. Rob, the twins, and Mary Lou sat with me in what felt comfortably close to a family pew. It was a wonderful vigil Mass.

What a week in scripture! What a week in history!

Even as I compose myself once again in that upper-room with Jesus and His disciples, it is hard for me to fully comprehend how far reaching the events of that night would be. Here we are, more than two thousand years later, still celebrating with those men that dinner, particularly the Eucharist, with which it ended. That is a big thing to truly grasp.

When I asked the disciples if they could appreciate what was happening, I was surprised that they seemed to have a pretty good idea. While they could not predict the future, the ones I spoke to seemed to understand the enormity of the new gospel.

They understood Jesus when He spoke of His impending departure, even though crucifixion was not one of the words used to describe what they expected to occur.

The other big news running through the room was the fact that one of the disciples was a traitor. In my contemplation, this rumor caused me to examine my own conversion. I have been on a long journey, stopping and starting and occasionally getting lost. However, with an extraordinary amount of God's grace and constant help from amazing people, I have arrived in Rome and begun to work around the edges of God's kingdom. As I reflect on the actions of Judas, it occurs to me that it would be similarly traitorous if I were to turn away from all that I have come to know and return to a life of selfish sin. Would my pieces of silver be so simple as the allure of self-importance? Obviously, what Judas did was vastly more important in its consequences, and significantly worse in terms of the magnitude of the sin. I guess he would be convicted today for conspiracy to commit murder in addition to treason. However, treason does not have to involve a further crime or sin. Betrayal, to state the obvious, is treason. It would be a major betrayal if I were to turn my back on the good news I have come to embrace over the past four years.

I prayed to feel sorrow, compassion, and shame. All of these feelings and more were generated each day through my prayers and in my contemplations. I love the prayer this week:

> God our Creator and Lord, I beg You that I may truly be a friend to Your Son and enter into His sufferings that He embraced for all the people You bring to life and for me.

2. The Night in the Garden

I ask God that I might feel sorrow because of what Jesus went through, even anguish and tears. And shame at what Jesus endures for me.

Monday, March 26   (Matthew 26:30-56)

After reading and re-reading Matthew's account of this incredible night, my prayer to feel sorrow, anguish and tears is granted more than I could imagine. I composed myself with Peter, James, and John, walking away from the main group of the disciples. We walked behind Jesus, who was clearly very troubled.

Even though He had asked us to wait behind and stand watch, we followed closely enough to see Him fall to the ground in anguish. We heard that mournful cry, "Father, if it is possible, may this cup be taken from me." At that moment, I could feel the pain of His suffering. I mean this literally. My stomach hurt. My heart hurt. This was Jesus incarnate, so real and so human. It was also Jesus divine, painfully asking His Father for an alternative. The moment then came when Jesus returned to the place where we had been asked to wait and watch. He awakened us with a rebuke so sharp that it pushed away my sorrow, replacing it with shame. "Couldn't you keep watch with me for one hour?" I had no answer. Sorry simply didn't cut it.

Tuesday, March 27   (Matthew 26:30-56, again)

Starting again this morning with Matthew, I did my best to get out of my shame and live with the sorrow of Jesus. Maggie and I went down to the garden when I returned from tennis. The garden by the lagoon became Gethsemane. The morning sunshine became moonlight. We heard Jesus say:

> *Are you still sleeping and resting? Look, the hour has come, and the Son of Man is delivered into the hands of sinners. Rise! Let us go! Here comes my betrayer.*

Hearing this, I felt enormous shame. Did He mean that simply by falling asleep when He had asked that I stand watch, I had betrayed Him? Likewise, had He suggested earlier that the three denials by Peter would be a form of betrayal? How was it possible that any of us could fail Him? We had personally and directly experienced His divinity. We had listened to His words from His mouth. We had watched Him perform miracles. Yet Peter, our leader, first among equals, would deny even knowing Jesus. We, smugly remembering our intimate dinner only hours earlier, simply fell asleep on the very night that Jesus was in greatest danger. These were not consoling thoughts.

Several scriptural passages had been suggested for additional readings this week. I read Luke 22:39-53 this morning, finding a few subtle differences from the account in Matthew about what happened in the garden that night. When Jesus walked ahead with Peter, John and James, He said to them:

> *Pray that you will not fall into temptation … When he rose from prayer and went back to the disciples, he found them asleep, exhausted from sorrow. Why are you sleeping? He asked them. Get up and pray so that you will not fall into temptation.*

This is a gentler Jesus, asking us to pray not to be tempted. Luke writes that we slept because we were exhausted from sorrow, not simply because we were slothful servants. While the account in Luke was nicer to read, I preferred the contemplative power of Matthew. The rebuke from Jesus matched my desolation.

Even as Jesus was reproaching us, Judas arrived with an armed mob, sent by the high priests to arrest Jesus:

> *"The one I kiss is the man; arrest him." Going at once to Jesus, Judas said, "Greetings, Rabbi!" and kissed him. Jesus replied, "Do what you came for, friend." Then the men stepped forward, seized Jesus and arrested him.*

One of our companions had the courage to grab a sword from one of the high priest's men and use it to cut off the swordsman's ear. I wished at once that I had shown such courage, in spite of the rebuke that followed:

> "Put your sword back in its place," Jesus said to him, "for all who draw the sword will die by the sword. Do you think I cannot call on my Father, and he will at once put at my disposal more than twelve legions of angels?"

Once Jesus said it, it was obvious that He and His Father had infinite power. Physical danger was not a threat to the divine Jesus. Jesus incarnate could and would experience indescribable pain and suffering. Jesus incarnate knew fear. He did not want this to happen. Jesus divine knew that the agony was the plan, and that it was necessary for an enormous purpose.

Once again, the account in Luke tells a gentler story. He reminds us of the loving, healing Christ, even in this moment of fear, anger, and confusion:

> But Jesus answered, "No more of this!" And he touched the man's ear and healed him.

Reflecting on this single act of "Christ-like" mercy, I marveled at the universal strength of His gospel. For two thousand years, men and women all around the world of all ages, races, and levels of intellect have been drawn to His message. Love God. Love your neighbor.

I returned to my contemplation, once again joining the crowd in the torch-lit garden:

> In that hour Jesus said to the crowd, "Am I leading a rebellion that you have come out with swords and clubs to capture me? Every day I sat in the temple courts teaching, and you did not arrest me. But this has all taken place that the writings of the prophets might be fulfilled." Then all the disciples deserted him and fled.

I fled with the others in sorrow and shame. I was little consoled by the argument that all this was necessary to fulfill some ancient prophecy. I wanted the cup of my knowledge to be taken from me.

The account of that night found in Mark 14 was another of the additional reading suggestions. As is almost always the case in the synoptic gospels, Mark, Luke, and Matthew tell very similar stories. The subtle difference in Mark that jumps out at me occurs after the report that all the disciples fled:

> A young man, wearing nothing but a linen garment, was following Jesus. When they seized him, he fled naked, leaving His garment behind.[77]

---

[77] Mark 14:51-52.

Even in my desolation, I had to smile.

Wednesday, March 28   (John 18:12-27)

I read John's account of the trials with great interest last night, and again this morning. History suggests that John the Evangelist was probably the same John, brother of James, son of Zebedee, who was in the small group that walked with Jesus in Gethsemane. The evidence suggests that John wrote his gospel in Ephesus more than half a century after the events occurred. His account is arguably the only one written by an eye witness.[78]

John tells us that the soldiers first took Jesus to the high priest Annas to stand trial.[79] In the first round of questioning by Annas, Jesus answered the questions put to Him clearly. He had preached openly in the synagogues and the temple. Annas was sufficiently satisfied with Jesus' answers that he dismissed Him, sending Him to the court of the high priest Caiphas, son-in-law of Annas.

I composed myself in that courtroom of Annas, standing with Jesus and the other two disciples. I felt shame when Jesus was slapped:

> *"Ask those who heard me. Surely they know what I said." When Jesus said this, one of the officials nearby slapped him in the face. "Is this the way you answer the high priest?" he demanded. "If I said something wrong," Jesus replied, "testify as to what is wrong. But if I spoke the truth, why did you strike me?"*

Why could I not step forward to defend Jesus? My shame was infinitely worse when I heard Peter deny Jesus for the third time, just as Jesus had predicted.

Thursday, March 29   (John 18:12-27, again)

There is something truly wonderful about physical exercise on a beautiful spring morning. The repetitive nature of these exercises is enhanced by (and enhances) the other routines and patterns in my life. So I returned from tennis this morning already in a spiritual place. Maggie was waiting at the garage door in her normal position of animated greeting. She ran to the library and took her position next to the meditation chair. I read aloud the passage from John.

---

[78] Raymond Brown writes that the Gospel was not written by the son of Zebedee nor by the Beloved Disciple (if he was not the son of Zebedee), but by an unknown Christian who was a follower or disciple of the Beloved Disciple. The author of the Gospel of John, therefore, was not an eyewitness.

[79] Ironically, the book of Acts, probably written by Luke around 62 CE, reports that, after Pentecost, Peter and John were taken before the Sanhedrin, which was presided over by this same Annas.

After thanking God for His grace of simply allowing me to live in this paradise, I began a conversation with Jesus about suffering. Richard Rohr has been writing for the last several days about the suffering of Jesus. It is beyond serendipitous that I began Week Three in the middle of the Lenten season, when Rohr's daily meditations seem to track the readings recommended by Ignatius. I particularly liked this thought from Rohr's meditation this morning:

> But Jesus teaches us, in effect, how to suffer graciously. He actually increases, it seems, our capacity for holding sadness and pain.

I asked Jesus about gracious suffering. Is a man more blessed by "grinning and bearing" pain and punishment? Or are civil disobedience and passive resistance preferred alternatives? Both bearing pain and resisting pain require a capacity to suffer. Jesus clearly stood His ground when confronted by His accusers. He did so with patient, courteous rebuttal questions:

> "Why question me? Ask those who heard me. Surely they know what I said."

I composed myself again with Jesus in the court of the high priest Annas. The crowd in the court room was wild and unruly, just as they had been when they arrived in the garden with Judas earlier. What was motivating them? How could the preaching of Jesus about justice, fairness, and love incite riot? Annas seemed to be asking similar questions. In fact, it was clear to me that Annas could find nothing guilty about Jesus, His followers, or His preaching. Annas did not have the courage to simply dismiss Jesus and send the crowd home. Instead, he chose the easy path and sent Jesus to Caiaphas, knowing full well that Caiaphas had promoted the idea that the commotion could only be ended with a death. Surely Annas knew that Caiaphas was the principal adversary of Jesus among the Sanhedrin. Just as surely, Annas knew that Caiaphas would only be satisfied with the death of Jesus.

I wanted to be brave. I wanted to speak out in support of Jesus. I wanted to clearly and persuasively show all the evidence to the court, proving incontrovertibly that Jesus was only about peace and love and justice. I remained quiet. My silence was as shameful as the denials of Peter or the cowardice of Annas.

Friday, March 30   *(Mark 14:53-72)*

The grace I am seeking this week is a deep, sorrowful, anguished knowledge of the suffering of Jesus Christ, particularly during that one night in the Garden of Gethsemane. I have begun my prayers each day with this simple, short prayer:

> Lord Jesus Christ, Did I know how I would break my heart with grief for You. Of all people in the world, You should have suffered least. I am ashamed of what we did to You while You broke Your heart with grief for me.

Reflecting on this, I am again amazed that the suffering of the Son of God is the very core of our faith. He embodied everything good about the human condition. Indeed, of all the people in the world, He should have suffered least. He suffered to show us how important suffering is. Richard Rohr wrote this earlier this week:

> *Suffering is the necessary deep feeling of the human situation. If we don't feel pain, suffering, human failure, and weakness, we stand antiseptically apart from it, and remain numb and small. We can't understand such things by thinking about them. The superficiality of much of our world is that it tries to buy its way out of the ordinary limits and pain of being human. Carl Jung called it "necessary suffering," and I think he was right. Jesus did not numb himself or withhold himself from human pain, as we see even in His refusal of the numbing wine on the cross (Matthew 27:34). Some forms of suffering are necessary so that we know the human dilemma, so that we can even name our shadow self and confront it. Brothers and sisters, **the irony is not that God should feel so fiercely; it's that His creatures feel so feebly.** If there is nothing in your life to cry about, if there is nothing in your life to yell about, you must be out of touch. We must all feel and know the immense pain of this global humanity. Then we are no longer isolated, but a true member of the universal Body of Christ. Then we know God not from the outside but from the inside!*

Maggie and I are in the library. We have just returned from the bench in the garden, where I composed myself again in the court of the high priest Caiaphas (at least I assume it is Caiaphas, since it does not end with Jesus remanded to another high priest). The two words spoken by Christ in Mark's account say everything:

> *Are you the Messiah, the Son of the Blessed One?* *"I am," said Jesus.*

Jesus might have spoken in oblique language. He might have used a parable or quoted some ancient scripture. However, He does not. He is as clear as it is possible to be. "I am." With these words, He subjected Himself to a beating, a mutilation, and crucifixion.

We are taught that Jesus had to die for our sins. I went to the Catholic Catechism to better understand the actual doctrine. How did the death of Christ redeem us? How could He die for us? As I understand it, the death of Christ is the beginning step only. The dance is not complete until we allow the death of our own artificial selves, when we "take up our cross and follow Him."[80]

---

[80] Here is a simplified version of the relevant sections from the Catechism: Accepting the Cup (612). In Gethsemane, Jesus accepted this cup of the New Covenant from his Father. He was "obedient even to death," saying "not as I will but as you will" (Mt 26:39). Although the human nature was assumed by the "Author of life," Jesus accepted death as part of our redemption. Surpassing All Other Sacrifices (613-615). Christ's death accomplishes man's redemption and restores man to God through the blood of the Covenant (Mt 26:28). Christ's unique sacrifice completes and surpasses all

Mary, His mother, was intimately involved in the cross. "Apart from the cross there is no other ladder by which we may get to heaven" (St. Rose of Lima)."

We have been called to take up our own crosses and to follow Jesus Christ. He left us an example of suffering so that we would suffer as well. It is through, and only through, this suffering, this "cross we bear" that we will be re-united with God.

Saturday, March 31   (Mark 14:53-72, again)

Tennis was magical this morning. We have a house full of guests, including Dick Ridge and Rod Denault from New York. The crowd from Savannah and Charleston (Andrea and Jim Walker and Jane Ries) is also "in the house." Good friends, good weather, and good tennis go well together!

I began this review morning by reading another of the additional passages, this one Psalm 35. Reading the Old Testament, particularly this week, highlights the great change introduced by Jesus with His gospel of love. Psalm 35 is filled with vengeance and retribution"

> *Contend, LORD, with those who contend with me; fight against those who fight against me. Take up shield and armor; arise and come to my aid. Brandish spear and javelin against those who pursue me. Say to me, I am your salvation. May those who seek my life be disgraced and put to shame; may those who plot my ruin be turned back in dismay. May they be like chaff before the wind, with the angel of the LORD driving them away; may their path be dark and slippery, with the angel of the LORD pursuing them...*

> *Contend for me, my God and Lord. Vindicate me in your righteousness, LORD my God; do not let them gloat over me. Do not let them think, "Aha, just what we wanted!" or say, "We have swallowed him up." May all who gloat over my distress be put to shame and confusion; may all who exalt themselves over me be clothed with shame and disgrace.*

It is hard to read this and accept the apparent fact that it was written long before Jesus confronted the crowds in Gethsemane. The words make a lot of sense. How

---

other sacrifices. It is a gift from the Father (who handed over his Son) and a gift from the Son (who freely accepted death). As prophesied by Isaiah, Jesus actually substituted himself for us. As the Suffering Servant, he bore "the sin of many" so the many would "be accounted righteous" (Isa 53:10-12). Becoming the Source of Salvation (616-617). Jesus gave the value of redemption and atonement to his sacrifice. Not even the holiest man can take upon himself the sins of others and offer himself as a sacrifice. However, because the divine person of the Son exists in Christ, this sacrifice is redemption for all. Christ's sacrifice was unique. Jesus is "the source of eternal salvation" and "merited justification for us" (Council of Trent). Invited to Drink His Cup (618). Christ can make us partners in his death in a way known only to God. He invites all to "take up their cross and follow him" (Mt 16:24). James and John were invited to drink the same cup (Mk 10:39) and Mary, his mother, was.

do I feel this morning? Do I want to hit back at those who so cruelly killed Jesus? Or will I make the choice I know Christ would want me to make? I went back to the prayer we used seven months ago when I began these exercises:

I choose to breathe the breath of Christ that makes all life holy.

I choose to live the flesh of Christ that outlasts sin's corrosion and decay.

I choose the blood of Christ along my veins and in my heart that dizzies me with joy.

I choose the living waters flowing from His side to wash clean my own self and the world itself.

I choose the awful agony of Christ to charge my senseless sorrows with meaning and to make my pain pregnant with power.

I choose you, good Jesus, you know.

I choose you, good Lord; count me among the victories that you have won in bitter woundedness.

Never number me among those alien to you.

Make me safe from all that seeks to destroy me.

Summon me to come to you.

Stand me solid among angels and saints chanting yes to all you have done, exulting in all you mean to do forever and ever.

Then for this time, Father of all, keep me, from the core of myself, choosing Christ in the world.

Amen.

As it did last September, praying this version of the Anima Christi consoled me. I commenced a conversation with Jesus in the garden, sitting on the bench with Him. I told Him I was deeply troubled by the current uproar over the killing of a young black man in Sanford, Florida. I want the guilty punished. I want the killer and the police department and the right-wing pundits to suffer for this outrage. I am not inclined to "choose the awful agony of Christ to charge my senseless sorrows with meaning and to make my pain pregnant with power." I want an eye for an eye and then some. He reproaches me with a silent smile. Vengeance accomplishes nothing. Justice will eventually come out of all of this noise, but it will only do so in the quiet space of reason.

Palm Sunday, April 1   *(Summary)*

What a glorious Palm Sunday!   On such a beautiful morning as this, I can only wonder what on earth he meant when T.S. Eliot wrote in <u>The Waste Land</u>:

> *April is the cruellest month,*
> *breeding Lilacs out of the dead land,*
> *mixing Memory and desire,*
> *Stirring Dull roots with spring rain.*

I came downstairs early this morning to prepare myself to Lector at the 9 am Mass. Not only was I scheduled to read the second reading, but also to participate in the multi-voice reading of the Passion.   I walked alone down to the garden bench, engaging Jesus in a conversation about humility, doing so because of the passage from Paul's letter to the Philippians that I was to read later in the morning:

> *Who, being in very nature God, did not consider equality with God something to be used to His own advantage; rather, he made himself nothing by taking the very nature of a servant, being made in human likeness.   And being found in appearance as a man, he humbled himself by becoming obedient to death— even death on a cross!*

He made himself nothing!   I explained that I considered this the greatest challenge in my life, perhaps the key to my salvation.   He nodded agreement.

In Luke's account of the Last Supper, Jesus expresses the same sentiment in beautiful language:

> *The greatest among you must behave as if you were the youngest, the leader as if he were the one who serves.*

I have returned from Mass, having experienced one of the best Eucharistic celebrations I can remember.   Father Steven summarized the story of the Passion in his homily.   Christ entered Jerusalem in glory, welcomed by the crowds with cloaks spread on His path and palm fronds waving in joy.   From this amazing high, Christ dropped to the incredible low of the night in Gethsemane.   Betrayed by one of His apostles and denied by another, Christ even cried out to His father, asking why He had been abandoned.   This Triduum week is all about falling from a high place to an incredibly low place.   Next Sunday, Easter, we will all bounce back to an even higher place as we experience the resurrection.

The week began with a prayer to experience sorrow, anguish and tears because of what Jesus endured for me.   I wanted to feel shame that He sacrificed Himself for me.   Celebrating Mass on this Palm Sunday completed my prayer cycle.   I walked back to the bench with Maggie, still listening to the sweet sounds of the children's choir singing "I can't live without you."   The amazing high walking into the church with Father Steven, waving my palm frond, was perfectly contrasted with the painful low looking up at the shrouded crucifix above the altar.   I did not weep in the church. I did weep in the garden.

3. Jesus faces His judges

I ask God for sorrow with Jesus sorrowing, anguish with Jesus in anguish, tears and deep grief because of the great affliction Jesus endures for me.

Monday, April 2   **(Matthew 27:1-2; 11-14)**

Spring in Ponte Vedra Beach is so beautiful it is hard to be anything other than grateful.   This Monday morning could not be more perfect.   Maggie and I have just come in from the garden, where we sat on the bench drinking in the beauty, peace, and pure joy of the simple gift of life.

Last night I read the three accounts of Jesus before Pilate in Matthew, Mark, and Luke.   As is so often the case, the synoptic gospels are very similar, obviously supporting the biblical scholarship behind the common sources.   I wanted to know more about this man Pilate, so I went to the upstairs library to do some historical research.

What intrigues me most is what we know (or think we know) about the structure of jurisprudence in Judaea at the time of the trial of Jesus.   Even though Judaea was a Roman province, it was not under the direct rule of Rome until 44 CE, a decade after the trial.   As I understand the implications of this, it seems to be largely about titles. Pontius Pilate was Prefect of Judaea, representing Rome under the direction of the legate of Syria.   After 44 CE, when Judaea came under direct Roman rule, the Prefect became a Procurator.

Whatever the title, this person was essentially the local governor.   As Rome's representative, Pilate was primarily responsible for commanding the military and for collecting taxes.   Most judicial functions, including civil and criminal courts, were the responsibility of the local government.   However, Herod was only a tetrarch or client-king, appointed by Tiberius, the Emperor in Rome.   The High Priest of the local judicial body – the Sanhedrin – was appointed by the Roman Prefect.   Caiaphas took the trial of Jesus to Pilate because the Sanhedrin was calling for a death sentence. The soldiers under Pilate's command would be the ones to carry out that sentence.

While in the garden this morning, I stood in front of the bench and looked south along the lagoon.   I composed myself with Jesus, in front of the judicial bench of Pilate.   It was clear from the outset that Pilate wanted nothing to do with this case.   Based on the evidence presented by the chief priests and elders, Pilate could find no guilt.   Yet the crowd had clearly become a mob.   A finding of innocence, Pilate seemed to think, would only anger this unruly horde.   So, like Annas, Pilate takes the cowardly course of sending the trial to another court.

As for me, I felt proud of Jesus. "You have said so." He did not deny it, nor did He confirm it. The stakes were incredibly high, and we all appreciated that fact. On one hand, I desperately wanted Him to mount a vigorous defense. Yet, on the other, I understood the dignity of silence in the face of injustice from the system, and anger from the mob.

Tuesday, April 3   (Matthew 27:1-2; 11-14, again)

Our house guests are departing one by one, leaving behind a certain amount of emptiness along with some peace and quiet. One of the blessings of a large house with many guest rooms is the company of friends and family. I have to confess to a relatively large amount of casual laziness with respect to our guests. I encourage them to enjoy themselves doing whatever it is they would like to do, and I devote myself to providing them a good example!

Sallie Ann, on the other hand, works almost non-stop from days before guests arrive, right through every hour of their visit, and even after they leave. It is due to her attention to the intimate details of the comfort and enjoyment of our guests that so many of our family and friends enjoy coming to Serendipity. She makes it pretty nice for me as well.

Richard Rohr wrote a particularly good meditation yesterday, once again calling attention to the importance of inclusion, as opposed to exclusion, in our faith. It is an interesting take on the idea of liberation theology:

> *Jesus enters the temple and drives out the dealers who are trying to buy and sell worthiness and access (Luke 19:45-46), which is the great temptation of all religion. He symbolically dismantles the system. The temple of religion (read "church" or "mosque" too) is henceforth to become personal, relational, embodied in people, and not a physical building. He came to say that God is available everywhere, and for some reason we like to keep God "elsewhere," where we can control God by our theologies and services.*

> *His public demonstration against the sacred space is surely the historical action that finally gets Him killed. The trouble with declaring one space sacred is that we then imagine other spaces are not! Here He takes on the detours of false religion: any attempt to "buy" God, purity and debt codes, and the primacy of "sacrifices" over mercy and compassion. Jesus has come to liberate God for humanity and humanity for God.*

Again this morning, the assignment is to read the account in Matthew of the first appearance of Jesus before Pilate. I turned again yesterday afternoon to a description of the roles of governors (prefects and procurators) under Roman rule. One interesting bit of information has to do with the number of Roman troops under the command of Pilate. It appears that Pilate commanded five cohorts, which were spread around Judaea. Each cohort consisted of approximately 500 troops, giving Pilate a grand total of 3,000 soldiers to enforce Roman rule throughout the province. If things were to get nasty, Pilate could call on the legate to Syria, who could dispatch a legion, consisting of 5,300 troops. Judging solely by the short distance from Damascus to Jerusalem, I suspect that Pilate could rule with relative impunity, even though his two cohorts in Jerusalem numbered only 1,000 men at most. The proximity of so many more would have dissuaded most potential revolutionaries. The threat of troops from Syria may have been illusory, however. The governor of Syria, a prestigious noble named Lucius Lamia, was in Rome for most of his term, almost certainly including the period of Christ's public ministry and the Passion.

The problem for Jesus, however, was not the heavy hand of Rome. It was the mob formed by angry Jews, all of whom shared a common religion, ethnicity, and culture with Jesus. Caiaphas, in my view the real villain in the plot, had advised Pilate early in Pilate's tenure as prefect. He must have assumed that he could eventually persuade Pilate to order the execution of Jesus. One historian, Jona Lendering writes:[81]

> The real reason why Caiaphas wanted to get rid of the man from Nazareth was -probably- that he had claimed to be 'the Son of Man sitting at the right hand of the Mighty One and coming on the clouds of Heaven,' which meant that Jesus was to share God's throne and to judge the Temple authorities. The high priest considered this blasphemy.
>
> Of course, Pilate was not interested in a blasphemer, and therefore Caiaphas presented him a different case: Jesus had claimed to be the 'King of the Jews'. In other words, he was charged with high treason. Although we learn about this from the sometimes biased gospels, we must consider this a historical fact, because it is too embarrassing to be invented.
>
> It is probable that Jesus considered himself a teacher, but it must have been easy for Caiaphas to interpret Jesus' action against the Temple in a military way. He had been arrested after a riot, was called 'king Messiah', claimed to be a descendant of David, had twelve disciples, had announced the destruction of the Temple, and had threatened to judge the high priest, stating that he was God's personal representative. Pilate had to crucify this would-be king. If he did not execute the pretender, he had failed as a governor.

Much of what is known about Pilate is derived from the gospels, particularly those of Mark and John. However, there are two independent sources, the Jewish historian

---

[81] According to Wikipedia, "Jona Lendering (born 29 October 1964 in Beneden-Leeuwen, Gelderland) is a Dutch historian and the author of books on antiquity, Dutch history and modern management. He taught history at the Free University, and worked as an archivist employed by the Dutch government, before becoming one of the founders of the history school Livius Onderwijs."

Josephus[82] and the Roman historian Tacitus. The brief description of the trial and execution of Jesus contained in the most famous writing of Josephus follows:

> *At this time there appeared Jesus, a wise man. For he was a doer of startling deeds, a teacher of the people who receive the truth with pleasure. And he gained a following both among many Jews and among many of Greek origin. And when Pilate, because of an accusation made by the leading men among us, condemned him to the cross, those who had loved him previously did not cease to do so. And up until this very day the tribe of Christians, named after him, has not died out.*

Sitting on the bench in the garden, I reflected on the age-old question, why bad things happen to good people. I explain it to myself using two important tenets of our faith. First, all of us have free will, and second, all actions have consequences.

So I view the trial and crucifixion of Jesus as foretold or prophesied, but not foreordained. In other words, Caiaphas and his angry cohorts acted with free will. They were free to choose to do something different from what they did. Judas had free will. He was not born to betray Christ. He chose to do so.

The choices made by these men had consequences, which were bad things that happened to the good person Jesus. Jesus incarnate acted with free will as well. He could have opted to avoid the suffering. He did things and went to places that He knew to be dangerous. His sacrifice was not a foreordained thing about which He could do nothing. No, in my view, Christ chose to be courageous. He chose to accept death to show us that death is a necessary part of eternal life. This is one of the reasons His crucifixion means so much.

The daily meditations from Richard Rohr this week are all appropriately devoted to Holy Week. This one, which arrived today, speaks to me:

> *Christians speak of the "paschal mystery," the process of loss and renewal that was lived and personified in the death and raising up of Jesus. We can affirm that belief in ritual and song, as we do in the Eucharist. However, until we have lost our foundation and ground, and then experience God upholding us so that we come out even more alive on the other side, the expression "paschal mystery" is little understood and not essentially transformative.*
>
> *Paschal mystery is a doctrine that we Christians would probably intellectually assent to, but it is not yet the very cornerstone of our life philosophy. That is*

---

[82] According to Wikipedia, "Titus Flavius Josephus (37 – c. 100), also called Joseph ben Matityahu (Biblical Hebrew: Yosef ben Matityahu), was a 1st-century Romano-Jewish historian and hagiographer of priestly and royal ancestry who recorded Jewish history, with special emphasis on the 1st century CE and the First Jewish–Roman War, which resulted in the Destruction of Jerusalem and its temple in 70."

the difference between belief systems and living faith. **We move from one to the other only through encounter, surrender, trust and an inner experience of presence and power.**

The faith experience seems to require suffering. I suppose there are a few very holy people, who have never suffered. They might be able to experience in some way the suffering of others. Most of us, though, must personally experience loss, pain, and suffering in order to know the grace of God.

Sallie Ann sent me a great C. S. Lewis quote this morning, which speaks to this as well:

Relying on God has to begin all over again every day as if nothing had yet been done.

I am reminded again of the saying, "Progress, not perfection."

Wednesday, April 4   (Luke 23:5-12)

I came down to the library this morning shortly before 5 AM, without Maggie. The Walkabout Foundation board meets this afternoon in New York. My flight is scheduled to leave Jacksonville at 7:30 AM. The house was extremely quiet! The stillness enhanced my experience of God's presence. We started talking during my prayer expressing gratitude.

I wanted to know more about how the followers of Jesus were feeling during this amazing week way back then. It is Wednesday, the day before Maundy Thursday. Jesus will not join His disciples for the candid conversation before and after the Last Supper until tomorrow night. We entered this city of Jerusalem in glory only three days ago.

Was the mood still one of exaltation? Or were the unruly crowds already being organized by the high priests and elders? Were the followers of Christ already beginning to fade into the background, hiding from the mob? How present was fear among the believers?

It was difficult for me to compose myself with Jesus on this day two thousand years ago. I could not get past my knowledge of what was about to happen. I told Him that whatever the rest of the small Christian community was thinking, I was afraid. I was afraid both for Him, and, candidly, for myself. In part reacting to my fear, Jesus agreed to join me in present time to continue our conversation. I talked excitedly about all that was happening in our local parish and around the world this week, obviously telling Jesus what He already knew. I think He appreciated my enthusiasm.

Wanting Him to know that I was "about His business," I told Him about the Walkabout Foundation. It was organized by the son of my good friend Rolando Gonzalez Bunster. Luis suffered a spinal cord injury twenty years ago, and has been confined to a wheelchair ever since. He and his sister organized the Walkabout Foundation for the purpose of providing wheelchairs to paraplegics in the poor countries of the world. I have agreed to serve on its board largely as a quid pro quo for Rolando joining the Woodstock board. In truth, I am delighted. It was with reluctance that I ended the conversation with Jesus in order to begin my contemplation of the passage from Luke's gospel.

I read the passage from Luke last night after teaching my class at UNF. Luke continues the story of the trial of Jesus. I composed myself in the court of Herod with Jesus. We were there because Pilate had cowardly refused to dismiss the charges against Christ, even though he knew they were groundless. Using the flimsy excuse that Jesus had been born in Nazareth, Pilate remanded the case to the Galilean king, Herod Antipas. In fact, neither Jewish nor Roman law at that time required the case to be tried in the jurisdiction of the accused's birth. To the contrary, jurisdiction belonged then as it does today, with the crime. The proper court is the one located where the crime is committed.

Nonetheless, Herod got the case. As Luke reports, the king was happy about this. Having heard of Jesus, Herod wanted to meet Him, and see Him perform a miracle. As I watched my Lord standing in front of the client-king, I desperately wanted Him to give Herod a sign, thus bringing this trial to an end. It did not happen the way I wanted. Jesus maintained His stoic silence, frustrating Herod as much as the handful of us who supported Him.

So Jesus, like a hot potato, is handed from one judge to another and back again. Herod sends Him back to Pilate. We knew this would not end well. The desolation I felt in my contemplation of that place and time returned with me to the library.

This is a very different Holy Week for me, not like any I have ever experienced. Of course, it is only my second Holy Week as a Catholic. This is a little misleading, however, because the Holy Week of 2010, the week leading up to my baptism, will, I hope, always be one of the "holiest" weeks in my life. My memory of that Holy Week is joyous, filled with the warm memory of the consecration of my marriage to Sallie Ann on Palm Sunday (she says "Harts of Palm Sunday"), and with the excited expectation of the sacraments that would be celebrated at the Easter Vigil. Holy Week last year went by too quickly, and may have been crowded with family and guests visiting Serendipity for the first time.

This week, however, I experience Holy Week in the active context of these exercises. I am acutely aware of the meaning of this week two thousand years ago in Jerusalem as well as right now in my local parish, my Woodstock community, and my personal relationship with Sallie Ann. My appreciation of the week is enhanced by the overlapping prayers and meditations of Ignatius, the Daily Missal, Richard Rohr, and even the messages copied in frequent emails from friends and family.

The daily meditation from Rohr arrived in my email inbox at 2:07 AM, so I read it before beginning my day at the insanely early hour of five. It begins with the statement by Jesus reported by Luke in his account of the Last Supper:

"The greatest among you must behave as if you were the youngest, the leader as if he were the one who serves."[83]

That statement is probably the simplest and most powerful definition of authority to be found in all four Gospels. "For who is the greater, the one at table or the one who serves?" Most of us would say immediately, "The one at table." He says, "Yet here I am among you as one who serves" (Luke 22:27). Jesus says, in effect, "I'm telling you that the way of domination will not build a new world. I have come to model for you the way to be human and the way to be divine—it is the way of loving service." Sometimes even the church does not understand this.

Why is it that everything I read these days seems to be perfectly aimed at me? This is especially true whenever the subject touches on humility. That is precisely the subject at the core of Christianity (and most other faith traditions). I ended the morning with a prayer expressing my gratitude for the grace of awareness. I thanked God for making me aware of this Holy Week, of my constant need for humility, and for the love and support of so many of those around me, particularly Sallie Ann. After the Our Father, I left for the airport.

Maundy Thursday, April 5   (Luke 23:5-12, again)

I began this Maundy Thursday saying a prayer of gratitude in my room at the Harvard Club in New York. It was 4 AM, and my cab would arrive at 4:45 AM to take me to LaGuardia for a 6 AM flight. I am truly too old for this!

However, I am grateful for the gifts that allow me to do it, especially for this amazing thing called the Walkabout Foundation. I learned yesterday at the board meeting that there are two program areas for the foundation: giving wheelchairs to poor people in poor countries and supporting spinal cord injury research. Money is raised through events, mostly "walkabouts," which are events in major cities that combine running, walking, and wheeling a wheelchair. The first walkabout followed the route of the pilgrimage of Saint James from France into Santiago de Compostela in Spain.

After sleeping on the flight from New York to Washington, I am back at the computer in the airport, waiting for the flight to Jacksonville. There is a chapel here in the airport! I have seen signs for them at airports in the past, but I have never been inside one. Well, this small room is perfect for private prayer and meditation.

---

[83] Luke 22:26

Thoughts from an unimportant argument at home intruded on my meditation. Is this the right thing on which to focus on this Maundy Thursday? Christ is having a really bad evening, following one of the most important dinners in the history of the world. An angry mob is out of control. Jewish high priests and Roman prefects are making terrible decisions. These seem to be more important matters than anything I am currently experiencing.

I avoided this unpleasantness by going back to Herod's court, joining Jesus and a handful of other disciples. Herod is asking questions and seeking answers that strike me as just noise. Herod has not been asked to rule on the issue of blasphemy or false teaching. He must know that he has been asked to decide whether Jesus will live or die. The reasons for the death penalty are nothing more than pretext. Herod must also know that sending the case back to Pilate is tantamount to deciding on death. At a bare minimum, it is not deciding to let Christ live. As heart breaking as this realization is, I find the mockery by the soldiers more grating. Jesus has already been beaten and spit upon. Herod now dresses Him in a fancy robe before sending Him back to Pilate. Reflecting on this mock trial, which is treated so casually by Herod and his men, does focus my mind on very different issues. I want to go to Mass this evening. I want to be at the altar of my new faith.

Good Friday, April 6   (Matthew 27:15-26)

Maggie and I went out to the bench very early this morning. It was cloudy, but warm and very still. We began our prayers expressing gratitude for the incredible experience of the Holy Thursday service last night. The Mass was wonderful, but even better was the closeness between Sallie Ann and me. We were both moved by the readings, the gospel, the homily, and the solemnity of the ceremony. Monsignor washed the feet of several parishioners, including the catechumens scheduled to be baptized at the Easter Vigil this Saturday.

I composed myself on that hill called Calvary or Golgotha, the place of the skull. Three crosses had been erected on the crest of the hill. Men, presumably criminals, were hung from the crosses on the left and on the right. The cross in the center awaited Jesus. Pilate was back in charge, as Herod had taken the easy way out and refused to rule on the case. Due primarily to pressure from the chief priests, led by Caiaphas, Pilate's court had found Christ guilty and sentenced Him to death. I watched as Pilate whispered to his associates that this death penalty was not the final word. Pilate said he had a way out, which was the custom of releasing one of the condemned men. However, I could sense the mood of the crowd. They were really an unruly mob, determined to see Jesus crucified. So they chose Barabbas to be released, ending all hope of saving the life of Christ.

I left that place to briefly reflect on the numerous occasions when I have watched and waited for a stay in the death penalty of a convicted criminal. Even when I knew (or thought I knew) that the conviction was right and the crime was truly heinous, I hoped for a stay of execution. I am truly opposed to the death sentence, and have been for as long as I can remember. We have executed almost 1,300 people in the United States since 1976, the year the death penalty was declared constitutional by the Supreme Court. This is a sad fact for a nation that ranks highest in the world for church goers!

I returned to Calvary. The madness of the crowd shouting "Crucify Him" sickened me. The courage and good will of Jesus amazed me. I felt helpless.

Easter Vigil Saturday, April 7   (Matthew 27:15-26, again)

It is still dark outside. I went out to the bench alone this morning before tennis. A cold wind was blowing up the lagoon. I started to compose myself on Calvary on that awful night, shivering against the cold, but I found Jesus and wanted to talk to Him about other things.   I was still very much under the spell of the Good Friday service yesterday. Monsignor Logan wore a simple white robe. He was completely in service throughout the afternoon, truly exemplifying the words of Christ at the Last Supper. The image of the altar stripped bare was still on mind. I could hear the painful, yet beautiful sounds of Jim Goodell's song at the end of Mass.

Sallie Ann and I read together for the first time. She had the first reading, a very long passage from Isaiah, and she pulled it off flawlessly. I was proud of her and happy for both of us.

The gospel reading consisted of a four-part reading of the Passion from the Gospel of John. Deacon Dan read the part of the Narrator. Father Steven read the part of Jesus. Sallie Ann read the part of the crowd. I read the part of the voice, which shifted from one person to another, including Peter and Pilate. I also read the part of the voice on Palm Sunday, when we read the Passion from the Gospel of Mark in four parts.

Reading the Passion together brought Sallie Ann and me closer to each other, and closer to the painful experience of Christ so long ago. Pain and sorrow were evoked by everything that happened in the ceremony yesterday. When two ladies in wheel chairs came forward to kiss the wooden cross, tears rolled down my cheeks. I cannot remember a more beautiful expression of faith.

Our prayer for this week means so much more to me now:

> *Lord Jesus Christ, Did I know how I would break my heart with grief for You. Of all the people in the world, You should have suffered least. I am ashamed of what we did to You while You broke Your heart with grief for me.*

Kneeling before that wooden cross yesterday allowed me to feel my grief for the suffering that He should not have suffered. Fairness was not part of the bargain.   Just as the idea that I have been saved because of the pain of another is beyond my rational comprehension, so is the idea that the Son of God would be the one to suffer that pain.

I came back from tennis to find Maggie waiting in excitement at the door. We sat on the bench, now bathed in warm sunshine. I started talking to Maggie, but soon found that I had entered another important conversation with God.

I said that I felt changed; that I was somehow different now from how I had been before. It is not clear to me whether I appear different to others. What is clear is that other people, other things, and other experiences appear different to me.

I described the Good Friday service. I pointed out how the red in the robes was brighter than I had ever seen it. The music was more beautiful than I had ever heard it. The readings and the Passion gospel had more meaning and more clarity than ever before.

Is this greater awareness a result of these exercises? Or is it simply a result of a combination of factors. I am retired, and am no longer obsessing on all the stressful things inherent in the international power business. I am involved in several spiritually healthy activities, including Woodstock, Arrupe, Lectoring, CRHP, Walkabout, and much of my reading. I am still so relatively new in my Catholic faith. Certainly, all these things should be having a cumulative effect on my awareness of God's presence in the world.

That said, I have no doubt that these Ignatian exercises are the primary component in the present phase of my spiritual journey. While reading some of my earlier entries in this journal, I am struck with the number of days last fall when I neither prayed nor wrote in my journal. This contrasts sharply with most days since Thanksgiving, when I have prayed and meditated for several hours, often more than once each day. The fact is that the exercises themselves are having a cumulative effect.

Ignatius planned it that way. Consider those weeks last fall when I contemplated my own sin day after day. While it initially seemed excessively repetitive, the fact is that I felt the sorrow and shame just a little more each day. That was the objective. During this Week Three, I have prayed, meditated about, and contemplated the events of a single twenty-four hour period for an hour or more on each of the past twenty days!

Especially when I composed myself in Jerusalem that night, as I have each of those twenty days, I feel like I am watching my own performance in a slow motion movie. The impact of each successive slow motion frame is itself greater than the frames before it. Each builds on the impact of all the other frames that have gone before it.

These thoughts were part of the conversation I had with God at the bench. I was reminded as I contemplated the importance of this day, Easter Vigil, of where I was two years ago, and what I was doing. To my surprise, Sallie Ann had invited my daughters, her sons, and some of our close friends to join us for this baptismal weekend. We had lunch at our house on Ella Lee Lane, an event I recounted vividly as I talked to my Friend in the garden.

Sallie Ann had hired Yvonne Washington, whose group we first encountered at Brennan's, to sing black Baptist gospel music. Yvonne had performed for Rob's wedding years earlier. Patsy Tudor was there, both for herself and representing Buddy. Father Tom, Father Al, and Father Jay were there from St. Anne's, again, for themselves and representing Father John. Barbara Munyak was there from RCIA, for herself and for all the members of our UB 2 group.[84] I remember being nervous about all that was scheduled to happen that night. Father Tom and I were both a little old to kneel in the baptismal font. We were clearly too old to get back up! I loved everything about that incredible day.

Easter Sunday, April 8 (Summary)

There was a special moment in my meeting with Sister Joan yesterday. Reading to her from this journal, I came to the last paragraph, recounting the lunch at our house on Ella Lee Lane in Houston. Reading the words caused me to choke up a bit, and tears came to my eyes. Maggie, who had until then been lying quietly on the floor at my feet, got up and put her paws on arm, patting me in sweet concern. Sister Joan was amazed! Frankly, so was I.

Maggie and I finally made our way to the library around 11 am this morning. Sallie Ann and I had just returned from the annual party at the Dotson's following the Easter sunrise service on the beach. The service and the crowd were decidedly Episcopalian, meaning, among other things, an abundance of pink and green clothing and Belgian loafers. The fact is that we enjoyed all of it. We have been coming to the sunrise service for almost fifteen years, beginning long before we moved to Ponte Vedra from Houston. There is just something quite special about singing "Christ the Lord is Risen Today," while watching the sun rise above the ocean.

As usual, the assignment on this Sunday is to review the prayers and meditations of the week. I normally include in my summary a consideration of anything during the week that affects my spiritual condition one way or the other.

In Jerusalem, two thousand years ago, this week was the most important week in the life of Christ. The Eucharist was formally introduced at the Last Supper. Judas betrayed Christ. Peter denied Christ. Our Lord Jesus Christ was brought before the courts of Annas, Caiaphas, Pilate, Herod, and Pilate again. An out-of-control crowd of angry Jews asked for the death of Jesus. When asked to choose between Jesus and the common criminal Barabbas, the mob chose to release Barabbas and crucify

---

[84] Candidates for membership in the Catholic Church are separated into two general categories: those who have been baptized in a recognized Christian church and those who have not been so baptized. Those who have been baptized take only one year of RCIA, while those who have not been baptized must go through two years. The "un-baptized" are referred to as UB 1 in their first year, and UB 2 in their second year.

Christ. Finally, on this morning two thousand years ago, the tomb of Christ was found empty. He had risen.

Well, after a week like that, it would be hard to win a "this week" contest, regardless of which week in history one were to choose. The week I reviewed this morning, the first week of April, 2012, in Ponte Vedra Beach, Florida (with a short side trip to New York), was a total non-event in comparison to that week so long ago. However, it was a week filled with spirituality - in the exercises, at our parish, and in my life outside of formal religion.

The Exercises. We began this week with the first part of the 27th chapter of Matthew (Matthew 27:1-2; 11-14), and we ended with another passage from the same chapter (Matthew 27:15-26). Oddly, we skipped the verses in Matthew reporting that Judas hanged himself. We turned to Luke 23:5-12 in the middle of the week to pick up the hearing of Jesus before Herod (which is not reported in Matthew's account of the Passion). Taken together, the readings provide an account of the various trials of Jesus on that Thursday night. He went first to Pilate's court, then to Herod's court, and, finally, back again to Pilate's court. Saint Jerome commented on this in the fourth century as follows:

> *I cannot sufficiently wonder at the enormity of the thing, that having purchased false witnesses, and having stirred up the unhappy people to riot and uproar, they found no other plea for putting Him to death than that He was King of the Jews; and this perhaps they set up in mockery.*

These so-called trials are frustrating to read about, and must have been even worse to experience. I composed myself in the courtrooms during the week, and felt that frustration. Precious little courage was shown by the representatives of Rome, who found no guilt on the part of Jesus, but nonetheless refused to deny the crowd an execution. My feelings progressed from deep sorrow for Jesus to anger at the courts. I felt powerless grief that the unfolding drama could not be stopped. Finally, I was ashamed that I showed no more courage than the judges and governors. I had prayed for sorrow, anguish, and grief. My prayers were answered.

Our Parish. Our Lady Star of the Sea celebrated something important each day from Palm Sunday through today, including particularly Palm Sunday, Maundy Thursday, Good Friday, Easter Vigil, and Easter itself. Sallie Ann and I participated on Palm Sunday and Good Friday, adding immeasurably to the quality of our experience. That said, however, I could not possibly exaggerate the spiritual value of the washing of the feet on Thursday night and the baptisms last night at Easter Vigil.

Both evenings brought back to me my own experience as a catechumen only two years ago. Father Tom washed my feet on that Thursday night, reducing me to tears and, quite simply, wrenching my heart. The feelings were so powerful that I can hardly remember anything from that Thursday night until the lunch on Saturday.

Just as I was thinking that nothing could ever touch me the way that foot washing had, I went through three different sacraments during a single service late on Saturday at the Easter Vigil service. Watching the catechumens last night here in Ponte Vedra Beach brought everything back to me. It was a good thing too, because I have to admit that most of my own baptismal night turned into a fog when I knelt in the baptismal font.

In my conversation with God this morning, I asked that He extend to me the grace never to forget the joy and fullness of that night.

Life Itself. While it sometimes seems not to be the case, I do have a life outside these exercises and my local parish. I did not expect to find spiritual sustenance from teaching at UNF, but I clearly have. We discuss ethical and moral questions every week. We bring fairness, justice, and "the good" into almost every class. I learn from the students, and I learn a great deal from Ben Hoffman, my co-professor.

I wrote earlier this week about the Walkabout Foundation. Like Woodstock, this board is inherently spiritual, simply because we are struggling to do something good and do it well. The other board members inspire me to be a better person. The discussion leads me to look for better answers to the tough questions involved in funding and implementing the foundation programs.

Perhaps the greatest source of spiritual growth and development outside of the parish and the exercises is my relationship with my family, particularly Sallie Ann. Rob and his daughters have been a major part of this Easter Sunday, beginning on the beach when it was lit by a beautiful full moon, and ending at the Easter egg hunt in the middle of the day. My relationship with Rob's family makes me grow.

Sallie Ann stands alone as the most important thing in my life. Sometimes she challenges me to no end. Sometimes I "mess up," creating problems, or making non-issues into major issues. However, through it all, she comes through with wisdom and depth. She has done so for thirty years. She may someday read this, and I am sure she will have suggestions for what I might have included or left out or simply said better. She will probably be right. On this Easter Sunday, I am moved to say that I love her, and that I could not live without her. I am a better person for knowing her.

4. The Way of the Cross and the Crucifixion

I ask God for sorrow with Jesus sorrowing, anguish with Jesus in anguish, tears and deep grief because of the great affliction Jesus endures for me.

Easter Monday, April 9   (Matthew 27:26-32)

Sister Joan gave me the assignments for this week last Saturday. All three scriptural readings are from the account of the Passion contained in Matthew 27. We read most of the first 26 verses last week, ending with the release of Barabbas.

After reading the passage through several times yesterday, I turned to the Catena Aurea for further elucidation. Several of the early commentators noticed that the mockery of Jesus with the fancy robe was reported by Luke to have occurred in the court of Herod, but by Matthew, to have occurred on Calvary before Pilate. I am not troubled by these slightly different accounts.

I find it strangely puzzling that anyone would adhere to a strictly-literal reading of the gospels. After all, they were written decades after the death of Jesus by men who, with the possible exception of John, were not eyewitnesses. They were transcribed by numerous scribes, and translated over centuries, again by numerous translators. As Father John loved to say, many of the things described in the bible probably happened differently than they are reported, or did not happen at all. Even so, they are all true!

What does come across in all of the accounts is the effort by the angry mob to mock Jesus. They did so using words. They did so by clothing him in the fancy robe, and by stripping him bare. They did so by crowning him with a crown of thorns. Commenting on this mockery, Rabanus[85] touches on an extremely important point:

> *And they mock Him with adoration, [those] who believe on Him, but despise Him with perverse works.*

It is easy to condemn all those involved in the events of that night two thousand years ago. I suspect it is very true, however, that Jesus accepted their mockery much more easily than He does our mockery, when we fail to live as we believe.

Maggie and I began the morning in front of the fire in the family room. We sat on the bench for a few minutes, but it was chilly in the clear spring air. I composed myself

---

[85] According to Wikipedia, "Rabanus Maurus Magnentius (c. 780 – 4 February 856), was a Frankish Benedictine monk, the archbishop of Mainz in Germany and a theologian. He was the author of the encyclopaedia De rerum naturis (On the Nature of Things). He also wrote treatises on education and grammar and commentaries on the Bible. He was one of the most prominent teachers and writers of the Carolingian age, and was called "Praeceptor Germaniae," or "the teacher of Germany.'"

on the hill with the crowd, watching helplessly as Pilate's soldiers abused Jesus Christ:

> *Then the soldiers of the governor took Jesus into the common hall, and gathered unto him the whole band of soldiers. And they stripped him, and put on him a scarlet robe. And when they had platted a crown of thorns, they put it upon His head, and a reed in His right hand: and they bowed the knee before him, and mocked him, saying, Hail, King of the Jews! And they spit upon him, and took the reed, and smote him on the head.*

I am embarrassed to admit that I always considered the letters **INRI** (Jesus, King of the Jews), often written on or above the cross, as high praise. I now understand that these letters, like the crown of thorns, also often included in a crucifix, are present to remind us of that painful mocking treatment of Jesus on Calvary. Reflecting on it now, I do relate personally and painfully to His suffering.

Maggie and I are about to walk down to the beach. Sallie Ann just sent me a wonderful quote from C.S. Lewis:

> *Remember He is the artist and you are only the picture. You can't see it. So quietly submit to be painted---i.e., keep fulfilling all the obvious duties of your station (you really know quite well enough what they are!), asking forgiveness for each failure and then leaving it alone. You are in the right way. Walk---don't keep on looking at it.*

For all kinds of reasons, this speaks to me. I must submit to be "painted." I must ask forgiveness for each failure and then leave it alone. I must do the next right thing, and I certainly and momently know what that is.

The path I am on now is "the right way." This is good advice as I leave to walk.

Easter Tuesday, April 10   (Matthew 27:26-32, again)

It is early on this Tuesday morning. I sat in front of the fire and listened to Taize as I prayed and meditated further on the passage from Matthew. I will play tennis in about half an hour. Reflecting on this morning in paradise, I thought of how Thomas Merton described happiness:

> *Happiness is not a matter of intensity but of balance, order, rhythm and harmony.*

The reading from Matthew ends with the encounter with Simon, the Cyrenian. Cyrene was a town in Libya, a long way across the North African desert from Jerusalem. Simon may have been a Gentile, leading some of the early Christians to consider him the first Cyrenian Christian. However, there was a Jewish community in Cyrene, which had its own synagogue in Jerusalem. So, it strikes me as more likely that Simon was in Jerusalem to celebrate the Passover at his own synagogue. Whatever the reason for his presence in that place at that precise time, Simon took up the cross of Jesus. I do not think it too much of a stretch to consider our acceptance of Jesus Christ through baptism to be symbolically "taking up the Cross."

I composed myself at the edge of the crowd as they delivered Jesus to Pilate's soldiers. Barabbas had just been released. I imagined that I stood in silence as this happened, watching helplessly as the soldiers stripped, beat, and mocked Jesus. I felt great shame.

Dressed in a scarlet robe and crowned by a crown of thorns, Jesus looked alone and forlorn. I felt like my feet were in concrete. I could not even look at Christ for fear that He would see me, and know that I had let Him down.

After He had been stripped of the fancy robe and was led away to be crucified, I watched as this stranger from Cyrene, Simon, stepped forward to answer the call to carry the cross. Even as I knew in my heart that I did not have the courage to do what Simon was doing, I wished that I had at least been asked. Even the soldiers knew I was a coward.

It was in this desolate mood that I read the daily meditation from Rohr. It spoke to me, but did not relieve my sorrow and shame:

> *The voluntary self-gift of Jesus on the cross was His free acceptance of all creation in its weakness and imperfection. He chose to become a divine brother to humanity, and by giving himself to God totally, he invites all of His brothers and sisters with him into that same relationship of belonging. "Chosen in Christ from all eternity" is the way Ephesians puts it (1:4).*

> *The raising up of Jesus (which is the correct way to say it) is the confirmation of God's standing and universal relationship with what he created ("covenant love"). Jesus stands forever as our Promise, our Guarantee, and our Victory (1 Corinthians 1:30) of what God is doing everywhere and all the time. The only way you can absent yourself from this victory is to stand alone and apart. Inside communion you are forever safe and saved.*

"The only way you can absent yourself from this victory is to stand alone and apart." I stand alone and apart when I refuse to surrender myself to the wonderful gift of faith. Simply by saying yes, I am allowed inside communion, where I will be forever safe and saved.

Easter Wednesday, April 11   (Matthew 27:33-38)

Matthew's account of the Passion continues today with these painful verses:

> *And when they were come unto a place called Golgotha, that is to say, a place of the skull, they gave him vinegar to drink mingled with gall: and when he had tasted thereof, he would not drink.* ***And they crucified him...***

Four simple words: And they crucified him. The horrendous act of crucifying requires unspeakable cruelty. They drove large nails through His hands into the wooden cross arm. They crossed His feet, and drove another nail through both feet into the upright wooden post of the cross. They did this while He was still alive.

I wanted to feel the pain and degradation of this truly awful event. I composed myself next to the soldiers as they held Jesus down on the cross and pounded the nails through His hands and feet. I watched as they lifted the cross into place, and dropped it into the hole. Christ moaned in agony. I moaned in disgrace.

I am seeking the grace of grief, anguish, and tears. Well, seek and ye shall find.

Rohr's meditations this week follow both the Liturgical Calendar and the pattern of these exercises. I particularly like the inclusive nature of his meditation today:

> *We cannot achieve our divine sonship and our divine daughterhood. All we can do is awaken to it and start drawing upon a universal mystery. We live with an inherent dignity by reason of our very creation, a dignity that no human has given to us and no human can take from us. All bears the divine fingerprint, as St. Bonaventure said. Our inherent dignity has nothing to do with our race or religion or class. Hindus have it, and Buddhists have it, and so-called "pagans" in Africa have it. They are just as much children of God as we are. Objectively. Theologically. Eternally. Where else do you think they came from? Did some other god create them, except THE GOD? Their divine DNA is identical to ours. We deny our supposed "monotheism" (there is one God) if we believe anything else.*

Easter Thursday, April 12   (Matthew 27:33-38, again)

Matthew's account goes on, reporting even more humiliating behavior on the part of the soldiers:

> *When they had crucified him, they divided up his clothes by casting lots.*

The soldiers literally cast lots – drew straws – to determine who would get which pieces of the torn garments of Jesus Christ. It is the essence of dehumanizing. It is hard for me to read this. I composed myself this morning on Calvary, watching in agony the agony of Jesus Christ.

I watched the Mel Gibson movie about the Passion of Christ several years ago. Sister Joan suggested I see it again now, but I resist because of how terribly painful it is to focus on what these people did to Jesus. After driving nails through His hands and feet into the wood of the cross, they tore the garments they had stripped off Him into pieces. Then they gambled to see which soldier would get what piece of clothing:

> *And sitting down, they kept watch over him there.*

After beating, disrobing, and nailing Him to a cross to die, they sat down to watch. I stood off to the side and listened to these men joking among themselves about what they had just done. I slipped from my position on the hill (the "place of the skull") to that place I found where I could see the whole earth and all time.

Two thousand years unfolded in front of my eyes, in communities on every continent and in every corner of the globe. What I saw was the emergence of a community of faith; faith in the very man about whom those soldiers were joking. The faith community consists today of almost two and a half billion people, one third of the earth's population. Over the two millennia that passed in front of me, I saw this faith community transform one country after another, one community after another, and one individual after another. The joke, it seems, was on those soldiers!

Easter Friday, April 13   (Matthew 27:39-47)

Matthew's account of the crucifixion continued in the reading this morning. Maggie and I began at the bench in the garden, in spite of a cold wind coming up the lagoon. I composed myself back on the hill, standing a bit to the side of the three crosses. Matthew described people "passing by." No one came to Golgotha to simply "pass by." Anyone coming to that awful place came to participate in the awful process of crucifixion, to mock the criminals on the crosses, or to collect the bodies of the crucified.

Those who came by taunted Jesus, asking where His God was now, and why He could not save Himself. One of the early Church Fathers noted the similarity of the language when the Devil was tempting Jesus at the beginning of His ministry (Matthew 4:6) and in this passage. The Devil said, "If thou be the Son of God, cast thyself down," and the crowds said while mocking Jesus on the cross, "If thou be the Son of God, come down from the cross."

Again, I stood silent, helplessly watching this painful, humiliating, public execution. In a very strange way, I began to notice a change in my relationship with Jesus Christ. For most of the past seven months, I have come to know Jesus incarnate. He has become a personal Friend. I came to know Him as a young man, and as the quiet, but powerful leader of a new approach to how people should relate to each other and to the Divine. As Pope Benedict and Bernard Lonergan and so many others have urged, I have fallen in love with Him.

The Jesus I talk to in the library, on the bench in the garden, and while walking on the beach, is filled with light and love. He smiles. He nods in approval, or gently signals disapproval. He played with Maggie on the beach.

Today, however, I feel as though the Jesus I came to know is gone, or is about to leave. Jesus incarnate has been beaten, spit upon, and nailed to the Cross. Jesus incarnate is writhing in pain, suffering unspeakable anguish, and even feeling abandoned by His Father. He obviously has other things to do than visit with me.

Jesus divine is harder for me to relate to. I am a little frightened of Him this morning. In my fantasy, I want to reach out and touch Jesus incarnate, consoling Him in His agony. I dare not touch Jesus divine. It is an unsettling feeling.

Easter Saturday, April 14   (Matthew 27:39-47, again)

It felt better than it usually does to play tennis this morning, and it usually feels very good. I needed the exercise. I needed the company of others playing and laughing and luxuriating in the springtime sun. I returned to the garden bench this morning to pray a new Easter prayer suggested by Richard Rohr:

Loving God, we love how You love us. We love how You free us. We love what You have given and created to surround us. Help us to recognize, and to rejoice in, what has been given, even in the midst of what is not given. Help us not to doubt all that You have given us, even when we feel our very real shortcomings. We thank You for the promise and sign of Your love in the Eternally Risen Christ, pervading all things in the universe, unbound by any of our categories of logic or theology.

We offer You our lives back in return. We offer You our bodies, our little lives, our racing minds and restless hearts into this one wondrous circle of Love that is You. My life is no longer just about me, but it is all about YOU.

I love the poetry in this prayer. I love the idea that we can give God our "little lives, our racing minds, and restless hearts." More than anything, I love that this prayer brings love back into the central focus of our relationship with God. I know that I will return to Calvary this morning, forced to face the cruelty of man and the agony of Jesus Christ. I am strengthened by this prayer.

Having composed myself once again at the back of the crowd watching Jesus literally dying in front of us on the Cross, I share the fear of all around me when the sky suddenly turns dark. It stays dark for three hours, making the suggestion of an eclipse impossible.

At the end of the third hour of frightening darkness, Jesus cried out:

My God, my God, why hast thou forsaken me?

These words, uttered at the very end of His life as a man, are the essence of Christ's humanity. He knows that He is the Son of God. He knows that He will be raised up in three days. He knows that His ministry cannot be fulfilled without His death.

Yet, faced with the imminent fact of that death, Jesus incarnate expresses fear, anguish, and forsakenness. In that moment, He is meek, defenseless, alone, and forlorn. In that moment, my love for Him could not be greater. In that moment, all the feelings of these daily meditations come together as one. In that moment, I say, You are not alone! I am with You!

Back in the library, I reflected on this moment of contemplative prayer. I left Jesus alone on that Cross, minutes before He would die. In the discomfort that I feel now, I wonder if I will be able to recover the intimacy that I have established with Jesus incarnate. He will soon be raised up. He will leave behind His incarnate being and become solely divine. What does that mean to our relationship?

C.S. Lewis, as is his want, wrote something that speaks to this possible dilemma:

> There are no ordinary people. You have never talked to a mere mortal. Nations, cultures, arts, civilizations - these are mortal, and their life is to ours as the life of a gnat. But it is immortals that we joke with, work with, marry, snub and exploit - immortal horrors or everlasting splendors. This does not mean that we are to be perpetually solemn. We must play. But our merriment must be of that kind (and it is, in fact, the merriest kind) which exists between people who have, from the outset, taken each other seriously - no flippancy, no superiority, no presumption.

Jesus was never an ordinary person, no "mere mortal," even at His most ordinary moment. The relationship between Jesus and me, especially the one established over the past seven months, was, in my belief, taken seriously by both of us. What gave it so much power was the absence of "flippancy, superiority, and presumption.

I approached Him open to the possibility of His gifts of grace. Even though I was early in my journey, I had long ago left the starting gate. His death on the cross does not signal the end of my journey or my relationship with Him.

However, I have a strong and growing sense that the relationship will now change. My friendship with Jesus incarnate must grow into a similar friendship with Jesus divine. Oddly, I suspect the disciples were experiencing very much the same kind of fear and trepidation as they awaited His return.

Sunday, April 15   (Summary)

It is early on this Sunday morning. I awakened with very warm feelings for Our Lady Star of the Sea parish. Sallie Ann and I attended the annual parish celebration of ministries, a dinner dance the parish gives to thank the hundreds of volunteers who make it all happen. Sister Joan was a star of the show, dancing as though she were still a teenager in Brooklyn. Sallie Ann danced with Father Stephen. She and I love to dance and last night was no exception. We felt connected to this community.

I will Lector at 9:00 o'clock this morning, reading from the first letter of Saint John:

> Everyone who believes that Jesus is the Christ is begotten by God,
> and everyone who loves the Father loves also the one begotten by him.

> In this way we know that we love the children of God when we love God and obey his commandments.

For the love of God is this, that we keep his commandments.

And his commandments are not burdensome, for whoever is begotten by God conquers the world. And the victory that conquers the world is our faith.

Who indeed is the victor over the world but the one who believes that Jesus is the Son of God?

This is the one who came through water and blood, Jesus Christ,
not by water alone, but by water and blood.

The Spirit is the one that testifies and the Spirit is truth.

This is a very good message for me to read today. I have been desolate since yesterday morning, thinking about Christ's words on the Cross. John's words reminded me that "whoever is begotten by God conquers the world." Jesus incarnate was most certainly begotten by God, and His resurrection is proof to all of us that He conquered the world. If we believe in Him, we must love Him.

There is more. We must love everyone begotten by God. That is the primary commandment. This is not burdensome, because by doing so, we too will, through our faith, conquer the world.

I have spent this Easter week in Matthew 27, focusing on just a few painful hours on that terrible night. The grace I sought this week was deeper sorrow, anguish, and grief because of the great affliction Jesus endured for me. I have achieved that and more.

Maggie and I are together, having just come in from the garden bench. Taize is singing in the background. The song is that wonderful chant based on Luke 23:42, "Jesus, remember me, when you come into your kingdom." It is perfect for my summary of this week.

Alongside the sorrow and grief I have felt for the agony of Jesus as He was mocked and crucified, I have felt a growing desolation. I have watched the life of my Friend, Jesus incarnate, come to a brutal end. I know how the story ends. I know that He will be raised up. After all, we celebrated the resurrection on Sunday, before this painful week in the exercises began. However, my focus this week has been on the end of His life incarnate, not the beginning of His new life.

I remember the eulogies for the small handful of my friends and family members who have died. Without exception, the emphasis was on the good news that my friends were now with God. They had returned home.

I wanted none of that. I was in pain. I hurt with the loss of my friends. I missed them terribly. Whatever my head might have known about another life, my heart was torn and anguished for the life that was ended.

That is precisely how I feel this morning about the death of Jesus on the Cross. What a cruel thing this contemplative process has been! I had never before regarded Jesus as a walking, talking, living, laughing, and loving Friend. Before these exercises, I never sat with Him on the bench, or chatted with Him while walking on the beach.

Sure, the terrible things that I watched the soldiers do to the historical Jesus Christ were awful and disgraceful and disrespectful. However, my greatest pain this week comes from the simple fact that they killed my Friend right before my eyes. He was not God. He was not a distant religious figure. He was not King of the Jews or the Savior of the whole world. He was my Friend. They killed Him. I miss Him.

My God, My God, why hast thou forsaken me?

Part of the grace I am seeking this week is tears. They have finally come.

5. Jesus Dies on the Cross

Monday, April 16   (Luke 23:33-43)

Maggie and I walked outside at six this morning. A crescent moon lit the dark sky. The sound of the waves was louder than usual. My conversation with Maggie became a conversation with God. I talked about the desolation I felt, which was even greater after reading Luke's account of those last few hours in the life of the incarnate Jesus:

Father, forgive them, for they do not know what they are doing.

I wondered how far that statement was meant to go. Did it apply only to the soldiers and others involved in the crucifixion and mockery? Or was it intended for a much wider audience, including even me? However, my sins were never committed in ignorance. I always knew better.

The bench seat was wet with the morning dew. It was, therefore, in some discomfort that I slipped back into the composition in that "place called the Skull." I listened to the criminals bickering with each other. I empathized with the one who defended Jesus:

We are punished justly, for we are getting what our deeds deserve. This man has done nothing wrong.

For some reason, the concept of injustice has not been part of my desolation over the past week. Of course the crucifixion was unjust. Oddly, that seems like a small sin compared with the overall atrocity of brutally killing Jesus Christ.

We are sitting in front of the fire in the family room, listening to the chanting of Cistercian monks. The sun is coming up over the palm trees across the lagoon. Maggie is sleeping next to me. The desolate hole in my side is becoming full with the peaceful grace of this place. Even in this moment of agony, these undeserved gifts surround me.

Tuesday, April 17   (Luke 23:33-43, again)

Reading through Luke's account of the crucifixion again this morning, I focused on verses 42 and 43:

> Then he said, "Jesus, remember me when you come into your kingdom." Jesus answered him, "Truly I tell you, today you will be with me in paradise."

I am reminded so much of the praise song, consisting largely of a repetition of verse 42, "Jesus, remember me when you come into your kingdom."

My first experience of this wonderful song was at Father John's funeral. It was the last song the choir sang at the service. As we pall bearers carried the coffin out of the church, the whole congregation repeated the song over and over again, until we had pushed the coffin into the hearse. I was weeping uncontrollably the whole time.

Now, I sing those words for hours after hearing the choir sing the song at Mass. I often listen to Taize sing it when I am writing in this journal after morning prayers.

This morning, however, I reflected for a long time on the two verses in Luke together. The criminal who defended Jesus was almost certainly not a religious man, by which I mean a devout Jew. It is even less likely that he was a follower of Jesus Christ. Yet he asked Jesus to remember him when He came into His kingdom!

Now, it is remotely possible that this criminal experienced some kind of conversion while hanging from a cross watching the crucifixion of Jesus Christ. It is more likely, however, that he simply said what he said out of desperation. In a sense, he was simply covering his bet by endorsing the revolutionary preacher Jesus.

It is Christ's answer that is most intriguing. Jesus told the criminal that he would be with Him, Jesus, in paradise that very day! How does a criminal get to paradise? If the criminal's simple, last minute request hanging on the cross is a sufficient expression of faith to qualify for salvation, then this whole thing is much easier than I thought.

I think Christ's statement about seeing the criminal in paradise says a great deal more about Jesus than it does about the criminal. Grace, we know, is unearned good favor; the granting of an undeserved gift. In exactly the same sense, mercy is unearned forgiveness. Christ was extending His grace to this criminal, giving him a gift he had in no way earned. In an act of incredible mercy, Christ was forgiving this criminal whatever sins might have prevented him from gaining access to paradise.

I tried to compose myself as the criminal on the third cross, listening to the exchange between Jesus and the other criminal.   I wanted to understand the situation as realistically and completely as possible.   I wanted to feel the pain that Jesus was feeling.

The composition was a failure.   I could not bring myself to experience the pain of crucifixion.   The word excruciating is derived from the act of crucifying.   It is aptly horrifying.   Even now, back in the library, my feet hurt where I imagined the nail breaking the skin.   I cringe when the crude hammer misses the nail and hits my fingers.   And that is the lesser pain!

Again I am overwhelmed at the unspeakable cruelty of crucifixion.   Yet hanging from these nails driven through their hands and feet, these men were having a conversation!   They must have been numbed by shock.

It was very early when we went outside to pray.   The crescent moon continued to light the sky.   The garden was eerily silent, seemingly more so in the empty space between the bench and the sound of the waves hitting the shore on the other side of the palm trees.   The morning chill was perfect for my desolation.   I was crying when I came back to the library.   Maggie is sleeping next to me.   We are listening to the choir of monks of a French abbey sing Gregorian chants.   I prayed the Our Father.

Wednesday, April 18   (John 19:25-30)

The reading from the Gospel of John is so appropriate for this sad morning.   Addressing a small group that included at least one disciple and three Mary's – His mother, His mother's sister, Mary the wife of Clopas, and Mary Magdalene – Jesus said:

> When Jesus saw his mother there, and the disciple whom he loved standing nearby, he said to her, "Woman, here is your son," and to the disciple, "Here is your mother." From that time on, this disciple took her into his home.

Reading John is appropriate because the disciple that Jesus loved was John the Evangelist, author of this very Gospel.   John was the disciple who took the mother of Jesus into his home.

The historians say that John wrote the Gospel in Ephesus, sometime near 90 CE.   It occurred to me this morning that John was writing his gospel from a memory of events he had personally witnessed about as far back in his life as my mission in Germany is in my life.

John goes on to provide a final, poignant reminder of the essential humanity of Jesus incarnate:

> Jesus said, 'I am thirsty'.   A jar of wine vinegar was there, so they soaked a sponge in it, put the sponge on a stalk of the hyssop plant, and lifted it to Je-

sus' lips. When he had received the drink, Jesus said, 'It is finished.' With that, he bowed his head and gave up his spirit.

In spite of the fact that I have not been an active member of any institutional religion for much of my life, I have been aware of the life and death of Jesus Christ for as long as I can remember. In all those six decades, I cannot remember ever being this close to the reality of His death. I wonder what I must have been thinking about on all of those Easter vacations. It was certainly no vacation for Jesus.

Composing myself in the small group that afternoon on Calvary came naturally to me this morning in my sadness. Lifting the vinegar soaked sponge up to Jesus; I realized that I was weeping. I heard Him say, 'It is finished," and, in my fantasy, I sat down and cried like a baby. In fact, I was crying as I sat on the bench. Maggie came up next to me and pawed my arm, as if to console me.

Thursday, April 19   (John 19:25-30, again)

Again, I was outside in the garden an hour before tennis. The dark morning is incredibly still and quiet. Sitting on the bench, I listened to the words over and over again in my mind:

> *It is finished.*

Just like that, Jesus could no longer feel the pain of His wounds, or taste the bitterness of the vinegar, or hear the words of the mocking crowd. Just like that, the short life of Jesus incarnate was over. Just like that, Jesus divine would continue the mission alone.

As I reflected on the immensity of what had happened, I thought about the criminal who had asked Jesus to remember him when He came into His kingdom. The criminal would not die for another day, when the soldiers would return to Calvary to break his legs in order to hasten death. I wondered if the criminal would see Jesus in paradise.

I thought for a long time about paradise. In modern usage, paradise means a place that is positive, harmonious, and timeless. That meaning certainly applies when I wake up each day here in Florida and exclaim that I have awakened to yet "another day in paradise."

I have learned from reading about Islam that paradise for Muslims is a garden, often contained within walls. It is rigorously symmetrical, and contains walks and waterways ("rills"), running straight and true along each axis. The Islamic gardens I have visited are the essence of contentment and timelessness. When I designed my own garden at Serendipity, I certainly aimed for something "positive, harmonious, and timeless."

So is that where the spirit of Jesus went?

And when Jesus had cried out again in a loud voice, he gave up his spirit.

My desolation lifted as I thought about paradise. I came back into the library. The monks were singing Gregorian chants. The space around me felt harmonious. I walked out into the south garden with its fountain and rill and walls of Japanese yew. There was indeed a timeless beauty to the place. I sensed that Jesus was there with me. We did not talk. We sat in silence by the fountain. Somehow, I knew that He was no longer in pain. That silent knowledge eased my own suffering. This had become more than just another day in paradise.

Friday, April 20   (John 19:31-42)

We are leaving later this morning for a weekend in Savannah to celebrate Rob's birthday. I read the passage from John last night. It stayed with me all night long. I read that crucifixion itself seldom killed those who were crucified. Thus, it was common practice to break the arms and legs of the crucified men (I have not read of any women crucified in the time of Christ, though I think it became somewhat common over the centuries) the day after they were hung on the cross in order to hasten death.

In this case, the Jewish leaders requested the leg-breaking in order to avoid the embarrassment of men on the cross on the Sabbath.

The soldiers therefore came and broke the legs of the first man who had been crucified with Jesus, and then those of the other.

The whole idea of crucifixion involves a level of atrocity that I can barely understand. I could not bring myself to contemplate the suffering of those men on Calvary that night. Imagine the distress I felt all night, trying to form a clear mental picture of these tortured men still alive twelve or eighteen hours after being nailed to their crosses. Did the soldiers break their legs by hitting them with some kind of hammer while the men were still hanging on the cross? Or were the men pulled down from the cross, their skin ripping from the nails, so that their legs could be broken while they were on the ground? Both images are simply awful.

But when they came to Jesus and found that he was already dead, they did not break his legs. Instead, one of the soldiers pierced Jesus' side with a spear, bringing a sudden flow of blood and water.

So, just to be certain that Jesus was indeed dead, the soldier "pierced His side with a spear." Even though Jesus was dead, the act of stabbing Him and causing blood and water to flow from His side is painful to contemplate.

There have been reports in the news over the past few days of US soldiers mutilating the bodies of dead Afghan insurgents. It is shameful, and shows neither respect for the dead nor any intelligence regarding relationships with the living. Of course, this was the intention of Pilate's soldier. The mockery continued after Christ died.

Like many others over the years, I found John's reference to a "day of Preparation" somewhat puzzling. So I made the mistake of researching the day of preparation that precedes the Passover Sabbath. I learned about the great "three days, three nights" controversy!

As I have often noted, I am not troubled by what might be small inconsistencies in the Bible. Many scribes and translators over many centuries are likely to make a small mistake or two. For those who insist upon the precise literal truth of every word, however, a great fuss has been made over the precise day and time of the death and resurrection of Jesus Christ.

Jack Kelley provided the clearest answer I could find:[86]

> So in the week Jesus died two Sabbaths that permitted no work were observed back to back: The Feast of Unleavened Bread on Friday the 15th, and the regular weekly Sabbath on Saturday the 16th. In Matthew 28:1 we read that at dawn on the first day of the week (Sunday the 17th) the women who were close to Jesus went to the tomb. Luke 24:1 tells us they were going to anoint His body for burial. The two Sabbaths had prevented them from doing so earlier. But He wasn't there. He had risen. Being the Sunday after Passover, at the Jewish Temple it was Feast of First Fruits. At the Empty Tomb it was Resurrection Morning.

Somehow, I think I would be just as moved to faith if Christ rose on the second day instead of the third. It is the resurrection itself that is special. I am happy there is a resolution for those who were bothered by this potential discrepancy.

Richard Rohr wrote a wonderful piece this morning:

> The great thing about God's love is that it's not determined by the object. God does not love us because we are good. God loves us because God is good. It takes our whole lives for that to sink in because that's not how human love operates.

> Human love is largely determined by the attractiveness of the object. When someone is loveable, nice, good, and attractive physically, or has a nice personality, we find it much easier to give ourselves to them. That's the way humans operate, outside of the economy of grace. Divine love is a love that operates in an unqualified way, without making distinctions between persons and without following our personal preferences. We don't have the capacity to receive that notion! Divine love is received by surrender instead of performance or perfection.

---

[86] Jack Kelley is an Evangelical Christian writer who apparently devoted a great deal of time to the careful study of this controversy. This explanation comes from his web site.

With painfully few exceptions, my whole life has been about "performing for approval." Frankly, it has often not worked all that well, since the approval I was seeking was from other humans. Divine love is unqualified. I am reminded of the phrase, "we cannot achieve it; we can only receive it."

Taize is singing "Jesus Remember Me" again in the background. I am writing this in the family room, next to the fire. Maggie is asleep on her pillow. The sun has come up, lighting a fire on the surface of the lagoon. The gentle magic of this place is working!

Saturday, April 21   (John 19:31-42, again)

We are in Savannah. I sat for half an hour in a quiet corner of the hotel lobby, praying and reflecting on the burial of Jesus. The morning provided a painful foretaste of what is to come in May. I missed Maggie. I missed the library and the garden. I walked down Liberty Street, but it was not the beach. My morning was not the same.

I was reminded of a passage from The Screwtape Letters, in which Wormwood is advised as follows:

> *If all else fails, redirect the patients prayers from God to an object. Any object would do, be it a crucifix hung on the wall, the upper-left hand corner of the ceiling, anything at all. Thus the patient would not be praying to God, but to something material.*

Of course, I looked up the exact language when I came back from my walk. The point is that my relationship with God was never about the library, bench, and beach. It was not about Maggie. In the course of the past eight months, I opened myself to God's presence, which is everywhere and always. I allowed myself to know and experience Him.

I composed myself this morning in the garden near Calvary. Joseph of Arimathea and Nicodemus were there with the body of Jesus. Even though I was intensely uncomfortable doing so, I assisted them as they wrapped His body in spices and linen. I tried in two ways to disassociate myself from the experience. First, I kept repeating to myself that this was just a contemplative fantasy. Second, I tried to think of the body of Jesus as simply a dead body, which could be anyone. It was just a cadaver.

Neither effort worked. My imagined presence in that garden with those men was extraordinarily real. I sensed their sadness. I watched them weep. I observed their gentle, caring movements as they handled the body of Jesus with almost professional skill.

The funerals of Father John, Buddy, and my father entered into my composition. I thought about the pause when, as a Lector at Mass, I read the intention for those who have died. It has always meant something to me, but will mean more now.

The three of us stood in silence for several minutes after we laid the body of Jesus in the tomb. It seemed a very insignificant way to honor the death of a king. I thought to myself that this burial part of the story was in fact insignificant. The real event was coming. Sunday morning was only three days away.

Sunday, April 22

Sallie Ann and I went to Mass at the Cathedral of St. John the Baptist here in Savannah last night. It was another incredible experience, made so in part by the soaring beauty of the cathedral itself. I still pinch myself each time I take communion. I am also still moved by great art and architecture. The combination is simply phenomenal.

This has been an extremely powerful week. I have experienced greater desolation than at any other time since I began these exercises. That is saying a lot. I remember the painful month of the First Week, when I kept drilling down on my sins. However, that was nothing like this.

All week long, I have found myself suddenly weeping, and not just in the privacy of my contemplation. I lost a good Friend this week. As I can only remember on a handful of other occasions, I am mourning that loss.

As I reflect on the week, I am struck with how little I have experienced true friendship in my life. There have been many men and women who have reached out to me, more than I ever deserved. Very few people have pierced my defensive façade. Stated differently, on very few occasions have I pierced through my obsessive absorption with myself.

The mourning moments I can remember involved those few occasions. I was deeply affected by the death of Rupert Simpson, the lawyer I worked with so intensely during the three years in Poland more than twenty years ago. There is a great picture of the two of us laughing with abandon while we danced together. We were at the wedding of Randy and Pam Phelps in Maine. The picture and the joyous event come back vividly, and bring tears.

I was deeply moved by the funerals of Sam Pardoe and Alice Gaither. I have written a lot in this journal about my relationship with Father John, and about how profoundly I mourned his death.

My friendship with Buddy Tudor is in a category all by itself. We were close friends for so long, more than forty years. We knew each other's parents, children, and grandchildren. We knew each other's employees, and business partners. We worked hard together. We played even harder together. He is the only person who knew everything about me. I knew just enough about him to assure his silence! As I think about it, he is probably the only person, other than Sallie Ann, with whom I have spent more time than I have spent over the past eight months in contemplation with Jesus.

That brings me back to this week and the loss of my Friend Jesus. Assuming an average of two hours a day for eight months, the total time "together" with Him comes to less than 500 hours. Malcolm Gladwell[87] wrote in <u>Outliers</u> that *"the key to success in any field is, to a large extent, a matter of practicing a specific task for a total of around 10,000 hours."* On that scale, then, I have certainly not applied myself to my relationship with Jesus Christ enough to make it successful. The goal of a friendship, however, is obviously different from the goal of a professional competition. The point of all this is that time, practice, and repetition matter.

Gladwell's 10,000-hour-test is tough. My rough calculation of time spent with Buddy over the term of our friendship comes to around 5,000 hours. Arun Sen and I probably spent close to 4,000 hours together, but most of that was work. Only Sallie Ann and I have spent enough true "friendship" time together to pass the test. My rough calculation comes up to more than 25,000 hours spent with her. A great deal of our time together has been concentrated in the last five years. We were apart for way too much time during the first 25 years of our marriage.

I mourned the death of Jesus each day this week. What strikes me as noteworthy, however, is that the week began with Easter Sunday. The joyous celebration of the resurrection this year was overshadowed by my intense contemplation of His death. From my present position at the bottom of this canyon of desolation, it is hard to imagine climbing successfully to the high cliff of celebration. That will be the challenge of Week Four.

6. The Longest Sabbath

Monday, April 23   *(Luke 23:56)*

Like last week, Father Tetlow did not suggest a grace to seek during this week. Again like last week, the appropriate grace seems to be quite obvious. I wanted to personally experience the death of Christ on the cross last week, feeling the pain of His suffering.

This week will be devoted to mourning His death. As the title of the week suggests, the mourning period will be limited to the two Sabbath days that fell between the death and resurrection of Jesus Christ.

Because of that rare occurrence of back-to-back Sabbaths, it was a long Sabbath for the disciples two thousand years ago. It must have been a miserable few days for the disciples, most of who believed that the death of Jesus was the end of Jesus. The Messiah was a dud. Not only did He not end the oppression of the Romans,

---

[87] According to Wikipedia, "Malcolm Gladwell is a Canadian journalist and author, whose books include The Tipping Point: How Little Things Make a Big Difference (2000), Blink: The Power of Thinking Without Thinking (2005), and Outliers: The Story of Success (2008)."

but He angered the leadership of the Jewish community, making any suggestion of reform that much more difficult. Everyone who had followed Him, or even attended one of His sermons, was a suspected terrorist. His death portended their deaths. They hid in their homes, quietly preparing their escape from the certain search for followers of Jesus that would ensue after the Sabbath celebrations.

So how did they spend their time? The short verse from Luke that I read this morning says simply that:

> [T]hey rested on the Sabbath in obedience to the commandment.

I composed myself in Jerusalem, "resting" with some of the other disciples. True rest was difficult. I was sad because Jesus was dead. I was deathly afraid for my own safety. I was nervous about my courage in the face of any accusations that might come from either the Roman soldiers or the Jewish hierarchy. I knew that my face would be familiar to those who had been watching Christ with so much anger and suspicion. Mourning in fear was a very strange feeling.

Richard Rohr adapted language from his CD entitled *The Four Gospels* for the daily meditation. Once again, it is spot on:

> *The Gospel of Mark (and all of the other gospels) leads up to Jesus finally standing alone, without anyone really comprehending what He's talking about when He teaches on the "Reign of God." Jesus realizes that He has to do it in His flesh. He's got to stop talking about it. He's got to let it happen. Maybe you've had the experience that it's not until someone dies that we ask the ultimate questions, and that's what we mean when we say Jesus had to die for us. It's not that He had to literally pay God some price (unfortunately, many Christians understand it that way, as if the Father is standing up there in heaven with a big bill, saying, "Until I get some blood, I'm not going to change my mind about the human race."). That puts us in a terrible position in relation to God, and it can't be true. As if God could not forgive without payment. It pulled God into our way of loving and forgiving which is always mercenary and tit for tat.*

> *Quite simply, until someone dies, we don't ask the big questions. We don't understand in a new way. We don't break through. The only price that Jesus was paying was to the human soul, so that we could break through to what is real and lasting.*

One of the great things about these exercises, at least for me, is that I began asking the big questions early in the life of Jesus. It is true that I was moved like never before by imagining myself with Him during His crucifixion and death. However, the power of contemplation had already been at work in my life several months before that awful week in Jerusalem.

I particularly like Rohr's clarification of the saving power of the death of Christ. It makes no sense to me as an Old Testament "eye for an eye"; His death for my sins. I hate the idea that His death was the "two-by-four up 'side the head"; a cruel gesture to get the world's attention. In fact, the mere death of Christ would not have mattered much at all in the history of the world. It was the resurrection that gave it power. I take communion to remember that He is risen, not to be reminded that He died.

Tuesday, April 24   *(Genesis 22:1-18)*

Maggie and I started the day this morning together, again in the library. After a genuinely heartfelt prayer of gratitude, we walked out into a chilly spring morning.

Sitting on the bench, I composed myself once again in Jerusalem, waiting through a long Sabbath weekend for what I knew would happen on Easter morning. In what seemed a little like a "play within a play," I imagined myself sitting on a bench in a Jerusalem garden, contemplating my experience with Jesus during the three years of His public ministry. That "contemplation within a contemplation" worked to create a peaceful center in my overall mood of mourning. I heard His Sermon on the Mount. I saw Him reach out to blind men, lepers, and women from the "other side of the tracks." I was proud to have known Him.

My reverie was interrupted by sounds of Roman soldiers passing by my secluded bench. Once again, I thought about my own safety; not about the life and meaning of Jesus Christ. I felt shame.

I left that uncomfortable place to return to the present time for my usual Tuesday morning tennis. The sense of belonging that pervades these thrice-weekly tennis games is powerful. On the court this morning were two other graduates of Harvard College, three other men who live on San Juan Drive here in Ponte Vedra Beach, and two members of Our Lady Star of the Sea parish!. I have not had that much in common with any group of people I can remember being around in the past fifty years. The big news this morning was that the parish bulletin had a picture of Sallie Ann dancing with Father Steven at the ministry party last Friday night.

Back in the library, my meditation focused on the Catholic celebration of the Triduum, the three days of Paschal stillness between Maundy Thursday and Easter Sunday. We are now in the sixth calendar week of exercise Week Three. Our readings for the rest of the week, beginning today, are similar to what the Lectors read at the Easter Vigil service.[88]

---

[88] Carl E. Olson described the Easter Vigil readings in the April 6 Ignatius Insight. "The Liturgy of the Word follows [the Service of Light], consisting of seven readings from the Old Testament and two from the New Testament. These readings include the story of creation (Genesis 1 and 2), Abraham and Isaac (Genesis 22), the crossing of the Red Sea (Exodus 14 and 15), the prophet Isaiah proclaiming God's love (Isaiah 54), Isaiah's exhortation to seek God (Isaiah 55), a passage from Baruch about the glory of God (Baruch 3 and 4), a prophecy of Ezekiel (Ezekiel 36), Saint Paul on being baptized into

Listening to Gregorian chants in the background, my mind wandered back to the Easter Vigil we just celebrated. Of course, that brought to mind the Easter Vigil of 2009, when I became a Catholic. I spent a long half hour remembering that wonderful night. The schedule for the evening, both then and now, was for the catechumens to be baptized before the Lectors read the scriptural passages. So on that big night two years ago, I was not altogether attentive when the Lectors went up to the ambo.

Some of the readings are focused on baptism, that sacrament which brings man into saving communion with God's divine life. Consider, for example, Saint Paul's remarks in Romans 6:

> *We were indeed buried with him through baptism into death, so that, just as Christ was raised from the dead by the glory of the Father, we too might live in newness of life.*

Easter is in many ways the season of baptism, the sacrament of Christian initiation, in which those who formerly lived in darkness and death are buried and baptized in Christ, emerging filled with light and life.

From the early days of the ancient Church the Easter Vigil has been the time for adult converts to be baptized and enter the Church. After the conclusion of the Liturgy of the Word, catechumens (those who have never been baptized) and candidates (those who have been baptized in a non-Catholic Christian denomination) are initiated into the Church by (respectively) baptism and confirmation. The faithful are sprinkled with holy water and renew their baptismal vows. Then all adult candidates are confirmed and general intercessions are stated. The Easter Vigil concludes with the Liturgy of the Eucharist and the reception of the Body, Blood, Soul, and Divinity of the Crucified and Risen Lord. As Eastern Catholics sing hundreds of times during the Paschal season,:

> *Christ is risen from the dead; by death He conquered death, and to those in the graves, He granted life![89]*

Jesus Christ (Rom 6), and the Gospel of Luke about the empty tomb discovered on Easter morning (Luke 24:1-21).

These readings constitute an overview of salvation history and God's various interventions into time and space, beginning with Creation and concluding with the angel telling Mary Magdalene and others that Jesus is no longer dead; "You seek Jesus of Nazareth, the crucified. He has been raised; he is not here." Through these readings "the Lord 'beginning with Moses and all the prophets' (Lk 24.27, 44-45) meets us once again on our journey and, opening up our minds and hearts, prepares us to share in the breaking of the bread and the drinking of the cup" (General Norms, 11).

[89] Carl E. Olson again, from his April 6, 2010, article in Ignatius Insight.

The reading today from Genesis 22 is the story of Abraham and Isaac. The command of God to Abraham that he sacrifice his only son has always seemed to me to be brutally "Old Testament."   Why would God ask such cruelty from Abraham? I found a very helpful commentary that suggests that God never desired the actual, physical sacrifice of Isaac:

> The issue shows, that God did not desire the sacrifice of Isaac by slaying and burning him upon the altar, but his complete surrender, and a willingness to offer him up to God even by death.
>
> Nevertheless the divine command was given in such a form, that Abraham could not understand it in any other way than as requiring an outward burnt-offering, because there was no other way in which Abraham could accomplish the complete surrender of Isaac, than by an actual preparation for really offering the desired sacrifice. This constituted the trial, which necessarily produced a severe internal conflict in his mind.[90]

I do not much like this notion that God used such clear language in asking Abraham to make the actual sacrifice only to be sure that Abraham truly felt tested.   It is similar to the idea that Rohr rejected in his meditation yesterday, which was that God demanded the death of Christ as a quid pro quo for our sins.   I ended my meditation period with a prayer for understanding.

Wednesday, April 25   *(Genesis 1:1-2:4)*

Last night was the final meeting of my class at UNF this semester. I came home late, but proud. That may seem commonplace to most people. There may have been a time in my own life when I would not have considered it noteworthy. Right now, however, I feel awfully good each time I finish something that I start. Our class, The Art of Civic Discourse, debated Ben Hoffman's other class, The Art of Conflict. The proposition they debated was Peter Singer's[91] argument that it is the moral obligation of every person to give a portion of his or her wealth to those with less. Singer is a leading advocate of the utilitarian philosophy that each of us should give until we reach the marginal utility of the gift. This argument leads logically to a world in which everyone is absolutely equal in terms of wealth and well-being.   It was a good ending to my second semester as a professor.

---

[90] Biblical Commentary on the Old Testament, by Carl Friedrich Keil and Franz Delitzsch [1857-78]

[91] According to Wikipedia, "Peter Albert David Singer (born 6 July 1946) is an Australian philosopher who is the Ira W. DeCamp Professor of Bioethics at Princeton University and Laureate Professor at the Centre for Applied Philosophy and Public Ethics at the University of Melbourne. He specialises in applied ethics and approaches ethical issues from a secular, preference utilitarian perspective."

Maggie and I came down to the library this morning to pray, and to read the story of the creation in Genesis. My prayer of gratitude slipped easily into a conversation with God. We talked about everything from the class debate last night, to my "compromise" position on evolution and creation. I told Him about the arrival today of Deacon Tom Bomkamp and his wife, Enza. We even talked about the cool weather!

As I read through the creation story in Genesis, I was struck more than a little with the amazing poetry of the language:

> *And God saw that it was good. And there was evening, and there was morning...*

Who were these poets? In what language was this poetry first written? It sounds so wonderful in English, but does it have the same poetic value in Hebrew or Greek or Latin? "And God saw that it was good" in Latin is *"et vidit Deus quod esset bonum."* The Latin for "there was evening, and there was morning" is *"est vespere et man."* Since I do not know Latin, I cannot say that these phrases sound as nice in Latin as they do in English. However, the poetic value of repetition is clearly present in the ancient language.

I found a timeline at the web site appropriately named "Greatsite.com."[92] If that timeline is correct, it was not until 995 CE that the first Anglo-Saxon version of the New Testament appeared. John Wycliffe, an Oxford professor, produced a hand-written copy of the first English language bible four hundred years later.

My guess is that the poetry emerged in the oral tradition, long before anything was written down in any language. I suspect those who told the stories found the rhythm of poetry easier to remember. Their audiences must have reacted well to the music of the poetry in these verses. The bible had already been translated into over 500 languages by 500 CE. I suspect much of the poetic quality found its way into every one of these translations.

Reading this story of creation feels good to me. I connect to all those who passed the oral tradition down from one generation to the next. I connect to all those who read the written word from one century to the next.

---

[92]The timeline according to Greatsite.com: **1,400 BC:** The Ten Commandments delivered to Moses. **500 BC:** Completion of all original Hebrew. **200 BC:** Completion of the Septuagint Greek manuscripts. **1st Century CE:** Completion of all original Greek manuscripts. **315 CE:** Athenasius, the Bishop of Alexandria, identifies the 27 books of the New Testament which are today recognized as the canon of scripture. **382 CE:** Jerome's Latin Vulgate manuscripts produced. **995 CE:** Anglo-Saxon (Early Roots of English Language) translations of the New Testament produced. **1384 CE:** Wycliffe is the produce an English manuscript of the complete Bible; all 80 books. **1526 CE:** William Tyndale's New Testament; the first New Testament printed in the English language. **1535 CE:** Myles Coverdale's Bible; The first complete bible printed in the English language. **1611 CE:** The King James Bible printed.

However, I know from science that our world was not made in six days. I am not troubled by the discrepancy. My faith is not based on a literal reading of Genesis or any other part of the bible. The more our best scientists learn about the origin of this earth and everything in it, the more amazed I am with its magic and majesty.

That works for me.

Thursday, April 26   *(Exodus 14:15-15:1)*

Maggie and I sat in the garden pavilion this morning. I had just returned from the tennis court. I read aloud the passage from Exodus. Maggie took little notice of my effort to include her, instead devoting herself to a frenetic lizard search. Paradise indeed!

Deacon Tom and Enza arrived last night in time to join Sallie Ann and me for dinner. The conversation picked up right at the place it left off, more than six months ago. It did not take long for us to get around to the political climate in the Catholic Church today. The Bomkamps sometimes feel as though they are not welcome in some Church circles. All four of us feel pressured to hide our political views around our friends in the Church.

Tom, who celebrated his 80th birthday last week, was over thirty when Vatican II was convened. All of the documents were released, and most of the changes in actions and attitudes of Catholics took place during the decade of his thirties. Enza and Sallie Ann were about ten years younger, but they were very much aware of the debates that took place in Rome, and the changes that resulted. For that generation of cradle Catholics, the divisions that only existed in vague theoretical discussions prior to Vatican II, became increasingly harder lines separating liberals and conservatives.

Listening to the talk last night about what it was like in the Church during the late sixties and the seventies, I could not help but see the parallels in the broader society. The painfully divided world we live in today is the result of the culture wars of that era.

I often talk about the political sea change that occurred in the United States during that period. As I understand it, a "big shift" in political views and party affiliations occurred between 1965 and 1975. That "big shift" sparked the increasing polarization of our country. The period began with the civil rights successes achieved during the administration of Lyndon Johnson.

Congress passed the Civil Rights Act of 1964, and the President issued an executive order that went even further in breaking down the barriers between the races. Almost immediately, the political parties in the United States began to change. The American South had theretofore been a solidly Democratic voting-block, forming a major part of the New Deal coalition of Franklin Roosevelt. The Civil Rights legislation caused conservative Southern Democrats to move into the Republican Party in massive numbers.

That one issue drove a wedge between liberals and conservatives that touched on almost every aspect of the relationship between the government (particularly the Federal government) and the individual. Basically, liberals argued that the government could and should intervene in virtually all aspects of life to ensure equal treatment of minorities (which rapidly grew to include anyone discriminated against for virtually any reason, including age, sex, ethnic background, religious preference, handicap, and sexual preference).

In 1973, the Supreme Court ruled in Roe vs. Wade that abortion was legal in the United States. A strange logical conundrum developed as a result of the pro-life movement. The Civil Rights conservatives argued that the state had no right to interfere in the private decisions of schools, clubs, and employers to discriminate. The pro-choice liberals took exactly the same position, arguing that the state has no right to interfere in the private decisions of a woman with respect to family planning and childbirth. However, Civil Rights conservatives joined with pro-life conservatives, that conundrum notwithstanding.

It seems to me that these two issues – reproductive rights and civil rights – are the primary wedges driving our society, our politics, and, ultimately, our Catholic Church into polarized camps. These two camps are finding it increasingly difficult to even talk to each other, much less find grounds for cooperation or compromise.

Reproductive rights include both abortion and contraception, and these issues are sometimes conflated with women's rights. The fact is that men are not biologically bound to the consequences of their actions in the same way that women are, and do not have the physical force of responsibility in those cases. Reproductive rights are not women's rights, but are certainly women's issues.

Many Catholics now believe that the constitutional separation of church and state has been crossed in recent efforts of the U.S. government to compel church affiliates to include reproductive rights in insurance policies.

The primary civil rights issue today is homosexuality, but may also include immigration policies. However, there are civil rights dimensions to many other problem areas as well. The so-called "war on drugs" overwhelmingly targets people of color, which explains most of the disproportionate number of black and Hispanic inmates in our prisons. A discrimination case has been filed against a Catholic school in Texas that dismissed a teacher for using *in vitro* fertilization.

So what does all of this have to do with Ignatius or my spiritual exercise today? This is a fair question. My answer has two dimensions. The first is that this journal is ultimately about my journey, and it would not be complete (or very honest) if it excluded my interest in politics. The second is that I became a Catholic at a time when Catholicism was part of many political discussions, and when the policies of government regularly come up in spiritual discussions.

I have many friends who have little or no interest in politics or political issues. Some of them do not vote. Others simply find political discussion boring. I know of very few people who are as politically interested (obsessed?) as I am. This is perfectly alright with me. Some people follow sports obsessively. Some people love to cook, and will discuss recipes day in and day out. Most hobbyists love to talk about their hobbies, including people who love to hunt and fish, people who love to play golf or tennis, and people who collect things. Now, what I do not know is whether any of these people would or have mentioned their outside passions and hobby interests in their journals.

It is my fervent hope that the current tensions between liberals and the Church will abate. After all, my Friend Jesus expounded some of the most liberal policies that have ever existed. He told us to feed the hungry, heal the sick, help the poor, and reach out to minorities. There has to be room in this big Catholic tent for those of us who consider these to be the truly non-negotiable tenets of our faith.

I ended the morning reading a line from Thomas Merton:

> If you want to study the social and political history of modern nations, study hell.

Friday, April 27   (Isaiah 54:5-14, 55:1-11)

It was a little cold outside this morning when Maggie and I went down to the bench. There was not a cloud in the sky, portending another beautiful spring day. I read from my journal before coming downstairs. Doing so forced me to include in my prayer a petition for some forgiveness. Sister Joan will remind me when I next meet with her that what I wrote yesterday was not in the spirit of these exercises. I am certain that she will be speaking not only for all the spiritual directors past and present, but also with the guidance and inspiration of the Holy Spirit. I will respond with those two words Father John sees at the center of our faith: inclusion and forgiveness.

Isaiah is one of my favorite Biblical authors. Over and over again, he anticipates the New Testament messages of concern for the people at the margins of life. He does it with great poetry:

> The LORD will call you back as if you were a wife deserted and distressed in spirit…For a brief moment I abandoned you, but with deep compassion I will bring you back.

> Come, all you who are thirsty, come to the waters; and you who have no money, come, buy and eat! Come, buy wine and milk without money and without cost. Why spend money on what is not bread, and your labor on what does not satisfy?
> For my thoughts are not your thoughts, neither are your ways my ways, declares the LORD.

Our readings from the Old Testament this week have been as wonderful to read as they were to listen to during the Easter Vigil. I wanted to understand how and why these particular verses were chosen for this important service.

I found a great article on the Franciscans web site, in which Father Nathan Mamo describes the passages well.[93] His description applies to this week's meditation just as well:

> Choose wisdom, life and salvation!

We celebrated the long Sabbath this week. I think I am well prepared for the fourth and final week of these exercises.

I ended the morning with a prayer from St. Francis of Assisi:

> Lord, make me an instrument of thy peace.
> Where there is hatred, let me sow love,
> Where there is injury, pardon;
> Where there is doubt, faith;
> Where there is despair, hope;
> Where there is darkness, light;
> And where there is sadness, joy.
>
> O Divine Master, grant that I may not so much seek
> to be consoled as to console,
> to be understood as to understand,
> to be loved, as to love.
>
> For it is in giving that we receive,
> It is in pardoning that we are pardoned,
> and it is in dying that we are born to eternal life.

---

[93] *The Old Testament lessons move us through the remembrances of the longer Genesis account of Creation as good (Genesis 1:1 – 2:2) and of God's great test of Abraham's obedience (Genesis 22:1-18). Exodus (14:15 – 15:1), essential for tonight's initiation rites, tells of the dramatic tension between Israel's saving God and Pharaoh's army (which symbolizes the power of evil to control and possess), culminating in the great victory song of salvation, a model for the Exultet perhaps. The first of two Deutero-Isaiah texts (Isaiah 54:5-14) is a prophecy of restoration and reconciliation between the merciful and faithful God and the recently chastened People of Ancient Israel. It is a love song of sorts on the occasion of renewal and reestablishment promising hope and salvation. The next prophetic lesson (Isaiah 55:1-11) is a further exhortation to hope in the ideal of restorative change and growth (insinuating repentance and conversion), and in the unfailing power of God's Word to persuade, reform and save the hearers. The sixth lesson (Baruch 3:9-15,32 – 4:4) is attributed to Baruch, legendary secretary and friend of the Prophet Jeremiah. Written as if early in the era of the Babylonian Captivity, Baruch (whose name means "the Blessed One") exhorts them to seek the very wisdom of God, hinting that the captivity is their own fault, but that real salvation is still possible.*

Fourth Week

(Five Weeks)

1. Jesus Christ rises from the dead

I ask God for the gift to feel glad and to rejoice intensely because Jesus Christ rises in exultation and in great power and glory.

Saturday, April 28   (The Risen Jesus Goes to His Mother)

Week Four begins today, the day before the Fourth Sunday of Easter in the Liturgical Calendar. I read through the scriptures and thought-pieces assigned to us for the next seven days. I saw that we will spend this week contemplating the events of the one day that Jesus rose from the dead. It will be a week to pray and reflect upon the Resurrection.

When Maggie and I went into the library after tennis, we spent more than the usual amount of time entering into God's presence. I prayed a long prayer of gratitude for the blessing of these exercises. I thanked God for Saint Ignatius. I thanked Him for Sister Joan and Father Gap. I thanked Him for Father Joseph Tetlow and Father Richard Rohr. I thanked Him for Saint Thomas Aquinas and Father Raymond Brown. I thanked Him for all the Church Doctors and Church Fathers. I thanked Him for the early Christians and the oral historians who passed the stories and wisdom of the Old and New Testaments from one generation to the next. I thanked Him for the Evangelists and the scribes and the monks and the translators and the printers who made it possible for me to share that wisdom.

Maggie and I walked out into a beautiful day, making our way down to the meditation bench in the lower garden. My prayer of gratitude continued. I thanked God for all the gifts that He has given me, so many of which I see all around me today. I thanked Him for Sallie Ann. I stayed in this grace-filled space of gratitude for a long time.

I explained to God in my prayer that I felt uneasy composing myself with Jesus, the Risen Lord. Jesus incarnate had become my Friend. We laughed and played together when He was a child. I learned from Him when He became an adult and began His ministry. I suffered with Him during those painful days leading up to His death. I mourned His death as much or more than I have mourned the deaths of my family and close friends.

How do I relate to Him now? I sensed more than heard an answer. Just do it. Compose a place. Compose the characters in the scene. Go with it.

So I composed myself with Lady Mary, the mother of Jesus. Her grief was greater than mine, yet she was serene. She knew that I had been grieving. She understood my pain. We were able to talk about her son, His life, His ministry, and His death.

Then He entered the place where we were talking. Mary embraced Him at once. She knew Him. She accepted His resurrection with as much simple faith as she had accepted the news from Gabriel that she was to be His mother.

He spoke in a beautiful deep voice. His words comforted Mary. He consoled His mother.

He reminded her of the joy she took from His birth and childhood. She reminded Him of His disappearance at the temple at the Passover. They talked about Elizabeth and John the Baptist. They talked about all the strong women Jesus had known in His life.

Listening to them together, I felt comforted as well. However, I was shy. I wanted very much to say something, but words would not come.

I heard Him say that He needed to show Himself to others. He hugged His mother, nodded at me, and left the room.

Mary came close to me, and offered to console me. She spoke to my shyness and my fear. She explained that she would always be available to intercede on my behalf with her son.

I left that place and time, but continued to pray. For as long as I can remember, I have resisted the notion of intercession. The idea was not part of the Mormon tradition. Like many Protestant religions, Mormons believed in direct communication with God. Intercession was viewed as an excuse for a clerical hierarchy.

For some reason, Mary was not a significant part of my RCIA training. This puzzles me today. I wonder if it was there all along, but I simply missed it. I have three shelves in my upstairs library for the books I read during RCIA. Prominent on the first shelf is a large book entitled Catechism of the Catholic Church. I remember the night we were told to turn to it whenever we wanted to know more about, or better understand Church doctrine.   I noticed quite a bit of dust on the book.   Isn't it a little odd that I have apparently not looked at the doctrinal "final word" before now?

Maggie joined me upstairs.   I shook the dust off of my Catechism and read.   I prayed and reflected.

Section 494 of the Catechism talks about Mary, quoting Irenaeus and other Church Fathers:

> *As St. Irenaeus says, "Being obedient she became the cause of salvation for herself and for the whole human race."   Hence not a few of the early Fathers gladly assert: "The knot of Eve's disobedience was untied by Mary's obedience: what the virgin Eve bound through her disbelief, Mary loosened by her faith."   Comparing her with Eve, they call Mary "the Mother of the living" and frequently claim: "Death through Eve, life through Mary."*

Sections 964-975[94] of the Catechism describe Mary's role as Mediatrix.   This role was further explained in *Lumen Gentium,*[95] promulgated in 1964 by Vatican II.   The Council sought both to reaffirm the important role of Mary, but also to clarify her limited role relative to that of the Trinity.   She is Mediatrix, not Co-Redemptrix:

> *There is but one Mediator as we know from the words of the apostle, "for there is one God and one mediator of God and men, the man Christ Jesus, who gave himself redemption for all."   The maternal duty of Mary toward men in no wise obscures or diminishes this unique mediation of Christ, but rather*

---

[94] According to the Catechism, her role in relation to the Church and to all humanity goes still further. "In a wholly singular way she cooperated by her obedience, faith, hope, and burning charity in the Savior's work of restoring supernatural life to souls. For this reason she is a mother to us in the order of grace."   "This motherhood of Mary in the order of grace continues uninterruptedly from the consent which she loyally gave at the Annunciation and which she sustained without wavering beneath the cross, until the eternal fulfillment of all the elect. Taken up to heaven she did not lay aside this saving office but by her manifold intercession continues to bring us the gifts of eternal salvation . . . Therefore the Blessed Virgin is invoked in the Church under the titles of Advocate, Helper, Benefactress, and Mediatrix."   "Mary's function as mother of men in no way obscures or diminishes this unique mediation of Christ, but rather shows its power. But the Blessed Virgin's salutary influence on men . . . flows forth from the superabundance of the merits of Christ, rests on his mediation, depends entirely on it, and draws all its power from it."   "No creature could ever be counted along with the Incarnate Word and Redeemer; but just as the priesthood of Christ is shared in various ways both by his ministers and the faithful, and as the one goodness of God is radiated in different ways among his creatures, so also the unique mediation of the Redeemer does not exclude but rather gives rise to a manifold cooperation which is but a sharing in this one source."

[95] According to Wikipedia, Lumen Gentium, the Dogmatic Constitution on the Church, is one of the principal documents of the Second Vatican Council. This dogmatic constitution was promulgated by Pope Paul VI on November 21, 1964, following approval by the assembled bishops by a vote of 2,151 to 5.   As is customary with significant Roman Catholic Church documents, it is known by its first words, "Lumen Gentium," Latin for "Light of the Nations."

shows His power. For all the salvific influence of the Blessed Virgin on men originates, not from some inner necessity, but from the divine pleasure. It flows forth from the superabundance of the merits of Christ, rests on His mediation, depends entirely on it and draws all its power from it. In no way does it impede, but rather does it foster the immediate union of the faithful with Christ...This maternity of Mary in the order of grace began with the consent which she gave in faith at the Annunciation and which she sustained without wavering beneath the cross, and lasts until the eternal fulfillment of all the elect. Taken up to heaven she did not lay aside this salvific duty, but by her constant intercession continued to bring us the gifts of eternal salvation. By her maternal charity, she cares for the brethren of her Son, who still journey on earth surrounded by dangers and cultics, until they are led into the happiness of their true home. Therefore the Blessed Virgin is invoked by the Church under the titles of Advocate, Auxiliatrix, Adjutrix, and Mediatrix. This, however, is to be so understood that it neither takes away from nor adds anything to the dignity and efficaciousness of Christ the one Mediator.

Maggie began to express her impatience with my research efforts, so we left our "Ivory Tower" to return to the downstairs library. We walked immediately out to the meditation bench.

I composed myself once again in the company of Mary. As before, she was serene. She seemed consoled to have seen her son, but there was a reverent quietness about her. I explained that I had been reading about her.

I read aloud the sentence from the Church Fathers:

The knot of Eve's disobedience was untied by Mary's obedience.

She seemed pleased. I asked if I could occasionally call upon her to intercede on my behalf. Again, she seemed pleased.

I returned to the bench in the garden. Maggie was looking for lizards. A family of ducks was swimming in the lagoon. I prayed the Our Father.

Sunday, April 29   *(Mark 16:1-11)*

Last night was the candlelight celebration for the Women's CRHP Team 13. One of my CRHP brothers reminded me that it was only one year ago that we walked from the Browning Center to the Church for our candlelight celebration. He mentioned this after noting that we had just emerged from the church into a group of more than forty friends. Neither of us knew the names of more than three people in the parish prior to our CRHP weekend.

Maggie is with me in the family room. Haydn is playing in the background. We lit a fire when we came in from our meditation outside in the garden. It is another day in paradise!

I began my prayer earlier this morning with more gratitude, picking up, to some extent, where I left off yesterday. My gratitude list is very long. The prayer flowed easily from gratitude to praise, and then to a conversation about the resurrection.

I composed myself in the tomb when the women came to anoint the body of Jesus. The "young man dressed in a white robe" said the words, "He is risen!" Hearing this, I left the tomb and returned to the family room. There was some commotion as the family prepared to go down to the beach for the annual ecumenical sunrise service. The extremely large congregation was singing along with the choir from Christ Episcopal Church. The song was "Christ the Lord is Risen Today." I joined in, singing louder than anyone else.

All around me, people were smiling. Their faces were shining, partly reflecting the rising sun, and partly as a result of their joy. Maggie, who was with me, expressed her joy by sprinting in circles in the sand.

Back on the bench in the garden, I marveled at the power of contemplative prayer. In the space of no more than thirty minutes, I had entered into a conversation with God in my garden, traveled back in time two thousand years to sit in the tomb in Jerusalem, and returned to Ponte Vedra to celebrate with friends and neighbors the rising sun (and the risen Son) on Easter morning:

Hallowed be your name, for yours is the power and the glory now and forever!

Monday, April 30   *(Luke 24:9-12, 34)*

The sky was bright in the east when Maggie and I went out to the garden bench this morning. The golden-pink horizon promised that the sun would be up soon. For some reason, there were many more birds than usual.

I composed myself back at the tomb, early on the morning of the Resurrection. The young man in the white robe was inside the tomb, explaining to the women that Jesus was gone. Matthew tells us that this young man was an angel, which is why the women were frightened. Presumably because I was in the middle of a fantasy, I was not troubled by that idea. So engrossed was I in determining the identity of the young man that I did not realize the sun was rising. The brilliance of the risen sun brought me out of my composition.

Luke identifies the women as Mary Magdalene, Joanna, and Mary the mother of James. There are so many women named Mary in the Bible that I remain confused, even after the intensity of my study over this past half-year. There are certainly enough men named James!

As I understand it, Mary Magdalene is the Mary from Bethany, sister of Martha and Lazarus. She is the Mary healed by Jesus when he removed seven evil spirits from her body. She is the Mary who anointed Jesus the week before the final Passover.

Pope Gregory the Great identified her as a prostitute, an identity she was not to lose for almost 1400 years. It was only in 1969 that Pope Paul VI said it wasn't so. However, he did so by saying that Mary Magdalene is a different Mary from the Mary from Bethany. This only tells me that there was another Mary in Bethany, different from Martha's sister.

Bede,[96] on whose authority I am able to identify Joanna, also states clearly that Mary Magdalene is the sister of Martha. Bede is quoted in the Catena Aurea saying that Joanna is the wife of Chuza, one of Herod's stewards. If this is true (and I certainly have no reason to doubt it), just think how amazing it is that the wife of a steward of Herod would join the closest woman-friend of Jesus at His tomb on the morning of the Resurrection! Life at the dawn of Christendom was odd indeed.

The other Mary at the tomb is the mother of the other apostle named James. James of Alpheus has the unfortunate distinction of being known down through the ages as James the Lesser. This is to distinguish him from James, son of Zebedee, and brother to John the Evangelist, who was also the most beloved friend of Jesus.

We know there were others, presumably women, with these three that morning. Mark identified one of them as Salome, who is sometimes referred to as Mary Salome (yet another Mary), and was probably the wife of Zebedee. Yes, that makes her mother of James the Greater.

The incredible power of women amazes me. Throughout the life of Jesus, he ministers to and is surrounded by women of different ethnic background, different social status, different health condition, and, presumably, different level of wealth. Think about Saint Monica, mother of Saint Augustine. Or consider Saint Helena, mother of the Emperor Constantine. Think about the women who practically managed the Underground Railroad in the years before the Civil War. Harriet Tubman, Sojourner Truth, Fanny Wright, and Harriet Beecher Stowe in the United States, and Hannah More and Elizabeth Heyrick, in England, come to mind. Of course I could go on forever.

I do not need to look in history books to find powerful women. Sallie Ann, my mother, my sisters Nancy and Connie, Phyllis Cox, Melissa, Jennifer, Sallie Ann's sister Mary Lou, Sister Kim, Sister Joan, and Mary Borg are just a few of the powerful women who have played important roles in my life. I cannot forget Maggie, one of the most influential women in my life today!

---

[96] According to Wikipedia, "Bede (672/673 – 26 May 735), also referred to as Saint Bede or the Venerable Bede (Latin: Bēda Venerābilis), was an English monk at the Northumbrian monastery of Saint Peter at Monkwearmouth and of its companion monastery, Saint Paul's, in modern Jarrow, both in the Kingdom of Northumbria. Bede's monastery had access to a superb library which included works by Eusebius and Orosius among many others."

Speaking of which, Maggie needed to go outside again.   I joined her so that I could return to my composition at the tomb.   Again, I reflected on the words of Luke:

> *...they told all these things to the Eleven...*

Just seeing that word – *eleven* – reminds me so vividly of the betrayer Judas.   Only four nights ago, Judas betrayed my Friend.   We are here in a tomb because of that betrayal.   Of course I know that it is highly likely that someone would eventually have betrayed Jesus.   That is a very weak argument.   Drug dealers often argue that, had they not sold the user his drugs, someone would have.   The act is the crime.   Betrayal is betrayal.

Luke goes on to remind us again that Peter was a difficult person to convince.   At first, he does not believe that the tomb was empty.   He has to go there himself to see the linens lying by on the ground.   Even then, Peter goes away wondering what happened!

As I reflect on it, however, it strikes me that this empty tomb on this particular morning is the single most important thing for any of us to believe.

David Lord Acton, one of the great English Catholics, agrees:

> *The whole point of Christianity is that the tomb is empty.*

The Resurrection is more than just the core of our faith.   It is the whole deal.   Without it, Jesus was a gifted man who said some very wonderful things, but He would have been forgotten within a generation.

I prayed the Our Father with great reverence.   In my mind, I was with the disciples, joining them in saying:

> *It is true!   The Lord has risen and has appeared to Simon.*

Tuesday, May 1   (Mark 16:1-11 and Luke 24:9-12, 34, again)

The assignment today is to reflect again on the readings from Mark and Luke that began the week.   Maggie was excited when I returned to the house from the tennis court.   She ran ahead of me to the meditation bench in the garden.   These exercises have brought Maggie and me much closer together.   I suspect that is largely the result of our doing the same thing at about the same time every day, and in the same place.   Dogs like predictability.   I like it more each day.

I prayed this morning about that other morning.   Mary Magdalene and her friends were with me outside the tomb.   They were in a state of fright, about to run to Peter and the other disciples to tell them about the empty tomb.   I did not share their fear. I did feel a sense of awe and amazement.   So it is true, I thought.   He really did rise from the dead!

I began a conversation with God about faith. As much as I have learned from, and benefited from, these exercises, I still spend a lot of time in my head. I rationalize some of the things that more devout people deeply believe. I include some rather fundamental tenets of our faith in the phrase "don't sweat the small stuff." I continue to gloss over my doubts about the virgin birth; the resurrection, transubstantiation, and the idea of heaven being a place good people go to after death to sit with God and the angels.

Which is better, I asked God, unquestioning faith in these fundamental aspects of our faith, or loving our neighbor and living a life of service? He answered that the operative phrase is "faith and works," not "faith or works." Christ preached that doing good was more important than strict observance of the religious laws.

God went on, however. He asked me about my life of service. He asked about my love of my family and friends. He cautioned me not to characterize the issue in a way that I was certain to lose, regardless of which is more important, faith or works.

Moments of doubt, He went on, have been common among people of faith from the beginning of time. The key is to accept them for what they are – moments of doubt – and move on. He told me that the best thing for me to do, when I question my faith, is talk to Him about it.

We left it there. I listened to the sound of the surf breaking on the beach. I prayed the Our Father in gratitude.

Wednesday, May 2   *(Summary)*

When Maggie and I were sitting on the bench earlier this morning, I looked back to the west, my left, where Sallie Ann has placed a little statue of the Virgin Mary. A bed of white petunias in full bloom surrounds the statue. It was magical.

It has been an extraordinary few days. Our time with the Bomkamps last week was a joy. They are fun and funny and, without dwelling on it, deeply spiritual. Sallie Ann spent the weekend at the CRHP retreat for the women's Team 13.

Again, I marvel at the strength of these women. I dropped by the cultural center a couple of times. I was quite careful to schedule my appearance at times I suspected relatively little would be available for me to do. All the "steel magnolias" were there: Joyce Moore, Cindi

Mona, Jenny Engmann, Carol Williams, and so many more. I am humbled by their commitment to service.

Monday was the major treat of the week. Our good friends from CRHP, Dianne and Dick Cook, had their marriage sacramentally blessed by the Church. Sallie Ann and I celebrated the same sacrament two years ago. We both read the scriptural readings at the service for the Cooks, and we joined the small wedding party for dinner afterward. As we listened to Dianne and Dick repeat their vows, we held hands and repeated our own as well. It was a deeply moving experience.

The grace I am seeking this week is "to feel glad and to rejoice intensely because Jesus Christ rises in exultation." Generally, I have not felt glad. I have not rejoiced. I am still mourning His death.

After writing in the journal earlier this morning, I left the library to run some errands. I spent some more time at the bench, thinking about the absence of joy in my prayers a few hours ago. When I was suffering from the extremely painful depression in 2006 and 2007, I continued to try different "solutions" to bring me back from the dark places. Most of my solutions at that time served only to deepen my depression.

Only after open heart surgery did I begin to search for joy in some better places. Sallie Ann and I talked about what was going on. We sought the help of a professional. We began to pray together, even though my idea of prayer was still distorted by the pain of my excommunication by the Mormons. I looked for and found some other resources.

First and foremost, I talked about my misery with Buddy Tudor, the only friend around whom I was completely honest. Later, when I started to look for solutions in Christ, I talked to Father John. Importantly, I became an active member of the St. Anne's RCIA community.

Buddy and Father John are no longer available to talk to in person. I have spent a lot of time with both of them in my daily contemplations. Right now, however, I feel like I need the fellowship of my living friends. I actually made a phone call to a good friend, and will have lunch with him today. Just having that on my schedule has begun to lift my mood.

2. Jesus Christ consoles his friends

I ask God for the gift to feel glad and to rejoice intensely because Jesus Christ rises in exultation and in great power and glory.

Thursday, May 3   *(John 20:19-23)*

It is a Thursday, which means tennis, one of the truly great delights of retirement! When I came back to the house, Maggie greeted me in her usual fashion, and we walked down to the garden bench together. I was already singing.

John tells us in the passage today about Jesus standing among His disciples in the house with its locked doors. I joined them in my composition.

I laughed to myself when Jesus said, "Peace be with you!" My immediate response was, "And with your spirit!"[97] Jesus actually smiled. For the first time since His death on the Cross, I felt joy in His presence.

All the others in the room were frightened, in part due to the appearance of Jesus with the wounds in His hands and side. They were more afraid, however, because the Jewish leaders and Roman soldiers were actively searching for followers of Jesus. As before, I realized I was in a fantasy, and did not share their fear. I could understand it. They had always known that they were risking the approval of their friends and families when they first began to follow Jesus. Over the past few weeks, however, it had become clear that their very lives were in jeopardy. I think they all knew that the danger would only grow.

Jesus called His disciples to receive the Holy Spirit and go out among the people. He gave them the power to forgive. This struck me at the time as an awesome responsibility, literally the power of life and death. I made a note to myself to research further this delegation of authority.

His charge to the disciples seemed to be aimed at me as well. "I am sending you." Not only was I honored to be included among His chosen few, I felt challenged to prove myself up to the task.

I left the composition and returned to the garden bench. It seems increasingly the case that a strong connection exists between joy and service. Being sent out by Jesus filled me with peace, serenity, and, simply, joy.

Friday, May 4   (John 20:19-23, again)

Morning after morning, I begin this journal with high praise for the meditation garden, or bench, or library corner, or beach. It may seem like a much-too repetitious refrain. However, I experience these places as very real gifts from God. It is as though He wants me to experience His presence in a place where I am sensitive to the sound of His voice, and the feel of His touch. Well, it works.

gain this morning, I sat on that bench totally in awe of my surroundings. The brightening sky, the rising sun, the awakening birds – all invite me to praise God and express my gratitude. Life could certainly be a lot worse!

I composed myself once again with the disciples in the room with the risen Christ.

---

[97] The English version of the Catholic Mass changed last November. We used to respond to the peace with the phrase, "And also with you." We now say "And with your spirit."

I am sending you.

These are such simple, direct words for what is, in the end, a simple, direct command. Jesus sent His disciples as His Father had sent Him. With that statement, Jesus breathed on them and said, "Receive the Holy Spirit."

As I understand this, it is a portent of the Pentecost. As its name suggests, this event occurred fifty days after the resurrection. I was not able to deepen my understanding of the difference between this call to the disciples on the first day after the resurrection and the call at Pentecost.

While seeking clarification on that point, however, I did read something very helpful from John Chrysostom in the Catena Aurea. In addition to showing Himself to them, Jesus gave the disciples the power to forgive sins that day in the loced room. I assume this is the same power used by priests in the sacrament of reconciliation. Chrysostom writes:

> *For not only cannot a priest, but not even angel or archangel do anything of themselves; the Father, Son, and Holy Ghost do all. The priest only furnishes the tongue, and the hand.*

The priests today and the disciples then, only furnish "the tongue and the hand." God does the actual forgiving of sin.

The consoling power of my prayers is working. Each day, the sadness I felt during the trial and crucifixion lifts a little more.

Saturday, May 5   (The Contemplation)

There was no tennis for me this morning. Because of our trip to Italy, I will not return to my thrice weekly group until June. Maggie and I sat on the dock this morning to pray. I think she senses that we are about to begin our longest period of separation since she was born. On reflection, I am the one feeling the separation anxiety! I cannot imagine a full month without this little dog.

We watched the sun come up. The meditation garden and pavilion look very different from across the grass. It seems a little odd that we have never begun our mornings on this side of the garden.

The full title of today's meditation is "The Contemplation for Learning to Love God." Ignatius called it *Contemplatio ad* Amorem, which is generally translated as The Contemplation to Gain Love. I will refer to it in this journal as "the Contemplation." I have been reading it from time to time since I met with Sister Joan on Wednesday. It is simply fabulous.

Kriztina and John Strangle[98] write that:

> [I]t serves as a magnificent crowning point of the entire retreat and as a transition to the aftermath, which we might call the 'Fifth Phase'.
>
> The Contemplation consists of four parts, each involving reflection rather than a fantasy composition. The first part is a reflection on the "splendors of the created world." While considering all the things He created in the world around me, I focus particularly on the gifts in this created world that He has given to me.
>
> The second part is a similar reflection, but one focused on the living creatures in the world, not the physical grandeurs. Every living thing was created by God. Every living thing is momently being created by God. He is present in all life. Again, I focus particularly on the fact that God is present in my life today, and He has been present since my conception.
>
> The third part is a reflection on how busy God has been, and is, as He creates and supports each of the parts of His creation. I think about all that I have been through over the past sixty-seven years. I imagine God's presence, offering grace and support throughout my life. He supported each achievement. He offered forgiving grace for each poor exercise of my free will.

Finally, I focus my reflection on the good in the world. His goodness can be found amid all this chaos around me. For all the frustration I feel for the mess mankind is making of our collective gift, I see glimmers of hope and light. I celebrate in my mind each of those individual acts of kindness, justice, and caring.

The following prayer is repeated at the end of each of the four reflections:

> Accept, O Lord and treat as your own my liberty, my understanding, my memory – all of my decisions and my freedom to choose.
>
> All that I am and all that I have You gave; now I turn and return all to You, looking to find Your hopes and will in all.

---

[98] Kriztina and John Strangle describe their book as follows: "The purpose of this book is to learn to live better. This can also be considered to be learning the art of discernment in a Christian context; that is, learning to make better choices by being open to the Creator and the inspirations of the Spirit while using one's reasoning and thinking powers to make these better choices. The method described and some of the principles are as old as philosophy and religion itself but the concrete form of these "Spiritual Exercises" were developed and practiced by St. Ignatius of Loyola in the 16th century and have been utilized by millions ever since. In this self-guided form that we present, the best of new understandings in psychology, philosophy, and theology are incorporated so as to 'modernize' the Ignatian Spiritual Exercises. Feel free to use this book as the Spirit inspires you and know that this book will accompany you. This is a scholarly work with many footnotes."

Keep giving me your holy love, Hold on me Your Life-giving gaze, and I neither need nor want anything else.

The Contemplation is clearly too important for one session. Each one of the four parts should be the focus of one or more morning sessions. I ended my prayer this morning somewhat frustrated by the effort required to get through all four parts of the Contemplation. I left each part too soon. More time will be devoted this week to all the little bits that make up each of the parts.

Sunday, May 6   (The Contemplation, again)

Sallie Ann and I spent most of the day yesterday involved with the parish. Our family joined the Keller family for a lunch in honor of Anna Grace, our god daughter. She celebrated First Communion, along with 125 of her CCD and Palmer classmates. We celebrated a second Mass at 5:30, where Sallie Ann sang with the praise choir.

I returned to the Contemplation this morning. Richard Rohr wrote in Radical Grace that:

> *What you quickly and humbly learn in contemplation is that how you do anything is how you do everything.*

As is occasionally the case, I like this thought from Rohr very much, even though I am not at all certain what it means. It is exciting to think that I will spend a week with him. The retreat is only two weeks from now.

Once again, I started with the first point of the Contemplation. I used one of the somewhat clumsy literal translations of the original Ignatius:

> *First Point. The First Point is, to bring to memory the benefits received, of Creation, Redemption and particular gifts, pondering with much feeling how much God our Lord has done for me, and how much He has given me of what He has, and then the same Lord desires to give me Himself as much as He can, according to His Divine ordination.*

This next part of the first point deals with the reciprocity of giving. The concept is wonderful. The challenge is, well, challenging.

> *And with this to reflect on myself, considering with much reason and justice, what I ought on my side to offer and give to His Divine Majesty, that is to say, everything that is mine, and myself with it, as one who makes an offering with much feeling: Take, Lord, and receive all my liberty, my memory, my intellect, and all my will -- all that I have and possess. Thou gavest it to me: to Thee, Lord, I return it! All is Thine, dispose of it according to all Thy will. Give me Thy love and grace, for this is enough for me.*

Sitting first in the library and then walking out into the garden toward the meditation bench, it was simply impossible not to be awed and humbled by His creation, and all within it that He has made available to me. Over and over again, it seems that the point of these Exercises, perhaps of our faith itself, is that we are to give everything we have to the benefit and service of God. I am not yet up to this challenge.

> *Second Point. The second, to look how God dwells in creatures, in the elements, giving them being, in the plants vegetating, in the animals feeling in them, in men giving them to understand: and so in me, giving me being, animating me, giving me sensation and making me to understand; likewise making a temple of me, being created to the likeness and image of His Divine Majesty; reflecting as much on myself in the way which is said in the first Point, or in another which I feel to be better. In the same manner will be done on each Point which follows.*

I compose myself in that wonderful place where I can see the whole of the universe and the fullness of all time. Among God's creatures made available to me and in support of my own creation are long hereditary lines of family, friends, teachers, mentors, and revered idols. Also among God's creatures that have helped make me who I am are tempters and bad influences. I know that I have resisted rather seldom. I like to think I have been more strengthened by recovery rather than by resistance. While most of the creatures I see in the "eyes of my soul" are human beings, there are also some animals, with Maggie standing proudly at the front of the pack.

Again, all of this creation is a gift made available to me. However, it is available to me to use for the benefit and service of God. The challenge continues:

> *Third Point. The third, to consider how God works and labors for me in all things created on the face of the earth -- that is, behaves like one who labors -- as in the heavens, elements, plants, fruits, cattle, etc., giving them being, preserving them, giving them vegetation and sensation, etc. Then to reflect on myself.*

I contemplate the labor of God. Early in the exercises, I was reminded by my CRHP brother, Ian Weldon, that God is infinite. As Ian told us then, infinity divided by two is not half of infinity. It is simply two infinities. God can work full time on my continuing creation, and still have all the time in the world to work full time on the continuing creation of each and every other person and creature. That is the meaning and power of infinity.

In this third point, Ignatius is asking me to work as hard for God as God has worked and is working for me. That is infinitely challenging. Yet it is what Ignatius did for the rest of his life.

Fourth Point. The fourth, to look how all the good things and gifts descend from above, as my poor power from the supreme and infinite power from above; and so justice, goodness, pity, mercy, etc.; as from the sun descend the rays, from the fountain the waters, etc.

Before attempting to compose myself in a place that would enhance my understanding and appreciation of this part of the Contemplation, I read more from the autobiography of Ignatius. He describes one of his first prayer fantasies in language that comes very close to a description of my own experience:

Near the road is a stream, on the bank of which he sat, and gazed at the deep waters flowing by. While seated there, the eyes of his soul were opened. He did not have any special vision, but his mind was enlightened on many subjects, spiritual and intellectual. So clear was this knowledge that from that day everything appeared to him in a new light. Such was the abundance of this light in his mind that all the divine helps received, and all the knowledge acquired up to his sixty-second year, were not equal to it. From that day he seemed to be quite another man, and possessed of a new intellect. This illumination lasted a long time. While kneeling in thanksgiving for this grace, there appeared to him that object which he had often seen before, but had never understood. It seemed to be something most beautiful.

The lagoon is my stream. The bench is my bank. When I enter a composition, the eyes of my soul open to something that is closer to a feeling than a clear vision. I sense it rather than see it.

Yet I can describe what happens in each composition in considerable detail. For example, there was a smile on the face of Jesus. There was a crowd of disciples sitting on the grass listening to Him preach. I had conversations with Jesus, and with others I know only from passages in the bible. I talked with Father John and Buddy. When I prayed, my mind was enlightened and all of my senses were made sharper.

Reflecting on my experience, it occurs to me that the smile I saw on the face of God was warm and comforting and knowing. However, I did not see His teeth. I did not see the corners of His mouth turn up. The "eyes of my understanding" see clearly, but very differently from my actual eyes.

Thomas Merton described contemplation extremely well in his book New Seeds of Contemplation:

Contemplation is a kind of spiritual vision to which both reason and faith aspire...Yet contemplation is not vision because it sees "without seeing" and knows "without knowing." It is a more profound depth of faith, a knowledge too deep to be grasped in images, in word or even in clear concepts.[99]

Back in the library, I composed myself once again where I could see the whole universe, both physical and temporal. I looked for love. I looked for goodness. I looked for bravery in the wars. I looked for caring in times of pestilence and disease. I looked for compassion for the poor. I looked for acceptance of minorities. Throughout all time, and everywhere in the world, I saw evidence of this goodness and love. It seldom, if ever, dominated, but it was always present. This is the message of the Fourth Point.

I sat in silence for a long time. In front of me was an article with a quotation from Joseph Kelly, the director of the Center for the Study of Jewish-Christian-Muslim Relations at Merrimack:

> *Heaven is the state of full and everlasting communion with the Holy Trinity . . . It is a state of perfect joy and happiness because we have reached the true purpose and only satisfying goal of our existence: loving union with our God. It is the fulfillment of all our longings, the completion of our being, the realization of our deepest capacities for surrender, ecstasy, and intimacy in a full and immediate knowing and loving the very Source of being . . . Heaven is being completely and fully loved by the Source of love. Heaven is our full and irrevocable acceptance of this divine self-giving. It is by God's grace that we become capable of eternal life and love . . . Heaven as such is the destiny of all, because in assuming our human nature Christ has made it possible for all people to enter into the life of God.*

This speaks to me in the place where I have arrived at the end of my morning of prayer. It speaks to me about the Contemplation. I prayed the Our Father. I added gratitude for an amazing morning.

Monday, May 7   *(Luke 24:13-35)*

The extraordinary beauty of this place - this wonderful corner of Paradise - overwhelmed me this morning. I sat in the garden wondering why in the world I would ever leave it! I know that I have never been to Italy as a Catholic. I know that spending time with Richard Rohr and the others in the retreat will be an incredible experience. However, the peace and serenity of this place cannot be surpassed.

When I finished the reading from Luke last night, I started chanting (in my mind) with our Parish CRHP community:

---

[99] Merton, New Seeds of Contemplation, p. 24.

Were not our hearts, burning within us?   Were not our hearts burning with fire.

That is what we chant when each new CRHP retreat team enters the church at the Saturday night candlelight ceremony.   Now for the first time, I realize where it comes from.   The symbolism of these words is powerful.   Cleopas and his friend exclaimed these words after breaking bread with and listening to the risen Christ talk directly to them.

The Cleopas in Luke shares a name somewhat similar to Clopas, whose wife Mary was with Mary Magdalene at the tomb of Jesus.   Clopas and this Mary were the parents of James the Lesser.   Could Cleopas and Clopas be one and the same person?   Bible scholars do not appear to feel very strongly about this, one way or the other.   It makes a lot of sense to me that Cleopas and Clopas were one and the same.   That would explain the knowledge Cleopas and his friend had of the events that had just transpired in Jerusalem.   It would also explain why the two of them encountered the Eleven so soon after returning to the city.

I composed myself walking along the dusty road.   My fantasy road was not in Israel, however.   I found myself walking along the road that ran behind our house on the farm, extending west in a more or less straight line all the way to the end of our property.   That road was always either extremely dusty or mired in angle-deep mud.   As a young boy, I remember the dust billowing up in clouds with each step.   The memory is so vivid that I can taste the dust.

This morning, however, I am not alone on the road.   My companions, Cleopas and his friend, were anxious to reach Emmaus, which was located about as far from Jerusalem, seven miles, as the little town of Moreland was from our farm.   I wondered whether I could make it that far.   Then Jesus appeared at our side, seeming to come out of nowhere.

It was clear that the others did not recognize Him.   I did.   I wondered whether there would be dust clouds when His feet touched the road.   I worried about the dust from our footsteps getting into His wounds.

Cleopas was anxious to share with this stranger the news of the crucifixion and, especially, of the empty tomb.   Jesus responded in a reproachful tone, challenging us to recall the many scriptural predictions of these very events.   I was quiet, not daring to speak lest the others would see that I was in awe of Jesus.

I was surprised when Jesus agreed to join us in Emmaus for our evening meal.   He repeated some of what He had done at the Last Supper.

When he was at the table with them, he took bread, gave thanks, broke it and began to give it to them.   Then their eyes were opened and they recognized him, and he disappeared from their sight.

I left my composition, returning to the library to reflect on the wonder of "life-giving bread." In a very real sense, my eyes are opened each time I take the Eucharist. The act of communion is itself a contemplative prayer. The eyes of my soul recognize Jesus.

I prayed the Our Father. I prayed for the grace to accept God's gifts in the right spirit. I prayed for the grace to rise to His challenge to give back.

Tuesday, May 8   *(Luke again)*

When we walked out to the garden bench this morning, there was an all-encompassing silence. The tide was at its lowest. There was absolutely no wind.I knelt at the bench to pray. As I entered the conversation with God, I became aware of my surroundings in what became a magical few minutes. A flock of egrets flew south along the lagoon, their dark shapes just becoming visible against the brightening eastern sky. Isolated sounds broke through the quiet. A turtle splashed into the water. An egret squawked.

Maggie rustled the privet, searching for lizards. Only when I finished the Our Father did I notice the western sky. A full moon behind the house captured the serenity of this bit of paradise.

The assignment this morning was to pray and reflect again on the extraordinary journey to Emmaus. Last night, as I prepared for my morning, I was reminded of something a lawyer told me years ago. The key to understanding a document is to read it carefully, then read it again. And then read it again.

Each time I read through the passage from Luke, I saw something else. This has been the case numerous times over the past eight months. It is also true of the mental spaces I visit in my compositions. Each time I return to a place, I see something more.

The passage that caught my eye this morning was Luke's description of the two men when Jesus joined them. I also noticed it when I reflected on what I had seen on the road that morning long ago:

They stood still, their faces downcast.

I reflected on how desolate I have felt since the trial and crucifixion of Jesus. It must be the case that anyone approaching me most mornings during the past three weeks would have found my face downcast.

The men on the road to Emmaus reported the news to the stranger they only later identified as Jesus:

> *In addition, some of our women amazed us. They went to the tomb early this morning, but didn't find his body. They came out and told us that they had seen a vision of angels, who said he was alive. Then some of our companions went to the tomb and found it just as the women had said, but they did not see Jesus.*

After hearing from their women that the tomb was empty except for angels, they heard from their companions that what the women had reported was true. Several witnesses report that the tomb was empty. Women, one of whom could very possibly be the wife of Cleopas, were told by angels that Jesus was alive. Yet, against all this evidence, the faces of the men were downcast.

My own desolation continued after Good Friday, the Easter Vigil, and Easter Sunday. I celebrated all of these days with my fellow parishioners. I stood next to them and recited the Nicene Creed. I took the life-giving bread. Yet my face remained downcast.

There have been several moments of consolation over the past nine months. Many days have been made happy by my experience of these exercises. I have met the risen Christ in my contemplations, though I have been nervously respectful of His divinity. I have given myself completely to the Contemplation, seeing and believing that all I have and all I am are gifts from God. I have been, and am still overwhelmed with the grace that surrounds me.

There remains, however, a strong sense of loss. I have read that others are similarly affected by the exercises. The constant intensity of the experience has been powerful in my life. The highs have been incredibly high. The lows have been painfully low. Both the highs and the lows have been emotionally draining. To some extent, I feel like I have been running a spiritual super-marathon.

Our trip to Italy, which begins today, will provide a much-needed change. We will visit one or more churches every day, seeking to celebrate my new Catholicity in some of the most beautiful buildings on the planet. We will spend a full seven days with other retreatants in Assisi. The retreat schedule shows many hours of discussion with Richard Rohr on mysticism and contemplative prayer!

Deacon Dan dropped by our house last night after dinner. I write that as though it is commonplace for a Deacon to drop by from time to time. In fact, it was an absolutely wonderful experience, one that speaks volumes about our faith community here in Ponte Vedra.

I ended my session this morning with a long prayer of gratitude, followed by the Our Father. My mood has lifted from downcast to mellow. I am comfortable not being exuberant.

Friday, June 1

It has been close to a month since I last wrote anything in this journal. On one hand, it feels like yesterday when I last walked down to the bench in the garden with Maggie. On the other hand, it seems like something I did years ago. In fact, Maggie and I reunited four days ago. We have walked in the garden every day, and walked on the beach twice this week.

Sister Joan and I plan to meet Sunday afternoon. I assume we will go through the plan and schedule for finishing the Fourth Week of the Exercises. I think there are Tetlow assignments for three more calendar weeks.

In addition to whatever Sister Joan assigns me, I want to focus some serious spiritual energy on a deeper understanding of the resurrection. It is so much at the heart of Christianity, and, metaphorically at least, central to many other wisdom traditions. Increasingly, I am coming to believe that I, along with everyone else, am resurrected anew each day. A resurrection requires a death, which, for each of us, must regularly be the death of the false self. It troubles me to think that my false self is born again so often, but to imagine the alternative is to deny reality.

I want to better understand the resurrected Christ. It has now been almost two months since those desolate days when I composed myself at the trial and crucifixion of Jesus incarnate. I slip back into that mind space easily and often, feeling the same sadness and pain each time. In church after church in Italy, I knelt at length before the various representations of the crucified Christ. They were created by great artists and sculptors for the express purpose of evoking those emotions among the faithful. I felt a deep connection with the hundreds of thousands who have knelt in those same chapels over the centuries.

Saturday, June 2

Walking on the beach with Maggie this morning, I attempted to bring at least some of the past month into sharper focus. I read through my notes from the Rohr retreat last night, and again this morning. Two concepts from the retreat stayed with me while I walked. First, Rohr talked about the idea of non-duality more than any other, regardless of the stated topic of the lecture or discussion. Second, he returned over and over again to connectedness.

Non-Duality

Before we left for Italy, the Rohr staff asked each of us to answer a series of questions. One of them was to identify a particular moment in our lives when we experienced non-duality. I answered honestly that I was not completely sure what the term non-duality meant.   As I now understand it, the concept is quite simple.   Non-dual thinking is "both/and," while dual thinking is "either/or."   Dualistic thinking separates the world into "good or bad," "right or wrong," and "we or they."

Rohr teaches that part of the normal process of growing up is to experience four "splits."   Each of these "splits" separates our conception and, therefore, experience of an aspect of reality into dualistic parts.   The process of growing up spiritually, of maturing, of fulfilling the challenge of the second half of life, consists of resolving each of these four "splits."   Rohr says the "splits" are illusory.   To Rohr, the entire spiritual journey is the process of overcoming the illusion of separateness.

The first "split" occurs in each of us as very young children.   It involves the separation of "me" from "others," including, significantly, our mothers.   Without this initial dualism, we would have insufficient definition or clarity to establish any kind of separate identity.   Its resolution requires that we focus on the universal oneness of man.   We must eventually come to realize that we are all more the same than we are different.   Much of human history is proof that this split is extremely difficult to resolve.   The resolution of this "split" is, in fact, connectedness, the other major theme running through the Assisi conference.

The second "split" separates body and mind.   The body becomes inferior to the mind.   It is associated with a variety of sins, ranging from obesity and sex to vanity and addiction.   Paul writes about it at length in his letters to the Romans.   It is frequently associated with Neo-Platonic thinking, and it became the official doctrine of the Catholic faith as a result of its strong embrace by Augustine.   We get stuck in the false notion that we can "think" our way into union with God.   I have been especially guilty of "feeding my mind and starving my heart."   Rohr likes to say "mind over what matters."   Resolving this split requires us to open our "heart space" and focus less on our "mind space."   True learning occurs when love precedes knowledge.

The third "split" is the separation of life from death.   Regarding things as either alive or dead is classic dualism.   In fact, life and death are two sides of the same coin.   This is one of the great teachings of the resurrection.   We cannot pretend that we will never die, or that those we love will never die.   Jesus teaches us that we die, but we are never dead.   When we die, our life changes, it does not end.

The final "split" is between our acceptable and our unacceptable selves.   We learn that one type of behavior is acceptable, and another type is unacceptable.   Each of us struggles with our shadow self.   I feel like I have come to know mine far too intimately.   I loathe my shadow self.   Rohr teaches us to embrace our unacceptable selves.   We are who we are.   We will stop presenting the world our false self of acceptability only when we resolve our dualistic sense of who we are.

Reading through what I have just written about the four splits reminds me of just how far I have to go to resolve the split between my mind and my heart.   The concepts are still too "heady."   I can say that I understand the difference between dual and non-dual thinking. I have experienced glimpses of non-duality in each of the four areas, especially during these exercises.

On balance, however, I have to confess to the predominance of dualism in my world view. I spend countless hours struggling with the polarization of the world into haves and have not's. My mind goes immediately to the conservative versus liberal position on every issue. I host regular debates between my good side and my dark side. It is worth mentioning that all of these dualistic notions are lessened during my periods of contemplative prayer.

I read something written by Elie Wiesel that speaks to me as I seek to understand this concept:

> *The opposite of love is not hate, it's indifference. The opposite of art is not ugliness, it's indifference. The opposite of faith is not heresy, it's indifference. And the opposite of life is not death, it's indifference.*

Connectedness

Saint Francis taught and lived a life of connectedness. His famous encounter with the leper early in his conversion was the transformational event that informs almost everything that follows. It forced him to see that he and the leper were connected. Francis and the leper were far more alike than they were different. Jesus taught us that time and time again.

Years ago, I met a sixteen-year-old who had already attempted to commit suicide three times. He was a high school dropout. He was unemployed. He suffered from incredible depression. Only after talking to him over the course of a weekend retreat did I realize there was more about us that was alike than different, exactly as Francis realized during his encounter with the leper. All of my sixty plus years of life, numerous courses, hundreds of books, and various achievements mattered less than the deep depression I shared with that young man. In that place where both of us hurt, the place that really mattered, we were exactly the same. That was a major breakthrough for me.

During the early years of my spiritual journey (early meaning four years ago, not forty!), I saw the connections between the various wisdom traditions. I thought then, as I think today, that Christians, Jews, Muslims, Buddhists, and serious humanitarians are connected in more ways than they are separate. Catholics and Protestants are connected. Conservative and liberal Catholics are connected. We all spend far too much time worrying about our differences. We spend too little time celebrating the core beliefs that we share.

I ended the morning by reading St. Francis's Canticle of Brother Sun and Sister Moon:

Most High, all-powerful, all-good Lord, All praise is Yours, all glory, all honour and all blessings.
To you alone, Most High, do they belong, and no mortal lips are worthy to pronounce Your Name.
Praised be You my Lord with all Your creatures,
especially Sir Brother Sun,
Who is the day through whom You give us light.
And he is beautiful and radiant with great splendour,
Of You Most High, he bears the likeness.

Praised be You, my Lord, through Sister Moon and the stars,
In the heavens you have made them bright, precious and fair.
Praised be You, my Lord, through Brothers Wind and Air,
And fair and stormy, all weather's moods,
by which You cherish all that You have made.
Praised be You my Lord through Sister Water,
So useful, humble, precious and pure.
Praised be You my Lord through Brother Fire,
through whom You light the night and he is beautiful and playful and robust and strong.
Praised be You my Lord through our Sister,
Mother Earth
who sustains and governs us,
producing varied fruits with coloured flowers and herbs.
Praise be You my Lord through those who grant pardon for love of You and bear sickness and trial.
Blessed are those who endure in peace, By You Most High, they will be crowned.
Praised be You, my Lord through Sister Death,
from whom no-one living can escape. Woe to those who die in mortal sin!
Blessed are they She finds doing Your Will.
No second death can do them harm. Praise and bless my Lord and give Him thanks,
And serve Him with great humility.

Sunday, June 3

I proclaimed the word at the 7:30 Mass this morning, reading the first passage, which was from Deuteronomy. I read the second reading, from Romans, last night at the 5:30 Mass. While I still struggle some with the temptation to read for the greater glory of Bob as opposed to that of God, I benefit hugely from this ministry. As part of my preparation to read, I apply what I have learned about composing myself in the scene – the space, the time, and the people – described in the passage. I attempt to find the voice of the Old Testament prophet admonishing the people of Israel. Or I imagine that I am Paul, speaking to the new Christians in Rome or Ephesus or wherever.   The process feeds me spiritually.   It certainly improves the quality of my reading.

I am making progress in my effort to understand the Resurrection.   I believe that Jesus incarnate died, but He is not dead.   He literally rose from that tomb in the hill above Jerusalem as Christ.   He is part of the triune God.   I want to learn more about the idea of His being the Cosmic Christ, present before Jesus incarnate, and, obviously, present after the Resurrection.   John's introduction to his Gospel makes it quite clear:

> In the beginning was the Word, and the Word was with God, and the Word was God. He was with God in the beginning.

I also see an enormously important metaphorical value in the story of the Resurrection.   My spiritual growth requires the death of my false self, and the birth of a new, authentic self.

Sadly, as I have said before, this process of death and resurrection must be repeated over and over again.   For me, at least, the false self is painfully difficult to kill.

T.S. Eliot provides a suitably enigmatic thought with which to end this morning:

> I had seen birth and death but had thought they were different.

3. Jesus Christ comes to the doubters

I ask God for the gift to feel very glad and to rejoice intensely, sharing in the delight and joy that Jesus Christ felt in rising from the dead and returning to console His friends.

Monday, June 4   *(John 20:24-29)*

While Maggie and I have visited all of our Ignatian places (the library, the bench, and the beach) almost every day since Sallie Ann and I returned from Italy, I have not followed the prescribed steps for the daily exercise.   It was with some pleasure, therefore, that I began this morning's session last night, as I have been instructed.   I read the passage from John about Jesus appearing to Thomas:

> Blessed are those who have not seen and yet have believed.

Reflecting on this earlier this morning, I considered the difference between seeing with the eyes of my body, on one hand, and seeing with the eyes of my mind, or of my soul, on the other.   I think it is the same distinction as that between literal knowing and spiritual knowing.   More than anything else, these exercises have helped me understand that spiritual knowledge matters more.   Compare the "proof" Thomas sought by putting his "fingers where the nails were" to the acceptance of Mary Magdalene, who apparently believed immediately when the angel told her that "he is risen." Of course, it was an angel! That notwithstanding, however, it strikes me that Mary had greater faith.

Obviously, the point of this passage from John is that most of us must base our belief most of the time on knowledge that we did not obtain conventionally. It points to the difference between experience and knowledge. Experiential learning only occurs when we open the eyes of our minds; when we allow it to happen to us; when we accept it.

Rohr wrote a piece about the resurrection in 2003 which speaks to me on this point:

> Once we have a personal experience in our own life of the risen Christ upholding us, naming us, loving us, freeing us, then we have nothing to fear. That's how secure Christ makes us. Because we have a reference point, we have a center point. We have received the gift of the Spirit.

As I have written before in this journal, I experienced great difficulty accepting the death of Jesus during the first few weeks after this past Easter. I was stubbornly refusing to accept the gift of the Spirit. I wanted to wallow more in my mourning of His death than in any celebration of His Resurrection.

Tuesday, June 5   *(John 20:24-29, again)*

It felt good to repeat the prescribed process again this morning. So much of the magic of these exercises comes from the repetitive pattern and practice of prayer. Like Maggie, I take special comfort from the familiar time, place, and movements of these morning sessions.

I composed myself with the disciples, including Thomas, when Jesus entered the room through the locked doors. It had been a full week since Thomas had first refused to accept the risen Christ.

I found it extremely easy – too easy - to identify with that refusal. Show me, I said. Prove to me beyond any doubt and then, only then, will I allow you to transform my life with this incredible gift! How preposterous this seems!

With the eyes of my mind, I watched Thomas touch the wounds of Christ. Strangely, but very palpably, the "skin of my mind" tingled as though I were personally touching the wounds. Kneeling next to the chair in the library, I felt my doubts fall away.

I mean that literally. It was as though something physically dropped to the floor. I was lighter. I was happy. These sensations must have lasted only a few seconds, but, recollecting them now, it seems to have been a much longer time. Even as I write this, I am "filled" with gratitude. It is as if that gratitude itself is a substance of very light weight, which lifts me up. I want this feeling to last all day.

Wednesday, June 6   *(The Contemplation)*

Before I record my thoughts about this morning, I want to briefly return to the incredible experience of yesterday. After my prayers, I left the library to join my tennis friends, still "floating" on a "pink cloud" of almost mystical joy. Throughout the day, I felt as though the Holy Spirit was my constant companion. It was one of the most magical days I can remember. All of the wonder of that day began when I "touched" the wounds of Christ in my mind. It is incredible.

Our instruction for today and tomorrow is to return to the Contemplation. Father Tetlow suggests a specific grace to be sought during prayer and meditation when using the Contemplation:

> *I want to have an intimate understanding of myself and my life as gift, and all my world as gift, so that I will be incandescent with gratitude, and then go beyond that to love the Giver of all this, who loves me vastly in deed and in sharing.*

Ignatius wrote a two-part preamble to the Contemplation, instructing his companions to *"reflect upon the unifying character of love in two aspects"*:

> *The first is that love ought to manifest itself in deeds rather than words. The second is that love consists in a mutual sharing of goods.*

Tetlow puts it a little differently; in my view, adding clarity:

> *Remember two things about love: First, love is act, not talk; it shows itself in the deed done, not simply in words spoken. Second, love works itself out in mutual sharing, so that the lover always gives to and receives from the beloved – everything: gifts, money, convictions, honors, position.*

One of the strongest messages running through the retreat in Assisi was expressed in a very simple statement: God is a verb, not a noun. He is an action, not a person or thing. The verb God is synonymous with verb love. As the first letter of John says:

> *Whoever does not love does not know God, because God is love.*

Reflecting on the preamble to the Contemplation, then, I can say with Tetlow that God is act, not talk. God shows Himself in deeds done, not simply in words spoken. God works Himself out in mutual sharing. He is lover, and He is beloved.[100] He gives, and He receives. This works for me.

---

[100] St. Augustine takes this concept further in describing the Trinity. God is the lover. Christ is the beloved. The Holy Spirit is the love itself.

As instructed, I composed myself standing in front of the throne of God. All around me were the Saints, Martyrs, Church Fathers, Church Doctors, and everyone I have ever known and admired. All of them, even the great men and women of history, seemed pleased that I had come to this place. Father John and Buddy Tudor were in the crowd. I saw my father and mother. They were smiling at me. I found myself weeping, and could not stop.

I tried to explain to them why I was so happy, but they looked at me with an expression that told me not to bother. So I simply said "I love you."

While it seemed superfluous, I did describe the extent of God's incredible gifts all around me. Both before and after the retreat in Assisi, Sallie Ann and I stayed in some of the most beautiful hotels in Italy. These amazing hotels were located in extraordinary gardens, either next to the sea or in park-like estates in the center of historic towns. We were blessed to be able to stay in such incredible examples of God's generous gifts to the planet. Yet, as I looked around me in the library and out in the garden, I realized that I truly awaken every day in paradise. The line from T.S. Eliot is perfect:

And the end of all our exploring will be to arrive where we started and know the place for the first time.

I ended the morning with the prayer suggested by Father Tetlow:

Accept, O Lord and treat as your own my liberty, my understanding, my memory – all of my decisions and my freedom to choose.

All that I am and all that I have You gave; now I turn and return all to You, looking to find Your hopes and will in all.

Keep giving me your holy love, Hold on me Your Life-giving gaze, and I neither need nor want anything else.

Thursday, June 7 *(The Contemplation)*

It rained heavily this morning, so tennis was cancelled. In an odd way, I felt connected to the world when I tried to watch the French Open and found that it was postponed due to rain in Paris. Maggie slept on her pillow as I organized the meditation space in the library. The rain outside enhanced the cozy feeling.

I composed myself once again in front of the throne of God. Everyone was there again, just like yesterday. I talked about the people God has put in my life. An amazing part of these exercises is how much I can remember when I focus my "memory search," and begin it with prayer.

Standing there in front of all those great people, I was able to recall people from almost every year and all the places I have lived or traveled during my life. It is humbling to think how much help I have received at each turn.   Some of the people mentored me at crucial times.   Some worked for me or with me in my various business pursuits.   Many were teachers.   Some were people I have hurt or offended.   All made my life better, or made me a better person.   All were gifts of God.

The gifts keep coming.   There are as many people in my life today as I can remember over all the years and places that led me here.   It seems so obviously the case that God's love grows with my capacity to receive it, and with my willingness to accept it.

I ended this morning's session with a slightly altered version of a prayer from the Jesuit Karl Rahner:

> Dear God, as I turn outward to the world, I must turn inward toward you, and possess you, the only One, in everything.

> Only through you can I be an 'inward' person.   Only through you am I with you within myself even as I am turning outward in order to be among things.

> Touch my heart with your grace.   You, who are love, give me love.   Give me yourself, so that all my days may eventually flow into the one day of your eternal life.   Amen

Friday, June 8   *(John 21:1-17)*

The account in John of the risen Christ causing His disciples to miraculously catch fish puzzles me.   By this time in His ministry, it seems to me that "signs" and "miracles" are no longer necessary.   Likewise, I am not clear as to why Peter was asked three times about his love for Jesus.   So I turned early this morning to Raymond Brown for clarification.   The biblical scholars generally agree on several points, all of which helped me put the passage in what I hope is the proper perspective.

First, Chapter 21 of John is considered to be "added on" to what the evangelist rather nicely ended in Chapter 20.   However, it seems to have been added extremely early in the redaction process, since there are no published copies of the Gospel of John without this Chapter.   Second, the style and approach of Chapter 21 is sufficiently close to that of the first chapter, called the prologue, as to convincingly argue that both were written by the same author or redactor.   Finally, in both cases, that of the prologue and of the epilogue, the author was not John the Evangelist.   The evidence all points to these two chapters having been redacted from various historical materials concurrent in time with the rest of the gospel of John, and agreeing both in form and substance with the Johannine tradition.

So, assuming that Chapter 21 was written by a redactor from the Johannine community, probably in Ephesus, and that it was added, like the prologue, to the very earliest copies of the Gospel, what can we say about the content?   There are two clear sections of the Chapter.   The first deals with the miraculous catch of fish, and the second involves the reinstatement of Peter by Jesus. Both sections are considered ecclesiastical, that is, dealing with the church that the disciples would establish and Peter would lead.

As I understand what I read this morning, the miraculous catch of fish was the last of several signs or miracles dealing with the missionary role of the disciples in the new church. The disciples, as fishers of men, were to teach people about the gospel of Jesus Christ, bringing them into the faith in much the same way that fish are brought into the net.[101]

The second section, dealing with the role of Peter, may be a bit redundant, but still makes a lot of sense to me. There is some logic in the story that allows Peter to affirm his love for Jesus three times, just as he earlier denied Jesus three times.

I have always enjoyed my prayer compositions involving the Sea of Galilee. It worked particularly well today, with hard rain falling on the lagoon from a very dark and windy sky. I imagined the boat tossing in the windswept sea, not surprisingly empty of fish. Unlike the disciples, I recognized the risen Christ immediately. I had been with the disciples in Jerusalem when Christ had first shown Himself.

The message from Jesus that we were to be active in spreading the gospel came through loud and clear. Somehow, I knew that most of us would soon separate into small groups, traveling far and wide to teach what we had been taught. Those who stayed behind, in and around Jerusalem, would be taking huge risks. Both the Jewish leadership and the Romans were actively searching for anyone connected with the "revolutionary," Jesus.

In my composition, I knew with a certainty that I would travel alone to far off lands, and that I would have success. Oddly, I knew that Jesus wanted me to use my gifts of motivating and teaching, and that He gave me the additional gift of wanderlust to speed me on my way to distant places.

I ended the morning with the Our Father. I felt at peace with my efforts to reconcile research into scholarship behind the passage, on the one hand, and the contemplative experience of the place, on the other.

Saturday, June 9 *(John 21:1-1, again)*

Rain threatened to prevent our tennis this morning, but we found a window and played a delightful three sets. Afterwards, the rain provided a perfect backdrop to

---

[101] The early fathers spent a great deal of energy working through the possible numerological implications of 153 fish in the catch and seven disciples. Frankly, I am left rather cold by this avenue of thought. It strikes me as trying too hard to find significance of something probably not present. Anyway, it seems to me that any numerological message would have been added in the redaction, and would reflect Greek influence more than anything otherwise present in the teaching of Jesus.

my prayer and meditation.

As I composed myself back at the Sea of Galilee with the disciples, I reflected again on the nature of contemplative prayer. I saw the rough water, the fishing boats, the gusting wind, and the wet sand along the water's edge. I smelled fish and wet earth and that strange smell of rain. I heard seagulls and surf and wind.

In contrast to centering prayer, or the meditative state we tried to achieve during the "sits" in Assisi, the experience was about as far away from "nothingness" as it is possible to be. Rohr seemed to be saying that only contemplation that finds negative space can generate the non-dualistic goal of prayer.

It seems to me to be possible to achieve union – to be non-dualistic - with the sensate experience of a heavily-populated contemplative space. When I focus solely on my contemplation, I become one with the people I see, the sounds I hear, the smells I smell, and the emotions of the event. It is a non-dual space.

I have seldom reached the center space of nothingness, even for a few seconds. I have certainly not been in that space for any length of time. In contrast to that, I have spent hours, even days, in the crowded places and spaces of my Ignatian compositions.

It was so again this morning. I not only talked to the disciples about the challenge of Christ's charge to us to be missionaries, I felt the excitement. More than that, I feel that excitement now, an hour later, as I write about it in this journal. It is as though the natural state of the contemplation is active. I cannot rest in the mental or imaginative state of my fantasy, but am compelled to take some action to realize the commitment expressed in the prayer.

In the final analysis, I am sure that both the centering prayer of the early mystics and Franciscans, and the fantasy prayer of Ignatius are valid approaches to the ultimate goal, which is to communicate with God. I like Merton's description of prayer:

> *Just remaining quietly in the presence of God, listening to Him, being attentive to Him, requires a lot of courage and know-how.*

The primary obstacle is self. Whatever gets us out of ourselves is an appropriate addition to our spiritual arsenal.

4. The Risen Lord shares His mission

I ask God our Lord to fill me with tremendous gratefulness, so that when I see how everything and my own self are gift, I may want to return thanks and praise and service to the One who gives and shares with such total generosity.

Monday, June 11   *(Matthew 28:16-20)*

Reading this passage today is puzzling to me, especially after all that I have read and prayed about over the past several weeks:

> *When they saw him, they worshiped him; but some doubted.*

This passage refers to the disciples who were with Jesus at the Last Supper.   How could any of them possibly still have doubts?   Jesus told the disciples several times that He would be resurrected.   They were told by Mary Magdalene that the tomb was empty, and that they, the women, had seen and touched the risen Lord.   The disciples had witnessed signs and miracles.   Here, they once again see with their own eyes the risen Jesus.   Yet the doubt persists.

What is nice about this passage is that it brings the Gospel of Matthew to a proper end.   The other gospels do not have such nice endings:

> *And surely I am with you always, to the very end of the age.*

The primary message in this last paragraph of the Gospel of Matthew is not about the doubts of the disciples or the benediction of Jesus.   It is the sending out of the disciples, called the Great Commission:

> *Therefore go and make disciples of all nations, baptizing them in the name of the Father and of the Son and of the Holy Spirit,*

I composed myself with the disciples at the mountain near Galilee.   Jesus made it clear that He had the authority to instruct and commission us to do virtually anything. He had been given "all authority in heaven and on earth."   So He used that authority to send us out to all nations.   It was a wonderful charge.   All of us felt emboldened. There was clear optimism with respect to our ability to actually make disciples throughout the world.

Once again, I traveled through time in my composition, leaving the Galilee region in the first century and arriving in Salt Lake City, Utah, in 1964.   I was standing among a group of fresh-faced young men, most of whom had only recently turned nineteen years of age.   A senior official of the Mormon Church repeated precisely these words from Matthew, sending us out to mission fields throughout the world.   We also felt emboldened and optimistic about our prospects for converting people to Mormonism. I departed for Germany the next morning.

I left the composition there, prayed the Our Father, and walked from the library down to the meditation bench in the garden. I continued to reflect on the two scenes. I had created in my mind the scene in first-century Palestine, albeit with as much study and research as possible. In contrast, I lived personally through the scene fifty years ago in Salt Lake City, and dug it out of my memory with only a little difficulty.

Yet the two scenes were profoundly real. In both scenes, I believed that I had been legitimately called to preach the true gospel. I pondered this for some time.

Clearly, the proselytizing efforts of the Mormon Church were extremely dualistic. That is, we were sent out to emphasize the differences between "us and them," regardless of who "they" were or what they believed.

I am not saying that all Mormons all the time are dualistic. I think there are many very good Mormons and there is a great deal of good in Mormonism. However, the strain of "the only true church" runs heavily through everything the Mormons say and do. That dominant dualistic belief was the very basis of the mission program.

Throughout His ministry, Christ taught non-dualistic thought and action. Father John was absolutely correct in saying that inclusion and forgiveness were the most important words in the new gospel. In part because he was so often writing to Gentiles, Paul's letters generally emphasize the inclusive nature of our faith.

Only in the Gospel of John do we find the "my way or the highway" language:

> I am the way and the truth and the life. No one comes to the Father except through me.

This passage was written by the evangelist half a century after the Great Commissioning described at the end of Matthew's Gospel. Did Jesus actually say something to that effect that day at the mountain near Galilee? Just as important, did the disciples think that is what Jesus meant, regardless of the actual words He used?

As much as it troubles me, I suspect most of the disciples preached the new gospel on those exclusionary, dualistic terms. The very nature of converting non-believers into believers is to emphasize the differences, not the similarities.

When John wrote verse 6 of chapter 14, I want to believe that he meant to say that the **teaching and message** of Jesus were the way, the truth and the life. Only by living non-dualistically, and by loving everyone – the poor, the sick, the outcast – could we come to the Father. Our charge was, and is, to love the non-believer as well. The face of God is in all that He has created, good and bad, believer and non-believer, sinner and saint.

Tuesday, June 12   **(Matthew 28:16-20, again)**

Since I left the house to play tennis after my prayers, Maggie did not join me in the library or at the garden bench this morning.   That turned out to be too bad.   It was a magical morning of clarity.

I prayed for understanding.   My conversation with the risen Jesus was as comfortable as it had become with Jesus incarnate.   It occurred to me that the nods and smiles of encouragement I saw with the eyes of my soul might have simply (simply!) been the Holy Spirit gently guiding me along the path.

Ilia Delio wrote in The Emergent Christ that "*as the mind begins to explore the deep mystery of God, the heart begins to change.*"   First, I love that thought.   However, second and more important, I believe it correctly describes much of what has been happening to me over the past few months.

I read something else in Ilia's book last night, something that truly helped me understand the Great Commission in a whole new light.   She quoted Paul Tillich writing in The New Being:

> *But I want to tell you that something has happened that matters, something that judges you and me, your religion and my religion.   A New Creation has occurred, a New Being has appeared, and we are all asked to participate in it. And so we should say to the pagans and Jews wherever we meet them: Don't compare your religion and our religion, your rites and our rites, your prophets and our prophets, your priests and our priests, the pious amongst you and the pious amongst us.   All this is of no avail!   And above all don't think that we want to convert you to English or American Christianity, to the religion of the Western World.   We do not want to convert you to us, not even to the best of us.   This would be of no avail.   We want only to show you something we have seen and to tell you something we have heard: That in the midst of the old creation there is a New Creation and that this New Creation is manifest in Jesus who is called the Christ.*

This is what Jesus called the disciples to go out to all the nations to say!   This has none of the "we are better than you" dualism generally associated with proselytizing.

As I reported all this to Jesus, I sensed the nod of assent and the smile of approval. As usual, there was a powerful sense that He was amused that it had taken me so long to understand.

Sunday, June 17   *(Summary)*

My week developed in a way I had not planned.   I left Wednesday morning for the airport, fully intending to pray and meditate each day in Washington and New York, precisely as called for in my weekly assignment.   It did not happen that way.

When I arrived in Washington for the Arrupe Board meeting, I got quite involved in the schedule of prayer and reflection followed by Gap LoBiondo and the rest of the Jesuits at Georgetown. We talked about Ilia Delio's book, The Emergent Christ, before Mass Wednesday evening. Much of what Sallie Ann and I learned during the retreat in Assisi is developed in depth by Ilia in several of her books, but particularly in this one. She brings a modern understanding of both the creation and the Incarnation into clear focus as she integrates them into a brilliant discussion of evolution and quantum physics.

After reading The Emergent Christ twice, I began to understand some of the science. It is exciting to see the connection between the best science of our time and a stimulating, deeply spiritual testimony of faith.[102] I love the concept of a Cosmic Christ incarnated out of God's love rather than as atonement for Adam's sin.

However, I believe more effort is needed to make all of the work being done to reconcile science and religion relevant to the day to day lives of people in the world today. I have offered to host a retreat later this summer to move that effort forward.

After yet another wonderful board meeting on Thursday, I flew to New York for the annual national meeting of the Council on Foreign Relations. General Martin Dempsey, the current Chairman of the Joint Chiefs, the highest ranking military officer in the United States, spoke that evening. It was amazing. Obviously, the speech changed the focus of my thoughts from matters of ethereal spirituality to the politics of global security, but I remained intensely engaged. The conversation and the company forced me to think. The real challenge was to approach the national and international political issues from the spiritual foundation of Ignatius.

That challenge stayed with me for the next two days. The focus on national and global security allowed me to introduce income inequality as a major impediment to any kind of reliable stability, either here at home or in the larger world. When the conversations turned to economic policy, income inequality rose even higher on the list of relevant issues. I talked a lot. I emphasized justice, fairness, equity, and consideration of the poorest among us in all of the meetings. A majority of the people involved in these meetings tended to agree with my views. However, most of

---

[102] Richard Rohr describes this in The Shape of God. "One reason so many theologians are interested in the Trinity now is that we're finding both physics (especially quantum physics) and cosmology are at a level of development where human science, our understanding of the atom and our understanding of galaxies, is affirming and confirming our use of the old Trinitarian language—but with a whole new level of appreciation. *Reality is radically relational, and the power is in the relationships themselves!* No good Christians would have denied the Trinitarian Mystery, but until our generation none were prepared to see that the shape of God is the shape of the whole universe! Great science, which we once considered an "enemy" of religion, is now helping us see that we're standing in the middle of awesome Mystery, and the only response before that Mystery is immense humility. Astrophysicists are much more comfortable with darkness, emptiness, non-explainability (dark matter, black holes), and living with hypotheses than most Christians I know. Who could have imagined this?"

them also agreed that we were living in national and global political environments that do not bode well for the people in the margins of life.

I read at Mass last night. Father Frank delivered a truly fabulous homily, in which he introduced the concept of heaven right here on earth. It is an idea consistent with my growing understanding and belief about our faith.

I am learning every day at a prodigious rate. Much of what I add each day to my store of knowledge expands the base of intellectual and spiritual agreement. That is, most of the new learning is consistent with and deepens what I have learned before. I sense that I am closing in on a convergence of understanding. I think this convergence is related to the exercises.

5. The Risen Lord hands on His Ministry

I beg the Lord God for the gift of living the joy of Christ Risen. I ask the gift to live . . . grateful for all that is in my life world, my life, and myself. And I ask for the great gift of bringing the Good News to others, in many forms.

Monday, June 18   *(Acts 1:1-12)*

Maggie and I began this morning on the bench in the meditation garden. We sat in silence for almost half an hour. It was the silence of the lagoon as the sun comes up, which means all manner of bird cries, occasional splashes from diving turtles, and surf in the distance. After only a few minutes, however, this chorus of nature acted like a heavy layer of insulation, creating a still, quiet space. Sitting in that space, I was suddenly overcome with melancholy. The recent pace of my life has been way too hectic. There have been too many airports and too many meetings. There has been way too much self-importance.

When I returned to the library, I found one of my favorite prayers:

> *Slow me down Lord.*
> *Ease the pounding of my heart*
> *By the quieting of my mind.*
> *Steady my hurried pace*
> *With a vision of the eternal reach of time.*
>
> *Give me, amidst the confusion of my day,*
> *The calmness of the everlasting hills.*
> *Break the tensions of my nerves and muscles*
> *With the soothing music of the singing streams*
> *That live in my memory.*
>
> *Help me to know*
> *The magical restoring power of sleep.*

Teach me the art
Of taking minute vacations,
Of slowing down to look at a flower,
To chat with a friend,
To pat a dog,
To read a few lines from a good book.

Remind me each day of the fable
Of the hare and the tortoise,
That I may know that the race
Is not always to be swift,
That there is more to life
Than its increasing speed.

Let me look upward
Into the branches of the towering oak,
And know that it grew great and strong
Because it grew slowly and well.

Slow me down Lord,
And inspire me to send my roots
Deep into the soil
Of life's enduring values,
That I may grow towards the stars
Of my enduring destiny.

Sister Joan suggested yesterday that I stop each day at the Holy Sacrament Chapel in our parish Church to sit in silence, listening to the Holy Spirit. I heard the words yesterday, but I only listened to their meaning this morning. Slow me down, Lord, slow me down.

Earlier this morning, while still in the garden, I composed myself with the disciples in Jerusalem. It had been forty days since Mary Magdalene told us about the empty tomb. As instructed, we had all stayed in Jerusalem, generally hiding from the Roman soldiers and the leaders of our own Jewish faith. We were afraid. We were disheartened.

When Jesus came to us, we wanted to hear Him announce the restoration of the kingdom. We wanted to hear that the Romans would leave Israel, taking with them their puppet leaders. That was not His message. Rather, He told us to wait for the Holy Spirit to "come upon us." When that happened, He said, we were to be witnesses to Him throughout the world.

Jesus led us out of Jerusalem toward Bethany. At the Mount of Olives, we watched Jesus ascend into the clouds. Two men in white robes suddenly joined our group, questioning why we were looking up at the sky. They told us Jesus would come again.

I left the composition. As I reflect on it now, I begin to understand the concept of Christ as distinguished from Jesus. As Rohr and others have said, Christ is not Jesus' last name. Christ means "the anointed one." Christ was anointed at the beginning of time, at the point of creation, at the very instant of the Big Bang. Christ became incarnate when He was born as Jesus. Jesus becomes Christ again at death. The physical and the divine are each part of the same wholeness.

Non-duality is a nuanced concept. It is not that body and spirit are one; or that life and death are one; or that good and bad are one. Neither, however, are they two. In an effort to bring together a concise summary of his teaching, Rohr has elaborated seven primary themes. The seventh theme describes this idea of a nuanced understanding of non-dual reality:

> Reality is "not totally one," but it is "not totally two," either! All things, events, persons, and institutions, if looked at contemplatively (non-egocentrically), reveal contradictions, create dilemmas, and have their own shadow side. Wisdom knows how to hold and to grow from this creative tension; ego does not. Our ego splits reality into parts that it can manage, but then pays a big price in regard to actual truth or understanding.

I mentioned a convergence of thinking in my journal entry yesterday. Some of that convergence is evident in my growing understanding of the divine Christ and His role in the world. At times in the past, I have simply tuned out when reading or hearing the story of the Ascension. If I thought about them at all, I considered the images of Jesus rising up into the clouds and angels in white robes as simple literary devices. They were intended to frighten or amaze the righteous.

This morning, however, I read, reflect, and experience the story in a radically different way. We were never meant to believe in the dualistic dichotomy of divine God "up there" and sinful mankind "down here." The Neo-Platonic idea of a righteous soul or spirit and an evil body was an unfortunate wrong turn for Christianity to take.

All of the world religions and "wisdom traditions" seem to share certain core elements, which have been described as the Perennial Tradition.[103] Rohr provides a concise statement of these shared beliefs:

> The Perennial Tradition encompasses the recurring themes in all of the world's religions and philosophies that continue to say:
>
> - There is a Divine Reality underneath and inherent in the world of things,
> - There is in the human soul a natural capacity, similarity, and longing for this Divine Reality, and

---

[103] See the recent books by Norman Livergood, John Carlson, Martin Lings, and Clinton Minnauer, just to name a few.

- *The final goal of existence is union with this Divine Reality.*

My Catholic faith teaches that this Divine Reality is the Trinity, of which God, Christ and the Holy Spirit are parts. All three elements of the triune godhead have been present from the beginning. One of the most important messages in the New Testament is the essential union between the divine and the human, evidenced by Jesus incarnate. The Trinity represents wholeness. Christ divine and Jesus incarnate represent wholeness. It is this wholeness that is the essential message inherent in all of the world's wisdom traditions, regardless of the names and terms used to describe it.

Rohr, again, adds to my understanding:

Everything makes sense when God is communion instead of domination.

I end this morning comforted by the concept of wholeness. The longer I continue on this spiritual journey, the more I appreciate the amazing men and women who have walked this way before me down through the ages. The more I read and listen, the more I appreciate those who are currently on the path with me all around the world. I feel whole with history and the world. During my RCIA training, I frequently expressed my sense of belonging to both a temporal and spatial universe. The questions we are asking today have been asked since the beginning of mankind, a "temporal universality" spanning the whole of time. These questions are being asked by people all around the world, a "spatial universality" spanning the globe. Again, it is wholeness.

Tuesday, June 19   *(Luke 24:50-53)*

Tennis Tuesday in the second half of June at Serendipity is pretty hard to beat. It was unusually cool this morning, perfect for tennis. Our granddaughters are playing in the hall, about to go to another one-week summer "camp." Maggie and I began our session in the library, but quickly moved out to the garden bench.

The theme of this week is the Lord passing on His ministry. Accordingly, we read another version of the story of the Ascension, this one from the gospel of Luke.[104]

The version of the Ascension in Acts is longer and more detailed than the brief paragraph we read from Luke this morning. Among other things, the account in Luke makes no mention of the two white-robed angels.[105]

---

[104] I personally find it interesting that the same author is credited with writing both the gospel of Luke and the Book of Acts. For a long time, it was thought that Paul's companion, Luke the Physician, authored both Luke and Acts. That view is generally disputed today. There seems to be general agreement that both books were written in the second half of the first century, possible sometime after the destruction of the temple in 70 CE.

Like yesterday, I composed myself with the disciples in Bethany. I listened to His message and watched as He "was carried up." We returned to Jerusalem and gathered at the temple. I thought it quite strange to be together at all, much less in the temple. To a very large extent, we were outlaws, presumably in grave danger should either the Romans or the most conservative Jews find us. Nonetheless, I imagined myself in the scene as is it written in Luke.

After leaving the composition, I reflected further on the idea that the twelve apostles simply stayed together in one place for the ten days between the Ascension and the day of Pentecost. Jerusalem must have been a tense place for followers of Christ during that period.

After all, Saint Stephen was killed by a mob of angry Jews very soon after the crucifixion of Christ. Paul, while he was still Saul, is reported in Acts as having participated in the killing of Stephen.

So I find it more than a little odd that the twelve men closest to Jesus would be hanging out together at the temple. When I think about who wrote the accounts of their doing so, and when those accounts were written, however, a somewhat different story seems more plausible. The author of Luke-Acts was likely writing these accounts more than fifty years after they occurred. It seems logical to me that the apostles were still in Jerusalem after the crucifixion. My guess, however, is that they were very much in hiding, and, at least for the first few weeks, quite unlikely to meet together in one place in the city.

It makes sense, however, that they would have agreed to meet outside the city in the relatively remote village of Bethany. It was there that the oral tradition said the Ascension took place. Bethany was presumably much safer than the temple in Jeru-

---

[105] Here are the two passages from the New International Version of the New Testament. **Luke 24:50-53.** When he had led them out to the vicinity of Bethany, he lifted up his hands and blessed them. While he was blessing them, he left them and was taken up into heaven. Then they worshiped him and returned to Jerusalem with great joy. And they stayed continually at the temple, praising God. **Acts 1:1-12.** In my former book, Theophilus, I wrote about all that Jesus began to do and to teach [2] until the day he was taken up to heaven, after giving instructions through the Holy Spirit to the apostles he had chosen. [3]After his suffering, he presented himself to them and gave many convincing proofs that he was alive. He appeared to them over a period of forty days and spoke about the kingdom of God. On one occasion, while he was eating with them, he gave them this command: "Do not leave Jerusalem, but wait for the gift my Father promised, which you have heard me speak about. For John baptized with water, but in a few days you will be baptized with the Holy Spirit." Then they gathered around him and asked him, "Lord, are you at this time going to restore the kingdom to Israel?" He said to them: "It is not for you to know the times or dates the Father has set by his own authority. But you will receive power when the Holy Spirit comes on you; and you will be my witnesses in Jerusalem, and in all Judea and Samaria, and to the ends of the earth." After he said this, he was taken up before their very eyes, and a cloud hid him from their sight. They were looking intently up into the sky as he was going, when suddenly two men dressed in white stood beside them. "Men of Galilee," they said, "why do you stand here looking into the sky? This same Jesus, who has been taken from you into heaven, will come back in the same way you have seen him go into heaven."

salem.   It would have been quite normal for people to gather in the week or ten days prior to Pentecost to prepare for the holiday.[106]

But so what?   The point of the two accounts, Luke and Acts, is not what the apostles were doing and where they were doing it.   The point is the Ascension.   It also matters little exactly when and how Christ ascends.   The point is the Ascension.   The message of the Ascension is that the incarnate Jesus became the divine Christ and reunited with His Father.

Wednesday, June 20   *(Acts 2:1-4)*

It was with a somewhat troubled heart and mind that I began my morning today.   I read the passage from Acts last night.   I read it again and again.

When the day of Pentecost came, they were all together in one place.   Suddenly a sound like the blowing of a violent wind came from heaven and filled the whole house where they were sitting.   They saw what seemed to be tongues of fire that separated and came to rest on each of them.   All of them were filled with the Holy Spirit and began to speak in other tongues as the Spirit enabled them.

Then I read the sections in the Catechism that deal with the Pentecost and the Holy Spirit.   The whole section was interesting, but this paragraph particularly appealed to me:

> *When the Father sends his Word, he always sends his Breath. In their joint mission, the Son and the Holy Spirit are distinct but inseparable. To be sure, it is Christ who is seen, the visible image of the invisible God, but it is the Spirit who reveals him.*

I am sure there are religious people all around the world, Catholics and non-Catholics, who have a comfortable understanding of the Trinity.   I am not among them.[107]

---

[106] Pentecost, or Shavuot, is the summer festival, celebrated fifty days after Passover by the Jews for centuries.   It is also called the Feast of Weeks.

[107] In his *The Shape of God: Deepening the Mystery of the Trinity*, Richard Rohr provides historical support for a very helpful view of the trinity. "Our Franciscan Saint Bonaventure, who wrote a lot about the Trinity, was influenced by a lesser-known figure called Richard of Saint Victor. Richard said, "For God to be good, God can be one. For God to be loving, God has to be two because love is always a relationship." But his real breakthrough was saying that "For God to be supreme joy and happiness, God has to be three." Lovers do not know full happiness until they both delight in the same thing, like new parents with the ecstasy of their first child.   The Holy Spirit *is* the shared love of the Father and the Son, and shared love is always happiness and joy. The Holy Spirit is whatever the Father and the Son are excited about; She *is* that excitement—about everything in creation!"

Nonetheless, I knelt at the meditation chair in the corner of the library to begin my morning session with prayer. I asked for understanding. I asked for faith.

Afterwards, I tried something that we did at the retreat in Assisi. They called it a "sit." Maggie and I were alone on the first floor of the house. She was sleeping. All electronic media was off. The heavily insulated doors and windows shut off all sound from outside. The quiet stillness was eerie. We sat in that quiet stillness for almost half an hour, which experienced sitters tell me is a long time. I cannot say that I ended my "sit" with clarity, but I was certainly less troubled.

After my "sit," I returned to my customary Ignatian prayer. I composed myself with the apostles in the house on that day of the Pentecost. All of the senses of my mind were attuned to the violence of the loud wind and bright fire that filled the space around us. I watched the apostles tremble with fear. I listened to them speak in what at first seemed like gibberish, but then sounded more like a cacophony of various foreign languages. Occasional words came through clearly. As I left the scene, however, it was more bedlam than anything else.

I wrote earlier this week that I believe there is a Divine Reality in the world. I believe that this Divine Reality is the Trinity. Each "person" in the Trinity - God the Father, Jesus Christ the Son, and the Holy Spirit – plays a separate and essential role in the universe. I am not at all clear about consubstantiality. Nor do I understand completely the particular roles played by the different members of this Triune Godhead.[108]

---

[108] Rohr goes on in *The Shape of God* to talk about the relationships between and among the Trinitarian Godhead: "In our attempts to explain the Trinitarian Mystery in the past we overemphasized the individual qualities of the Father, Son, and Holy Spirit, but not so much the relationships between them. That is where all the power is! That is where all the meaning is! The Mystery of God as Trinity invites us into a dynamism, a flow, a relationship, a waterwheel of love. The Mystery says God is a verb much more than a noun. God as Trinity invites us *into* a participatory experience. Some of our Christian mystics went so far as to say that all of creation is being taken back into this flow of eternal life, almost as if we are a "Fourth Person" of the Eternal Flow of God or, as Jesus put it, "so that where I am you also may be" (John 14:3). Paul says, "God's weakness is stronger than human strength" (1 Corinthians 1:25). That awesome line gives us a key into the Mystery of Trinity. I would describe human strength as self-sufficiency or autonomy. God's weakness I would describe as *Interbeing*. Human strength admires holding on. The Mystery of the Trinity is about each One letting go into the Other. Human strength admires personal independence. God's Mystery is total mutual dependence. We like control. God loves vulnerability. We admire needing no one. The Trinity is total intercommunion with all things and all Being. We are practiced at hiding and protecting ourselves. God seems to be in some kind of total disclosure for the sake of the other. Our strength, we think, is in asserting and protecting our boundaries. God is into dissolving boundaries between Father, Son, and Holy Spirit, yet finding them in that very outpouring! Take the rest of your life to begin to unpackage such a total turnaround of Reality. A Threefold God totally lets go of any boundaries for the sake of the Other, and then receives them back from Another. It is a nonstop waterwheel of Love. Each accepts that He is fully accepted by the Other, and then passes on that total acceptance. Thus "God is Love." It's the same spiritual journey for all of us, and it takes most of our life to accept that we are accepted—and to accept everyone else. Most can't do this easily because internally there is so much self-accusation (self-flagellation in many cases). Most are so convinced that they are not the body of Christ, that they are unworthy, that we are not in radical union with God. The good news is that the question of union has

However, I do believe that one of them is behind the Big Bang, and is out in front of the evolutionary process. It makes sense to me that this is God the Father.

In no small part thanks to these exercises, I have come to know Jesus incarnate. I believe He is the Cosmic Christ He was present with His Father at the beginning. After His death, Jesus incarnate became one, again, with the Cosmic Christ. Christ is the Word; the Anointed One. As Ilia Delio says, God is Love; a force-field of Love. Christ is the Form of that field. The Holy Spirit is the energy of that field. I believe I have experienced the very real presence of the Holy Spirit. While much of the time I did not appreciate it, I believe that Spirit has been with me on this incredible journey all my life.

For as long as I can remember, the day of Pentecost has been the day the saints were called to give witness to the Lord Jesus Christ. Of course, the saints in my distant memory were the Latter Day Saints of the Mormon Church! However, even during the forty years between my excommunication by the Mormons and the beginning of my education to become a Catholic, I thought of the day of Pentecost as the day the early Christians received the gift of the Holy Spirit. It was this gift that would energize and support them in fulfilling the charge they had been given by Jesus Christ to spread the gospel to all nations.

Somewhere along the way, I began to associate "Pentecostal" with various Christian churches that were "way out" in their approach to faith. At the extreme, I think about snake handlers from the hollows of West Virginia and Kentucky. Moving back from the extreme, many of the traveling preachers who gather crowds in large tents engage regularly in faith healing, and often break out in tongues. While I do recognize the role of prayer, faith, and spirituality in healing, I am skeptical of those for whom religion becomes as much spectacle as it is worship.

The description Luke provides, in the second chapter of Acts, of apostles speaking in tongues is obviously the source of its identification as Pentecostal. There are clearly two ways to interpret speaking in tongues.

One way would simply be the ability of a person or persons to speak in several languages, some or most of which were not known to them. As I read the verses in Acts, this strikes me as the intention of Luke. The apostles were able to speak to people from various tribes in their native languages. When I was a missionary in Germany, some of the Germans suggested that my early fluency in German was a form of the gift of tongues.

Another way to interpret the idea of speaking in tongues involves uttering sounds that are essentially gibberish. For those not able to understand the various languages

---

already been resolved once and for all. We cannot create our union with God from our side. It is objectively already given to us by the Holy Spirit who dwells within us (Romans 8:9—and all over the place!). Once we know we are that grounded, founded, and home free, we can also stop defending ourselves and move beyond our self-protectiveness, too."

being spoken by the apostles that first day Pentecost, it sounded like the mumbling of drunkenness.

I returned to my composition. I was among those gathered to celebrate the Feast of Weeks for the first time since the crucifixion of Christ. Since it was the fiftieth day since the Passover, the celebration would be referred to commonly as the day of Pentecost. The roaring wind and blazing fire had attracted all of us to gather outside the house where the apostles had been meeting. The apostles came outside to talk to us.

My family and I had traveled all the way from Rome for the celebration. We were amazed, therefore, when the Aramaic-speaking apostles addressed us in Latin. We heard other languages being spoken by other apostles as they preached to Jews from other countries. At a distance, the sound of all of these different languages being spoken at one time sounded strangely similar to the chirping of birds!

I left the composition, returning to the garden bench and the wonderful quiet of the early dawn. I thought about the Holy Spirit as the source of energy for the universal Love that is God. As it has been in the past, this energy was palpable all around me. It moved my hand, even as I touched it with my hand.

What could I do with the power of this Spirit? A better question would be what could I not do with its incredible power? I felt confident that I could understand difficult things, speak about them with clarity and authority, and even do so in German or Spanish or Italian. All of the gifts God has given me are brought to life through the energy of the Holy Spirit. It is new wine. I am a new bottle.

Thursday, June 21 *(Acts 2:5-36)*

Venus and Jupiter were visible in the dawn sky this morning. Looking up into that incredible sky, I reflected on the vastness of this universe. I wondered at the magic of its mystery. Is it truly possible that I am one with all of this? Is it so that, like that sky, I am infinite? I sat on the bench for some time, praying in gratitude for the simple, overwhelming gift of life.

Then I composed myself among the crowd listening to Peter speak. When he pointed out that the actions of the apostles could not have been drunkenness since it was only nine in the morning, I smiled inwardly. Peter had apparently not seen all there is to see at nine in the morning!

Peter quoted the wonderful words from the prophet Joel:

> [Y]our young men will see visions; your old men will dream dreams.

Somewhere in the vast storehouse of cosmic wisdom, I must have heard that when I was young. I certainly saw visions and dreamt dreams. For the better part of my life, I have struggled to discern the difference between the visions and the dreams. When did I become old?

I left the composition and returned with Maggie to the library. She slept. I listened to Gregorian chants. It is hard to imagine anything more peaceful.

Peter touched on some of the themes that I have been working through during the past several weeks. Referring to Christ, Peter said it was "impossible for death to keep its hold on him." I read last week that life and death are two sides of the same coin. Jesus died, but He is not dead. He is not gone. He has simply changed form. What could once be seen and experienced as matter, can now be sensed and experienced as energy.

Later, Peter quoted the prophet David, who said to the Lord:

> You have made known to me the paths of life; you will fill me with joy in your presence.

Luke tells us that the power of Peter's preaching that morning resulted in the baptism of "about three thousand." Even allowing for a certain amount of hyperbole, that is impressive.

I ended the morning with the Our Father. I was filled with gratitude. I was at peace.

Friday, June 22 *(The Contemplation)*

Our assignment this morning was to return to the Contemplation. I did so in an odd way, sitting in the waiting room of a local Lab Corp office, about to have blood drawn for some tests. There was something very appropriate about that particular space.

It was a simple room. Only slightly-padded metal chairs lined two walls. The window into the office space was on one of the remaining walls. The door leading out to the parking area was on the final wall. Some long outdated magazines were in a rack in a corner. There was no television. I was alone in the room, waiting for a single phlebotomist to finish with another patient.

I began by reflecting on the two Ignatian "aspects" of the Contemplation. First, love ought to manifest itself in deeds rather than words and, second, love consists in a mutual sharing of goods.

As I looked around the very plain room, I considered the enormous amount of knowledge, experience, and technology that existed behind the service desk. My cardiologist had generated a prescription for the laboratory tests, which could have been performed in any one of literally dozens of laboratories within easy driving distance of my house. Each of these laboratories employed well-trained, committed technicians whose ability to draw the blood, handle it properly, and correctly analyze it was developed through education and training from equally qualified and committed teachers and technicians. The whole enterprise consisted of separate individuals working at separate small companies, all interconnected by an amazing array of technology. All of this has been given to modern man through the creative energy of God.

I considered the idea that much of that knowledge and experience was the result of deeds done out of love. Men and women had learned, and were still learning, enough about our bodies to understand how everything works. They and others had invented procedures and machines to see into our bodies and, thus, predict the future. All of those hours spent resulted in deeds done, and all of it must have come from love. All of it is so interconnected that a great deal of sharing of goods, knowledge, technique, and understanding must exist.

The phlebotomist called for me, ending my reverie. However, the thought pattern continued throughout the morning. I played very poor tennis in a club match at the Sawgrass Racquet Club, embarrassing myself and my team. When I arrived back at the house, Maggie was beside herself. She led me excitedly to the library and jumped into the chair in the corner.

So I started the day again. I composed myself standing before the throne of God. All the Angels and Saints and Doctors and Fathers of the Church were standing around me. They were praying that I might see and understand.

Ignatius wrote that perfection consists of finding God in all things. The only way to develop the faith necessary to meet God in all things is to cultivate it in a personal relationship with Him. I expressed my deep gratitude for the personal relationship I have begun to cultivate with God over the past nine months. I prayed for a deeper knowledge and closer relationship.

Combining both the first and second points of the Contemplation, I prayed the *Suscipe*:

> *Take, Lord, and receive all my liberty, my memory, my understanding, and my entire will – all that I have and call my own. You have given it all to me. To you, Lord, I return it. Everything is yours; do with it what you will. Give me only your love and your grace. That is enough for me*

The third point of the Contemplation is that God works in all creation. It is sometimes called the theology of work. Just as God works in all creation, He makes us fully aware of the need for us to work - on our own continuing conversion and in the constant creation of the world. God is love. We are connected to God through love. That love must be manifest in deeds, and the love and the deeds must be mutually shared.

The fourth point in the Contemplation is perhaps the most important. God descends on us. Ignatius said it a little differently:

This is to consider all blessings and gifts as descending from above. Thus, my limited power comes from the supreme and infinite power above, and so, too, justice, goodness, mercy, etc. descend from above as the rays of light descend from the sun, and as the waters flow from their fountains.

It seemed fitting for me to be talking to God about this point at the very moment that it occurred. In my fantasy, God stepped down from His throne and descended upon me and the others in the crowd around me. Just as I described the obvious role of the Divine in the interconnected enterprise of the medical laboratory, I was overcome by His presence.

I left the composition filled with gratitude. I thanked Him. I prayed the Our Father. I wept.

Saturday, June 23 *(Ephesians 4:7-16)*

As I read the passage from Ephesians again this morning, several phrases seemed to jump off the page. I am reminded again of the sense of convergence, of various strands of understanding coming together here at the end of the exercises.

Paul talks about Christ "descending and ascending," suggesting that descent is a necessary part of ascent. Or, as Paul says, descent and ascent are necessary "to fill the whole universe." When I first considered the idea that I had to fall down in order to rise back up, I saw up and down dualistically. Down was bad. Up was good. Thinking about it now, I am beginning to see up and down as necessary parts to the whole. The whole, or wholeness, is the purpose of life.

Paul goes on to say that all of Christ's people are to be equipped for service so that His "body" (think, His kingdom here on earth) "may be built up until we all reach unity...and become mature, attaining to the whole measure of the fullness of Christ." Unity, maturity, whole measure, fullness – these are words and concepts that express and encompass the goal of wholeness.

The letter to the Ephesians goes on to say:

Instead, speaking the truth in love, we will grow to become in every respect the mature body of him who is the head, that is, Christ. From him the whole body, joined and held together by every supporting ligament, grows and builds itself up in love, as each part does its work.

I thanked God for the clarity. I thanked Him for this journey. I prayed for strength to serve others as He has equipped me to serve them.

Sunday, June 24   *(Romans 8:18-27)*

Paul writes to the small Christian community in Rome, consoling them in what must have been reported to him as some trouble. The trouble, it seems, is some activity involving sins of the flesh, almost certainly sexual.

Generally, I love Paul's writing. However, Chapter 8 in his letter to the Romans is about my least favorite. It is one of the most starkly Platonic passages in the New Testament.

We read often from his letters during the First Week of the exercises. I alternated between composing myself in the company of Paul as he wrote his letters and composing myself in the company of the Christian community that received the letters. I found both places to be filled with an amazing aura.

This morning, I composed myself in Rome, listening to the leader of our small group read to us from the letter we had just received from Paul. As I listened to the words in Paul's letter, I tried to think back on just what had happened, either in our community or in Corinth, where Paul wrote the letter, to cause Paul to go on at such length about the badness of our bodies and the goodness of our spirits. Whatever it was, Paul makes a very big deal out of it, and, I am afraid, leads the Church in an unfortunate direction.

I left the composition and returned to the library, stopping in my mind along the way. The first stop was at a Woodstock board meeting at Georgetown. The second stop was the large lecture room at the conference center in Assisi. In both places, I had learned something about Neo-Platonic philosophy, and its powerful role in the early theology of our Catholic faith. Now, for the first time, I could see it in what Paul wrote to the Romans:

> *For if you live according to the flesh, you will die; but if by the Spirit you put to death the misdeeds of the body, you will live.*

This is about as stark a dualistic distinction as could possibly be made. St. Augustine is said to have based a good part of his Neo-Platonic thinking on Paul. Of course, once Augustine enshrined that kind of dualistic thinking in official doctrine, it would govern the Church for almost a thousand years.

As usual, Rohr says it extremely well:

> *I'm sure that so many of the problems we have—addiction, obesity, anorexia—they're all this rejection of the body; a result of feeling the body is not good, not holy. I'm sure sexual addiction also is just a body trying to compensate; feeling so unloved, so disconnected, it tries to connect in False Self ways that don't really work.*

There's no point in hating this—which Jesus never does. Jesus shows tremendous compassion for what we later called "the sins of the flesh." Jesus is only hard on what we call "the sins of the spirit": arrogance, pride, hypocrisy; these are the sins that really destroy the soul. Jesus is not localizing sin in the material universe (sins of the flesh or sins of weakness). Sins of the spirit and the mind—these are the sins that really separate you from God. So the alternative orthodoxy that's emerging is orthopraxy instead of verbal orthodoxy: adopting an orthodox, gospel-based way of life instead of just saying the right words and thinking the right thoughts.

Here I am at the end of the Ignatian exercises and I am just now coming to understand, and agree with, the concept of non-dualistic thinking. I wonder now if this has been the point all along. Could my friendship with Jesus incarnate have been possible otherwise? Certainly, everything He preached was about wholeness, acceptance, inclusion, and forgiveness. I fell in love with Jesus before it became clear to me that falling in love is what this whole thing is about.

Father John had emphasized inclusion and forgiveness long before I had ever heard of the Spiritual Exercises of Ignatius Loyola. The Jesuits at Woodstock included me before I accepted them. I love how Thomas Merton said it:

We have what we seek, it is there all the time, and if we give it time, it will make itself known to us.

At the end of my session this morning, I sat for a long time on the bench. I prayed and prayed for clarity. I am at the end of the Exercises, yet barely at the beginning of understanding.

Epilogue

When I began these exercises more than nine months ago, I considered myself a fervent convert to Catholicism. I had been transformed by baptism. The conversion had continued for another two years of intense activity in the parish life of Our Lady Star of the Sea, complete with CRHP, the Men's Group, and regular proclamation of the word as a Lector. As Paul wrote to the Corinthians:

> *Therefore, if anyone is in Christ, he is a new creation. The old has passed away; behold, the new has come.*

I continued and had even intensified my involvement with both Woodstock and Arrupe. In short, I was in a pretty good place spiritually. The new had come.

So I did not choose to undertake these exercises because I felt my faith life was missing something. To the contrary, I embarked upon the Spiritual Exercises precisely because I felt close to God, and strong in my faith. I expected this effort to move me along that path, following the trajectory I had already chosen and maintaining my already-rapid pace.

That is not what happened. Both the trajectory and the pace of my spiritual growth changed dramatically over these months. Through the incredible power of contemplative prayer, I became truly familiar with Jesus Christ. While I have always read a great deal, the written word had always been two dimensional on the page. The Ignatian approach to contemplative prayer radically changed my reading experience. Words became active, three-dimensional space. I moved around in that space. I talked to the other people I encountered there. I smelled the smells, heard the sounds, and even felt the wind and the changes in temperature.

More than anything else, I participated in the birth, youth, ministry, and death of Jesus incarnate. I read and researched many passages from the letters of Paul and the Gospels. I imagined myself present in the cave in Judaea when the infant Jesus was circumcised, on the long walk with the Holy Family into exile in Egypt, and in the temple in Jerusalem with the precocious young man that Jesus became. I was there with Jesus for all His major sermons, and for His miracles. I sat at the table for the Last Supper. I agonized with Him on Calvary.

He became a friend. I cared about Him. I fell in love.

It took weeks of painful mourning before I was willing to move past the events that night on Calvary. Slowly, cautiously, I allowed myself to befriend the Resurrected Christ. I learned what C. S. Lewis meant when he said:

> *The Christian does not think God will love us because we are good, but that God will make us good because He loves us.*

Day by day, I opened myself more to His love. Each day, I said "yes" just a little more loudly. Each day, He made me better.

The exercises officially ended on the last day of June. It is obviously appropriate, therefore, that I end this journal. While I will stop writing about it, I do not intend to end the practice of daily prayer and meditation. I will continue my spiritual journey. There is no rush. It is a journey I hope never to finish.

Contemplative Prayer

There have been so many significant benefits for me from the Exercises that I could spend a week just making the list. Very high on that list would be learning how to pray contemplatively using fantasy. What began as merely a technique became a mainstay in my daily spiritual routine.

Of course I used it each day when praying about the daily assignment. By composing myself in the time and place of the reading, I could experience each scene with all the senses of my soul. I saw the surroundings in color. I smelled the smells. I recognized the people. I trembled with cold on the windy sea, and trembled out of fear standing before the chief priests.

I often become too engrossed in extracurricular reading and research. The most effective way to get back to the daily reading was to compose myself in that time and place. I used this form of contemplation to prepare myself when I proclaim the word at Mass.

I know that the centering prayer of the medieval mystics is an alternative preferred by a lot of people, many of whom I truly respect. I have concluded that there is a place for both the *"via negativa"* of the Franciscans and the *"via imaginativa"* of the Ignatians.[109] For me, the primary purpose of contemplative prayer, its function, is to know oneself and to communicate with the Divine Reality. In my opinion, the form is less important than the function.

---

[109] Pseudo-Dionysius and Thomas Aquinas discussed these two approaches to contemplation in terms of *cataphatic prayer* (with images, sometimes called the *via affirmativa* or the *via imaginativa*) and *apophatic prayer* (without images, sometimes called the *via negativa*). Ken Wilber is one of the primary contemporary advocates of apophatic spirituality. My own efforts to completely empty my mind to the point of mystical unity with the Divine have largely failed. In contrast, my experience with the compositions I mentally create has frequently led to a sublime sense of connection.

The simple fact is that I want to deepen my understanding of contemplation. There is a great deal of truth in the notion that the best way to do that is through constant practice. I will augment my daily prayers by reading from my embarrassing library of books by numerous authors on the many forms of contemplative prayer. In addition to what I can and will do in the library and the meditation garden, there are some exciting ways to expand my understanding.

As for the Ignatian approach, I will continue to work with at least two spiritual advisors. Sister Joan and I will continue to meet in her office on a more or less monthly basis. Father Gap and I are talking about formalizing our discussions. We will continue our practice of finding time to talk at the various Woodstock meetings. We will augment those face to face conversations with regular spiritual updates by phone.

Beyond the one-on-one conversations, I hope to participate in various Ignatian retreats. Weekend retreats, week-long retreats, and "long retreats" of thirty days are offered at several Ignatian retreat houses around the country.

I will turn once again to Richard Rohr to increase my understanding of Franciscan contemplation. The Rohr Institute has launched the Living School for Action and Contemplation.[110] This two-year program will involve onsite study in New Mexico, along with online study from home. I have requested the application package for the first class of students. Assuming I submit the completed application by the September deadline, I will learn in mid-December whether I have been accepted into the class graduating in 2014. My friend, Sister Ilia Delio, has been invited to join the faculty of the Living School as a Master Teacher.

More Reading

Throughout this journal I have quoted from various sources outside the Ignatian tradition. Happily, the passion for reading that my parents inspired in me six decades ago continues unabated. Neither Sister Joan nor Father Gap had much success in their attempts to rein in my research and reading. In fact, however, I added many more books to my reading list than I actually read during the nine-month exercises.

Richard Rohr is far and away the most frequently cited "outsider," followed at some

---

[110] The Living School for Action and Contemplation is a two-year academic program of the Rohr Institute. At its core, the Rohr Institute is strongly guided by the Franciscan heritage and spiritual lineage that have influenced Fr. Richard Rohr and the themes he has developed over his career. In keeping with the Franciscan Alternative Orthodoxy, the Rohr Institute's Living School program emphasizes an embodied lifestyle made up of practices that deepen a more conscious union with Divine Reality. We believe that lived practices are much more important for awakening to this union than verbal or intellectual beliefs alone. Through both varied teachings and practices, the Living School creates opportunities for students to experience moments of awakening that bring about profound changes to the self. These changes allow each of us to live in more conscious union with all that is and to express that union actively through works of engagement and compassion which are so needed in our world.

distance by Thomas Merton and C.S. Lewis. From time to time, all three of these men have been considered by some Catholics to be a little too unorthodox. Merton and Lewis are not criticized as much today as they were when they were alive, but they are certainly "edgy."

In addition to re-reading everything these three have ever written, I have whole shelves of books waiting to be read. Some of the books I want to read came up as I explored the topics assigned during the exercises. Others were suggested by speakers at the retreat in Assisi, or by fellows and board members at Woodstock, or by friends, both in the Catholic Church and from other wisdom traditions. I hope I live long enough to read them all.

Giving Back

James Russell Lowell once observed:

> *Creativity is not the finding of a thing, but the making something out of it after it is found.*

The first several months of these exercises increased my awareness of the enormous gifts I have been given throughout my life. In the last few weeks of the exercises, I became increasingly aware of the importance of "making something out of" those gifts by giving them back. I intend to redouble my efforts to do so.

Barbara Munyak, the head of my RCIA group in Houston, challenged me (and the other catechumens) to begin searching for new "ministries" months before we were baptized. Among other things, she advised us to sign up for one or more of the service ministries in the parish. Significantly, she advised us to also look outside our parish and outside Catholicism. Barbara taught us that our new faith would only have meaning when we "made something out of it."

Sallie Ann and I have long believed that charity begins at home. Accordingly, my primary form of "giving back" is to be a better husband, father and grandfather than I have been in the past. You will notice that I am setting a fairly low bar, since my past performance has at times been far from acceptable. However, I have come a long way since I began my spiritual journey, and I continue to make progress each day.

In addition, I am currently sitting on four different boards (one of which I chair), teaching at the University of North Florida, and serving as a Lector in the proclamation ministry of our parish. While I derive enormous satisfaction from all of these activities, I want to do more.

Particularly now that the exercises are over, I want to become involved in one of the local programs dealing with people in the margins of life. My experience has been that hands-on, direct care has the greatest healing effect, both on the healed and the healer. Mission House, the MaliVai Washington Foundation, Habitat for Humanity,

Interfaith Dialogue and various prison ministries are just a few of the programs constantly seeking volunteers for projects within a ten-mile radius of my house.

Next Steps

What happens now?   All that I know for certain is that I do not know for certain.   As Nils Rohr, the Nobel laureate in Physics, once famously said:

> *Prediction is difficult, especially when it involves the future.*

Most mornings, I suspect that Maggie and I will continue to meet in the library.   We will walk down to the bench in the garden.   We will walk on the beach.

Try as I may to make it not so, most of my sins will continue.   I will still struggle with selfishness.   I will frequently overthink things, and will attempt to remedy that by reading as many books as I can find.   I will search the internet for answers, and, more often than not, be tempted to shop for yet another unnecessary bit of stuff.

Father James Martin, SJ, wrote something in the April issue of America Magazine that continues to speak to me:

> *Most of our lives are spent in Holy Saturday.   In other words, most of our days are not filled with the unbearable pain of a Good Friday.   Nor are they suffused with the unbelievable joy of an Easter.   Some days are indeed times of great pain and some are of great joy, but most are in between.   Most are, in fact, times of waiting, much as the disciples waited during Holy Saturday. We're waiting - waiting to get into a good school; waiting to meet the right person; waiting to get pregnant; waiting to get a job; waiting for things at work to improve; waiting for diagnosis from the doctor, or waiting for life just to get better.*

> *But there are different kinds of waiting.   There is the wait of despair.   Here we know - at least we think we know - that things could never get better, that God could never do anything with our situations.   This may be the kind of waiting that forced the fearful disciples to hide behind closed doors on Holy Saturday, cowering in terror.   Then there is the wait of passivity, as if everything were up to fate.   In this waiting there is no despair, but not much anticipation of anything good either.*

> *Finally, there is the wait of the Christian, which is called hope.   It is an active waiting; it knows that, even in the worst of situations, even in the darkest times, God is at work.   Even if we can't see it clearly right now.   The disciples' fear was understandable, but we, who know how the story turned out, who know that Jesus will rise from the dead, who know that God is with us, who know that nothing will be impossible for God, are called to wait in faithful hope.   And to look carefully for signs of the new life that are always right around the corner - just like they were on Holy Saturday.*

I do know what happened at the end of the story.   It is the essence of my faith.

Maggie and I walked in the garden this morning.   The sky was, as they say, "darkest before the dawn."   It was extremely quiet.   Not even the sound of the waves hitting the beach broke the silence.   Thomas Merton describes it well:

> *I suppose what makes me most glad is that we all recognize each other in this metaphysical space of silence and happening, and get some sense, for just a moment, that we are full of paradise without knowing it.*

I whispered to Maggie that I thought we were not alone.   Then we sat in the stillness, "full of paradise," watching the eastern sky slowly brighten.

Made in the USA
Coppell, TX
01 December 2021

66864738R00168